Contributions to Finance and Accounting

The book series 'Contributions to Finance and Accounting' features the latest research from research areas like financial management, investment, capital markets, financial institutions, FinTech and financial innovation, accounting methods and standards, reporting, and corporate governance, among others. Books published in this series are primarily monographs and edited volumes that present new research results, both theoretical and empirical, on a clearly defined topic. All books are published in print and digital formats and disseminated globally.

Slađana Benković • Aleksandra Labus •
Miloš Milosavljević
Editors

Digital Transformation of the Financial Industry

Approaches and Applications

Springer

Editors
Slađana Benković
Faculty of Organizational Sciences
University of Belgrade
Belgrade, Serbia

Aleksandra Labus
Faculty of Organizational Sciences
University of Belgrade
Belgrade, Serbia

Miloš Milosavljević
Faculty of Organizational Sciences
University of Belgrade
Belgrade, Serbia

ISSN 2730-6038 ISSN 2730-6046 (electronic)
Contributions to Finance and Accounting
ISBN 978-3-031-23268-8 ISBN 978-3-031-23269-5 (eBook)
https://doi.org/10.1007/978-3-031-23269-5

This Springer imprint is published by the registered company Springer Nature Switzerland AG
The registered company address is: Gewerbestrasse 11, 6330 Cham, Switzerland

Preface

This book is aimed to be a collection of state-of-the-art research findings in digital transformations across the financial industry from the Central and East European markets. Digitalization is fundamentally changing financial services in the last few decades and tends to reshape the landscape of financial industry in an unprecedented manner. This book seeks to extend the concurrent body of knowledge on digital transformation in the financial industry by encompassing significant conceptual contributions, innovations in methods and techniques and by delineating the main applications of digital transformation in the CEE region. Although the books elaborating digital transformation in finance can be found in the market, these books dominantly focus on developed market. The aim of this book is to progress one-step forward—to focus on practice in developing and transitional/post-transitional countries.

When any technology disrupts an industry, trailblazers are usually from the highly developed countries. Diffusion of tech-related disruption is, however, only rarely linear and uninterrupted. Thusly, we were highly motivated to collect the evidence on the development of fintech from the CEE countries.

This book can serve to all important fintech stakeholders—students, academic community (with both technical and social science background), and practitioners (decision-makers and policy holders in various organizations of the financial systems). As for the students, typical users are master or doctoral level of education with major subjects covering business, finance, accounting, economics, management science, and other fields in social science and/or engineering. As for the academic community, the book might be interesting for lecturers and scholars from CEE countries. Finally, the book is aimed at practitioners—economic analysts, information technology developers and information system experts, small investors, institutional investors, as well as regulators of the financial system and national finance policy makers. Particularly important practical niche are fintech developers—entrepreneurs who change the landscape of financial industry.

Belgrade, Serbia

Slađana Benković
Aleksandra Labus
Miloš Milosavljević

Introduction

Abstract

In this section, we give a brief description of fintech and its development in Central and East European (CEE) countries. Afterwards, we provide an outline of this book by explaining each chapter at a glance.

Fintech Development in the CEE Region

Ever since the first coin was minted, financial industry has been steadily developing. This development has never been linear as it was shaped by a myriad of different factors. Merchants and practitioners modernize the industry and give birth to innovations that reshape financial industry, as it was in the case of renaissance-time Italian "banchieres". Sometimes, great minds were the ones to remodel the landscape of financial services as was with the Adam Smith's free-market banking. Sometimes, wars and crisis were the dominant factors, as was the case in the Great Depression from the early 1930s. Today, we still have billions of dollars-worth financial practices, gigantic body of knowledge on finance and related scholarly disciplines, and sadly—devastating wars and strong hurricane-like economic crises. It seems, however, that none of these factors dominate the transformation of financial industry. It seems that a baton in this relay race has been given to her majesty Technology.

Technology development became such an influential factor for the development of age-old industry of finance—that finance and technology started combining their power. Many scholars and practitioners have seen this allegorical combining so important that we gained a new portmanteau (combination of words)—FinTech.

The book has a biangular view on the development of FinTech. On the one hand, it seeks to collect evidence on transformation of financial industries and services. There is ample evidence from around the globe that technology has changed the landscape of many financial services, such as moneylending (Jagtiani and Lemieux 2018), digital payments (Jun and Yeo 2016; Kang 2018), cryptocurrencies (Lee and Deng 2018), wealth management (Sironi 2016), auditing, risk and compliance (Schmitz and Leoni 2019), or insurance (Eling and Lehman 2017). On the other hand, the most important technologies disrupting financial sector are artificial intelligence (Ashta and Herrmann 2021), big data (Hasan et al. 2020), Internet-of-Things (Maiti and Ghosh 2021), blockchain (Chen and Bellavitis 2020), cloud computing (Meng et al. 2021), and mobile technologies (Jocevski et al. 2020).

From a historical perspective, the term Fintech has been mentioned for the first time five decades ago by the vice-president of a Hanover Trust bank from New York (Bettinger 1972). As of that time, Arner, Berberis, and Buckley (2015) infer that we have two turning points in the development of financial technologies—(1) the emergence of ATMs and (2) Global Financial Crisis from 2008. Accordingly, we have witnessed three distinct periods in the Fintech development:

- Fintech 1.0 (1866–1967),
- Fintech 2.0 (1967–2008), and
- Fintech 3.0 (2008–today).

Traditional leaders and pioneers of the technology adoption in financial industry are the USA, West European countries, Japan, and few others. During this period, majority of the CEE countries were first behind the 'Iron Curtain' and only have started transition in the early 1990s.

Now, however, the CEE countries have embraced Western lifestyle and modern technologies are proliferating in the financial industry and services in these countries. We have seen the first unicorn in fintech industry from this part of the world in 2021 (CFTE 2021). This book aims to collect evidence on the development of financial technologies from this specific region.

Outline of the Book

This book is divided in two major parts, both with a different purpose. The first part provides financial aspect of fintech development. This part should be viewed as less technical and more human-oriented. Contrary to that, the second part of the book deals with the technical and technology aspects of the development of fintech.

Part I

The first eleven chapters dominantly explain the financial side of fintech development. The outline of this part of the book is given below:

Chapter "Effects of ERP on Accounting Information System: Analysis of Accountants' Attitudes" uses a primary data collected among accounting professionals to explain the effect of ERP system on the changes in accounting processes and procedures.

Chapter "Impact of Digitalization on the Accounting Profession" is a logical extension to the previous chapter. Using a structured literature review, it explains how accounting information is communicated in the modern setting, both internally and externally.

Chapter "The Impact of Digitalization on Audit" is based on primary data collected from auditors. By using a Smart PLS analysis, this chapter focuses on than interrogative: To what extent auditors use digitalisation in performing audits in Serbia?

Chapter "The Effect of Innovation Through Intangible Assets on Company's Profitability" uses the secondary data from 194 Serbian companies during the period of 2017–2020 to investigate the impact of investment in intangible assets on the companies' business performances which are observed as profitability.

Chapter "Disrupting the Stock Market: Stocks Gone Crypto" focuses on the financial markets from the CEE region. In particular, this chapter addresses the question on whether or not investors from the emerging and developed markets do react uniformly to the blockchain-related announcements globally.

Chapter "The Future of banking in FinTech Era: Decentralised and Embedded Finance" is based on a qualitative exploratory research design aiming to provide evidence on the impact of FinTech innovations on financial services industry in South-East Europe.

Chapter "Digital Transformation of the Serbian Car Insurance Industry: A Mixed-Method Approach" uses a mixed-method approach to evaluate the capacities of the Serbian insurance industry for the comprehensive digital transformation.

Chapter "InsurTech: New Competition to Traditional Insurers and Impact on the Economic Growth" provides an economic analysis of the importance of InsurTech as a new competition to traditional insurers and its impact on the economic growth by using the data from EU27 member states.

Chapter "Customers' Intention in Terms of Using Mobile Banking Services in Serbia" explores the customer side of technology acceptance in baking. Based on the famous TAM model, the study examines the most important factors for the use of mobile banking services in Serbia.

Chapter "New Ways of Providing Public Services: Platforms of Service Provision and the Role of Artificial Intelligence: In the Light of the Development of the Hungarian Public Administration" reports on the Hungarian case of the use of platforms by the public administration system. This chapter also reviews possibilities for the use of artificial intelligence by the Hungarian public administration.

Chapter "Preventing the Abuse of the FinTech Sector for Money Laundering and Fiscal Fraud in Terms of Polish Law: Legal Measures and Postulates of Normative Changes" explains the methods for the prevention of the abuse of fintech in the Polish legal and economic setting. This study is based on a formal-dogmatic method.

Part II

Chapter "Digital Payment Systems: State and Perspectives" provides a comprehensive overview of existing digital payment systems and points out their key capabilities, strengths, and limitations.

Chapter "Leveraging Open Banking: Challenges and Opportunities" explains various applications of innovative open banking models and services through the lens of end users. The potential benefits of enabling open banking through blockchain are being analysed.

Chapter "FinTech Innovations as Disruptor of the Traditional Financial Industry" provides insight into how FinTech companies are changing the financial industry and how FinTech innovations are disrupting financial markets and tending to eliminate existing established financial companies.

Chapter "Cybercrime and Cyber Security in Fintech" describes financial technology cybercrime. A systematic analysis of cyber threats and cyber security issues in the context of Fintech was done, resulting in a list of recommendations for different stakeholder groups (banks, fintech companies, and end users).

Chapter "Mobile Applications for Personal Finance Management: Technology Acceptance Perspective" describes the perspectives of the adoption of mobile application technologies in the function of managing personal finances. Research on this topic was conducted for the first time in Serbia.

Chapter "Digital Payment Systems for Small to Middle-Sized Enterprises in Serbia" provides an overview of digital payment systems with an emphasis on their implications for SMEs (small and medium-sized enterprises) and entrepreneurs with the aim of identifying and classifying current payment technologies, focusing on trends and researching their application in SMEs and entrepreneurs in Serbia.

The last chapter "Digital Payment Systems on High-Speed Railway Belgrade - Novi Sad with a Comparative Analysis" presents a comparative analysis of the forms and means of implementing the digital payment system on Serbian railways in the previous decade.

Faculty of Organizational Sciences,
University of Belgrade,
Belgrade, Serbia

Slađana Benković
Aleksandra Labus
Miloš Milosavljević

References

Arner DW, Barberis JN, Buckley RP (2015) The evolution of Fintech: a new post-crisis paradigm? SSRN Electron J. https://doi.org/10.2139/ssrn.2676553

Ashta A, Herrmann H (2021) Artificial intelligence and fintech: an overview of opportunities and risks for banking, investments, and microfinance. Strat Change 30(3):211–222. Portico. https://doi.org/10.1002/jsc.2404

Bettinger A (1972) FINTECH: a series of 40 time shared models used at manufacturers Hanover Trust Company. Interfaces 2(4):62–63

CFTE (2021) Top Fintech unicorns: 2021 review. Centre for Finance, Technology and Entrepreneurship. Available at: https://courses.cfte.education/wp-content/uploads/2022/01/Top-Fintech-Unicorns-in-2022.pdf. Accessed 17 Oct 2022
Chen Y, Bellavitis C (2020) Blockchain disruption and decentralized finance: The rise of decentralized business models. J Bus Ventur Insights 13:e00151. https://doi.org/10.1016/j.jbvi.2019.e00151
Chuen DLK, Deng RH (eds) (2017) Handbook of blockchain, digital finance, and inclusion, vol 1: cryptocurrency, FinTech, InsurTech, and regulation. Academic
Eling M, Lehmann M (2017) The impact of digitalization on the insurance value chain and the insurability of risks. Geneva Pap Risk Insur – Iss Pract 43(3):359–396. https://doi.org/10.1057/s41288-017-0073-0
Hasan MdM, Popp J, Oláh J (2020) Current landscape and influence of big data on finance. J Big Data 7(1). https://doi.org/10.1186/s40537-020-00291-z
Jagtiani J, Lemieux C (2018) Do fintech lenders penetrate areas that are underserved by traditional banks? J Econ Bus 100:43–54. https://doi.org/10.1016/j.jeconbus.2018.03.001
Jocevski M, Ghezzi A, Arvidsson N (2020) Exploring the growth challenge of mobile payment platforms: a business model perspective. Electron Comm Res Appl 40:100908. https://doi.org/10.1016/j.elerap.2019.100908
Jun J, Yeo E (2016) Entry of FinTech firms and competition in the retail payments market. Asia-Pac J Financ Stud 45(2):159–184. https://doi.org/10.1111/ajfs.12126
Kang J (2018) Mobile payment in Fintech environment: trends, security challenges, and services. Hum-Centric Comput Inf Sci 8(1). https://doi.org/10.1186/s13673-018-0155-4
Lee D, Deng RH (2018) Handbook of blockchain, digital finance, and inclusion: cryptocurrency, FinTech, InsurTech, and regulation
Maiti M, Ghosh U (2021) Next generation Internet of Things in Fintech ecosystem. IEEE Internet of Things J 1–1. https://doi.org/10.1109/jiot.2021.3063494
Meng S, He X, Tian X (2021) Research on Fintech development issues based on embedded cloud computing and big data analysis. Microprocess Microsyst 83:103977. https://doi.org/10.1016/j.micpro.2021.103977
Schmitz J, Leoni G (2019) Accounting and auditing at the time of blockchain technology: a research agenda. Austral Account Rev 29(2):331–342. https://doi.org/10.1111/auar.12286
Sironi P (2016) FinTech innovation: from robo-advisors to goal based investing and gamification. Wiley

Contents

Effects of ERP on Accounting Information System: Analysis of Accountants' Attitudes

Mirjana Todorović and Milan Čupić

Abstract Enterprise Resource Planning (ERP) is one of the popular information communication technologies (ICT) in the contemporary business environment, adopted by many companies around the world. It is usually considered that ERP allows rapid information flow, minimal response time to the requirements of buyers and suppliers, better interactions with business partners, higher quality of services, and increased customer satisfaction. It is also often found that ERP influences accounting information systems (AISs), the application of different accounting methodologies, and the accounting profession. We, therefore, aim at identifying the effects of ERP implementation on the AIS and accounting professionals. We use a questionnaire to investigate the attitudes of 37 persons working in accounting and related departments of 37 companies operating in Serbia. Our results show that accountants believe that ERP implementation strongly influences data processing and recording, as well as preparing and publishing financial reports. They believe that ERP increases accountants' efficiency and work performance, although the level of accountants' satisfaction with ERP is relatively weak. Our results also show that accountants do not find it difficult to adapt to the new working conditions in the ERP environment.

Keywords Accounting information · ERP systems · Accountants' work · Accountants' satisfaction · Accountants' performance

1 Introduction

Digitalization and digital transformation are our reality, permeating all spheres of life and business. Accounting information systems (AISs) and accounting professionals are not immune to these processes. Blockchain and big data analytics, supported by

M. Todorović · M. Čupić (✉)
Faculty of Economics, University of Kragujevac, Kragujevac, Serbia
e-mail: mtodorovic@kg.ac.rs; mcupic@kg.ac.rs

S. Benković et al. (eds.), *Digital Transformation of the Financial Industry*, Contributions to Finance and Accounting,
https://doi.org/10.1007/978-3-031-23269-5_1

cloud-based analytical tools and artificial intelligence (AI) automate decision-making, release accountants from routine tasks, and reduce the risk of human errors, but on the downside also increase the cybersecurity risks (Gonçalves et al. 2022). Consequently, digitalization is attracting the attention of researchers trying to analyze and explain the challenges that technologies bring and thus contribute to the realization of the goals and tasks of the accounting professionals (Knudsen 2020; Möller et al. 2020; Lombardi and Secundo 2021; Agostino et al. 2022). This is not an easy task given the dynamics of changes, expectations from the accounting profession, and the complexity of the issue. The focus of these researchers is often on the effects of Enterprise Resource Planning (ERP) implementation (Grabski et al. 2011; Kanellou and Spathis 2013; Heinzelmann 2017; Youssef and Mahama 2021).

Youssef and Mahama (2021) point out that the ERP is software for corporate resource planning consisting of "a single database that integrates a software suite to streamline business processes and facilitate data and information flow between a firm's business processes and its trading partners." They further stress that ERP is considered to "provide an integrated solution for planning, executing and controlling business processes horizontally across the value chain." ERP was developed as an answer to the continuously growing information needs of management (Bradford and Florin 2003; Malinić and Todorović 2012) and is often observed as a factor of the company's competitive advantage (Tarigan et al. 2020). ERP implementation is also associated with organizational changes, process reengineering, and changes in the functions of employees (Martins and Santos 2021).

ERP is often found to influence the organization and performance of AIS, the application of different accounting methodologies, and the accounting profession. The most important effects of ERP implementation on AIS are better quality of reports, stronger organizational integration, and empowered personnel (Abbasi et al. 2014; Zamani and Valmohammadi 2014). ERP implementation allows the application of various advanced accounting techniques and tools (Malinić and Todorović 2012; Todorović 2014, 2016) and accounting techniques used with ERP can affect company performance (Wajdi 2018). ERP also changes the way accountants work and seek new knowledge (Martins and Santos 2021). We, therefore, aim at identifying the effects of ERP implementation on the AIS and accounting professionals of Serbian companies. More specifically, we aim to answer the following research questions:

RQ1. What changes does ERP bring to AIS?
RQ2. How does ERP affect the efficiency, motivation, and satisfaction of accounting professionals?

By addressing our research questions, we address several research gaps and thus make several contributions to the extant literature. Gonçalves et al. (2022) argue that "the impact of digital transformation on accounting is still very unclear." Our research, therefore, contributes to the dissemination and further development of knowledge on modern trends in AIS and to a better understanding of the changes to the role of professionals in accounting, management accounting, controlling, and financial management in companies adopting and implementing digital technologies. Youssef and Mahama (2021) similarly note that "the extant literature has offered inconclusive evidence on the impact of ERP on management accounting practices." Consequently, our research contributes to the literature on the impact of ERP on AIS and accountants, which is also important given the relatively scarce literature on this topic, especially in developing and emerging economies.

The structure of the paper is as follows. The second part provides the theoretical background, while the third provides a review of the previous research. The fourth part presents the methodology. The fifth part presents the results and discussion of our results, while the sixth part presents our conclusions.

2 Theoretical Background

The key word to describe ERP is integration. ERP integrates all the departments, processes, and functions of the company into one information system and offers a holistic and integrated view by using a single database (Davenport 1998; Ghosh et al. 2013). Integration also means that the data are available to all personnel in the organization at all times. The main benefits of data integration are the following: (a) information flow among fundamental processes becomes easier; (b) real-time and reliable data sharing contributes to the business processes automation; and (c) the company can handle its dispersed activities by defining a unified standard of practices (Heinzelmann 2017; Eker and Aytac 2017). ERP also contributes to transparency by providing a detailed overview of processes and divisions, improving data availability, and increasing the visibility of local actions (Davenport 1998).

ERP can meet the specific needs of various users and is often viewed as a critical success factor for companies (Dezdar 2017). ERP was developed as an answer to the continuously growing information needs of different users, most notably company management (Bradford and Florin 2003; Malinić and Todorović 2012). It allows rapid information flow, minimal response time to the requirements of buyers and suppliers, better interactions with business partners, higher quality of provided services, and increased customer satisfaction (Malinić and Todorović 2012). ERP also supports decision-making at all company levels, efficient control of business functions, and planning of strategic actions (Koch 2007). ERP helps companies respond to rapid market changes, increase operational efficiency (Laudon and Laudon 2018) and productivity, reduce costs, and improve sales conditions in the long run (Andres et al. 2012; Su et al. 2013). Companies across various industries use ERP to improve their competitiveness (Dechow and Mouritsen 2005), organizational efficiency and effectiveness, and ultimately performance (Arnold 2006).

Grabski et al. (2011) argue that ERP systems are typically the largest, most complex, and most demanding information systems implemented by companies. Although traditionally implemented by large companies, they are rapidly implemented by medium-sized and small companies (Antoniadis et al. 2015). The implementation of an ERP system is a complex and large-scale project requiring considerable time, money, and expertise (Umar et al. 2016). Umar et al. (2016) point out that there are more than 60 critical success factors of ERP software implementation identified in the literature. The failure rate of ERP is very high, and problems can arise during and after its implementation. Therefore, the implementation project should be adequately planned and implemented.

The changes for the better and continuous business improvements are often listed as the motives for ERP implementation (Todorović and Čupić 2017). The successful ERP implementation is expected to result in a significant change in business philosophy, culture, and operations, i.e., to be a turning point in the company's business (Erwanto and Zusi 2020). Martins and Santos (2021) point out that ERP implementation is associated with changes in the organizational structure, business processes, management strategies, and employees' skills and functions. They argue that ERP directly influences the business processes and their changes, reflected in the functions of the employees, and verify that ERP provides the opportunity for companies to change their organizational structure. Finally, they stress that these changes interact and mutually influence each other, making it difficult to identify the origin and sequence of changes related to ERP implementation.

Motives for ERP implementation can be viewed from different perspectives, such as different hierarchical levels or needs of different functional areas (departments). Spathis and Constantinides (2004) show that the most important motives for ERP implementation are "integration of applications, real-time information, and particularly information for decision making." From the perspective of different functional areas, accounting and finance usually have the greatest need for ERP implementation (Hyvonen 2003). Kanellou and Spathis (2013) argue that ERP implementation has been the most important and substantial IT project interacting with the accounting function at the beginning of the twenty-first century. ERP brings significant changes to the whole company, but mostly to AIS (Malinić and Todorović 2011).

Kanellou and Spathis (2013) argue that there are no studies examining perceptions and attitudes regarding the accounting benefits of ERP implementation and the satisfaction of ERP users, including IT professionals and accountants. They emphasize that there is generally little research on the accounting benefits of ERP implementation, the way these benefits are evaluated by managers and employees, and the interaction of these benefits with ERP users' satisfaction. Sutton (2006) points out that ERP affects the accounting process by significantly changing the way business data are collected, stored, disseminated, and used. Given that ERP is not just software and that it also influences how people work and often imposes its logic on a company's strategy, organization, and culture, the number of research papers focusing on ERP is expected to increase (Grubišić 2014).

3 Literature Review

AIS is one of the most important company success factors and its efficient and effective implementation increases efficiency and reduces risk exposure of the company (Kamal 2015). On the other hand, information communication technology

(ICT) strongly affects AIS performance. Effects of ERP—as one of the ICTs, on accounting, however, attract limited attention in the literature, leaving many questions open. Granlund (2011) and Rom and Rohde (2007) argue that researchers fail to produce a clear understanding of the relationship between ERP and management accounting, while Abbasi et al. (2014) argue that the research on the impact of ERP on management accounting is still at a foundational stage. The empirical results are contradicting—while Hassan and Mouakket (2016) show that ERP has limited or no impact on accounting practices, Eker and Aytac (2017) and Wagner et al. (2011) argue that ERP fosters accounting change. All of this creates the need for new research on the influence of ERP on AIS and accountants.

3.1 *Effects of ERP on the Accounting Process*

The creation of information and preparation of various reports are still among the most important activities of accountants, relying on the efficient collection, processing, and manipulation of large volumes of data (Macura and Gajić 2022). ERP can be a useful tool for the realization of these activities. For example, after ERP implementation, accountants are found to spend significantly less time on data entry but more time on data analysis (Suhaimi et al. 2016). ERP can directly influence the quality of the reports through real-time data transfer (Zamani and Valmohammadi 2014) and increase flexibility in information generation and integration of accounts applications (Spathis and Constantinides 2004). It is found to provide better support to the decision-making process by providing timely and reliable accounting information and enterprise integration (Colmenares 2009).

ERP improves financial management and provides more opportunities for employees to deal with financial management issues (Newman and Westrup 2005). Sánchez-Rodríguez and Spraakman (2012) find that ERP allows the development and use of a more detailed chart of accounts and more extensive, standardized, and thorough performance measurement. They argue that ERP supports the use of both financial and nonfinancial measures, as well as access to standardized operational data. It also provides more efficient cash flow management and enables various forms of analysis, e.g., variance analysis or financial statement analysis.

ERP improves the capacity of management accounting and cost accounting (Malinić et al. 2012). ERP is an excellent tool for management control because it is often found to provide transparency. It facilitates and improves the planning and control of all business units and activities (Suhaimi et al. 2016), and allows the application of various advanced accounting and management techniques and tools (Malinić and Todorović 2012). Galani et al. (2010) show that ERP improves the quality of AIS, decreases expenses, and improves company performance. Eker and Aytac (2017), Wajdi (2018), and Youssef and Mahama (2021) similarly find the positive impact of ERP on company performance.

We aim to identify the impact of ERP on financial reporting, financial statements analysis, financial management, and decision-making. Given that AISs still face many obstacles due to accountants' errors or delays (Rahman et al. 2017), our focus is also on changing accountants' roles and work under influence of ERP.

3.2 *Effects of ERP on Accountants*

ERP is changing the work environment of accountants and automating routine accounting (Newman and Westrup 2005; Malinić and Todorović 2012; Schulze and Nuhn 2020). It contributes to much quicker, more quality transaction processing, and shortens the time required for the realization of regular and routine tasks. The simplification of accounting procedures, while enhancing their efficiency and effectiveness, reduces the efforts of the accountants and contributes to reducing unintended errors (Jasim and Raewf 2020). Also, the number of accountants needed usually decreases (Mamić-Sačer and Žeger 2007). ERP supplies accountants with more accurate and timely information and consequently contributes to better decision-making (Sánchez-Rodríguez and Spraakman 2012).

ERP is expected to improve the efficiency of accountants' routine work. It enables the recording of business events at the place and time of occurrence, as well as daily reporting. ERP, however, still cannot perform creative tasks, analyses, and interpretations (Todorović and Ljubisavljević 2019). Accountants are, therefore, expected to spend more time on financial analysis, informing middle and top management, and performance measurement, which makes their job more complex, demanding, and future oriented. Hence, ERP changes the way accountants work and seek new knowledge.

ERP is expected to be one of the most important factors shaping the demand for accountants' expertise, knowledge, skills, and responsibilities in the future. Accountants are, for example, expected to have more complex knowledge of ICT and different ICT tools, to embrace digital technologies and improve their digital competencies (SAIPA 2019; Demko-Rihter 2021). In other words, besides the skills of compiling data and preparing financial statements, accountants also need to improve their abilities to communicate effectively and perform analytical analyses accurately (Chen et al. 2012). Activities that require experience, intuition, creativity, and multidisciplinarity are also becoming more important (Schulze and Nuhn 2020). Accountants should be able to work in teams, to improve their strategic thinking, communication, and different soft skills.

As already mentioned, there are no studies examining attitudes toward the influence of ERP implementation on the efficiency and satisfaction of accountants. This topic is important because accountants' satisfaction with ERP comes from the accounting benefits of ERP (Kanellou and Spathis 2013; Nguyen et al. 2021). ERP quality is also positively associated with accountants' performance and satisfaction (Weli 2018). ERP system reliability, response time, flexibility, integration, and convenience of access are important factors contributing to the satisfaction of ERP users (Lin 2010). In addition, an increase in ERP quality can result in better accountants' performance and a higher level of accountants' satisfaction (Costa et al. 2016; Dezdar 2017). We aim to identify and understand the impact of ERP on the efficiency, motivation, and satisfaction of accountants.

4 Methodology

The main activities of the research methodology used in this study are the following: (a) questionnaire design, (b) sampling and data collection, and (c) analysis of the data.

The questionnaire consists of three groups of questions. The first group includes general questions about the ERP software used, ERP use, and the training during the ERP implementation. The second group is aimed at identifying the attitudes of respondents toward the effects of ERP on the accounting process and AIS, accountants' efficiency, and the level of accountants' satisfaction with ERP. It includes a total of 16 statements. We use a five-point Likert scale—accountants are offered responses ranging from 1—strongly disagree to 5—strongly agree. The final, third part of the questionnaire includes questions about the respondents, including gender, age, and level of education.

The questionnaire was made available in *Google forms* and 150 persons who work in the accounting department and related departments of 150 companies operating in Serbia were invited via email to fill it out. In total, our sample consists of 37 respondents from 37 companies, giving a response rate of 24.7%. Alreck and Settle (2004) point out that a response rate of 5–10% can be considered satisfactory in social sciences research. Our sample consists of companies of different sizes and from different industries, all of which use ERP. The majority are small (43.2%), but the sample also includes medium-sized (21.6%) and large companies (35.1%). Also, the majority of companies are manufacturing (56.8%). Sample companies use different ERP packages, but most often SAP (in 30% of cases). They mostly have many years of experience in the use of ERP—a total of 33 companies (89%) use ERP for more than 3 years.

All the respondents went through training for ERP use. The training lasted 1 month in most of the cases and more than 8 months in only one case. Professional education and training are often considered significant factors of successful ERP implementation (Kiran and Reddy 2019; Odoyo and Ojera 2020), as well as of some other activities involving accountants, such as continuous improvement processes (Todorović and Čupić 2017) and quality financial reporting (Obradović et al. 2018). Table 1 presents the information on respondents in the sample. The majority of respondents are female (73.0%) and age less than 40 years (56.75%). The sample mainly includes respondents who have a bachelor's degree (45.9%).

We analyze the data using the *Statistical Package for Social Sciences (SPSS, Version 20.0)*. We measure the reliability and internal consistency of the variables (statements) using Cronbach's Alpha coefficient. Cronbach's Alpha of 0.950 suggests that the list of statements has a high degree of internal consistency in measuring the respondents' attitudes (Hair et al. 2019). Jamieson (2004) points out that Likert

Table 1 Characteristics of the respondents

	Frequency	%
Gender		
Male	10	27.0
Female	27	73.0
Age		
Up to 30 years	12	32.4
31–40 years	9	24.3
41–50 years	5	13.5
More than 50 years	11	29.7
Level of education		
Secondary education	7	18.9
College	2	5.4
Bachelor's degree	17	45.9
Master	11	29.7

scales produce ordinal data, requiring the median or mode as the measure of central tendency. We will base our conclusions on the median, but will also determine and interpret the mean. The five-point Likert scale implies that a median and mean higher than 3.00 indicate that the respondents agree with the statement, while a median and mean lower than 3.00 indicate that the respondents disagree with the statement. To analyze the relationships between respondents' attitudes, we use both the Pearson and Spearman correlation tests.

5 Results and Discussion

5.1 Descriptive Analysis

We rely on descriptive statistics to analyze the degree of agreement of the respondents with the defined statements and the homogeneity/heterogeneity of the attitudes of the respondents. Table 2 shows the mean and median level of the respondents' agreement with each of the statements together with the standard deviation and the number of respondents who opted for the extreme positions (1 = absolute disagreement; 5 = absolute agreement).

The first part of Table 2 allows the examination of respondents' attitudes toward the effects of ERP on the accounting process and AIS. Given that the median level of agreement is 4 (85.7%) for six statements and 5 (14.3%) for one statement, we conclude that the respondents generally agree with the statements and believe that ERP has a significant impact on the accounting process and AIS. In addition, it should be noted that respondents seldomly absolutely disagree with the statements—only up to 2 out of 37 respondents (5.4%). Respondents believe that ERP has the strongest impact on processing and recording the data (given the highest median and mean) and preparing and publishing financial reports. On the other hand, they

Table 2 Descriptive statistics

Statement		Mean[a]	Stdev	Med	F1	F5
Effects of ERP on the accounting process and AIS						
1	Collecting, checking, and importing the data	3.97	1.01	4	0	14
2	Processing and recording the data	4.22	1.03	5	1	19
3	Adjusting and changing the data	3.70	1.20	4	2	12
4	Preparing and publishing financial reports	4.11	0.94	4	1	14
5	Analyzing financial reports	3.95	1.20	4	2	16
6	Cash flow management	3.65	1.16	4	2	11
7	Support for decision-making	3.65	1.03	4	1	7
Effects of ERP on the efficiency of accountants						
8	Tasks realization in real time	3.70	1.02	4	1	9
9	Reduction in the time necessary for tasks realization	3.76	0.96	4	5	8
10	Reduction in routine workload	3.68	1.06	4	7	9
11	Reduction in the frequency of errors in tasks realization	3.70	1.05	4	2	8
12	Reduction in the number of accountants	3.76	1.16	4	1	13
13	Reduction in the routine work volume	3.57	1.04	4	1	7
Effects of ERP on the accountants' satisfaction						
14	Improved work performance	3.78	1.06	4	1	10
15	Improved employees motivation	3.24	1.26	3	4	7
16	Complexity to adjust to a new way of work	2.78	0.95	3	4	1

Notes: Stdev is standard deviation, Med is median, while F1 and F5 indicate the number of respondents who express absolute disagreement or absolute agreement with the specified statement, respectively. A total of 37 respondents expressed their attitude toward all specified statements

[a] On a five-point Likert scale where 1 denotes complete (absolute) disagreement with the statement and 5 denotes complete (absolute) agreement

believe that ERP has the weakest impact—although not weak, given the mean value of 3.65, on cash flow management and decision-making. Respondents have the most homogeneous (given the standard deviation) attitudes toward the impact of ERP on preparing and publishing financial reports, and the most heterogeneous attitudes toward the impact of ERP on adjusting and changing the data and analyzing financial reports.

Our results imply that ERP significantly changes and improves the way business data are collected, stored, disseminated, and used. It improves data manipulation and contributes to the improvement of the accounting process. The respondents also believe ERP has a strong impact on preparing and publishing financial reports. We identify the highest level of homogeneity of attitudes on this statement. Such a result is expected and in accordance with the results of some previous studies. Suhaimi et al. (2016), for example, conclude that accountants spend significantly less time on data processing after ERP implementation. Some traditional and routine accounting tasks are transferred to ERP and the time required for these tasks is reduced (Waelter et al. 2018). ERP provides stronger information support, a higher level of flexibility in information generation, information integration, real-time information, and better report quality (Abbasi et al. 2014; Colmenares 2009; Zamani and Valmohammadi

2014). Kanellou and Spathis (2013) find a reduction in the time for and frequency of financial statements preparation after the ERP implementation, while Malinić and Todorović (2012) show that the time needed for operational reporting is shorter and for strategic reporting longer.

The respondents believe that ERP has the weakest impact on cash flow management and decision-making. These activities of accountants are more specific, complex, and demanding. For example, previous research shows that the time needed for performance measurement and data analysis is longer after the ERP implementation (Malinić and Todorović 2012). In an ERP environment, accountants can devote more time to financial analysis and decision-making rather than to data input (Arora and Kumar 2021). ERP provides a lot of information that needs to be adequately analyzed. That is why it is necessary to use additional tools, like Excel and Business Intelligence (BI). The specificity of these activities, as well as the impact of ERP on their implementation, may be the primary reasons for the lower scores.

The second part of Table 2 is related to the examination of respondents' attitudes toward the effects of ERP on the efficiency of accountants. Given that the median level of agreement with the statements is four in all six statements, we conclude that the respondents generally agree with the statements and believe that ERP has a significant impact on accountants' efficiency. It should be, however, noted that the average level of respondents' agreement is lower (ranging from 3.57 to 3.76) than in the first part of the questionnaire. A relatively large number of respondents absolutely disagree with statements on the reduction of time necessary for tasks realization and reduction of routine workload. Despite that, on average, respondents believe that ERP has the strongest impact on the reduction of time necessary for tasks realization and reduction in the number of accountants. On the other hand, they believe that ERP has the weakest impact on reduction in routine work. Respondents have the most homogeneous attitudes toward the impact of ERP on the reduction of time necessary for tasks realization, and the most heterogeneous attitudes toward the impact of ERP on the reduction in the number of accountants.

Our results imply that accountants' efficiency increases after ERP implementation. This is in accordance with the results of some previous studies. For example, Bejjar (2017) shows that ERP improves the efficiency and effectiveness of accountants. ERP also shortens the time for accounting procedures as these can be realized in an automated manner. This gives more time to accountants, for example, for preparation and analysis of the financial statements. Several studies show that ERP reduces the volume of routine work (Newman and Westrup 2005; Schulze and Nuhn 2020) and that ERP contributes to more efficient use of accountant's time due to the elimination of routine reports (Etemadi and Kazeminia 2014). Interestingly, however, the respondents in our study believe that ERP has the weakest, although not weak, impact on the reduction in the volume of routine work. We also find that respondents on average strongly believe that the number of accountants in the accounting department is decreasing after ERP implementation. ERP enables accountants to carry out activities in real time and contributes to the reduction of work errors.

The third part of Table 2 is related to the examination of respondents' attitudes toward the effects of ERP on the accountants' satisfaction. Given that the median level of agreement with the statements is 4 (33.3%) in one statement and 3 (66.7%) in two statements, we conclude that the respondents agree with the statements and believe that ERP influences accountants' satisfaction. Their agreement is, however, relatively low, especially when compared to the first two groups of statements. The respondents, nevertheless, rarely absolutely disagree with the statements—only up to 4 out of 37 respondents (10.8%). Respondents believe that ERP has the strongest impact on work performance improvement (given the highest median and mean). They generally believe that the adjustment to the new way of work after ERP implementation is not complex. Finally, they also believe that ERP does not have a strong impact on improving employees' motivation. Respondents have the most homogeneous attitudes toward the impact of ERP on the complexity to adjust to a new way of work, and the most heterogeneous attitudes toward the impact of ERP on improving employees' motivation.

Our results show that it was not too demanding for accountants to adjust to the new working conditions after ERP implementation. The ERP implementation is a complex task that requires money, time, and expertise (Umar et al. 2016) and is associated with significant changes in the company. Small companies very often do not have enough qualified staff and enough knowledge and resources (Ou et al. 2018; Goumas et al. 2018), which can be the cause of greater difficulties in accepting a new way of work. On the other hand, large companies usually do not have significant financial constraints, but can have problems with business complexity, which makes it difficult to adopt a new way of work (Umar et al. 2016). Customizations of ERP are, therefore, necessary to meet the size and scale of operations in different companies (Baker and Yousof 2017). Our results also show that the respondents believe that ERP contributes to improvement in their work performance, but not that much to their motivation. We, therefore, conclude that the level of satisfaction with ERP is relatively weak. This differs from the results of some previous studies. For example, Nguyen et al. (2021) find that ERP generally has a positive effect on accountants' satisfaction, while Etemadi and Kazeminia (2014) find that ERP implementation improves job satisfaction for management accountants.

5.2 *Correlation Analysis*

To determine the sign and degree of correlation between pairs of statements, we compute Spearman's and Pearson's correlation coefficients for each pair of statements. Given that the number of coefficients calculated is large, Table 3 shows only pairs of statements with statistically significant correlation coefficients ($p < 0.05$). Correlation coefficients with absolute values greater than 0.5 can be considered as strong according to Cohen (Pallant 2013). The Pearson's coefficient is larger than 0.5 when the Spearman's coefficient is smaller than 0.5 in 4 cases, while we find

Table 3 Correlation analysis

	1	2	3	4	5	6	7	8	9	10	11	12	13	14	15	16
Effects of ERP on the accounting process and AIS																
1		0.78	0.45	0.56	0.55	0.75	0.68	0.61	0.83	0.77	0.62	0.70	0.75	0.75	0.70	
2	0.77		0.59	0.75	0.77	0.72	0.73	0.56	0.76	0.65	0.68	0.62	0.76	0.68	0.67	
3	0.45	0.59		0.60	0.51	0.46	0.47	0.38	0.54	0.43	0.39		0.36	0.41	0.49	
4	0.50	0.63	0.52		0.82	0.60	0.73	0.50	0.62	0.60	−57	0.46	0.62	0.67	0.64	
5	0.56	0.70	0.48	0.84		0.68	0.70	0.44	0.57	0.60	0.43	0.55	0.71	0.60	0.54	
6	0.72	0.72	0.50	0.64	0.73		0.73	0.59	0.75	0.74	0.57	0.72	0.81	0.64	0.69	
7	0.61	0.60	0.43	0.65	0.69	0.71		0.69	0.76	0.81	0.75	0.53	0.76	0.74	0.73	
Effects of ERP on the efficiency of accountants																
8	0.65	0.60	0.44	0.54	0.52	0.59	0.76		0.78	0.68	0.64	0.40	0.61	0.71	0.73	
9	0.82	0.72	0.52	0.50	0.56	0.71	0.68	0.80		0.83	0.70	0.65	0.79	0.77	0.86	
10	0.77	0.63	0.41	0.54	0.63	0.71	0.77	0.73	0.81		0.64	0.64	0.73	0.71	0.77	
11	0.56	0.55	0.34	0.46	0.35	0.53	0.71	0.72	0.67	0.62		0.53	0.64	0.74	0.71	
12	0.68	0.63	0.20	0.48	0.59	0.68	0.48	0.42	0.63	0.63	0.50		0.71	0.61	0.55	
13	0.69	0.74	0.34	0.58	0.70	0.79	0.74	0.64	0.74	0.69	0.61	0.67		0.77	0.68	
Effects of ERP on the accountants' satisfaction																
14	0.73	0.59	0.35	0.62	0.61	0.57	71	0.75	0.75	0.69	0.71	0.60	0.75		0.79	
15	0.70	0.63	0.47	0.56	0.53	0.67	0.68	0.78	0.83	0.74	0.71	0.55	0.64	0.77		
16																

Notes: The numbers in the column and row headers represent the statements listed in Table 2. Numbers below the table diagonal represent Spearman's correlation coefficients statistically significant at 5%. The numbers above the table diagonal represent Pearson's correlation coefficients statistically significant at 5%

only two opposite cases. All correlation coefficients are positive, except in one case—the Pearson's correlation coefficient for statements 4 and 11. We find no statistically significant correlation coefficients involving statement 16, which refers to the complexity to adjust to a new way of work. We continue our discussions by focusing on the strongest Spearman's coefficients presented in Table 3.

Respondents who believe that ERP positively affects and facilitates the processes of data collection, control, and entry, as well as the processes of data processing and recording, also believe that ERP positively affects the reporting process. Ou et al. (2018) similarly argue that firms implementing ERP can provide strong technical support for accounting information collection, processing, and reporting, as well as for the improvement of accounting information quality. Respondents who believe that ERP has a positive effect on the process of preparing and publishing financial reports also believe that ERP has a positive effect on the process of analyzing financial statements. Given the procedure and flow of the accounting process, these findings are expected—ERP automates certain accounting tasks and contributes to their efficient implementation (Bejjar 2017; Etemadi and Kazeminia 2014). Although the time required to analyze financial reports is often found to increase after the ERP implementation (Malinić and Todorović 2012; Arora and Kumar 2021), respondents in our study believe that the improvement in financial reporting is accompanied by improvements in the analysis of the financial reports. This implies that more quality and meaningful financial reporting provides a better basis for financial analysis.

Respondents who believe that ERP has positive effects on the processes of data collection, control, and import, i.e., on data manipulation, believe that ERP contributes to a reduction of time necessary for implementing the tasks and a reduction in the number of employees in accounting. One of the most important advantages of ERP is the increase in the efficiency of data processing and routine tasks implementation, which consequently leads to a reduction in time and number of employees necessary for the realization of accountants' tasks. Ou et al. (2018) argue that automation in the context of ERP reduces the chances of excessive human intervention and opportunistic behavior. It should also be noted that the respondents in our study believe that ERP, by contributing to the reduction of the time required for the implementation of tasks, contributes to the reduction of workload and enables the implementation of tasks in real time.

Respondents in our study who believe that ERP contributes to the improvement of work performance also believe that ERP reduces the time necessary for the implementation of accountants' tasks, reduces the volume of routine work, and increases the capacity for tasks realization in real time. ERP improves the quality of accounting information and the quality of accountants' work (Bejjar 2017). Given the identified effects of ERP on work performance and the efficiency of accountants, we could expect that ERP has a positive effect on the motivation of employees. The question, however, arises about the causes of the relatively low average score for the effect of ERP on the motivation of accountants (statement 15). The effect of ERP on the satisfaction and motivation of employees is possibly mediated or moderated by some other factors relevant to the very complex and multidimensional motivational system of employees.

6 Conclusions

We aim to identify the effects of ERP implementation on the AIS of Serbian companies. Our focus is on the ERP effects on the accounting process and work of accountants, as well as on the accountants' efficiency and satisfaction. Our results show that ERP implementation strongly influences data processing and recording, as well as preparing and publishing financial reports. In other words, it affects data manipulation and contributes to the improvement of accounting reporting. It increases accountants' efficiency, given that the accountants spend less time on routine tasks and the volume of routine work reduces. Finally, ERP improves the work performance of accountants, although the level of accountants' satisfaction with ERP is relatively weak. Our results also show that accountants do not find it difficult to adapt to the new working conditions in the ERP environment.

Our research contributes to the literature in several ways. We fill the gap in the literature on the changes in AIS after ERP implementation by examining the accountants' attitudes. The attitudes of accountants and other employees toward ERP, as well as training, education, and user acceptance, are very often listed as critical factors of successful ERP implementation. Our research further contributes to the dissemination and development of knowledge on modern trends in AIS and a better understanding of the changed role of accountants in the ERP environment. Our research also has significant practical implications. It can be beneficial to companies seeking to implement ERP, improve AIS, create additional training, and promote the need for continuous education of accountants.

Our research has several limitations. Our sample is small and includes companies from only one country. A larger and more diverse sample could allow the use of more advanced statistical methodology and different conclusions. Another important limitation of our research stems from the potentially biased or wrong answers of the respondents as well as answers the respondents might have provided randomly or without an understanding of the statement. Hence, more detailed and precise results could have been obtained if the interview was used in addition to the questionnaire. Future research should be directed toward the factors that influence the efficiency and effectiveness of accountants in the ERP environment as well as their satisfaction. This could contribute to the success of some future ERP implementation projects.

References

Abbasi S, Zamani M, Valmohammadi C (2014) The effects of ERP systems implementation on management accounting in Iranian organizations. Educ Bus Soc 7(4):245–256

Agostino D, Saliterer I, Steccolini I (2022) Digitalization, accounting and accountability: a literature review and reflections on future research in public services. Financ Account Manage 38(2): 152–176

Alreck PL, Settle RB (2004) The survey research handbook. McGraw-Hill/Irwin, Boston, MA

Andres J, Lorca P, Emilio Labra J (2012) The effects of ERP implementations on the profitability of big firms: the case of Spain. Int J Technol Manag 59(1–2):22–44

Antoniadis I, Tsiakiris T, Tsopogloy S (2015) Business intelligence during times of crisis: adoption and usage of ERP systems by SMEs. Procedia Soc Behav Sci 175:299–307

Arnold V (2006) Behavioral research opportunities: understanding the impact of enterprise systems. Int J Account Inf Syst 7(1):7–17

Arora M, Kumar D (2021) Enterprise resource planning (ERP) has an impact on the management control system and the work of accountants. J Adv Scholarly Res Allied Educ 18(1):279–284

Baker MB, Yousof Z (2017) Factors influencing knowledge sharing in enterprise resource planning system usage in small and medium enterprises. J Theor Appl Inf Technol 95(8):1–10

Bejjar MA (2017) The impact of enterprise resource planning (ERP) on the performance of accounting processes. Int J Inf Technol Manage Inf Syst 8(1):22–39

Bradford M, Florin J (2003) Examining the role of innovation diffusion factors on the implementation success of enterprise resource planning systems. Int J Account Inf Syst 4(3):205–225

Chen HJ, Yan Huang S, Chiu AA, Pai FC (2012) The ERP system impact on the role of accountants. Ind Manag Data Syst 112(1):83–101

Colmenares L (2009) Benefits of ERP systems for accounting and financial management. Proc Acad Inf Manage Sci 13(1):3–7

Costa CJ, Ferreira E, Bento F, Aparicio M (2016) Enterprise resource planning adoption and satisfaction determinants. Comput Hum Behav 63:659–671

Davenport TH (1998) Putting the enterprise into the enterprise system. Harv Bus Rev 76(4):1–12

Dechow N, Mouritsen J (2005) Enterprise resource planning systems, management control and the quest for integration. Account Org Soc 30:691–733

Demko-Rihter J (2021) Uloga i perspektive računovodstvene profesije u kontekstu industrije 4.0. In: Računovodstvena znanja kao činilac ekonomskog i društvenog napretka. Ekonomski fakultet Kragujevac, pp 324–336

Dezdar S (2017) An integrative model for realising benefits from enterprise resource planning implementation. Int J Bus Inf Syst 24(4):423–451

Eker M, Aytac A (2017) The role of ERP in advanced managerial accounting techniques: a conceptual framework. Bus Econ Res J 8(1):83–100

Erwanto ED, Zusi H (2020) Factors affecting success of ERP (Enterprise resource planning) system implementation. Int Hum Appl Sci J 1(1):12–24

Etemadi H, Kazeminia S (2014) Impact of enterprise resource planning systems (ERP) on management accountants. Manage Admin Sci Rev 3(4):507–515

Galani D, Gravas E, Stavropoulos A (2010) The impact of ERP systems on accounting processes. Int J Econ Manage Eng 66:418–423

Ghosh B, Yoon T, Fustos J (2013) Enhancing functional fit with continuous training during the ERP post-implementation phase. Int J Inf Syst Serv Sect 52:30–45

Gonçalves MJA, da Silva ACF, Ferreira CG (2022) The future of accounting: how will digital transformation impact the sector? Informatics 9(1). https://doi.org/10.3390/informatics9010019

Goumas S, Charamis D, Tabouratzi E (2018) Accounting benefits of ERP systems across the different manufacturing industries of SMEs. Theor Econ Lett 8:1232–1246

Grabski SV, Leech SA, Schmidt PJ (2011) A review of ERP research: a future agenda for accounting information systems. J Inf Syst 25(1):37–78

Granlund M (2011) Extending AIS research to management accounting and control issues: a research note. Int J Account Inf Syst 12(1):3–19

Grubišić I (2014) ERP in clouds or still below. J Syst Inf Technol 16(1):62–76

Hair JF, Black WC, Babin BJ, Anderson RE (2019) Multivariate data analysis. Cengage Learning EMEA, Andover

Hassan MK, Mouakket S (2016) ERP and organizational change: a case study examining the implementation of accounting modules. Int J Organ Anal 24(3):487–515

Heinzelmann R (2017) Accounting logics as a challenge for ERP system implementation: a field study of SAP. J Account Org Change 13(2):162–187

Hyvonen T (2003) Management accounting and information: ERP versus BoB. Eur Account Rev 12(1):155–173

Jamieson S (2004) Likert scales: how to (ab)use them? Med Educ 38(12):1217–1218

Jasim Y, Raewf M (2020) Impact of the information technology on the accounting system. Cihan Univ-Erbil J Hum Soc Sci 6(1):50–57

Kamal S (2015) Historical evolution of management accounting. Cost Manage 43(4):12–19

Kanellou A, Spathis C (2013) Accounting benefits and satisfaction in an ERP environment. Int J Account Inf Syst 14:209–234

Kiran TS, Reddy AV (2019) Critical success factors of ERP implementation in SMEs. J Project Manage 4:267–280

Knudsen DR (2020) Elusive boundaries, power relations, and knowledge production: a systematic review of the literature on digitalization in accounting. Int J Account Inf Syst 36:100441

Koch C (2007) An introduction to ERP. Available via http://escc.Army.mil/doc/ERP/ERP_white_papers/ABC-An_Introduction_to_ERP. Accessed 12 Oct 2009

Laudon KC, Laudon JP (2018) Management information systems: managing the digital firm. Pearson, London

Lin HF (2010) An investigation into the effects of IS quality and top management support on ERP system usage. Total Qual Manag 21(3):335–349

Lombardi R, Secundo G (2021) The digital transformation of corporate reporting – a systematic literature review and avenues for future research. Meditari Account Res 29(5):1179–1208

Macura P, Gajić P (2022) Modeling the interdependence of marketing and accounting information systems. Acta Economica 20(36):53–74

Malinić S, Todorović M (2011) Implementacija integrisanog računovodstvenog-informacionog sistema – teorijsko metodološke osnove i rizici. Računovodstvo 55(1–2):20–34

Malinić S, Todorović M (2012) How does management accounting change under the influence of ERP? Econ Res 25(3):722–751

Malinić S, Todorović M, Jovanović D (2012) ERP and management accounting changes of industrial enterprises in Serbia. Industrija 40(2):189–208

Mamić-Sačer I, Žeger K (2007) Računovodstveni informacijski sustavi. Zajednica računovođa i finansijskih djelatnika, Zagreb

Martins JL, Santos C (2021) The influence of ERP systems on organizational aspects of accounting: case studies in Portuguese companies. Account Res J 34(6):666–682

Möller K, Schäffer U, Verbeeten F (2020) Digitalization in management accounting and control: an editorial. J Manag Control 31(1):1–8

Newman M, Westrup C (2005) Making ERPs work: accountants and the introduction of ERP systems. Eur J Inf Syst 14:258–272

Nguyen TH, Nguyen QT, Hoang Vu LD (2021) The effects of accounting benefit, ERP system quality and management commitment on accountants' satisfaction. Account Forum 7:127–136

Obradović V, Čupić M, Dimitrijević D (2018) Application of international financial reporting standards in the transition economy of Serbia. Aust Account Rev 28(1):48–60

Odoyo CO, Ojera PB (2020) Impact of top management support on accounting information system: a case of enterprise resource planning (ERP) system. Univ J Manage 8(1):12–19

Ou P, Zhao H, Zhou Z (2018) Does the implementation of ERP improve the quality of accounting information? Evidence from Chinese A-share listed manufacturing firms. J Appl Bus Res 34(1): 43–54

Pallant J (2013) SPSS survival manual: a step by step guide to data analysis using IBM SPSS. McGraw Hill, New York

Rahman M, Ahammed M, Abdur RM, Main UM (2017) Obstacles and implementation of accounting software system in small medium enterprises (SMEs): case of south Asian perspective. Int J Sci Bus 1(1):7–15
Rom A, Rohde C (2007) Management accounting and integrated information systems: a literature review. Int J Account Inf Syst 8(1):40–68
SAIPA (2019) Industry 4.0 – fight or flight for accounting. Available at https://www.saipa.co.za/wp-content/uploads/2019/04/SAIPA-ProfessionalAccountant_35_d9.pdf. Accessed 2 Apr 2021
Sánchez-Rodríguez C, Spraakman G (2012) ERP systems and management accounting: a multiple case study. Qual Res Account Manag 9(4):398–414
Schulze M, Nuhn HFR (2020) Robotic process automation in controlling - results of an empirical study. International Group of Controlling – IGC, St. Galen
Spathis C, Constantinides S (2004) Enterprise resource planning systems' impact on accounting processes. Bus Process Manag J 10(2):234–247
Su NH, Chang JS, Chen KL (2013) The impact of enterprise resource planning implementations on firm's long-term operating and market performance. In: Paper presented at the international conference on business and information, Bali
Suhaimi NSA, Nawawi A, Salin AS (2016) Impact of enterprise resource planning on management control system and accountants' role. Int J Econ Manage 10(1):93–108
Sutton SG (2006) Enterprise systems and the re-shaping of accounting systems: a call for research. Int J Account Inf Syst 7(1):1–6
Tarigan ZJH, Siagian H, Jie F (2020) The role of top management commitment to enhancing the competitive advantage through ERP integration and purchasing strategy. Int J Enterp Inf Syst 16(1):53–68
Todorović M (2016) Time-driven activity-based costing as a tool of building an integrated management system. Facta Univ Series: Econ Org 13(1):45–57
Todorović M, Čupić M (2017) How does 5S implementation affect company performance? A case study applied to a subsidiary of a rubber goods manufacturer from Serbia. Eng Econ 28(3): 311–322
Todorović M, Ljubisavljević S (2019) Primena informacionih tehnologija u računovodstvu - izazovi za reviziju. In: Šapić S, Kostić M, Obradović V, Todorović V, Drenovak M (eds) Ekonomski efekti tranzicije i restrukturiranja privrede Srbije u funkciji evropskih integracija. Ekonomski fakultet, Kragujevac, pp 351–362
Todorović M (2014) Ključni aspekti kreiranja i primene jednačina vremena u obračunu troškova. Ekonomski Horizonti 16(3):253–264
Umar M, Khan N, Agha MN, Abbas M (2016) Exploring the factors affecting ERP implementation quality. J Qual Technol Manage 7(1):137–155
Waelter A, Kaplan B, Gibson AB, Krumwiede K (2018) Stepping outside the box: elevating the role of the controller. Institute of Management Accountants – IMA & Deloitte's Center for Controllership
Wagner EL, Moll J, Newell S (2011) Accounting logics, reconfiguration of ERP systems and the emergence of new accounting practices: a sociomaterial perspective. Manag Account Res 22(3): 181–197
Wajdi F (2018) The role of management accounting practices in the use of the mediate relation the quality of information and the quality of an ERP system on performance of companies in Indonesia manufacture. Akuntabilitas 11(2):257–280
Weli W (2018) The accountant satisfaction in using ERP systems. Commun Inf Technol J 12(1): 27–34
Youssef M, Mahama H (2021) Does business intelligence mediate the relationship between ERP and management accounting practices? J Account Org Change 17(5):686–703
Zamani M, Valmohammadi C (2014) The effects of ERP systems implementation on management accounting in Iranian organizations. Educ Bus Soc 7(4):245–256

Impact of Digitalization on the Accounting Profession

Bojan Savić and Vladan Pavlović

Abstract The goal of the paper is to provide a comprehensive insight into the implications that the process of business digitalization has on the roles and competencies of accountants. Due to current technological changes, all integral parts of accounting as a business function have undergone or will undergo corresponding changes shortly. Research is based on secondary sources of materials. A structured review of academic literature on the impact of digital technologies on accounting and corporate reporting has been performed by collecting peer-reviewed papers from the Web of Science and Scopus databases. The contribution of the paper is reflected in highlighting innovative ways of communicating accounting information, both internally and externally. In that sense, the paper points out the changes that have occurred in the financial reporting process and current regulations, then in the field of management accounting, as well as recent changes in the scope of integrated reporting. The accounting profession will continue to evolve, and accountants will acquire new knowledge and competencies to respond to numerous challenges adequately. These findings are important for accountants and management and other participants in the corporate reporting chain, such as investors, creditors, capital market regulators, and auditors.

Keywords Digitalization · XBRL · Accounting profession · Corporate reporting

B. Savić (✉)
Agricultural Faculty, University of Belgrade, Belgrade, Republic of Serbia
e-mail: bsavic@agrif.bg.ac.rs

V. Pavlović
Faculty of Economics, University of Pristina in Kosovska Mitrovica, Kosovska Mitrovica, Republic of Serbia
e-mail: vladan.pavlovic@pr.ac.rs

S. Benković et al. (eds.), *Digital Transformation of the Financial Industry*, Contributions to Finance and Accounting,
https://doi.org/10.1007/978-3-031-23269-5_2

1 Introduction

The growing trend of the presence of digital technologies in everyday life and the economy has conditioned the need to change the way a company conducts business. Digitalization requires continuous communication with stakeholders to maintain the race with growing competition, better meet customers' needs, operate at lower costs, and more efficiently realize the defined company's goals (Monterio 2016a). Digitalization, on the other hand, provides an opportunity to find new modalities of cooperation between a company and different stakeholders, both within the supply chain and within the company (Verneeten and Heinen 2021). Introducing innovative products and services, forming new markets and business opportunities, and reengineering business processes imply implementing effective strategies in response to new business conditions (Brands 2018). The strategy's definition, implementation, and validation must be based on relevant information. The digitalization of the economy and business model has not remained without an impact on the accounting profession, in the sense that it generates certain risks, but it also represents a kind of source of opportunity (Verneeten and Heinen 2021). As such, digitalization not only affects the scope of work and its implementation in the finance and accounting sector but also provides new opportunities to support the accounting profession in realizing company goals (Galarza 2017). Digitalization touches on numerous segments of financial reporting, starting with recording business events and transactions through preparing financial statements and their disclosure (Phornlaphatrachakorn and Na-Kalasindhu 2021). Changes are also inevitable in management accounting, business reporting, integrated reporting, auditing, and forensic accounting.

The digital environment that emerged as a result of technology entering all parts of society and the emergence of numerous innovations and trends, such as Big Data, XBRL (eXtensible Business Reporting Language—XBRL), Cloud Computing, Blockchain, Artificial intelligence (AI), have repercussions on the scope, as well as the extent and type of knowledge and skills that is necessarily expected from accountants so that they can successfully respond to new challenges (Howell 2015). Although accountants have long been more than mere notaries of business changes, digitalization implies a further evolution of their competencies. For professional accountants, digitalization reduces the volume of manual work, allowing them to use part of their efforts for more creative purposes, supporting management in its efforts to improve competitiveness and create company value (Boyle 2021).

Several questions arise from the previously stated, such as whether the accounting profession is endangered by the process of digitalization, i.e., whether AI will replace the human factor. How can the accounting profession contribute to managing current risks and value creation? What are the additional competencies and knowledge that accountants must master? Will the role of accountants, and thus the scope of their work, undergo significant changes in the coming period?

Since it has direct implications for accounting reports in terms of format and the time frame in which they become available to users, it is essential to consider how digitalization affects the company's communication with stakeholders. Digitalization implies tagging financial reports in the financial reporting segment, which is highly regulated by professional and legal regulations. Improving the availability, accuracy, and timeliness of information provides an opportunity for report users to perform appropriate analyses and comparisons and to make adequate decisions on the allocation of financial resources on that basis. This further affects financial markets' efficiency by reducing information asymmetry and related risks (Tarca 2020).

XBRL is used to tag financial data in such a way that a large amount of information in reports can be automatically loaded through software and is thus much easier to sort, aggregate, compare, and finally use by many stakeholders (Monterio 2016a). In the European Union, the turn toward digitalization of financial statements envisages that public companies operating in the EU will prepare statements by the Inline XBRL (iXBRL) starting in 2020 (Colgren 2018). These reports must also be subject to external audit, which requires the audit profession to make adjustments and acquire new skills. Leading companies strive to disclose additional relevant information to investors using the XBRL technology for more efficient communication. However, it is essential to note that the application of XBRL standards is not exclusively in the domain of financial reporting. Because the company's management is responsible for compiling financial reports, management accountants, as a kind of support to the management, also have competencies in this area (Mccullogh et al. 2017). Namely, their task is to reduce errors that may occur during data generation, and they have partial responsibility for verifying compliance with the relevant regulations. The importance of this support is evidenced by the high costs that may occur due to inadequate quality of information, which are manifested in the form of wrong business and investment decisions, reputational risk, legal obligations, and others (Dallavia and Garbellotto 2015).

Management accountants' contribution to improving the quality of information can be provided through adequate education and training, the advising of management when choosing investments in information technology and equipment, but also by pointing out to the management the importance of efficient and timely internal and external communication based on contemporary technologies (Brands 2018). The added significance of the profession is reflected in supporting the management of new types of risks, such as cybersecurity risks (Monterio 2016b).

This paper aims to point out the implications that the process of business digitalization has on the scope of work and competencies of accountants. All integral parts of accounting as a business function due to the dynamics in the selection and implementation of digital business strategy and current technological developments, all integral parts of accounting as a business function have undergone or will undergo appropriate changes shortly. Emphasized initiatives, generating new knowledge and competencies of accountants in response to current business circumstances, is an adequate response to support the decision-making process, and improve competitiveness and risk management.

Research is based on secondary sources of materials. A structured review of academic literature on the impact of digital technologies on accounting and corporate reporting has been performed by collecting peer-reviewed papers from the WoS and Scopus databases. Highlighting innovative ways of communicating accounting information internally and externally is the main contribution of this paper. In that sense, the paper points out the changes that have occurred in the financial reporting process and current regulations, then in the field of management accounting, as well as recent changes in the scope of integrated reporting.

2 XBRL as an Instrument to Support Corporate Reporting

The emergence and broader use of the Internet initiated an information revolution, which is manifested in the fact that billions of information in electronic form are available at relatively low costs or completely free of charge upon request initiated with just one click. In the context of corporate reporting, the environment described has significantly influenced the communication system between the company and its stakeholders because their information needs have evolved and become highly complex. In addition, unfavorable market conditions, and particularly crises periods, often encourage data manipulation in financial statements (Pavlović et al. 2019b, 2022b), as well as some characteristics of management that could additionally contribute to that practice (Pavlović et al. 2018, 2019a, 2022a).

By applying specific software programs and standards, it is possible to do this faster and simpler, than in the conditions of manual compilation and publishing of corporate reports. Extensible Markup Language—XML is an Internet technology used to exchange company data electronically. The use of XML for processing accounting data and reporting is called eXtensible Business Reporting Language—XBRL. It is a key language implemented in the form of accepted dialects required by specific business processes. Although initially introduced to improve financial information, it was soon realized that XBRL could also be adapted and successfully applied to non-financial reporting (Willis 2002).

XBRL represents an international standard for preparing and using corporate business reports. As a software language, it is aimed at supporting investors, analysts, regulators, and other stakeholders by providing the ability to obtain and exchange information quickly and efficiently. This is achieved through the information marking protocol, more precisely so that each segment of data in electronic form is automatically added to the appropriate identification code (label). One of the advantages of using the XBRL electronic language is that computers can select, analyze, store, exchange, and present information (Piechocki and Servais 2010).

The foregoing suggests that XBRL represents a revolutionary approach to corporate reporting as it provides stakeholders with access to necessary information. The main characteristic of XBRL is that it is platform neutral, which means that the content it transmits remains unchanged. It also provides the ability to efficiently transform reports from one system to another, between different companies, without losing their essential meaning. More precisely, financial (or other) reports can be compiled using specific accounting software, and users have the opportunity to download the report in the desired format through the XBRL standard (Monterio 2016a).

The two main components of XBRL as a standard for financial and non-financial information are technical specifications and taxonomies. Technical specifications contain fundamental definitions of how XBRL works. Taxonomies indicate what data is displayed and how it relates to other reports' positions. These are categorized schemes that define specific labels for individual items of information. The basic XBRL specification defines three dimensions: the reporting period, the reporting entity, and the more broadly defined reporting scenario. The listed XBRL specification tags are organized into logical structures known as taxonomies, i.e., data classification systems (Gonzalbez and Rodriguez 2012).

The advantages of the XBRL standard are reflected in the following (PriceWaterhouseCoopers 2003):

- Lower costs of preparation, publication, and use of reports (time and necessary interventions of reporting authorities are reduced).
- Greater reporting flexibility and timely information for company management and stakeholders.
- Simplified and international access to information.
- Standardized information recognized and understood by all users.
- Increased reporting transparency and reliability of information through the reduction of errors, distribution of information while preserving its integrity.
- Supports analytical skills.

In addition to the imposed legal obligation to publish reports using the XBRL standard in certain countries such as the United States, Australia, Canada, and Japan, numerous companies worldwide opt for its implementation voluntarily. These proactive companies strive to improve dialogue with their stakeholders (Dallavia and Garbellotto 2015). Regarding the authority for forming and maintaining taxonomies, the USA US GAAP XBRL taxonomies are defined and updated by the FASB), while the IASB defines IFRS XBRL taxonomies. One of the solutions for taxonomies in the field of integrated reporting is to define them by the International Integrated Reporting Council (IIRC).

Although XBRL was initially intended for financial information, this standard business reporting language is flexible and can be applied to sustainability reporting. The XBRL framework can be designed to meet a variety of information needs. Automating business reporting is part of the path to integrated reporting that includes technological innovations such as XBRL standards, Internet reporting, and real-time reporting. The Consortium XBRL states that significant benefits in efficiency and lower business costs arise from the automatic collection and systematization of information. Still, there are challenges in establishing the credibility of the information in business reports (Dallavia and Garbellotto 2015). The XBRL standard facilitates the adoption and implementation of the integrated reporting concept and enables stakeholders to have a more comprehensive knowledge of the company's performance and prosperity.

Analogous to financial reporting, the Global Reporting Initiative has defined taxonomies for reporting on sustainable development (specific categorized schemes and labels for a particular industry), such as taxonomies for carbon dioxide emissions, reduction of carbon dioxide emissions compared to the previous year, and similar. The taxonomy is a comprehensive set of XBRL files that cover numerous entry points at different points in time and provide concepts relevant to specific purposes. Taxonomies refer to both financial and non-financial information (Rowbottom et al. 2021). The XBRL taxonomy for environmental, social, and corporate governance information increases its value by making it available in real-time alongside financial information, based on which it is possible to see cause-and-effect relationships between them. The XBRL standard should also make it likely to increase the expressive power of financial and non-financial information. Namely, non-financial information in the reporting process is often presented in isolation, resulting in no insight into their connection with financial performance (Monterio 2010). The report on sustainable development in XBRL format is always based on the entry points defined by GRI or the extension created by the reporting entity. Defined taxonomies allow companies to easily mark information on sustainable development in their report, allowing users to recognize and analyze the required information (Global Reporting Initiative 2010).

The XBRL standard contributes to the quality of comparability and timeliness of the information. The question of comparability is particularly important for the information on sustainable development. Considering how it is possible to achieve comparability of content between individual companies requires identifying an objective reporting framework that supports comparability of information where it exists and simultaneously encourages comparability if the information is incomparable (Watson and Wray 2022).

A widely accepted framework is necessary for integrated reporting to provide globally comparable information, and XBRL provides just such a framework. Using the XBRL standard, information on sustainable development should be tagged according to a taxonomy so that it can be easily understood and processed by computers and transferred between available applications. Labels representing a kind of bar code provide relevant information and describe each element of environmental, social, and corporate governance information in a way that enables their computer processing and is easily understood by the users. The above codes are based on accounting principles that can be used to classify the different elements of the report. Labels should also indicate the connection of specific categories of information and references to the relevant non-financial reporting framework (Watson and Monterio 2010).

Integrated reports show three levels of indicators. For each key performance indicator, it is possible to determine via XBRL whether it represents information about the state or current, historical or prospective, or quantitative or qualitative information. XBRL dimensions and formulas play an essential role in solving technical architecture challenges. Based on the defined dimensions, the integrated report can show the multidimensional nature of key value drivers such as key performance indicators and strategic goals, economic efficiency, energy efficiency, reducing pollution, increasing the value of human and social capital, and effective corporate governance. The fundamental performance indicators are expressed in absolute value and belong to one of the selected areas from the sustainability domain: economic, environmental, social, and corporate management (Beusch et al. 2017).

In contrast, the derived performance indicators represent the relative relationship between the selected fundamental indicators. Using the formulas enables us to verify whether the displayed information respects the defined complex indicators and whether these values are coherent with the basic and derived indicators When financial and sustainable development information is marked in an integrated report, all participants within the information support chain—investors, creditors, analysts, capital market, auditors, regulation, and others, can quickly, precisely, and easily access valid and comparable information. This contributes to the credibility of integrated reports (Gonzalbez and Rodriguez 2012).

XBRL Global Ledger—XBRL GL enables the codification of financial and non-financial information in a suitable way for conducting various analyses. With this, it is possible to contribute to the digitalization of integrated reports since different business dimensions, such as economic, ecological, and social, are covered. That could facilitate data integration in the CSR reporting practice (Knežević and Pavlović 2019). The innovative way of generating reports, through the provision of information in real time, supports the decision-making process and contributes to the efficient communication of the company with stakeholders (Dallavia and Garbellotto 2015).

Automating corporate reporting provides the opportunity for accountants to devote more time to activities that add value to the company, the opportunity for key stakeholders to gain better insight from the reports presented, and enable more efficient capital allocation decisions—financial, natural, social/relational, human and intellectual capital (Verneeten and Heinen 2021). It is essential to point out that XBRL has the potential to be applied to the information that circulates within the company, primarily for performance management, process improvement, data mining, etc.

3 The Role of Accountants in the Business Digitalization

The imperative to improve business processes and the ubiquitous digitalization of business had implications for the scope of the accounting function and, thus, for the role and competencies of accountants. Digital technologies have contributed to the automation of numerous activities in the company, as a result of which routine operations such as data entry and documentation records have been significantly accelerated and facilitated. The described circumstances initiated numerous questions, such as: will the need for the services of accountants disappear in the future, and should accountants think about retraining in other activities?

With the development of AI and the automation of numerous activities within the accounting function, accountants have gained more time to focus on activities that contribute to value creation (Sun et al. 2020). The above implies the development of new activities in the field of accounting, as well as the emergence of new roles that accountants will have to contribute to the strategic positioning of companies and the creation of value. Some include technology management and data analysis, cross-functional collaboration, risk management, performance monitoring, and more (Verneeten and Heinen 2021).

Since machines cannot replace people, that is, thinking at a strategic level, it is considered that the digitalization process does not threaten the survival of the accounting profession. Still, the fact is that the accountant's scope will undergo significant changes. Expect that in the coming period, the accountant's scope of work will change by more than 30% compared to the current one, which requires the accounting profession to adequately prepare for the upcoming changes (Galarza 2017). The former confirms that accountants are still crucial in supporting strategic decision-making. Accountants will support management by creating various scenarios based on real data, assessments, and risk management through financial modeling and strategic planning (ICAEW 2019).

The above indicates that accountants are expected to become multi-specialized professionals possessing considerable skills. This implies continuous learning and improvement competencies. In addition, the faculties play a significant role in listening to the market's needs; they should strive to update their curricula to prepare new generations of accountants who will be able to provide substantial support to the adaptation of companies to changed business circumstances (Lundy et al. 2021). This is especially important if one considers that senior accountants have excellent accounting competencies but have not kept up with accelerated technological changes, due to which new technologies are not close to them (Verneeten and Heinen 2021). Professional accountants must be educated and develop additional skills through various continuing education programs. The evolution of the accounting function implies that accountants develop advanced skills in data management, their analysis, and visual presentation of the obtained information, to provide insight and foresight as business partners. The focus on strategic issues and assistance in formulating, validating, and implementing the strategy becomes the center of their activity. Furthermore, accountants are expected to focus on innovation and change management. This implies critical and creative thinking as well as the skills of timely recognition of threats and opportunities in the environment (Lawson 2019).

The previously described trends in contemporary business have caused changes in the field of information needs of both strategic stakeholders and management, and a new challenge has been set before the accounting profession. Namely, it is about financial and non-financial information being given the status of strategically important assets. Creating and maintaining the company's strategic resources requires appropriate investment in appropriate equipment and technologies. Accounting and financial experts participate significantly in technological projects, providing support through assessing expected effects and implementing innovative technical solutions (Brands 2018). Also, it is essential for accountants in the early stages of specific technological changes must anticipate the impact on business in the short, medium, and long term (ACCA-IMA 2013).

In light of the digitalization of business and the improvement of the accounting function, it is necessary to invest in data strategy, data management, and data analytics. The introduction of new processes in the company presupposes the existence of skilled personnel who will initiate and support the proposed changes. In this sense, the reporting team must be equipped with knowledge (knowledge of the specifics of the company's business, strategy, business model, clear awareness of what information needs to be created, how to analyze and present it), as well as the skills to effectively implement the entire process while ensuring the integrity and reliability of the displayed information (Bray 2018). A company's information strategy is vital to gaining and maintaining a competitive advantage. That is why it is crucial for management to know where information is located, who is responsible for it, for what purposes it was created, the degree of information aggregation, and its importance in the context of performance management (Corban 2021).

One of the leading risks of the digitalization of business is cyber risk. The role of accountants in this area is to support the protection of strategic information through an adequate system of internal control, monitoring, and innovative technologies (Monterio 2016b). Accountants must be extremely proactive in terms of contributing to the initiation and timely implementation of changes in companies in such a way that the business can successfully adapt to the dynamic environment and improve its competitive position (Boyle 2021).

It is important to note that the success of a digital strategy does not depend only on the purchase of state-of-the-art equipment and advanced software. Each company has its specifics, and the digital strategy implemented by one company may not be adequate for others. Critical thinking, problem-solving creativity, and business understanding make human capital still a key player in the race with digital Darwinism (Gibson et al. 2020). The importance of human capital as a part of intellectual capital has been recently widely explored in various industries (Pavlović et al. 2021). Its unique qualities make it a factor of competitive advantage of rising importance in the Digital Age. It is a detailed understanding of customer needs, strategic and integrated thinking, creative problem solving, effective communication, ethical issues, regulatory compliance, leadership, and more (Serafeim 2016; McDonald 2022). Some researchers find evidence that ethics conduction is connected with age (Pavlović et al. 2019a).

Integrated thinking as the basis of successful digitalization of business means that the decision-making process is carried out with an overview of the long-term implications of each decision and action on various forms of capital, as well as the potential of creating company value. Integrated thinking starts at the board of directors level and then, through a "top-down" approach, is transferred to lower hierarchical levels—senior management and employees, including accountants (Deloitte 2015). Integrated thinking requires implementing changes within a company's traditional performance measurement and reporting system. It has already been pointed out that digitalization enables the creation of detailed information, as a result of which companies can introduce certain more advanced performance measures and thereby better understand the efficiency of certain aspects of the business (Brockhaus et al. 2022). As such, integrated thinking implies a change in the business concept and is essential in effectively implementing a business digitalization strategy.

To successfully implement the digitalization strategy, it is not enough just for the management to declare that they want to leave the traditional thought algorithm. The problem is much more complex; the "silo" mentality does not arise spontaneously. A silo is the result of a combination of several elements—organizational culture, traditional way of thinking, and process factors. Correcting the mentioned elements makes it possible to change the mentality in the company. The accountant's role in this domain is to present to the management all the advantages that digitalization brings for the company and to initiate the idea of the necessity of digitalization of business and reporting (Savić 2015).

Through integrated reporting, accountants have the opportunity to innovate corporate culture and improve the company's reporting process, which contributes to freeing relevant information from corporate silos and making it available to management and numerous stakeholders at the same time. The innovative content of the report, through the integration of information on realized value and used capital together with information on implemented strategies and the business model, represents a strong incentive to generate and distribute added value in the short, medium, and long term (Ridehalgh et al. 2018).

The survival of the accounting profession in the future requires a reorientation toward management accounting and its support for internal decision-making. This presupposes that the competencies and knowledge available to management accountants are used to support management decision-making while preserving the traditional role of accountants in the field of financial reporting. Additionally, accountants must improve their IT skills for collecting, validating, and reporting purposes in the digital era. They are expected to conduct cost/benefit analysis and support when choosing a data management strategy, data analysis using business intelligence software, interpretation of results, and generation of predictive information. In this regard, Frigo and Krumwiede (2020) indicate that management accountants are in a unique position to participate in and guide the process of strategic analysis. The above requires strategic thinking and strategic analysis skills. To be reliable advisors, they must understand the company's operations in detail. They need to know how the business is doing, key influences, customers' buying habits, satisfaction level, and competitors' strengths and weaknesses.

For cost-benefit analysis and cost control that is related to digitalization, it is necessary to extend the concept of life e cycle to include a broader set of costs, not only directly but indirectly, through externalities or impacts in the broader environment (Savić et al. 2019). To design the digitalization of business operations and achieve profitability, accountants have at their disposal different budgeting techniques. They are used for various purposes, and besides defined goals and business conditions, the choice is determined by the type of activity (Savić et al. 2016).

Finally, due to the change in reporting, it is necessary to choose an adequate model for presenting reports to stakeholders (Lawson 2019). In this sense, integrated reports that strive to show financial and non-financial performance in a way that shows their mutual connection and conditioning have shown numerous benefits compared to other forms of reports. The foregoing assumes that accountants take on the part of the tasks previously reserved for IT experts, such as mapping XBRL GL data, codifying and decoding data, and advanced analysis tools (Dallavia and Garbellotto 2015).

Through various forms of cooperation between companies and key stakeholders, it is possible to collect the necessary information to define strategies, plans, and internal and external reporting. In the given circumstances, integrated reporting is recognized as an instrument that allows a comprehensive overview of the company's performance. Building trust and consequently securing long-term support from the public, including commercial and financial market participants, requires selecting and implementing an appropriate reporting strategy that will guide the corporate reporting portfolio, along with an integrated report as a leading instrument. To achieve adequate results in the mentioned area, the reporting strategy must be conceived and supported by an efficient system that will manage the entire implementation process of the integrated reporting undertaking. Accountants inevitably have a significant role in the mentioned process, which is first of all recognized through the initiative of introducing integrated reporting, and then through information support for the definition and implementation of the digital reporting strategy (Todorović et al. 2020).

Integrated reporting and digitalization should enable a reorientation from displaying historical information to predictive analysis. This further presupposes the introduction of accounting engineering, which includes redesigning and innovating the accounting function by the changes (digitalization, AI; cloud) for accountants to respond to the challenges they face successfully. Accounting must adopt an interdisciplinary approach to problem solving. Effective use of digital systems in daily work requires accountants to improve their knowledge since digital accounting is much more comprehensive than the use of individual digital systems. Hence, digitalization requires more than technological innovation. More precisely, digital transformation radically changes key elements of the accounting profession, such as concept, business philosophy, education, the definition of accounting and qualifications of professional accountants, accounting thought, practice, and culture (Tekbas 2022).

Digitalization paves the way for introducing new KPIs based on new information. Also, it is possible to predict the future, that is, to create prospective information based on real-time web search data. Thus, for example, financial accountants can anticipate stakeholder demand for information before earnings announcements, and management accountants can predict customer sentiments before launching a new product. Big Data helps companies track their costs, i.e., improve cost control and productivity, thereby enabling sustainable value creation (Knudsen 2020).

Regarding cost management and control as an essential assumption for developing and preserving competitive advantage, it is undeniable that the accounting profession has significantly contributed to practice so far. Successful cost management primarily requires precise cost measurement. Information obtained based on traditional costing systems is not suitable for managing the challenges faced by enterprises. The solutions could be found in the contemporary cost accounting systems that eliminate the weaknesses of the conventional approach and provide more precise information (Savic et al. 2014).

The fact that integrated reporting and business sustainability require the consideration of not only economic aspects but also the social and environmental dimensions of business has created the need for cost management to understand the implications of business operations for the broader environment of entities. The most significant number of contemporary techniques and methods of cost calculation and analysis focus on the costs arising from the production phase. From the perspective of global competition, considering the imperative of maintaining sustainable business in the long run, the information obtained is insufficient for designing, implementing, and revising competitive strategies. Cost accounting information that goes beyond the traditionally understood operating costs to quantitatively encompass and give a monetary presentation of environmental business aspects is very important in a contemporary business environment for capturing, analyzing, managing, and improving the overall performance of an entity (Savić et al. 2020).

Digital transformation of accounting can help to reach that goal through cost modeling. Two fundamental principles of cost modeling are the principles of causality and analogy. This will ensure more comprehensive knowledge of costs, more rate budgeting, better insight into the cause-and-effect relationships between certain decisions and incurred costs, and more efficient decision-making (Clinton and England 2016).

4 Conclusion

The process of automatization and digitalization of business has significantly affected the accounting profession in such a way that accountants have become more efficient in creating high-quality information. New challenges in business have led to the expansion of the scope of accountants to more effectively use opportunities and manage risks in business. The accountant's role has evolved from the creation of financial information for accounting to capital owners to a partner and management advisor in the strategic decision-making process. Accountants are expected to support management in assessing and managing existing and potential risks and simultaneously contribute to finding innovative solutions that will create sustainable value for all stakeholders. In addition to numerous advantages, digitalization also brings a new type of risk, cyber risk, reflected in the possibility of unauthorized access to data. Hence, the internal control system supported by IT controls should prevent potential damage.

Analytical skills and logical thinking remain essential elements of accountants' competencies to manage Big Data effectively. The focus on strategic issues and assistance in formulating, validating, and implementing the strategy becomes the center of their activity. Furthermore, accountants are expected to focus on innovation and change management. In this sense, accountants must master digital knowledge and be ready to learn and improve continuously.

With the change in the business environment, the information needs of both management and stakeholders change, which presents a new challenge to the accounting profession. Namely, it is about the fact that financial and non-financial information received the status of strategically important assets. Accountants are expected not just to prepare past-oriented information but also to create prospective information to see the future. Integrated reports emerged as a response to the changing culture of reporting and the need for more effective communication with stakeholders. By showing the interrelationship of financial and non-financial performance, it is possible to see the impact of different forms of capital (financial, production, natural, human, intellectual, relational, and social) on business sustainability.

Integrated reporting and digitalization should enable a reorientation from displaying historical information to predictive analysis. This further presupposes the introduction of accounting engineering, which includes redesigning and innovating the accounting function by the resulting changes. Accounting must adopt an interdisciplinary approach to problem solving, and accountants must master the application of IT technologies, statistics, modeling, scenario analysis, and more.

Each company has specifics that must be considered when choosing a digital strategy. It is important to note that success in implementing a digital strategy does not depend only on purchasing state-of-the-art equipment and software. Thinking, understanding specific situations in the company and its environment, as well as creativity in overcoming challenges are qualities that technology still does not possess. This speaks in favor of the importance of human capital, i.e., accountants, as an essential element not only of the successful digitalization of business but also of the long-term survival and prosperity of the company. For the successful improvement of business processes and the implementation of a digitalization strategy, it is not enough just for the management to declare that they want to leave the traditional thought algorithm. The problem is much more complex since the "silo" mentality does not arise spontaneously. Digitalization of corporate reporting is much more comprehensive than the use of individual digital systems. It presupposes a review and redefinition of key elements of the accounting profession, such as concepts, definitions, philosophy, education, the definition of accounting and qualifications of professional accountants, accounting thought, practice, and culture.

The future survival of the accounting profession requires greater attention to management accounting as significant support for internal decision-making and management consulting. The foregoing assumes that accountants take over some of the tasks previously reserved for IT experts, codifying and decoding data and advanced tools of analysis.

Acknowledgments This paper is a result of the research project financed by The Ministry of education, Science and Technology Development of the Republic of Serbia No. 451-03-68/2022-14/200116 and No. 451-03-1/2022-14/25.

References

ACCA-IMA (2013) Digital Darwinism: Thriving in the face of technology change. https://www.accaglobal.com/content/dam/acca/global/PDF-technical/futures/pol-afa-tt2.pdf. Accessed 17 June 2022

Beusch P, Frisk JE, Rosen M, William D (2017) Management control for sustainability: towards integrated systems. Manag Account Res 54(2022):1–14

Boyle M (2021) Finance and accounting in the virtual world. Strat Financ 102(12):40–45

Brands K (2018) Digital demands. Strat Financ 100(10):68–70

Bray M (2018) Building an integrated reporting management system. KPMG https://home.kpmg/au/en/home/insights/2018/02/building-integrated-reporting-management-systems.html.. Accessed 20 June 2022

Brockhaus J, Buhmann A, Zerfass A (2022) Digitalization in corporate communications: understanding the emergence and consequences of CommTech and digital infrastructure. Corp Commun Int J. https://doi.org/10.1108/CCIJ-03-2022-0035

Clinton D, England B (2016) Principles of healthy managerial costing. Strat Financ 98(3):40–45

Colgren D (2018) XBRL, Blockchain, and new technologies. Strat Financ 99(7):62–63

Corban T (2021) Data as a strategic asset. Strat Financ 102(10):60–61

Dallavia N, Garbellotto G (2015) Internal reporting with XBRL global ledger. Strat Financ 97(4): 46–54

Deloitte (2015) A Directors' guide to integrated reporting. Deloitte and Touche, London http://www2.deloitte.com/content/dam/Deloitte/nz/Documents/risk/directors-guide-int-rep.pdf. Accessed 27 June 2022

Frigo M, Krumwiede K (2020) Strategic analysis - methods for achieving superior and sustainable performance. Statement on Management Accounting, Institute of Management Accountants, The Association of Accountants and Financial Professionals in Business. https://wwwimanetorg/insights-and-trends/the-future-of-management-accounting/strategic-analysis-methods-for-achieving-superior-and-sustainable-performance?ssopc=1 Accessed 10 July 2022

Galarza M (2017) The changing nature of accounting. Strateg Finance 98(8):50–54

Gibson A, Kaplan B, Cutbill D (2020) From mirage to reality: bringing finance into focus in a digital world. IMA-Deloitte. https://wwwimanetorg/-/media/1556f3868820422ea39760b48abd4755ashx. Accessed 13 July 2022

Global Reporting Initiative and Deloitte & Touche (2010) GRI taxonomy: implementation guide. Global Reporting Initiative, Deloitte & Touche, 2012. https://www.globalreporting.org/resourcelibrary/GRITaxonomy-Implementation-Guide-2012.pdf. Accessed 15 June 2022

Gonzalbez J, Rodriguez M (2012) XBRL and integrated reporting: the Spanish accounting association taxonomy approach. Int J Digit Account Res 12:59–91

Howell J (2015) Moving to the cloud. Strat Finance 97(6):30–37

ICAEW (2019) Big data and analytics: the impact on the accountancy profession. https://www.icaew.com/-/media/corporate/files/technical/technology/thought-leadership/big-data-and-analytics.ashx. Accessed 24 July 2022

Knežević G, Pavlović V (2019) CSR reporting practice: is there room for integration? – evidence from Serbian foreign investors. J East Eur Manage Stud (JEEMS) 24(2):280–304. https://doi.org/10.5771/0949-6181-2019-2-280

Knudsen DR (2020) Elusive boundaries, power relations, and knowledge production: a systematic review of the literature on digitalization in accounting. Int J Account Inf Syst 36:1–22

Lawson R (2019) Management accounting competencies: fit for purpose in a digital age? Institute of Management Accountants Montval. https://wwwimanetorg/insights-and-trends/the-future-of-management-accounting/management-accounting-competencies%2D%2D-fit-for-purpose-in-a-digital-age?ssopc=1. Accessed 20 July 2022

Lundy B, Sergeant A, Jiles L (2021) Accounting curricula in digital age. Strateg Financ 103(2): 28–33

Mccullogh A, Mcguire B, Smith D (2017) XBRL, and the cloud: a case study. Strateg Financ 99(5): 40–47
McDonald P (2022) AI is transforming finance, but it won't replace you. Strat Financ 103(10): 19–20
Monterio B (2010) Sustainability reporting and XBRL – part 2. Strat Finance 92(3):56–61
Monterio B (2016a) Improving data quality: people, process, technology. Strat Finance 97(10): 62–63
Monterio B (2016b) Technology trend to watch. Strat Finance 98(2):86–88
Pavlović V, Knežević G, Bojičić R (2018) Board gender diversity and earnings management in agricultural sector - does it have any influence? Custos e Agronegócio on line 14(2):340–363
Pavlović V, Knežević G, Bojičić R (2019a) Does board of director's age impact earnings management in agriculture? - Case study Serbian agricultural sector. Custos e Agronegócio on line 15(1):254–272
Pavlović V, Knežević G, Joksimović M, Joksimović D (2019b) Fraud detection in financial statements applying Benford's law with Monte Carlo simulation. Acta Oeconomica 69(2): 217–239. https://doi.org/10.1556/032.2019.69.2.4
Pavlović V, Knežević G, Petković M (2021) The impact of intellectual capital on financial performance in the fishing industry - evidence from France. Custos e Agronegócio on line 17(4):445–467
Pavlović V, Knežević G, Bojičić R (2022a) The impact of gender and age on earnings management practices of public enterprises: a case study of Belgrade. Econ Stud (Ikonomicheski Izsledvania) 31(3):130–148
Pavlović V, Knežević G, Cunha Callado AA (2022b) Is the corporate solvency conundrum primarily a Balkan issue or a broader European continental misunderstanding? Econ Stud (Ikonomicheski Izsledvania) 31(1):72–93
Phornlaphatrachakorn K, Na-Kalasindhu K (2021) Digital accounting, financial reporting quality, and digital transformation: evidence from Thai listed firms. J Asian Financ Econ Bus 8(8): 409–419
Piechocki M, Servais O (2010) The role of XBRL and IFRS in integrated reporting, the landscape of integrated reporting: reflection and next steps. In: Eccles R, Cheng B, Saltzman D (eds) The landscape of integrated reporting: reflection and next steps. Harvard Business school, Boston, pp 155–159
PriceWaterhouseCoopers (2003) Trusted and efficient financial reporting. Working paper. https://www.pwc.com/en_GX/gx/xbrl/assets/pwc_trusted_efficient_financial_reporting.pdf. Accessed 10 June 2022
Ridehalgh N, Bray M, Dumble K (2018) Trust through transparency. https://home.kpmg/au/en/home/insights/2018/02/trust-through-transparency-integrated-reporting.html. Accessed 26 June 2022
Rowbottom N, Locke J, Troshani I (2021) Digitalization the tail wags the dog? Digit Corporate Report Account Org Soc 92(2021):1–18. https://doi.org/10.1016/j.aos.2021.101226
Savić B (2015) Integrisano izveštavanje kao podrška integrisanom upravljanju i održivom kreiranju vrednosti (Integrated reporting as support for integrated management and creating sustainable value). In: Kaličanin D, Lončar D, Bogetić Z, Todorović M (eds) Stvaranje vrednosti: teorijsko-praktični aspekti (Value creating: theorical and practical aspects), Ekonomski fakultet Univerzitet u Beogradu, Beograd, pp 223–241
Savic B, Vasiljevic Z, Đorđević D (2014) Strategic cost management as instrument for improving competitiveness of agribusiness complex. Econ Agric 61(4):1005–1020
Savić B, Vasiljević Z, Popović N (2016) The role and importance of strategic budgeting for competitiveness of the agribusiness supply chain. Econ Agric 63(1):295–312
Savić B, Milojević I, Petrović V (2019) Cost optimization in agribusiness based on life cycle costing. Econ Agric 66(3):823–834. https://doi.org/10.5937/ekoPolj1903823S

Savić B, Vasiljević Z, Milojević I (2020) Costing system as an instrument for enhancing environmental performance of entities in agribusiness. J Bus Econ Manag 68(3–4):294–302. https://doi.org/10.5937/EKOPRE2004294S
Serafeim G (2016) Integrated reporting. Institute of Management Accounting, Montvale. https://www.imanet.org/-/media/0830fcd907cd41a7bd760b8900fe7b94.ashx. Accessed 24 July 2022
Sun H, Rabbani MR, Sial MS, Yu S, Filipe JA, Cherian J (2020) Identifying big data's opportunities. Chall Implicat Financ Math 8(10):2–20
Tarca A (2020) Digital reporting – questions for practitioners, standard-setters and researchers. IFRS Foundation. https://www.ifrs.org/news-and-events/news/2020/07/digital-reporting-questions/. Accessed 20 July 2022
Tekbas I (2022) Accounting engineering and space accounting. Cosmo Publishing Company, Waldorf
Todorović M, Savić B, Jovanović D (2020) Integrisano izveštavanje novi model korporativnog izveštavanja (Integrated reporting new model of corporate reporting). Ekonomski fakultet Univerziteta u Kragujevcu, Kragujevac
Verneeten F, Heinen J (2021) Managing digital transformation. Stateg Finance 102(8):46–53
Watson L, Monterio B (2010) Bringing, order to the chaos: integrating sustainability reporting framework and financial reporting into one report with XBRL. In: Eccles R, Cheng B, Saltzman D (eds) The landscape of integrated reporting: reflection and next steps. Harvard Business school, Boston, pp 160–166
Watson L, Wray D (2022) The digital transformation of sustainability data. Strat Finance 103(10):36–41
Willis M (2002) XBRL: corporate communications for the 21st century. PriceWaterhouseCoopers http://wwwxbrlorg/Business/General/PwC-Corp-Comms-21st-Century-2002-10pdf. Accessed 20 June 2022

The Impact of Digitalization on Audit

Bojana Vuković, Dejan Jakšić, and Teodora Tica

Abstract Digital business starts with the development of a new business model using digital technologies. Technological development and digitalization have had considerable influence on the globalization of the business world and led to structural changes that also affect the audit profession. In the era of digital transformation, companies must be fast to adapt to new circumstances and rely on IT audits. The aim of this paper is to discover to what extent auditors use digitalization in performing audits in Serbia. The research was conducted using a specially designed questionnaire, filled in by a total of 110 respondents. Smart PLS analysis was used for processing and analyzing the data. The findings show that as a result of digitalization, audit quality in Serbia is significantly positively affected by audit users' perception changes, auditors' work changes, and also auditors' professional profile changes. Audit regulation changes as a result of digitalization do not have a significant impact on the quality of audits in Serbia. Bearing in mind that digitalization represents a challenge as well as an opportunity for audit, the obtained results reveal valuable information to all interested stakeholders that rely on the results of audit work in decision-making.

Keywords Digitalization · Digital technologies · Audit quality · Serbia

1 Introduction

Today, information technology and the auditing profession are closely linked, with IT impacting auditing, particularly in two areas. These are, on the one hand, the subject of the audit, since the task of the auditor is to evaluate the quality of the system in which accounting and other data are processed (Jakšić 2001a, b, 2002;

B. Vuković (✉) · D. Jakšić · T. Tica
Faculty of Economics in Subotica, Subotica, Serbia
e-mail: bojana.vukovic@ef.uns.ac.rs; dejan.jaksic@ef.uns.ac.rs; teodora.tica@ef.uns.ac.rs

S. Benković et al. (eds.), *Digital Transformation of the Financial Industry*,
Contributions to Finance and Accounting,
https://doi.org/10.1007/978-3-031-23269-5_3

Jakšić and Mijić 2010). On the other hand, auditors today can use a whole range of computer-assisted tools and techniques (Andrić et al. 2011; Jakšić and Mijić 2009b).

Aditya et al. (2018) claimed that digital transformation offered new opportunities for IT auditing, positively contributing to the company's activities. The importance and complexity of IT audit increase as technology is embedded into the critical operations of most organizations (Gray and Abdolmohammadi 2016). Dzuranin and Cand Mălăescu (2016) emphasized that there were at least three significant challenges facing IT audits in the context of digital transformation, such as the increased volume of available data, the emergence of new technology, and reform requirements and regulations. The use of computers in the processing of accounting data has affected the skills and competencies requirements for auditors (Aditya et al. 2018; Jakšić and Mijić 2009b; Mijić and Vuković 2013). In changing work conditions, the auditor must respond to these growing needs.

Keeping in mind how vital digitalization in auditing is, the authors formulated two main goals in this study: one is to examine the extent to which auditors use digitalization when performing the main auditing tasks, the other aim is to gauge to what degree the advantages of digitalization are recognized and integrated into auditing in Serbia. The research further aims to show whether and to what extent digital tools such as Big Data, Artificial Intelligence, Blockchain Technology, and Robotic Process Automation are used in auditing. To the author's knowledge, there have been no similar studies conducted in Serbia to date. In the few previous investigations on the impact of digitalization on audit, the authors used a different methodology and explored other countries (Tiberius and Hirth 2019; Ramesh 2019; Adiloglu and Gungor 2019; Nguyen et al. 2020; Manita et al. 2020; Kend and Nguyen 2020; El- Monem Serag and Al- Aqiliy 2020; Almaleeh 2021; Anh and Anh 2021; Lugli and Bertacchini 2022). The obtained results lend a useful insight into digitalization levels in Serbia to all interested stakeholders using audit reports, which will, in turn, lead to better business decisions on all sides.

2 Digital Technologies in Audit

The auditor role may be impacted in numerous ways by the digitalization of the corporate field. One of the main driving forces behind the change in the audit process toward digitalization is the stakeholders themselves. The quality of decision-making by internal and external stakeholders is based on the reliability and completeness of disclosed information in financial statements (Vuković et al. 2020b). They perceive the external audit as an assurance that the financial statements are exempt from material errors. Consequently, the introduction of digitalization in auditing could be comprehended as a reduction of the time required for issuing an audit opinion (Manita et al. 2020). In that manner, financial statements, assuming that they consist of true and objective data (Vuković et al. 2022a), could serve as the basis for future decisions, rather than be considered historical. To management boards of audit clients, the traditional audit represents an additional financial burden rather than an added value to their business.

2.1 The Need for a Digital Audit

Contemporary economic conditions pose high demands on auditors regarding the expected quality of audit work (Mijić and Vuković 2013). The environment in which auditors express a competent opinion is increasingly complex as companies are globalizing, expanding the scope and types of their activities, processing their data electronically, etc. (Andrić et al. 2015). Furthermore, auditors are always subjected to strict price and time constraints when performing assurance procedures and expressing opinions as efficiently as possible with limited resources (Jakšić and Mijić 2012; Mijić 2014). Taking responsibility for the expressed opinion is unfavorable since it is difficult for the auditor to obtain reasonable assurance that the findings are sufficient and adequate to form an opinion (Mijić and Jakšić 2010). In addition to long-term, competitive advantages that are achieved by maximizing the requirements for profitable business (Vuković et al. 2017), the competitive advantages of audit companies are based on implementing the latest technologies in the audit process. Considering that business diversity affects more stable business conditions and reduces business risk (Vuković et al. 2022c), audit firms tend to expand their service supply by including the provision of new digital services.

Various regulators issue various professional practice frameworks. It must also be noted that the audit of the information system differs depending on whether it is performed as part of an external, internal, or government audit (Andrić and Jakšić 2005; Jakšić and Mijić 2009a). It not only differs in the scope of work, but in the execution framework itself, too, since there are different regulations for each of the traditional types of audits.

In a modern business environment, corporate performances are significantly influenced by globalization, competitive struggle, and rapid changes (Vuković et al. 2022b). The incredible technological advancement and the prompt introduction of digitalized processes have altered the way the corporate world does business. As corporations implemented the new, highly automated processes they now depend on, finance, accounting, and internal audit departments were forced to adapt (Betti et al. 2021). Consequently, external auditors were forced to consider the reform and modernization of their business. Corporations and their accounting departments must face substantial challenges, risks, and opportunities arising as a direct consequence of advancements in digitalization and processing capacity, along with the expansion of information (Bhimani and Willcocks 2014).

2.2 Current Trends and Opportunities of Big Data in Audit

In an era characterized by Big Data sets, data is considered a new business asset that can fundamentally transform the global economy (Hamdam et al. 2022). The term Big Data relates to databases that are exceedingly large to be recorded, stored, processed, or assessed using the ordinary computer software tools currently available. Generally, information in Big Data refers to the gathering of various categories of information which may include a mix of conventional structured financial and non-financial data, logistics data, sensor data, emails, phone calls, and social media data (Yaqoob et al. 2016). Big Data offers highly relevant corporate insights and higher-level audit proof. The introduction of several sources of audit evidence is made possible by the automated data collection provided by sensors, RFID (Radio Frequency Identification), and GPS data streams (Zhang et al. 2015). The financial market files, emails, Internet pages, social media posts, and media news are examples of Big Data components. Currently, a growing number of corporations are increasingly combining large datasets with innovative corporate techniques to provide finest information for decision-making (Gandomi and Haider 2015).

The latest literature discussions emphasize how crucial the function of Big Data is in audit engagement in terms of enhancing the accuracy, productivity, and effectiveness of the auditor's opinion. Big Data Analytics affects audit processes at various levels of the audit engagement, especially in assuming the auditing responsibility, preparing for the auditing procedure, analyzing the effectiveness of the internal control process, conducting the preparatory processes of the analytical review, and defining the thresholds of risk exposure and materiality. Considering the human psychological limitations, auditors are unable to assess the whole population of corporate transactions, hence, auditors must rely on sampling techniques in order to process data, which may be avoided by using Big Data analytical platforms. Additionally, Big Data provides auditors with a far wider basis for evaluating the reliability of transactions, flows, assets, liabilities, as well as financial statements in general (Brown-Liburd et al. 2015). However, there is a strong likelihood that the implementation of digitalization in the form of Big Data analytical tools will cause rising audit engagement fees (Dagilienė and Klovienė 2019).

In terms of barriers to the introduction of Big Data, the difficulty in accessing the client's data must be mentioned, primarily referring to the form, as well as breaking through the protective walls that are set up by each company to preserve business secrets. Moreover, auditors have a problem adapting their software to the client's accounting software, especially with multinational clients. Moreover, regardless of the origin, auditors demand that the data should be reliable and accurate (Brown-Liburd et al. 2015). Occasionally, the use of Big Data may lead to non-fulfilment of those requirements, due to a high data volume collected from various unstructured sources. Finally, although technologies are not as limited as human mental capacity, a similar deficiency could occur in their use. In the context of Big Data, analytical software may face a similar problem of information accumulation and overload, resulting in the selection and analysis of irrelevant information cues, which may mislead auditors during deeper analysis (Ahmad 2019).

2.3 Current Trends and Opportunities of Artificial Intelligence in Audit

Artificial Intelligence, also known as machine intelligence, refers to the ability of devices to imitate the natural intellect seen so far only in humans and animals. The underlying notion of the Artificial Intelligence mechanism is the ability to understand data, learn from its content, and consequently, use the acquired knowledge to achieve future tasks and goals. The built-in algorithm can repeat a certain process as many times as possible, e.g., review invoices or control inventory and payments, enhance AI experience and become even more effective and precise.

AI can be programmed to recognize extreme values, negative entries, unauthorized changes, unusually large out-of-season payment amounts, or double entries of invoices or suppliers. Instead of having the audit team manually review tens or even hundreds of thousands of transactions and balances from a predetermined sample, Artificial Intelligence makes it possible, in a short time period, to evaluate how accurately the entire set of transactions or business activities was recorded (Munoko et al. 2020). In this regard, auditors can focus on logical reasoning that is the result of their cognitive abilities, which still cannot be replaced by technology to the extent of providing their experienced judgment (Kend and Nguyen 2020; Fedyk et al. 2022).

One of the most common applications of Artificial Intelligence in audit engagements is to improve warehouse operations and inventory issues, making them less subject to human errors. Visual recognition systems can "interpret" a drone snapshot, resulting in fast identification of the physical object and categorization into a specified category. This approach automates asset and stock-related controls, and subsequently replaces traditional inventory inspections, a crucial task, especially given the importance of adequate inventory management for efficient working capital management (Vuković et al. 2020a).

The greatest technical advantage that AI brings is the continuous audit of financial loggings and transactions throughout the fiscal year. AI's abilities enabling such a process include automated collection of data, documentation scanning, payment tracking, and logical error testing, among others. Furthermore, with the introduction of Artificial Intelligence, it is possible to improve the detection of fraudulent activities using advanced machine learning.

Nevertheless, it must be mentioned that corporate implementation of Artificial Intelligence also involves certain underlying risks. Firstly, there is a risk of an improperly set algorithm by insufficiently trained employees. Also, the disparity in the legal regulation of AI between different jurisdictions could motivate certain corporations to move their branches to other countries, more suitable for further development. Since Artificial Intelligence collects a large amount of sensitive data, such as personal information, there is also the rising risk of abusing such information, which is hard to control.

2.4 Current Trends and Opportunities of Blockchain Technology in Audit

Following the initial development of blockchain technology triggered by the introduction of a new unit of value known as bitcoin, many corporations realized that this type of technology could be beneficial for accounting and financial purposes. Blockchain technology functions according to the principle of a chain and the participants in the chain can perform various exchanges of value, transactions, payments, as well as exchanges of property rights or obligations between each other. Blockchain is a global virtual ledger that tracks and encrypts transactions between two parties, ensuring that all parties involved in the chain have an identical data presentation. What makes blockchain unique is the promptness and uniqueness of data, in the sense that every alteration in the chain in the form of instruction or transaction is initiated by one participant, but also visible to everyone and is unchangeable. Moreover, transaction or activity initiated by one user must be approved by all other participants in the chain.

Auditors as well as other users in general, may benefit in many ways from the use of blockchain-based technology. Because blockchains keep records of all the prior actions that have occurred inside the chain, a person can access each one from past periods. Given that the system does not permit the alteration, erasure, or destruction of any of the activities that were previously realized, the importance of the system's transparency cannot be overstated. While still in the process of development, blockchain is a technology that has the potential to fundamentally alter how corporations operate and consequently, how they will be audited. One aspect of audit engagement that takes up a considerable part of the audit team members' time is the formation of a sample of transactions or balances that is to be examined in more detail. Their assessment reveals whether the evidence is reliable, relevant, or if it there were any material errors during recording and reporting. Blockchain technology can replace this most time-consuming part of the engagement. Considering the volume of transactions performed by clients, the blockchain can ensure greater trustworthiness of all transactions. Furthermore, auditors could rely on the blockchain mechanism itself, and not just on a subjectively determined sample. Another vital aspect of blockchain is that its records are unchangeable, assuring that once data is entered, it cannot be altered or removed unless to be merged with a subsequent entry.

However, the audit profession believes that blockchain cannot yet compensate for the wide range of audit engagement performed by a human (Gauthier and Brender 2021). In addition to the final judgment of the auditor and the extensive experience that took years to amass, blockchain technology is still not advanced enough to unfailingly recognize whether a transaction has been carried out between related parties or whether assets and liabilities are correctly classified and properly valued in accordance with International Accounting Standards/International Standard of Financial Reporting. Also, the recognition of fraud and evasion that can generally be detected by physical presence, e.g., by inventorying cannot yet be reliably detected by blockchain. In addition, the legal teams of audit firms maintain that in some countries blockchain technology is not legally regulated.

2.5 Current Trends and Opportunities of Robotic Process Automation in Audit

Robotic Process Automation is a state-of-the-art software form that utilizes standard operating procedures and predetermined task action choreography to finish the automated performance of a mix of recordings, operations, actions, payments, and repetitive tasks in software systems to offer either an outcome in a form of product or service, or to provide suggestion with error detection by a human. The automation process itself implies a software that enables the execution of low-complexity activities according to predetermined rules, by combining different application sources and programs, without human intervention.

The goal of any digitalization-oriented corporation is to automate and robotize as many actions as possible. For activities to be performed by robotic process automation, they must be defined by rules, constant repetition, operations that include interaction with a variety of distinct software applications, low complexity, digitally structured data, and ought to have a predetermined form or template (Eulerich et al. 2021). Activities suitable for robotization include opening and closing accounts, sending requests for bank payments, sending payment reminders, monitoring spent employee working hours and comparing to planned, changing employee records, standardized template fillings, receiving new purchase orders, monitoring raw material consumption, sending alerts when stocks are low, data analysis, automatic change of protection systems, such as passwords.

A great advantage of robot-based technologies is that they have simplified reporting, especially if it was previously standardized (Kokina and Blanchette 2019). Reports that used to be written on a yearly or twice-a-year basis could now be achieved on a daily basis, with minimal final control by a human. Furthermore, a significant contribution to the audit lies in the robotization of accuracy control of data entries, whereby the automated software evaluates whether the data form is correct, whether it was entered correctly, whether the format is appropriate or if it was entered by mistake as a negative value, etc.

Provided that the tasks are correctly programmed, activities, processes, or transactions should become more efficient and effective compared to human actions (Cooper et al. 2019). An additional advantage of this mechanism is lower procurement and programming costs compared to the paid time spent on members of the audit team (Huang and Vasarhelyi 2019). However, what is holding corporations back from applying robotics in auditing is the shortage of specialized workforce with abilities to program the automated process. It is essential to highlight that despite all the advantages of robotization, the human factor and the power of reasoning in auditing should not be replaceable by automation (Zhang et al. 2021).

3 Research

3.1 Data and Methodology

To measure the impact of digitalization on audit quality in Serbia, the authors created a specially designed questionnaire consisting of personal and survey parts and conducted a nationwide study. The personal information set of questions asks about gender, age, and workplace in auditing. The survey part consists of 20 statements divided into five groups based on audit quality dimensions. The target group of the questionnaire included 110 respondents who were engaged in auditing in one of the following ways: employed in auditing at the accounting company Big Four, employed in auditing at any audit company, employed in the field of internal audit, employed in public sector audit, employed as lecturers in their specialty in auditing, or employed in accounting and auditing association. The survey was conducted May–June of 2022. The respondents' answers were rated on a Likert scale from 1 to 5, where 1 was "completely disagree" and 5 was "completely agree." Based on research by Anh and Anh (2021), the authors defined the following four dimensions of audit quality: audit users' perception changes as a result of digitalization, audit regulation changes as a result of digitalization, auditors' work changes as a result of digitalization and auditors' professional profile changes as a result of digitalization. Each dimension of audit quality consists of a certain number of indicators based on investigations by Zhang et al. (2015), Brown-Liburd (2015), Frey and Osborne (2017), Tiberius and Hirth (2019), Manita et al. (2020), Almaleeh (2021). The indicators are presented in Table 1.

Bearing in mind the previously listed theoretical and empirical studies, presented dimensions, and indicators, the authors formulated the following hypotheses:

Hypothesis 1 (H1): Audit users' perception changes as a result of digitalization have a significant positive impact on audit quality in Serbia.

Hypothesis 2 (H2): Audit regulation changes as a result of digitalization have a significant positive impact on audit quality in Serbia.

Hypothesis 3 (H3): Auditors' work changes as a result of digitalization have a significant positive impact on audit quality in Serbia.

Hypothesis 4 (H4): Auditors' professional profile changes as a result of digitalization have a significant positive impact on audit quality in Serbia.

Table 1 Digital audit quality

Second-level construct	Indicators (measurements)
Audit quality	
Q1	Audit risk reduction
Q2	Audit fees reduction
Q3	Complete population analysis instead of sampling
Q4	Regulatory audit framework changes
First-level construct	
Audit users' perception changes as a result of digitalization	
P1	More reliable and credible audit report
P2	Obsolete personal judgment of auditors
P3	Large cost savings and profit growth
Audit regulation changes as a result of digitalization	
R1	Use of Artificial Intelligence
R2	The regulatory gap between auditing standards and the digital environment
R3	Auditing standards' adjustments
Auditors' work changes as a result of digitalization	
W1	Automation of simple, repetitive tasks
W2	Expansion of auditor's scope of work
W3	Use of continuous audit
W4	Use of Big Data Analysis
W5	Use of blockchain technology
W6	Use of robotic process automation
W7	Fraud detection and auditor's forecasting
Auditors' professional profile changes as a result of digitalization	
PP1	Auditing as a less attractive job
PP2	Auditor's employment reduction
PP3	Audit profession's reputation growth

Source: Authors' illustration based on Grubor et al. (2021)

In the research, the software package Smart PLS3 was implemented with a specially created database, according to Grubor et al. (2021). The PLS-SEM model was previously only used in the investigation by Alrashidi (2022) who studied the impact of Big Data analytics on audit procedures in the Middle East. In this study, the authors set out from a formative-formative type model (Becker et al. 2012) for measuring the impact of digitalization on audit quality in Serbia. The audit quality as a formative construct of the second level is determined by four formative constructs of the first level. The created model is presented in Fig. 1.

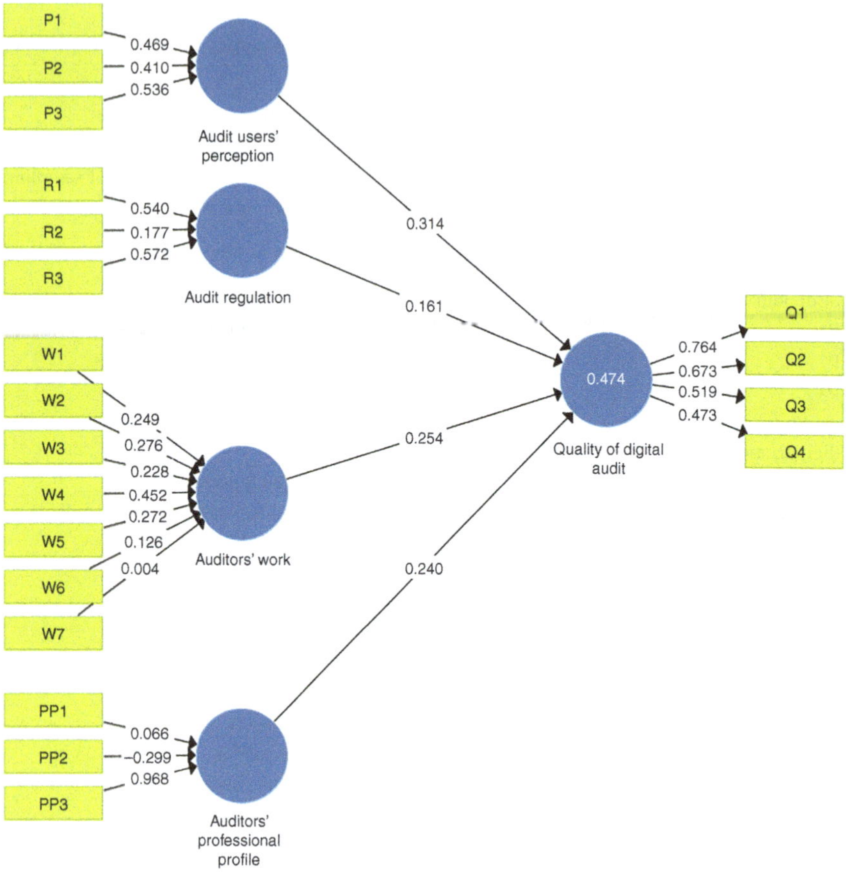

Fig. 1 Quality of digital audit model (Source: Smart PLS, authors' calculation)

3.2 Results

First-level formative constructs require testing for convergent validity, collinearity, significance, and relevance of indicators (Hair et al. 2017). In order to evaluate the convergent validity, a redundancy analysis was conducted for each of the model segments, four new variables were added to the questionnaire, one for each construct, relying on research conducted by Brown-Liburd (2015), Zhang et al. (2015), Appelbaum et al. (2017), Anh and Anh (2021). New variables were presented in Table 2.

The results obtained for each part after running the PLS algorithm are summarized in Figs. 2, 3, 4, 5, and 6.

From Fig. 2 it can be seen that the regression coefficient value was 0.906, while the determination coefficient value was 0.821, which was in accordance with both the reference value of the regression coefficient, i.e., greater than 0.70, as well as the coefficient of determination (R2), whose minimum value should be 0.50. These

Table 2 General variables

	Variables
QQ:	The growth in audit quality encourages audit improvement.
PQ:	Automated audits and information transparency bring greater confidence in the auditor's judgments and decisions.
RQ:	The regulation framework creates an environment for faster and better auditor work through the reliance on technological advancements.
WQ:	Digitalization facilitates the work of auditors in generating more accurate and timely audit reports.
PPQ:	Digitalization requires higher information technology and data analysis skills of an auditor.

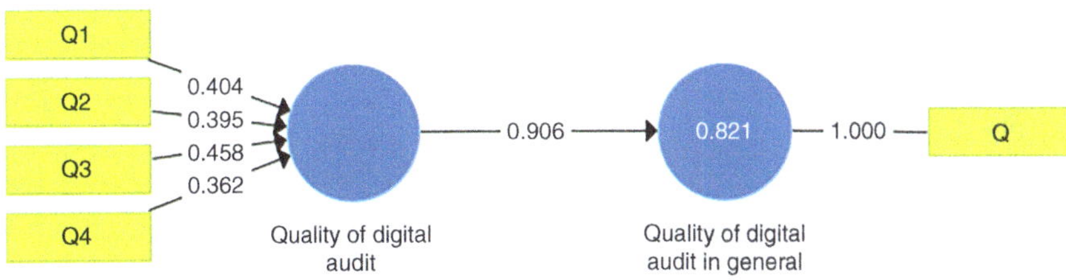

Fig. 2 Redundancy analysis for digital audit quality (Source: Smart PLS, authors' calculation)

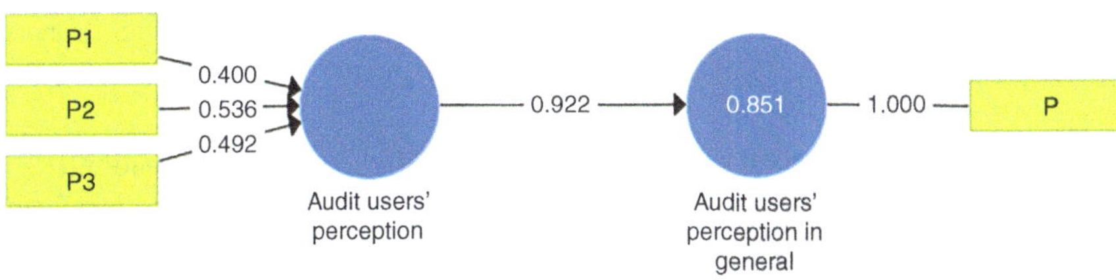

Fig. 3 Redundancy analysis for the audit users' perception (Source: Smart PLS, authors' calculation)

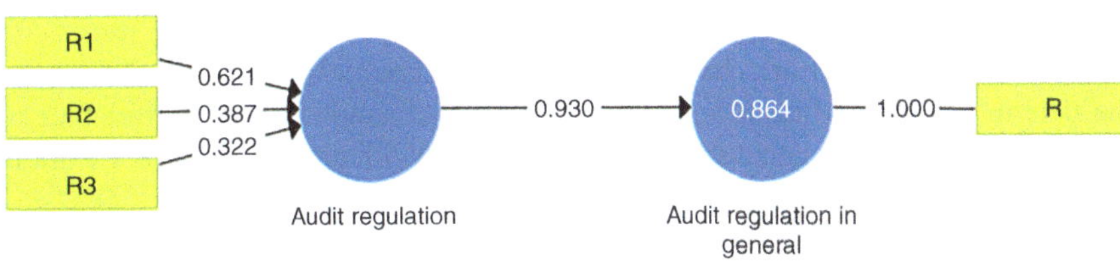

Fig. 4 Redundancy analysis for audit regulation (Source: Smart PLS, authors' calculation)

values clearly indicate that all observed audit quality variables significantly encourage audit improvement.

Figure 3 shows that the regression coefficient value was 0.922 and the determination coefficient value was 0.851, which again is in accordance with the reference

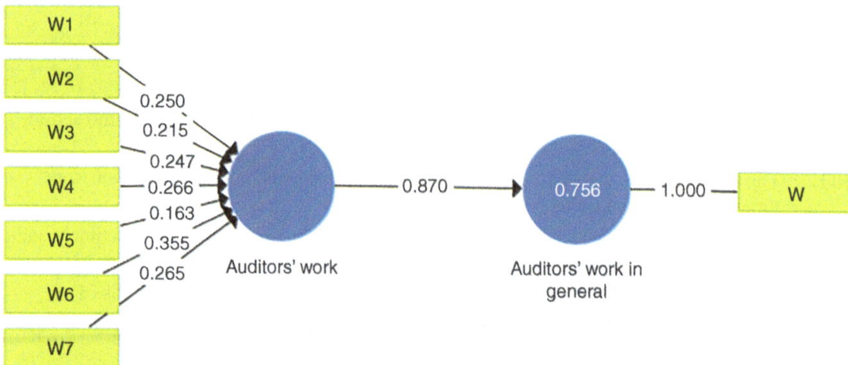

Fig. 5 Redundancy analysis for auditors' work (Source: Smart PLS, authors' calculation)

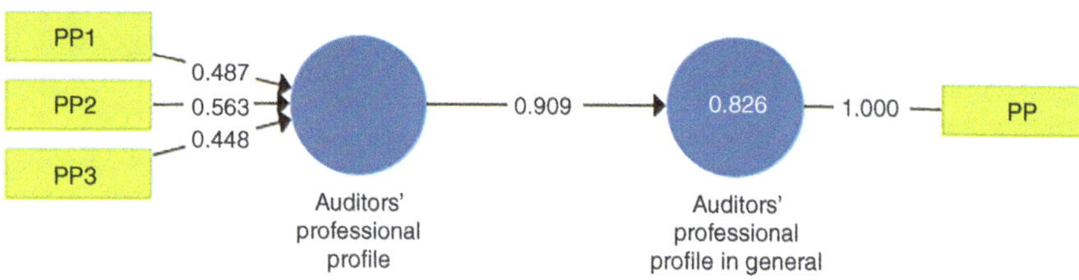

Fig. 6 Redundancy analysis for auditors' professional profile (Source: Smart PLS, authors' calculation)

value of the regression coefficient as well as the coefficient of determination (R2). This means that all observed indicators of audit users' perception had a significant impact on a higher degree of confidence in the auditor's judgments and decisions.

In the case of audit regulation, the regression coefficient value was 0.930, (greater than 0.70), and the determination coefficient value was 0.864 (also greater than 0.50). These figures confirmed that all variables of audit regulation changes had a significant impact on a regulatory environment in which auditors worked faster and better.

As for the auditors' work changes, the regression coefficient value was 0.870 and the determination coefficient value was 0.756 which implied that all variables of auditors' work changes had a significant impact on facilitating the auditor's work in order to generate more accurately and timely audit reports.

In terms of the auditors' professional profile, the following values were determined: the regression coefficient value was 0.909 and the coefficient of determination was 0.826, which signalled that all variables of the auditor's professional profile significantly influenced the level of required information technology and data analysis skills of an auditor.

In order to assess the collinearity of the variables that form the first-level construct, the authors ran the PLS algorithm. The obtained results are presented in Table 3.

Table 3 VIF at an indicator level (Source: Smart PLS)

	VIF
P1	1.150
P2	1.071
P3	1.223
PP1	1.143
PP2	1.139
PP3	1.006
Q1	1.138
Q2	1.144
Q3	1.050
Q4	1.054
R1	1.130
R2	1.356
R3	1.464
W1	1.170
W2	1.208
W3	1.153
W4	1.220
W5	1.341
W6	1.243
W7	1.132

The results summarized in Table 3 highlight that for all observed indicators or quality measures, the VIF value was smaller than 5, which showed that there was no problem from the aspect of multicollinearity. Therefore, the Bootstrapping procedure was used to examine whether or not, or to what extent the variables' influence was significant. The initial model after starting the bootstrapping procedure is demonstrated in Fig. 7.

The Bootstrapping procedure first examined the outer weight of the indicators and their significance levels (Grubor et al. 2021). For the obtained results of indicators outer weight, see Table 4.

The results in Table 4 show that for the indicators PP1, PP2, PP3, R2, W1, W2, W3, W5, W6, and W7 outer weight was not statistically significant, considering that $p > 0.05$. Thus, the corresponding Outer loadings of the indicators had to be investigated in order to determine whether the loadings were high or statistically significant. The resulting values of indicators' outer loadings are given in Table 5.

The results presented in Table 5 led to the following steps: all indicators whose outer loadings were greater than 0.5 or statistically significant ($p < 0.05$) were retained, and thus the indicators PP1, PP2, and W7 were eliminated. The indicator PP3 was $p < 0.05$, but the value of the outer loadings was 0.959, i.e., greater than 0.5, therefore, this indicator was kept. The values portrayed that all retained indicators significantly affected the quality or represented a significant measure of the audit quality in Serbia.

The final model, without the indicators PP1, PP2, and W7, is presented in Fig. 8.

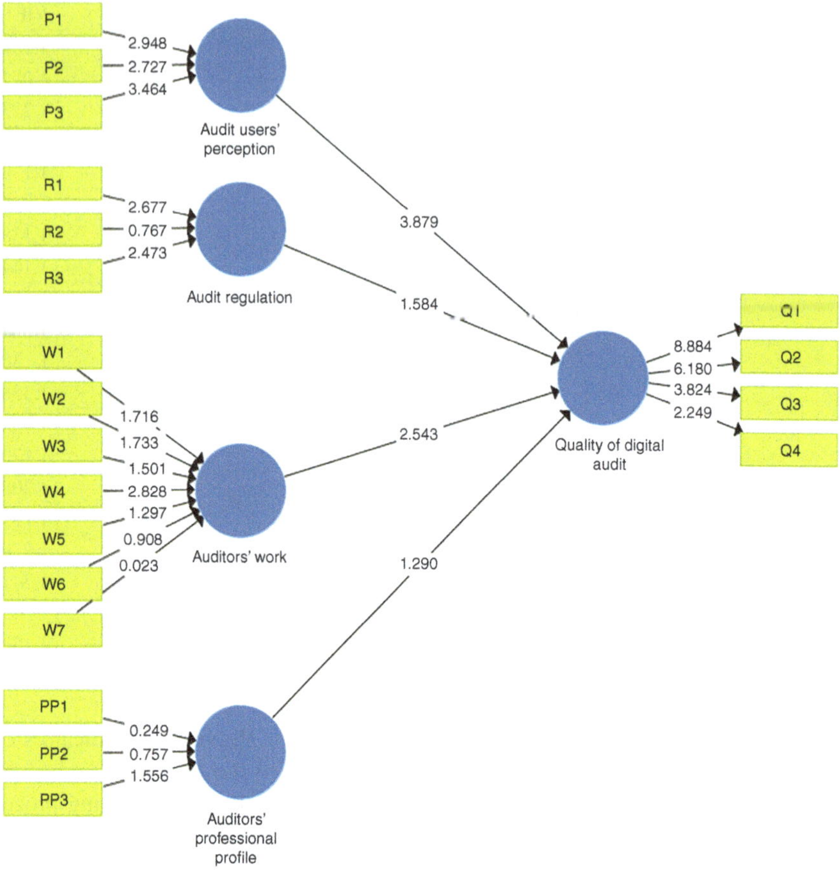

Fig. 7 The initial model of digital audit quality after the Bootstrapping procedure (Source: Smart PLS, authors' calculation)

The last aspect to be investigated was the relationship between audit quality (second-level construct) and its four dimensions (first-level constructs) through the path coefficient which indicates their relevance and weight. The path coefficients values were determined (see Table 6).

4 Discussion

Based on the results given in Table 6, it can be stated that audit users' perception, auditors' professional profiles, and auditors' work all had a significant positive impact on audit quality in Serbia ($T > 1.96$; $p < 0.05$). Thus, the hypotheses H_1, H_3, and H_4 were confirmed. Present findings confirmed those of Tiberius and Hirth

Table 4 Outer weight

	Original Sample (O)	Sample Mean (M)	Standard Deviation (STDEV)	T Statistics (|O/STDEV|)	*P* values
P1 → Audit users' perception changes	0.469	0.455	0.159	2.948	0.003
P2 → Audit users' perception changes	0.410	0.397	0.150	2.727	0.007
P3 → Audit users' perception changes	0.536	0.521	0.155	3.464	0.001
PP1 → Auditors' professional profile changes	0.066	0.104	0.263	0.249	0.803
PP2 → Auditors' professional profile changes	−0.299	−0.105	0.394	0.757	0.449
PP3 → Auditors' professional profile changes	0.968	0.651	0.622	1.556	0.120
Q1 ← Quality of digital audit	0.542	0.535	0.090	6.047	0.000
Q2 ← Quality of digital audit	0.409	0.406	0.092	4.458	0.000
Q3 ← Quality of digital audit	0.334	0.317	0.097	3.439	0.001
Q4 ← Quality of digital audit	0.291	0.259	0.131	2.225	0.027
R1 → Audit regulation changes	0.540	0.536	0.202	2.677	0.008
R2 → Audit regulation changes	0.177	0.170	0.230	0.767	0.444
R3 → Audit regulation changes	0.572	0.519	0.231	2.473	0.014
W1 → Auditors' work changes	0.249	0.250	0.145	1.716	0.087
W2 → Auditors' work changes	0.276	0.236	0.159	1.733	0.084
W3 → Auditors' work changes	0.228	0.203	0.152	1.501	0.134
W4 → Auditors' work changes	0.452	0.440	0.160	2.828	0.005
W5 → Auditors' work changes	0.272	0.247	0.209	1.297	0.195
W6 → Auditors' work changes	0.126	0.113	0.139	0.908	0.364
W7 → Auditors' work changes	0.004	0.002	0.152	0.023	0.981

Source: Smart PLS

Table 5 Outer loadings

	Original sample (O)	Sample mean (M)	Standard deviation (STDEV)	T statistics (|O/STDEV|)	*P* values
P1 → Audit users' perception changes	0.694	0.674	0.150	4.631	0.000
P2 → Audit users' perception changes	0.585	0.570	0.143	4.102	0.000
P3 → Audit users' perception changes	0.811	0.788	0.123	6.599	0.000
PP1 → Auditors' professional profile changes	0.030	0.118	0.250	0.121	0.904
PP2 → Auditors' professional profile changes	−0.234	−0.025	0.359	0.651	0.515
PP3 → Auditors' professional profile changes	0.959	0.647	0.610	1.571	0.117
Q1 ← Quality of digital audit	0.764	0.763	0.086	8.884	0.000
Q2 ← Quality of digital audit	0.673	0.668	0.109	6.180	0.000
Q3 ← Quality of digital audit	0.519	0.497	0.136	3.824	0.000
Q4 ← Quality of digital audit	0.473	0.429	0.210	2.249	0.025
R1 → Audit regulation changes	0.769	0.751	0.142	5.422	0.000
R2 → Audit regulation changes	0.581	0.545	0.214	2.719	0.007
R3 → Audit regulation changes	0.844	0.788	0.143	5.905	0.000
W1 → Auditors' work changes	0.563	0.525	0.156	3.607	0.000
W2 → Auditors' work changes	0.612	0.551	0.147	4.179	0.000
W3 → Auditors' work changes	0.532	0.486	0.165	3.224	0.001
W4 → Auditors' work changes	0.742	0.712	0.117	6.354	0.000
W5 → Auditors' work changes	0.668	0.622	0.145	4.616	0.000
W6 → Auditors' work changes	0.416	0.381	0.150	2.777	0.006
W7 → Auditors' work changes	0.213	0.199	0.179	1.193	0.233

Source: Smart PLS

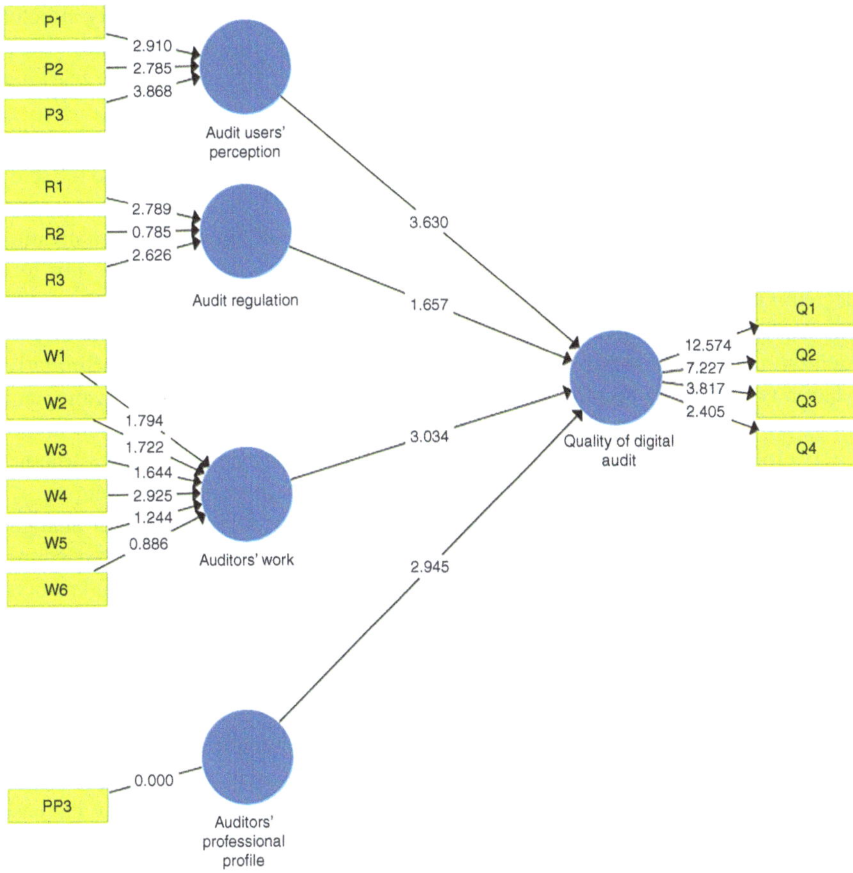

Fig. 8 The final model of digital audit quality (Source: Smart PLS, authors' calculation)

Table 6 Path coefficients

	Original sample (O)	Sample mean (M)	Standard deviation (STDEV)	T Statistics (|O/STDEV|)	*P* values
Audit regulation → Quality of digital audit	0.168	0.176	0.101	1.657	0.098
Audit users' perception → Quality of digital audit	0.301	0.282	0.083	3.630	0.000
Auditors' professional profile → Quality of digital audit	0.215	0.211	0.073	2.945	0.003
Auditors' work → Quality of digital audit	0.264	0.301	0.087	3.034	0.003

Source: Smart PLS

(2019), Anh and Anh (2021) who established that audit quality was highly affected by audit users' perception changes. Manita et al. (2020) and Anh and Anh (2021) also found that audit quality was significantly affected by auditor's professional profile and auditor's work changes. The obtained findings for Serbia were in accordance with the research carried out by Almaleeh (2021) who claimed that digitalization led to changes in the audit quality determinants, which were reflected in the competence of auditors, audit procedures, and the timeliness of audit reporting. Further, the results of Almaleeh research underlined that digitalization would not lead to a decrease in the auditing profession's attractiveness, nor to a decrease in the number of employees in auditing. Moreover, El- Monem Serag and Al- Aqiliy (2020) believed that digitalization raised the audit judgment quality by identifying abnormalities and proposing solutions for highlighted issues. Similarly, Manita et al. (2020) emphasized that digitalization improved audit relevance and provided an innovation culture within auditing companies. Adiloglu and Gungor (2019) followed a similar line of research, focusing on investments in infrastructure and continuous education in audit companies from the aspect of digitalization.

Audit quality in Serbia was most affected by audit users' perception changes (0.301), bearing in mind that the audit users relied on automated audit procedures and information transparency. Given the importance of the transparency and responsibility principles in the public sector, the digitalization of the State Audit Institution work was introduced in Serbia in order to increase the audit quality. Audit quality in Serbia was further significantly affected by auditors' work changes due to digitalization (0.264) that included more complex and sophisticated tasks, providing higher assurance levels, meeting the stakeholders' needs through real-time audit approaches and diminishing audit constraints. This relationship was in accordance with the research of Earley (2015) who held that digitalization led to audit quality increase because it enabled a more comprehensive insight into the client's processes and environment. Finally, audit quality in Serbia was the least affected by auditors' professional profile (0.215), which assumed that auditors should diligently provide competent professional service in accordance with technological progress. These findings were supported by the research results of Lugli and Bertacchini (2022) who showed that digitalization led to offering of new audit services and encouraged the increase of the audit quality. Similarly, Ramesh (2019) pointed out that digitalization significantly improved audit quality and client satisfaction, affecting skills, qualification, perception of auditors, and audit tenure. On the other hand, the audit regulation changes as a result of digitalization did not have a statistically significant influence on the quality of audits in Serbia, therefore hypothesis H2 was rejected. This, in fact, means that Artificial Intelligence has not yet been deemed vital in setting and applying auditing standards in Serbia. The data indicated that making the necessary adjustments to narrow the gap between auditing standards and current practices did not affect the audit quality in Serbia. Conversely, by analyzing the impact of emerging technologies on the Australian audit profession, Kend and Nguyen (2020) emphasized that despite being aware of the obstacles that emerging technology would pose, regulatory authorities should still keep up with the change through the appropriate regulatory framework.

5 Conclusion

Digitalization highlights the importance of information technology while providing new opportunities for the company's added value. In the current age of digitalization business complexity, data expansion, data review, and data audit are just some of the challenges that the accounting and auditing professions are faced with. The use of IT affects the growth of audit efficiency and effectiveness through review and analysis of large data volumes, simplified and implemented procedures on the entire client data population as well as improved and continuous detection and monitoring of high-risk transactions and fraud. Digitalization has brought about the automation of simple, repetitive tasks and impacted the methods of conducting an audit, the audit planning process, the assessment of materiality and risk, documentation, as well as the scope and content of audit procedures and audit evidence assessment (Nezhyva and Miniailo 2020). The key advantages of digitalization include flexibility, simplified working conditions of auditors in terms of time and space, and more reliable and credible audit reports thanks to the reduced risk of human error.

New technologies such as blockchain, Artificial Intelligence, process automation, robotics, collaboration platforms, and mobile applications are changing the nature of accounting and auditing jobs by eliminating the need for labor-intensive tasks and even some creative tasks. Using Big Data analytics as a crucial digital tool could improve the effectiveness, efficiency, and quality of the auditor's judgment about the truthfulness and objectivity of financial statements (Appelbaum et al. 2017). Cognitive technology based on the concept of machine learning and AI influences the methodology of auditing, optimization of the control process, and the interpretation of data in greater detail and in real time by providing added value to customers. Blockchain technology also has a positive impact on the internal control system in terms of efficiency, effectiveness, and reliability and may lead to audits becoming obsolete in the future due to decentralized verification of all transactions. The use of robotic process automation in auditing automates electronic communication via e-mail, monitors changes in the annual audit plan and key risk indicators, and also automates reporting activities and data quality assessment.

Based on the obtained results, audit quality in Serbia is most affected by audit users' perception changes as a result of digitalization. Hence, the application of digital tools in auditing leads to greater confidence in the audit and the increased quality of insights into services and products, both from the perspective of clients and auditors. Further, the audit quality in Serbia is significantly affected by auditors' work changes due to digitalization. The use of modern IT tools in order to automate audit procedures results in better controlled, higher quality auditing and enhanced productivity. Finally, the auditors' professional profile as a result of digitalization has a significant positive impact on audit quality. Given that the competence of the auditor is a key determinant of its effectiveness, auditors must monitor current IT trends and possess specific IT skills and abilities in order to achieve a satisfactory level of competence and quality in performing audit engagements. However, audit regulation changes as a result of digitalization have no significant impact on audit quality in Serbia. While it was expected that changes in regulations and regulatory requirements due to digital transformation and novel technology would reflect on the quality, the results indicated that this was not the case in Serbia.

The presented results contribute to the existing literature on audit quality and reveal the need for all audit employees in Serbia to acquire new competencies and develop their capabilities in the field of digitalization because it is certain that this contributes to additional value creation for both auditors and their clients. As technology advances, so should auditors modify the audit approach and improve their understanding of digital transformation strategy so as to be able to provide accurate audit services. Although the regulatory framework guidelines do not significantly affect the audit process quality in Serbia, the regulation should make an effort to update the existing standards in step with IT developments. The lack of guidance in audit standards can be seen as an opportunity for innovation, as stated by Salijeni et al. (2021). Relevant stakeholders would observe those findings as drivers of change in Serbian audit profession digitalization. Future research areas include other dimensions of audit quality or expanding to a larger sample. Another direction of investigation is a future comparative analysis on the effects of digitalization on audit quality in other countries.

References

Adiloglu B, Gungor N (2019) The impact of digitalization on the audit profession: a review of Turkish independent audit firms. J Bus Econ Financ 8(4):209–214. https://doi.org/10.17261/Pressacademia.2019.1164

Aditya BR, Hartanto R, Nugroho LE (2018) The role of IT audit in the era of digital transformation. Paper presented at the International Conference on Informatics, Engineering, Science and Technology, Bandung, Indonesia, 9 May 2018. https://doi.org/10.1088/1757-899X/407/1/012164

Ahmad F (2019) A systematic review of the role of big data analytics in reducing the influence of cognitive errors on the audit judgement. Rev Contabilidad Spanish Acc Rev 22(2):187–202. https://doi.org/10.6018/rcsar.382251

Almaleeh NMS (2021) The impact of digital transformation on audit quality: exploratory findings from a Delphi study. Sci J Commerc Res 3:9–36

Alrashidi M, Almutairi A, Zraqat O (2022) The impact of big data analytics on audit procedures: evidence from the Middle East. J Asian Financ Econ Bus 9(2):92–102. https://doi.org/10.13106/jafeb.2022.vol9.no2.0093

Andrić M, Jakšić D (2005) The role of internal audit in modern conditions. Auditor 8:44–53

Andrić M, Mijić K, Jakšić D, Vuković B (2011) Implementation of accounting software as a support to company management. TTEM:296–309

Andrić M, Jakšić D, Mijić K (2015) The current impact of information technologies on the audit process. The University of Novi Sad, Faculty of Economics in Subotica, Subotica

Anh TTK, Anh HH (2021) Perception of digital transformation effect on audit quality: the case of Vietnam. J Int Econ Manage 21(3):91–107. https://doi.org/10.38203/jiem.021.3.0037

Appelbaum D, Kogan A, Vasarhelyi MA (2017) Big data and analytics in the modern audit engagement: research needs. Auditing J Pract Theory 36(4):1–27. https://doi.org/10.2308/ajpt-51684

Becker J, Klein K, Wetzels M (2012) Hierarchical latent variable models in PLS-SEM: guidelines for using reflective-formative type models. Long Range Plan 45(5–6):359–394. https://doi.org/10.1016/j.lrp.2012.10.001

Betti N, Sarens G, Poncin I (2021) Effects of digitalisation of organisations on internal audit activities and practices. Manag Audit J 36(6):872–888. https://doi.org/10.1108/MAJ-08-2020-2792

Bhimani A, Willcocks L (2014) Digitisation, 'big data' and the transformation of accounting information. Account Bus Res 44(4):469–490. https://doi.org/10.1080/00014788.2014.910051

Brown-Liburd H, Issa H, Lombardi D (2015) Behavioral implications of big data's impact on audit judgment and decision making and future research directions. Account Horiz 29:451. https://doi.org/10.2308/acch-51023

Cooper L, Holderness K, Sorensen T, Wood DA (2019) Robotic process automation in public accounting. Account Horiz 33(4):15–35. https://doi.org/10.2308/acch-52466

Dagilienė L, Klovienė L (2019) Motivation to use big data and big data analytics in external auditing. Manag Audit J 34(7):750–782. https://doi.org/10.1108/MAJ-01-2018-1773

Dzuranin A, Cand Mălăescul I (2016) The current state and future direction of IT audit: challenges and opportunities. J Inf Syst 3.0:7–20

Earley CE (2015) Data analytics in auditing: opportunities and challenges. Bus Horiz 58(5):493–500. https://doi.org/10.1016/j.bushor.2015.05.002

El-Monem Serag AA, Al-Aqiliy LM (2020) A proposed framework for big data analytics in external auditing and its impact on audit quality with a field study in Egypt Alexandria. J Account Res 4(3):1–60. https://aljalexu.journals.ekb.eg/article_124109.html

Eulerich M, Pawlowski J, Waddoups NJ, Wood DA (2021) A framework for using robotic process automation for audit tasks. Contemp Account Res 39:691. https://doi.org/10.1111/1911-3846.12723

Fedyk A, Hodson J, Khimich N, Fedyk T (2022) Is artificial intelligence improving the audit process? Rev Acc Stud 27:938. https://doi.org/10.1007/s11142-022-09697-x

Frey CB, Osborne MA (2017) The future of employment: how susceptible are jobs to computerization? Techol Forecast Soc Change 114:254–280. https://doi.org/10.1016/j.techfore.2016.08.019

Gandomi A, Haider M (2015) Beyond the hype: big data concepts, methods, and analytics. Int J Inf Manag 35:137–144. https://doi.org/10.1016/j.ijinfomgt.2014.10.007

Gauthier MP, Brender N (2021) How do the current auditing standards fit the emergent use of blockchain? Manag Audit J 36(3):365–385. https://doi.org/10.1108/MAJ-12-2019-2513

Gray JM, Abdolmohammadi M (2016) Information technology audits by internal auditors: exploring the evolution of integrated IT audits. In ProQuest Dissertations and Theses

Grubor A, Đokić N, Milićević N, Đokić I (2021) Marketing research. Faculty of Economics in Subotica, Subotica

Hair JF, Hult GTM, Ringle CM, Sarstedt M (2017) A primer on partial least squares structural equation modeling (PLS-SEM). Sage

Hamdam A, Jusoh R, Yahya Y, Abdul Jalil A, Zainal ANH (2022) Auditor judgment and decision-making in big data environment: a proposed research framework. Account Res J 35(1):55–70. https://doi.org/10.1108/ARJ-04-2020-0078

Huang F, Vasarhelyi MA (2019) Applying robotic process automation (RPA) in auditing: a framework. Int J Account Inf Syst 100433:100433. https://doi.org/10.1016/j.accinf.2019.100433

Jakšić D (2001a) Computer systems security controls. Auditor 4(16):89–102

Jakšić D (2001b) Experiment planning procedures for evaluating control risk. Ann Facul Econ Subotica:122–130

Jakšić D (2002) Segregation of computer duties. Auditor:88–102

Jakšić D, Mijić K (2009a) The scope of the audit of information systems. Finrar:17–23

Jakšić D, Mijić K (2009b) Integration of computer aided tools and techniques in audit process. Auditor 12:5–1

Jakšić D, Mijić K (2010) Planning of IT audit based on risk assessment. Auditor 13:39–52

Jakšić D, Mijić K (2012) The methodology of business process management using software solution. Paper presented at the international symposium engineering management and competitiveness, University of Novi Sad, technical faculty "Mihajlo Pupin," Zrenjanin, 22–23rd June 2012

Kend M, Nguyen LA (2020) Big data analytics and other emerging technologies: the impact on the Australian audit and assurance profession. Austral Account Rev, CPA Aust 30(4):269–282. https://doi.org/10.1111/auar.12305

Kokina J, Blanchette S (2019) Early evidence of digital labor in accounting: innovation with robotic process automation. Int J Account Inf Syst 35:100431. https://doi.org/10.1016/j.accinf.2019.100431

Lugli E, Bertacchini F (2022) Audit quality and digitalization: some insights from the Italian context. Meditari Account Res 1–20. https://doi.org/10.1108/MEDAR-08-2021-1399

Manita R, Elommal N, Baudier P, Hikkerova L (2020) The digital transformation of external audit and its impact on corporate governance. Technol Forecast Soc Chang 150(C):119751. https://doi.org/10.1016/j.techfore.2019.119751

Mijić K (2014) Integration of the audit process of financial statements in order to improve the audit firm performance. Ann Facul Econ Subotica 32:219–234

Mijić K, Jakšić D (2010) Application of computer tools and techniques according to the phases of the audit of financial statements. Auditor 13(49):65–86

Mijić K, Vuković B (2013) How to improve the efficiency and quality of the financial statement audit process? Paper presented at VIII congress of Montenegro accountants and auditors, Institute of Chartered Accountants of Montenegro, Becici, 17–19 October 2013

Munoko I, Brown-Liburd HL, Vasarhelyi M (2020) The ethical implications of using artificial intelligence in auditing. J Bus Ethics 167:209–234. https://doi.org/10.1007/s10551-019-04407-1

Nezhyva M, Miniailo V (2020) Digitalization of audit in the conditions of the Covid-19. Herald Kyiv Natl Univ Trade Econ 131:123–134. https://doi.org/10.31617/visnik.knute.2020(131)09

Nguyen AH, Ha HH, Nguyen SL (2020) Determinants of information technology audit quality: evidence from Vietnam. J Asian Financ Econ Bus 7(4):41–50. https://doi.org/10.13106/jafeb.2020.vol7.no4.41

Ramesh V (2019) Digitalization and audit profession. Int J Innov Technol Explor Eng 8(6):33–39

Salijeni G, Samsonova-Taddei A, Turley S (2021) Understanding how big data technologies reconfigure the nature and organization of financial statement audits: a sociomaterial analysis. Eur Account Rev 30:531. https://doi.org/10.1080/09638180.2021.1882320

Tiberius V, Hirth S (2019) Impacts of digitalization on auditing: a Delphi study for Germany. J Int Account Audit Tax 37(C):100288. https://doi.org/10.1016/j.intaccaudtax.2019.100288

Vuković B, Andrić M, Jakšić D (2017) The impact of working capital management on company's profitability: empirical evidence from Serbia. Custos e Agronegocio on line 13(1):333–349

Vuković B, Milutinović S, Milićević N, Jakšić D (2020a) Corporate bankruptcy prediction: evidence from wholesale companies in the Western European countries. J Econ 68(5):477–498

Vuković B, Milutinović S, Mirović V, Milićević N (2020b) The profitability analysis of the logistics industry companies in the Balkan countries. Promet-Traffic Transport 32(4):497–511. https://doi.org/10.7307/ptt.v32i4.3311

Vuković B, Mijić K, Jakšić D, Saković D (2022a) Determinants of cash holdings: evidence from Balkan countries. E and M Econ Manage 25(1):130–142. https://doi.org/10.15240/tul/001/2022-1-008

Vuković B, Milutinović S, Peštović K, Krsmanović B, Jakšić D (2022b) Analysis of financial performance determinants: evidence from the European agricultural companies. Custos e agronegocio online 13(1):285–306

Vuković B, Peštović K, Mirović V, Jakšić D, Milutinović S (2022c) The analysis of company growth determinants based on financial statements of the European companies. Sustainability 14:770. https://doi.org/10.3390/su14020770

Yaqoob I, Hashem I, Gani A, Mokhtar S, Ahmed E, Anuar N, Vasilakos A (2016) Big data: from beginning to future. Int J Inf Manag 36:1231. https://doi.org/10.1016/j.ijinfomgt.2016.07.009

Zhang J, Yang X, Appelbaum D (2015) Toward effective big data analysis in continuous auditing. Account Horiz 29:469–476. https://doi.org/10.2308/acch-51070

Zhang CA, Thomas C, Vasarhelyi M (2021) Attended process automation in audit: a framework and a demonstration. J Inf Syst 36:101. https://doi.org/10.2308/ISYS-2020-073

The Effect of Innovation Through Intangible Assets on Company's Profitability

Ivana Medved, Kristina Peštović, and Dušan Saković

Abstract The aim of this paper is to investigate the impact of investment in intangible assets on the companies' business performances which are observed as profitability. Investment in intangible assets is one of the crucial activities and resources that contribute to achievement of competitive advantage, company growth, and development. According to previous research papers and significant impact of intangible assets on firm performance, the effect of intangible assets on companies' profitability in Serbia was conducted. The research is based on the financial statements of 194 observations of companies listed on Belgrade stock exchange during 2017–2020. The sample consisted of small, medium, and large enterprises from manufacturing sector (Section C). The results of the models have clearly documented that there is a significant positive relationship between intangible assets and financial performance of companies measured as profitability ratios. Investment in intangible assets affects profitability of companies positively. This paper has helped to expand the theoretical concept of intangible assets and the impact of investment in intangible assets on profitability of companies. The results of research should encourage the managers of listed manufacturing companies to invest more in intangible assets in order to increase profitability.

Keywords Intangible assets · Investment in intangible assets · Financial performance · Company's profitability · Listed manufacturing companies

I. Medved (✉) · K. Peštović · D. Saković
Faculty of Economics in Subotica, University of Novi Sad, Subotica, Serbia
e-mail: ivana.medved@ef.uns.ac.rs; kristina.pestovic@ef.uns.ac.rs; dusan.sakovic@ef.uns.ac.rs

S. Benković et al. (eds.), *Digital Transformation of the Financial Industry*, Contributions to Finance and Accounting,
https://doi.org/10.1007/978-3-031-23269-5_4

1 Introduction

Investments in various forms of tangible assets are well-known contributors to shareholder wealth and company growth. Tangible assets are traditionally a regular form of material and physical assets investments and also common financial statement positions. However, over the past decades, intangible assets have become increasingly important for knowledge creation, innovation, company's competitive advantage (Kramer et al. 2011; Bagna et al. 2021), and their contribution to company's profitability and value is more noticeable (Seo and Kim 2020). Therefore, there are expectations from those who use information in companies to adequately assess the effect of innovations on intangible assets, and from accounting standards establishment to adapt accounting regulations to the needs of measuring, evaluating, and reporting on intangible assets (Lopes and Rodrigues 2007; Lev and Gu 2016). Intangible assets are often disregarded in favor of tangible assets (Li and Wang 2014).

Intangible assets are a very important part of any company struggling to survive in a changing and uncertain environment. These assets are crucial for modern companies, especially in the circumstances of the increasingly widespread use of digital technologies and other forms of knowledge. Intangibles occur in all aspects of the company (in particular, in knowledge-based company), from R&D, to production and sale, but also have a great impact on company functions and policy, especially accounting, finance, and strategic management. The impact of intangible assets on company operations is important at both the macro and the micro levels. On a macro level, macroeconomic and monetary policy have mostly indirect impacts on companies' intangibles. According to Ahn et al. "only a few intangible assets are currently capitalized in national accounts (SNA 2008/ESA2010 standards), namely R&D, mineral exploration, computer software and databases, as well as entertainment, literary and artistic originals. Expenditures for design, branding, new financial products, organizational capital and firm-provided training are instead currently treated as intermediate costs" (2020, 1). On the micro level, that influence is predominant in terms of measuring changes in financial and non-financial indicators of business success of company, knowledge creation, and competitive advantage creation, determining the degree and importance of their connection, as well as the overall connection with innovation and investment promotion.

Intangible assets are known as "intellectual assets," "knowledge assets," "knowledge-based capital," or "intellectual capital." There are many different definitions of intangible assets. Most of them imply the usual differences between intangible and tangible assets. Intangibles are nonphysical assets with a main focus on investing in human capital, intellectual property, computerized information, and economic competencies in the form of training/education of workers (key personnel), innovation and technology development, public and private research and development expenditures (R&D), market exploration and development (marketing), organizational and management efficiency, customer and institutional networks, and software and information technology (Barker et al. 2021; Thum-Thysen et al. 2017, 2019).

According to Seo and Kim (2020) and Thum-Thysen et al. (2017) intangibles are fundamental, long-run strategic assets because they can provide a company with vital and valuable financial performances and competitive advantages and the economy as a whole. An intangible asset, according to International Accounting Standards 38 (IAS 38), is an identifiable nonmonetary asset without physical substance (IAS 38 is used by European listed companies for financial reporting of intangibles). Such an asset is identifiable when it is separable, or when it arises from contractual or other legal rights. Intangible assets can be a key driver of innovation, which is why both internal and external users of accounting information are interested in reliable information about intangible assets. Despite accounting regulations, accounting practitioners have serious difficulties with the identification, measurement, and systematic disclosure of intangibles. There is a significant gap between market value of companies and reported book values with potential to fail in reporting intangibles (Haji and Mohd Ghazali 2018; Sardo and Serrasqueiro 2018).

The issue of profitability of companies in relation to investments in intangible assets is a twofold issue: firstly, it is important which intangible assets are recognized in the Balance Sheet (intangible assets acquired in acquisitions) and secondly, investments in intangible assets are important for measuring profitability are accounted as an expense (which reduces current income for future benefits) (Barker et al. 2021; Lev 2018).

The aim of this paper is to investigate the effect of intangible assets on companies' profitability in the Republic of Serbia. The research is based on the financial statements of 194 observations of companies listed on Belgrade stock exchange during the period of 2017–2020. The sample consisted of small, medium, and large enterprises from manufacturing sector (Section C). This study contributes to the accounting practice in the Republic of Serbia because of the importance it attaches to the analysis of intangible assets and its connection with the profitability of the listed companies in Serbia. The results of the models have clearly documented that there is a significant positive relationship between intangible assets and financial performance of companies measured as profitability ratios. Investment in intangible assets affects profitability of companies positively. According to these finding, it can be concluded that growth of the value of intangible assets influence on the achievement of the higher rate of return on assets and return on equity.

This paper is structured into five sections. Section 2 illustrates the literature and theoretical framework. Section 3 describes the methodology, sample, and used variables. Section 4 explores results and discussion. In addition, the fifth section provides contributions, further recommendations of study, limitations, and conclusions of paper.

2 Literature Review

Intangible assets appear in many different forms, which have some common characteristics. According to Barker et al. (2021), intangibles can be grouped as relating to human capital (training), organizational capital (intellectual property, processes, IT), and social capital (customer relationships, external networks, reputation). Human capital, according to Radonić et al. (2021) was the first aspect of intangible assets that became interesting for the academic community. From the point of view of the wider academic community, intangible assets are a subject of interest for economic, legal, and statistical disciplines. International Financial Reporting Standards and International Accounting Standards have measurement and recognition principles for intangible assets. Intangibles are resources controlled by the entity as a result of previous events (purchase or self/creation) and from which future economic benefits (inflows of cash or other assets) are expected (IAS 38). According to IAS 38, critical attributes of an intangible asset are: identifiability, control (power to obtain benefits from the asset), and future economic benefits (such as revenues or reduced future costs).

The basic forms of intangibles are: (1) intangibles created through innovation and discovery, (2) intangibles that underlie organization practices (including also investments in customer satisfaction, product quality, and brand reputation), and (3) intangibles related to human capital (Thum-Thysen et al. 2017).

The specifics of intangible assets are systematic risks, high uncertainty, firm-specificity, the absence of rivalry between uses, human capital intensity, high sunk costs, nontradability of most intangible assets, and synergies and complementarities among intangible asset types (Mohammed and Al Ani 2020; Thum-Thysen et al. 2017).

There are many research papers, the last three decades, which investigate the impact of intangible assets on companies' performances, especially accounting-based financial performance indicators (Tadić et al. 2020) displayed by return on assets (ROA), return on equity (ROE), earnings before interest, taxes, depreciation, and amortization (EBITDA) divided by total revenue (EBITDA margin), net and gross profit margin, growth in revenue, current accounts receivables, inventory turnover, operational cash flow and other. This study demonstrates that "new product releases and patent production have the strongest" (Tadić et al. 2020, 993) effect on company performances, in meaning of notable influence on productivity and consequently a very significant impact on profitability.

According to Andrašić et al. (2018), many empirical studies have investigated internal factors of profitability of the company—such as size, sales growth, debt ratio, quick ratio, age, inventory level, fixed assets to total assets ratio, capital turnover, and others. Research by Andrašić et al. (2018) explores the performance of medium and large agricultural companies in the region of Vojvodina in the Republic of Serbia. Data are collected from the financial reports of companies for the period 2006–2015. This study shows a statistically significant impact of company size, current liquidity, debt, market share, sales revenue growth, insurance, and export on return on assets as the main profitability determinant. According to Andrašić et al. "in order to improve the performance of medium and large companies in the agricultural sector, and primarily profitability, companies should focus on payment cycles of short-term liabilities and collection of receivables. It is necessary to coordinate time for collecting receivables and paying liabilities so companies provide their liquidity and solvency" (2018, 236).

Economic success is increasingly based on the effective utilization of intangible assets, but despite their significance, the literature reveals a low level of interest in their identification, measurement, and disclosure, especially in the public sector (Bunget et al. 2014). Empirical study of intangible assets in Romanian municipalities was conducted by Bunget et al. (2014). The research results indicate the performance of public sector measured through disclosure index is greater in larger municipalities and the municipalities with the largest value of intangible assets. According to these findings, it can be concluded that the higher value of intangible assets have a positive significant effect on performance in the public sector.

Research study by Sardo and Serrasqueiro (2018) analyzed panel data of a dynamic model based on a sample of non-financial listed companies in 14 Western European countries for the period between 2004 and 2015. This research indicates the importance of intellectual capital for companies' financial performance regardless of being high-tech, medium-tech, or low-tech companies. Findings show a positive effect on the relationship between growth opportunities and companies' financial performance with impact of intellectual capital. Also, according to this study, there is a non-linear relationship between growth opportunities and companies' financial performance and between ownership concentration and companies' growth opportunities. Intellectual capital has a positive influence on companies' growth opportunities. According to this research, managers bear in mind that intellectual capital has a positive effect on the financial performance of the company and the exploitation of growth opportunities.

Denicolai et al. (2014) performed the empirical analysis of a proprietary database of 294 listed companies headquartered in Europe. This study shows the impact of intangibles (distinguishing between internally and externally generated intangible assets) on company growth and analyze the effect of company size, measuring if it can alter the relationship between intangibles and performance. The intangibles are vital in boosting company performance, and "this effect varies with firm size and an additional boost is created by externally generated intangibles" (Denicolai et al. 2014, 219).

The research on the impact of internally generated intangible assets on the performance of companies measured as the market value was conducted by Cosmulese et al. (2021). The research includes a sample of 180 NASDAQ and NYSE-listed entities between 2007 and 2016 in Romania. The research results indicate that the using and implicitly increasing the share of intangible assets of the Romanian entities will reach to the higher profitability.

Corrado et al. (2016) showed evidence of cross-country and cross-industry dataset on investment in tangible and intangible assets for 18 European countries and the US. Findings provides the diffusion of intangible investment across Europe and the USA over the years 2000–2013. Also, this research provided a growth of accounting evidence before and after the Great Recession in 2008–2009. This research model distinguishes free and commercialized knowledge. Free knowledge is freely available to companies. Commercialized knowledge is produced using inputs and the company must pay for it to use it in their production process (knowledge). This type of knowledge is "accumulated over time, generating the stock of commercial knowledge via the standard perpetual inventory relation and with its own user cost (explicit or implicit)" (Corrado et al. 2016, 3). According Corrado et al. (2016) intangible assets are investments that allow knowledge to be commercialized. Findings of this study show that intangible investments are more dynamic than tangibles. Also, intangible intensity and the intangible-to-tangible ratio are positively correlated with the level of GDP per head and negatively associated with the financial shock of the Great Recession (in 2008–2009). Higher intangible investment rates and higher intangible-to-tangible investment ratio, according to this study have countries with higher average company sizes and less stringent regulations in product and labor markets.

Li and Wang (2014) performed a study reviewing the listed technology companies' annual reports for a 5-year period (from 2008 to 2012) in Hong Kong. They examined the influence of intangible assets (R&D cost, employee benefits expense, and sales training) on financial performance by using ROA as a financial measure of the company. The result of regression model in this study demonstrates both R&D expenditure and sales training have a positive relationship to ROA in statistics but employee benefits expense is not.

Wang et al. (2016) analyzed the different effects of R&D policy choices on accounting performances and market values of listed companies in the Chine Stock Exchanges during the period 2007–2014. According to this study, different R&D policy choices provided different implications for company value and company strategy to the market. If the company is choosing to capitalize on their R&D investments, they will have higher market value, implying that the strategy was focused on sustaining their long-term development. On the contrary, the companies selecting to expense their R&D expenditure have higher accounting performance and the focus was on improving short-term gains. The conclusions are that the policy choice on R&D capitalization and expensing is a trade-off result between the accounting performance and the market value of a company.

Mirović et al. (2019) stated in their research that large companies compared to small companies show more interest in improving performance measurement and they are encouraging higher levels of disclosure because of increasing investor confidence. This observation indicates that for stakeholders or external users higher levels of information is necessary.

"The main measure of the success of enterprise, sector, as well as the economy, is a profitability. Profitability indicates the ability of enterprises to generate a profit in relation to investment" (Mijić and Jakšić 2017, 155). With the intent to analyze factors that affect the profitability of agricultural enterprises in the countries of Southeast Europe (Hungary, Romania, Bosnia and Herzegovina, and Serbia), Mijić and Jakšić (2017) guided a panel data analysis for the period 2011–2014.

The profitability determinants of agricultural enterprises in Hungary and Romania are the same, according to this study and positively affected by leverage, quick ratio, growth, and lagged profitability. In Serbia, and Bosnia and Herzegovina important profitability determinants (quick ratio, lagged profitability, and growth, and in Bosnia and Herzegovina, leverage, is also significant) have only positive influence.

Milić et al. (2018) inspected reliability of reported earnings of agricultural companies in the Republic of Serbia. The research was based on a sample of 1983 agricultural companies - a year observation. This study utilized various regression models and univariate tests. The conclusion is that profitability and leverage have a significant influence on earnings management. According to Milić et al. "research shows that the practice of income-decreasing behavior is associated with companies' profitability, while as income-increasing behavior is associated with profitability and leverage" (2018, 127) of companies.

The findings, among academics and practitioners, indicate that there is a positive relationship between intangible assets investment and companies' performance. Seo and Kim (2020) examined the relationship between investment in intangible assets and performance in small and medium enterprises. The research is based on 173 companies in Korea. Results indicate that intangible assets have a positive effect on a company's profitability and value.

According to Dakić et al. "more information about the impact of some internal factors on profitability will enable investors easier choice of the company they need to invest in and which will allow them to return invested funds with greater certainty" (2019, 489). A study (Dakić et al. 2019) performed in the Republic of Serbia in the period from 2007 to 2015 (9 years) on a sample of 657 observations of companies and includes three groups (samples) of food processing companies (meat, fruit, vegetable, and milk processing companies). The business success in this survey was measured by companies profitability (return on assets), while size, debt ratio, quick ratio, inventory, sale growth, and capital turnover ratio were defined as the independent determinants. The results show that among all three types of food processing industry sale growth has a positive significant influence on profitability.

Glova and Mrazkova (2018) investigated the impact of intangibles on firm value. They examine the value relevance of intangibles expressed by R&D expenditures and intangible fixed assets and other variables with the firm value. Using the regression approach for 1520 observations in the years 2011–2015, they found out that R&D expenses to total assets can significantly explain market to book value ratio of selected companies. One of the findings indicates that intangible fixed assets to total assets are not statistically significant (Glova and Mrazkova 2018).

Bagna et al. (2021) investigated the effect of innovation through patents and intangible assets on growth and profitability of European companies. The research was based on a sample of 6677 observations of listed European companies. Among the findings, the results indicate that there are positive relationship between intangible intensity and growth of companies.

A research study by Cordazzo and Rossi (2020) investigates if the mandatory IFRS adoption influenced the value relevance of intangible assets of non-financial firms listed on Borsa Italiana from 2000 to 2015. This study isolates the impact of several classes of intangible assets on stock prices and then classifies firms according to intangible asset intensity.

Arianpoor (2021) investigated the impact of intangible assets on company performance in the Tehran Stock Exchange companies. The research was based on the use of multiple linear regression analysis and the sample of 1350 companies. This research investigates intangible assets' role in company performances from 2008 to 2018. The findings show that intangible assets positively impact company performance (return on assets, return on equity, net profit, and profit margin). The author observed that, in emerging economies, intangible assets have notable part in company performance.

Mohanlingam et al. (2021) provided the results of the effects of intangible assets on financial performance and financial policies of listed technology firms in Thailand. The research is based on the data of 33 out of 38 technology companies listed on the Stock Exchange of Thailand for the 5-year period from 2015 to 2019. The results indicated that intangible assets have a significant positive relationship with profitability measured as return on equity. Furthermore, the study found that intangible assets also had a significant positive relationship with financial policies measured as debt to equity. Moderating variables such as company size and leverage were found to significantly influence these relationships.

3 Methodology and Sample

In order to investigate the impact of investment in intangible assets on profitability two regression models are defined. Profitability as a dependent variable is defined as return on assets and return on equity as the two most commonly used variables. The following independent variables are defined: investment in intangible assets, fixed assets ratio, size of company, current ratio, and leverage on return on assets. Investment in intangible assets represents the trend of intangible assets between two period (Table 1).

Model 1/ROA:

Table 1 Definition variables of models

Variables	Character	Mark	Method of calculation
Return on assets	Dependent	Y1	Net income/Total assets
Return on equity	Dependent	Y2	Net income/Capital
Intangible assets	Independent	X1	Intangible assets$_t$/Intangible assets$_{t-1}$
Fixed assets ratio	Independent	X2	Long-term fixed assets/Total assets
Size	Independent	X3	Nat Log of Total assets
Current ratio	Independent	X4	Current Assets/Current Liabilities
Leverage	Independent	X5	Total debt/Capital
Sales growth	Independent	X6	Sales$_t$/Sales$_{t-1}$

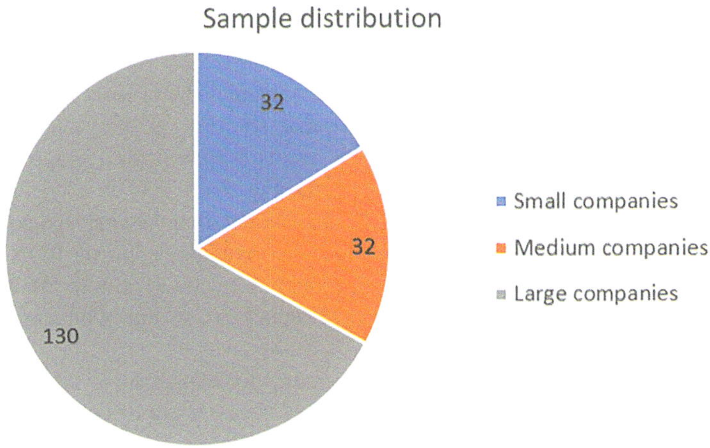

Fig. 1 Distribution of companies by the size in sample

$$Y_{1\mathrm{it}} = \beta_0 + \beta_1 X_1 + \beta_2 X_2 + \beta_3 X_3 + \beta_4 X_4 + \beta_5 X_5 + \beta_6 X_6 + \varepsilon i \quad (1)$$

where $Y_{1\mathrm{it}}$ t—Return on assets (dependent variable); β_0—model constant; βi—coefficiency of independent variables; X_1—Intangible assets (independent variable); X_2—Fixed assets ratio (independent variable); X_3—Size (independent variable); X_4—Current ratio (independent variable); X_5—Leverage (independent variable); X_6—Sales growth (independent variable); *E*—error with a normal distribution; *i*—signify each company ($i = 1,\ldots, n$); *t*—signify the period of time ($t = 1,\ldots, t$).

Model 2/ROE:

$$Y_{2\mathrm{it}} = \beta_0 + \beta_1 X_1 + \beta_2 X_2 + \beta_3 X_3 + \beta_4 X_4 + \beta_5 X_5 + \beta_6 X_6 + \varepsilon i \quad (2)$$

where $Y_{2\mathrm{it}}$ t—Return on equity (dependent variable); β_0—model constant; βi—coefficiency of independent variables; X_1—Intangible assets (independent variable); X_2—Fixed assets ratio (independent variable); X_3—Size (independent variable); X_4—Current ratio (independent variable); X_5—Leverage (independent variable); X_6—Sales growth (independent variable); *E*—error with a normal distribution; *i*—signify each company ($i = 1,\ldots, n$); *t*—signify the period of time ($t = 1,\ldots, t$).

The research is based on the financial statements of 194 observations of companies listed on Belgrade stock exchange during 2017–2020. The sample consists of small, medium, and large companies belonging to the manufacturing sector (C sector) (Fig. 1).

All data were taken from the website of the Business Agency Register of the Republic of Serbia and covered the period from 2017 to 2020. For the data processing, statistical software SPSS v. 23 was used.

4 Results and Discussion

In the assets structure among manufacturing companies the primary is fixed assets. Fixed long-term assets on average represent 49.85% of the total assets of manufacturing companies, while intangible assets represent on average 3.29% of total assets or 5.1% of fixed assets (Table 2 and Fig. 2).

The minimum values of ROA and ROE show that within the analyzed companies there are those with negative profitability. The average value of ROA for the observed sample is 3%, and for ROE 2%, which is relatively low profitability. As for the independent variables, their average values are in line with the expected results (Table 3).

Table 4 presents the Pearson correlation matrix for explanatory variables, showing moderate correlations between them. This is necessary to discover the possible problem of multicollinearity which can cause disorders in estimating the value of parameters, their significance, and the direction of influence on the dependent variable. All values of correlation coefficients are not at a level that could lead to multicollinearity problems. In multiple regression analysis, the variance inflation factor (VIF) is used as an indicator of multicollinearity. The acceptable level of tolerance value is 10 and it is recommended as the maximum level of tolerance (Dakić and Mijić 2020). Since all VIF values are less than 10 (see Tables 7 and 10), it is concluded that there is no multicollinearity between the variables.

Table 2 Structure of intangible assets in total assets and fixed assets

	Average of Intangible assets % of total assets	Average of Intangible assets % of fixed assets
2017	3.4628	5.7721
2018	3.4771	5.3514
2019	3.1451	4.7165
2020	3.1190	4.5822
Grand Total	3.2992	5.1008

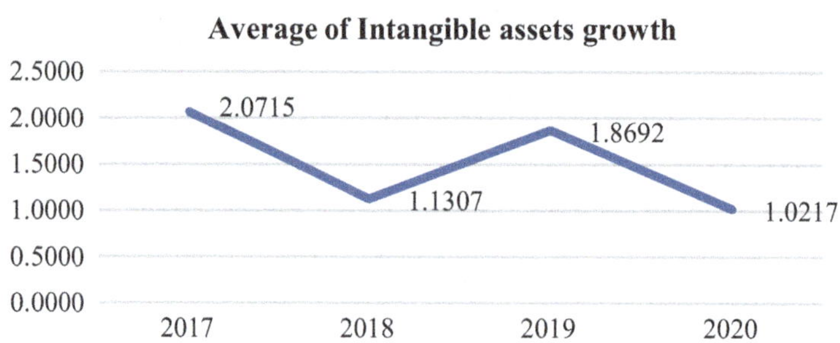

Fig. 2 Trend of average of intangible assets growth

Table 3 Descriptive statistics of dependent and independent variables

Descriptive statistics					
	N	Min.	Max.	Mean	Std. deviation
ROA	194	−0.4017	0.2767	0.032418	0.0841073
ROE	194	−9.3382	3.0589	0.022731	0.7613069
Intangible assets growth	194	0.0163	34.4638	1.522475	3.2018087
Fixed assets %	194	0.0186	0.9211	0.498582	0.2186930
Size ln	194	9.0604	17.8831	14.605450	2.0536015
Current ratio	194	0.2716	17.9751	2.799296	3.4856134
Leverage	194	0.0349	42.7393	2.075730	5.2350954
Growth	194	0.0125	4.4174	1.050215	0.3875414
Valid *N* (listwise)	194				

Table 4 Result of correlation analysis of variables in the models

	1	2	3	4	5	6	7	8
ROA	1							
ROE	0.172	1						
Intangible assets growth	0.029	0.229	1					
Fixed assets %	−0.101	−0.009	−0.047	1				
Size ln	0.285	0.090	0.109	0.157	1			
Current ratio	0.161	0.037	−0.036	−0.320	−0.091	1		
Leverage	−0.172	−0.292	0.405	−0.149	0.158	−0.175	1	
Growth	0.190	0.160	−0.031	0.065	0.026	−0.110	0.102	1

The results of the regression models show that investment in intangible assets, or intangible assets growth, has a positive and significant impact on profitability measured as return on assets and return on equity. According to these findings, it can be concluded that growth of the value of intangible assets influences the achievement of a higher rate of return on assets and return on equity. The results show that intangible assets are significant at the level of 90%. On the other side, the following independent variables have a significant impact on return of assets at the level of 95%: fixed assets ratio, size, leverage, and sales growth. Size and sales growth have a positive significant impact on return on assets, while fixed assets ratio and leverage have a significant negative relationship to the return on assets (Table 5).

R Square is 0.238 adjusted 0.214 which indicates that 21% of variance of depended variable can be explained with defined independed variables (Tables 6 and 7).

The results of the second model are almost the same as the results of the first model. The difference is that independent variable intangible assets are significant at

Table 5 Model 1 summary

Model summary				
Model	R	R Square	Adjusted R Square	Std. error of the estimate
1	0.488[a]	0.238	0.214	0.0745839

[a] Predictors: (constant), growth, size ln, intangible assets growth, current ratio, fixed assets %, leverage

Table 6 Results of ANOVA model 1

ANOVA[a]						
Model		Sum of squares	df	Mean square	F	Sig.
1	Regression	0.325	6	0.054	9.739	0.000[b]
	Residual	1.040	187	0.006		
	Total	1.365	193			

[a] Dependent Variable: ROA
[b] Predictors: (Constant), Growth, Size ln, Intangible assets growth, Current ratio, Fixed assets %, Leverage

Table 7 Results of regression analysis of model 1

Coefficients[a]								
		Unstandardized coefficients		Standard. Coefficients			Collinearity statistics	
Model		B	Std. error	Beta	t	Sig.	Tolerance	VIF
1	(Constant)	−0.201	0.043		−4.695	0.000		
	Intangible assets growth	0.003	0.002	0.118	1.675	0.096	0.827	1.210
	Fixed assets %	−0.068	0.027	−0.177	−2.512	0.013	0.825	1.212
	Size ln	0.014	0.003	0.352	5.348	0.000	0.940	1.064
	Current ratio	0.003	0.002	0.113	1.623	0.106	0.841	1.189
	Leverage	−0.005	0.001	−0.306	−4.142	0.000	0.746	1.341
	Growth	0.052	0.014	0.240	3.710	0.000	0.972	1.029

[a] Dependent variable: ROA

the higher level of 95%. All other variables (fixed assets ratio, size, leverage, and sales growth) have the same level of impact on return on equity. The results also indicate that current ratio does not effect significantly to the profitability ratios in both regression models (Table 8).

R square is 0.305, adjusted 0.282 which indicates that 28% of variance of depended variable can be explained with defined independed variables (Tables 9 and 10).

Table 8 Model 2 summary

Model summary[a]				
Model	*R*	*R* Square	Adjusted *R* Square	Std. error of the estimate
1	0.552[b]	0.305	0.282	0.6449143

[a] Dependent variable: ROE
[b] Predictors: (Constant), Growth, Size ln, Intangible assets growth, Current ratio, Fixed assets %, Leverage

Table 9 Results of ANOVA model 2

ANOVA[a]						
Model		Sum of squares	df	Mean square	*F*	Sig.
1	Regression	34.085	6	5.681	13.658	0.000[b]
	Residual	77.776	187	0.416		
	Total	111.861	193			

[a] Dependent Variable: ROE
[b] Predictors: (Constant), Growth, Size ln, Intangible assets growth, Current ratio, Fixed assets %, Leverage

Table 10 Results of regression analysis of model 2

Coefficients[a]								
		Unstandardized coefficients		Standard. Coefficients			Collinearity statistics	
Model		*B*	Std. error	Beta	*t*	Sig.	Tolerance	VIF
1	(Constant)	–0.951	0.371		–2.565	0.011		
	Intangible assets growth	0.103	0.016	0.432	6.442	0.000	0.827	1.210
	Fixed assets %	–0.416	0.234	−0.120	–1.781	0.077	0.825	1.212
	Size ln	0.051	0.023	0.137	2.177	0.031	0.940	1.064
	Current ratio	–0.009	0.015	−0.042	–0.632	0.528	0.841	1.189
	Leverage	–0.078	0.010	−0.538	–7.616	0.000	0.746	1.341
	Growth	0.448	0.121	0.228	3.691	0.000	0.972	1.029

[a] Dependent variable: ROE

The results are according to the findings of other similar research papers (Seo and Kim 2020; Bagna et al. 2021; Qureshi and Siddiqui 2020), which clearly documented that there is a significant positive relationship between intangible assets and financial performance of companies measured as profitability ratios.

In relation to the set models of this research, Seo and Kim (2020) investigated the impact of investment in intangible assets on better company performance by focusing on specific intangible assets such as human capital, advertising, and research and development. In this sense, the key difference compared to this research which gathers all intangible assets for balance sheet is the inclusion of specific intangible assets. In their model, the authors set the profitability and value of the company as the dependent variable. The independent variables, according to them, are the size of the company, the age of the company, human capital, advertising, and research and development. All VIF values are less than 10, so there is no multicollinearity. *R* Square is 0.16 which indicates that 16% of variance of a depended variable can be explained with defined independed variables. All results are significant at 1% significance level. The author's conclusion is that managers should increase investments in these three types of intangible assets and as a result, there will be an increase not only in the profitability of the company but also in the value of the company for investors. One of the interesting findings is that investment in advertising affects the profitability and value of the company. Given that companies can invest separately or simultaneously in human capital, advertising, research and development to improve their performance, managers should strategically use these three key factors and adopt investments in intangible assets to achieve their managerial goals.

Bagna et al. (2021) put innovation as one of the most important drivers of company growth. They analyzed whether there is a significant relationship between investment in specific forms of intangible assets, such as patents, and better company performance. In relation to this research, which includes all forms of intangible investments that are recorded in the company's balance sheets, Bagna et al., focused on those that have the patent value shown in their balance sheets. As the first dependent variable, the authors set the growth of the company, which they calculated as the difference in consecutive periods in the position of sales revenue, while as the second dependent variable they set ROIC, as a measure of profitability. The authors emphasize that the use of ROIC in this analysis is more suitable than the use of ROE, primarily because the numerator includes operating profit that is not influenced by the capital structure. Indicators related to patents were set as independent variables, where the intensity of intangible investments (INT) is the most important variable. *R*-squared is equal to 0.30 in the full Model, supporting good reliability for findings. The regression results are at the significance level of 1%, 5%, and 10%.

Qureshi and Siddiqui (2020) analyzed the impact of intangible assets on profitability, efficiency, capital structure and dividend policy, and market value of technology companies. The main purpose of this study is to determine whether intangible assets affect the financial indicators of a company or not. Unlike this research, where we measured the impact through changes in ROA and ROE, they analyzed the movement of other financial indicators of the company, such as ROIC, Leverage, P/E, P/sales, and P/book value. As a dependent variable, the authors set the value of the company's intangible assets, and as independent variables, they listed the financial indicators of profitability and company value. The first significant conclusion of their research, at the same time the opposite conclusion of this research, is that investments in intangible assets have a significant negative impact on ROE, ROA and other listed indicators, at the significance level of 1%. Also that they have an insignificant positive impact on the profit margin, P/E, and a significant positive impact on dividends policy. Additionally, looking separately at the countries included in the research in Finland, Japan, Pakistan, and the USA, the intangible assets have a significant positive impact on ROA and ROE, which is fully consistent with the results of this research.

5 Conclusions

Investment in intangible assets affects profitability of companies positively. The objective of the empirical research was to determine whether there is a significant relationship between the growth of investment in the company's intangible assets and its business performance in the form of profitability. From the empirical research, which was set up through two models, two conclusions were drawn: The first is that there is a significant positive relationship between investment in intangible assets and the growth of return on assets (ROA) and the second is that there is an even more significant positive relationship between the growth of investment in intangible assets and return on equity (ROE). These results are supported by previous research that dealt with the relationship between investment in intangible assets and changes in company performance.

This paper has helped to expand the theoretical concept of intangible assets and the impact of investment in intangible assets on profitability of companies. This paper also has practical implications.

The manufacturing sector is a very important part of the overall economy of the Republic of Serbia, with a significant share of the total GDP. It is crucial for a developing country to recognize and invest in those factors that will contribute to faster growth. Investing in intangible assets in the modern economy is a necessity, given the rapid technological changes. Only by consensual investment in software, patents, licenses, and other forms of intangible assets, companies will readily meet the challenges that await them in the business operations of the twenty-first century. The research results can be of interest to managers of listed manufacturing companies in Serbia in order to make decisions about future business policy, adjustment to changes, and as a final goal—achieving a higher rate of profitability, growth, and company value. The results of research should encourage the managers of listed manufacturing companies to invest more in intangible assets that are crucial for their business strategy.

The limitations of research can be observed in the point of based on the one sector manufacturing companies and one country. Future research should include comparative analysis with other sectors and other countries. Another limitation of this research may be that the intangible assets used in the analysis were taken as a whole from the balance sheet. The growth of intangible assets was taken as a change in the complete BS position, and thus it is not possible to emphasize the role of specific forms of intangible assets, which may have a more significant contribution to the profitable growth. The recommendation for further research can be to analyze the links of specific forms of intangible assets to financial indicators, with the aim of focusing future investments in those intangible assets that create the most value for company.

Investment in intangible assets affects profitability of companies positively. This paper has helped to expand the theoretical concept of intangible assets and the impact of investment in intangible assets on profitability of companies. The research results can be of interest to managers of listed manufacturing companies in Serbia in order to make decisions about future business policy and achieving a higher rate of profitability. The results of research should encourage the managers of listed manufacturing companies to invest more in intangible assets in order to increase the profitability. The limitations of research can be observed in the point of based on the one sector manufacturing companies and one country. Future research should include comparative analysis with other sectors and other countries.

References

Ahn J, Duval R, Sever C (2020) Macroeconomic policy, product market competition, and growth: the intangible investment channel. Working paper research. IMF - International Monetary Fund. WP/20/25. https://www.imf.org/-/media/Files/Publications/WP/2020/English/wpiea2020025-print-pdf.ashx. Accessed 25 Jun 2022

Andrašić J, Mijić K, Mirović V et al (2018) The modelling factors of agricultural companies performances. Custos E Agronegocio On Line 14(4):223–240

Arianpoor A (2021) The impact of intangible assets on firm performance: evidence from an emerging economy. Iran J Account Audit Financ 5(2):61–77

Bagna E, Cotta Ramusino E, Denicolai S (2021) Innovation through patents and intangible assets: effects on growth and profitability of European companies. J Open Innov: Technol Market Complex 7(4):220

Barker R, Lennard A, Penman S et al (2021) Accounting for intangible assets: suggested solutions. Account Bus Res. https://doi.org/10.1080/00014788.2021.1938

Bunget OC, Blidisel RG, Feleaga L et al (2014) Empirical study of intangible assets in Romanian municipalities. E+M Ekon Manage 17(3):136–151

Cordazzo M, Rossi P (2020) The influence of IFRS mandatory adoption on value relevance of intangible assets in Italy. J Appl Acc Res 21(3):415–436

Corrado C, Haskel J, Jona-Lasinio C et al (2016) Intangible investment in the EU and US before and since the great recession and its contribution to productivity growth. EIB Working Papers 2016/08, European Investment Bank (EIB)

Cosmulese CG, Socoliuc M, Ciubotariu M et al (2021) Empirical study on the impact of evaluation of intangible assets on the market value of the listed companies. E+M Ekon Manage 24(1):84–101

Dakić S, Mijić K (2020) Regression analysis of the impact of internal factors on return on assets: a case of meat processing enterprises in Serbia. Strat Manage 25(1):29–34

Dakić S, Mijić K, Jakšić D (2019) Multiple regression approach to modelling determinants of business success based on financial statements: evidence from food processing companies in the Republic of Serbia. Custos E Agronegocio On Line 15(4):485–501

Denicolai S, Cotta Ramusino E, Sotti F (2014) The impact of intangibles on firm growth. Tech Anal Strat Manag 27(2):219–236

Glova J, Mrazkova S (2018) Impact of intangibles on firm value: an empirical evidence from European public companies. Ekonomický Časopis 66(6):665–680

Haji AA, Mohd Ghazali NA (2018) The role of intangible assets and liabilities in firm performance: empirical evidence. J Appl Acc Res 19(1):42–59

IAS 38 – Intangible Assets. https://www.ifrs.org/content/dam/ifrs/publications/pdf-standards/english/2021/issued/part-a/ias-38-intangible-assets.pdf Accessed 15 Jun 2022

Kramer JP, Marinelli E, Iammarino S et al (2011) Intangible assets as drivers of innovation: empirical evidence on multinational enterprises in German and UK regional systems of innovation. Technovation 31(9):447–458

Lev B (2018) Ending the accounting-for-intangibles status quo. Eur Account Rev:1–24

Lev B, Gu F (2016) The end of accounting and the path forward for investors and managers. Wiley

Li H, Wang W (2014) Impact of intangible assets on profitability of Hong Kong listed information technology companies. Bus Econ Res 4(2):98–113

Lopes I, Rodrigues AMG (2007) Intangible assets identification and valuation – a theoretical framework approach to the Portuguese airlines companies. Electron J Knowl Manage 5(2): 193–202. https://www.researchgate.net/publication/228508687_Intangibles_Assets_Identification_and_Valuation-A_Theoretical_Framework_Approach_to_the_Portuguese_Airlines_Companies Accessed 30 Jun 2022

Mijić K, Jakšić D (2017) The determinants of agricultural industry profitability: evidence from Southeast Europe. Custos E Agronegocio On Line 13(1):154–173

Milić D, Mijić K, Jakšić D (2018) Opportunistic management behavior in reporting earnings of agricultural companies. Custos E Agronegocio On Line 14(1):125–142

Mirović V, Milenković N, Jakšić D et al (2019) Quality of biological assets disclosures of agricultural companies according to international accounting regulation. Custos E Agronegocio On Line 15(4):43–58

Mohammed ZO, Al Ani MK (2020) The effect of intangible assets, financial performance and financial policies on the firm value: evidence from Omani industrial sector. Contemporary Econ 14(3):379–391

Mohanlingam S, Phuong Nguyen LT, Mom R (2021) The effects of intangible assets on financial performance and financial policies of listed technology firms in Thailand. Apheit Int J 10(1): 1–17

Qureshi J, Siddiqui DA (2020) The Effect of Intangible Assets on Financial Performance, Financial Policies, and Market Value of Technology Firms: A Global Comparative Analysis. Asian J Finance Account 12(1):26-57

Radonić M, Milosavljević M, Knežević S (2021) Intangible assets as financial performance drivers of IT industry: evidence from an emerging market. E&M Econ Manage 24(2):119–135

Sardo F, Serrasqueiro Z (2018) Intellectual capital, growth opportunities, and financial performance in European firms: dynamic panel data analysis. J Intellect Cap 19(4):747–767

Seo HS, Kim Y (2020) Intangible assets investment and firms' performance: evidence from small and medium-sized enterprises in Korea. J Bus Econ Manag 21(2):421–445

Tadić J, Medved I, Bojanić R et al (2020) R&D product development KPIs and performance of companies in Serbia. Tehnički Vjesnik-Technical Gazette 27(3):990–995

Thum-Thysen A, Voigt P, Bilbao-Osorio B et al (2017) Unlocking Investment in Intangible Assets. Economic and financial affairs, discussion paper 047. European Commission. Publications Office of the European Union, Luxembourg

Thum-Thysen A, Voigt P, Bilbao-Osorio B et al (2019) Investment dynamics in Europe: distinct drivers and barriers for investing in intangible versus tangible assets? Struct Chang Econ Dyn 51:77–88

Wang Y, Du R, Koong KS et al (2016) Effects of R&D policy choice on accounting performance and market value. R&D Manag 47(4):545–556

Disrupting the Stock Market: Stocks Gone Crypto

Milica Latinović

Abstract Financial technology development is disrupting industries throughout the world. More and more companies are embracing some type of these innovative technologies because their executives believe that those technologies have value-increasing potential. But do investors share their point of view? Do investors react uniformly to the blockchain-related announcements globally? The purpose of this research is to determine, what is investors' reaction to such changes in a corporate strategy. Investors' reaction to corporate signals and announcements is best explored with the event study methodology. We focus our analysis on the large-cap publicly traded companies from the Central and Eastern Europe, more specifically, on the three companies from technology sector which are among the largest companies from this region. Our results show that there is a difference in the reaction between the investors in the emerging and developed markets. Cumulative abnormal returns are significant, but the investor reaction in Poland and the Czech Republic is positive, while investors in developed market's reaction is a negative one.

Keywords Cryptocurrency · Blockchain · Stock market · Investors' reaction · Event study

1 Introduction

In this research, we are going to examine the ways in which corporate strategy can be altered with the adoption of blockchain technologies and whether such alterations are value enhancing. Innovative technologies are gaining recognition worldwide, but different regions exhibit different exposure. Therefore, we are going to try to put the Central and Eastern Europe (CEE) region on the global blockchain map and determine the investors' attitudes toward the adoption of disruptive technologies.

M. Latinović (✉)
Faculty of Organizational Sciences, University of Belgrade, Belgrade, Serbia
e-mail: milica.latinovic@fon.bg.ac.rs

S. Benković et al. (eds.), *Digital Transformation of the Financial Industry*,
Contributions to Finance and Accounting,
https://doi.org/10.1007/978-3-031-23269-5_5

To do that, we use research reports and classification of technological companies from CEE region, which group tech companies depending on their market capitalization (Digital Poland 2021),[1] and we find companies listed on the stock markets. We use public companies because we can observe investor's reaction. We use companies with large market capitalization, to be able to capture the true nature of the reaction. Countries from the CEE region are mostly classified as emerging and frontier markets. Their stock markets are still not as developed, and as liquid as, the stock markets of developed countries. However, sampled companies are large cap even in the developed markets and therefore, can offer us an important insight into investors' preferences. Technological companies are used since they can be considered more reliable when issuing blockchain announcements (Chen et al. 2022), and the reaction to their announcements is expected to be a more genuine one. Our main findings suggest that investors approve blockchain-related news and that they disapprove FinTech-related announcements.

Since their inception blockchain technologies and cryptocurrencies made a huge commotion in the financial markets. FinTech, blockchain, cryptocurrencies, and tokens are some of the new words in financial terminology. Those are also new elements of the financial sector and can be an indicator of its innovativeness, development, or opportunity. Countries have holdings of cryptocurrencies. Each traditional industry has experienced certain changes due to the advances in blockchain technology. Last year JP Morgan released a report and presented findings that traditional financial companies are at risk, since digital finance came into prominence. Their reaction to the emerging trend was to enter a digital arena, with debt security tied to the "crypto basket." This leads us to the question—are public companies at risk as well? What are the ways public companies can adapt to the emergence of a blockchain-based assets and technology? If we know that theory says that each company has shareholders that they deserve, are their shareholders ready for such a change and how will they react to disruption?

So far, if we look at the corporate finance domain, finance professionals have several ways in which they can implement blockchain technology like in their supply chain, financing, payment, and settlements (JP Morgan 2018). Furthermore, a certain number of public and private companies worldwide have substantial holdings of bitcoin. Do cryptocurrencies present a good investment opportunity for a company? If there is a link between markets for different asset classes and there is a high degree of integration between them, there is no diversification opportunity. But if markets are not fully integrated, that could represent an investment opportunity (Jebran et al. 2017). There are plenty of tech companies, mainly in the USA and Canada that adopted the crypto. Companies in the countries of Central and Eastern Europe are following their path, but their number is much more modest. European companies are a bit more cautious now.

[1] https://digitalpoland.prowly.com/164485-phoenixes-dragons-and-wolves-meet-100-digital-champions-who-are-building-digital-economy-in-central-and-eastern-europe

Does corporate adoption of innovative technologies create long-lasting shareholder value? Why do public companies consider and include cryptocurrencies in their businesses? Numerous corporate executives believe that blockchain technologies present a value-creation vehicle. Therefore, many corporations invest substantial capital in blockchain technologies. However, there is evidence that this technology is value creating only in the case when corporate blockchain plans are credible (Autore et al. 2021). Schlecht et al. (2021) expect that blockchain technologies will have a huge impact on the business and society and find evidence of considerable efficiency gains through technological progress.

So, how do investors look at the blockchain technology, cryptocurrencies, and the companies that embraced some form of disruption? How do they react when a company goes "crypto"? There are different kinds of investors based on their risk preferences. Some investors are risk-takers, and they invest in fungible and non-fungible tokens directly. Some investors are more risk averse, and they do not invest directly in the new digital asset classes; rather, they choose traditional asset classes which have exposure to the various types of blockchain technology. Cahill et al. (2020) show that on the day that a company announces that will connect in some way with blockchain technology, investors have a positive reaction to such news.

But market participants should be cautious since with every novelty there are the ones who will try to misuse it. Words that often arise in the research investigating blockchain and cryptocurrencies are words like credible, familiarity, and trust. Therefore, appropriate legislation is the key to investors' protection, building trust, and further increasing companies' involvement in blockchain technologies and cryptocurrencies. But regulation is still in its infancy. There are very large discrepancies regarding what market participants have at their disposal in each country. Nonetheless, due to expansion in cryptocurrency ecosystem, there is a challenge for regulators to decrease legal uncertainty, and provide adequate investor protection while promoting technological change (Ferreira and Sandner 2021). Europe adopted a Digital Finance Package in September 2020, which will come into effect by 2024. Since China has banned crypto mining and trading (Quiroz-Gutierrez 2022),[2] Europe became the largest cryptocurrency economy.

However, in this research, we are not going to analyze all European markets, rather we focus on Central and Eastern Europe, and try to find the largest and the most influential technology companies listed on the stock exchanges. Thus, we are going to investigate the adoption of innovative technologies by publicly traded companies originating from Poland and the Czech Republic. In our research, we are going to examine "crypto" stock characteristics and explore investors' reaction to the relevant corporate announcements of "crypto" related events. By "crypto" we are going to assume not just cryptocurrencies, but we are going to define that term more broadly and incorporate blockchain, FinTech, and tokens into discussion and analysis. In the second part, we are going to present the way innovative technologies can

[2] https://fortune.com/2022/01/04/crypto-banned-china-other-countries/

be implemented in a corporate domain. In the third part, we explore value creation potential of the innovative technologies and their implementation. Forth part presents business models of three companies from Poland and the Czech Republic, the ways they adopted the "crypto" and investor's reaction to shifts in their strategy. Fifth part offers concluding remarks.

2 Disruption in the Corporate Setting

Corporations operate either domestically or globally, and the development of the financial system defines the opportunities that they have at their disposal. Inequality throughout the world is substantial. With the technological development and the disruption of the financial service sector, FinTech will enable financial inclusion of the ones that do not meet bank requirements. Financial inclusion can decrease poverty and inequality in countries where people are mostly unbanked or underbanked (Mushtaq and Bruneau 2019). Financial technology development can help to increase job openings. Moreover, there is evidence that private sector development with job creation potential, will decrease inequality (Le and Tran 2022). Financial system development has an impact on income inequality, but there is a certain threshold after which it has a decreasing effect on inequality. New financial technologies will enhance the financial sector's development. For example, by improving securities markets in emerging economies, such as those in the regions of Central and Eastern Europe, inequality can be reduced and not at the cost of credit expansion (Latinovic and Milosevic 2019). If the company's business model includes some type of financial innovative technology, that can potentially make companies more attractive to investors globally. That can make stock markets more attractive and bring more capital flows to those markets. In turn, that will improve the overall economy, development, and decrease a possibility of a market crisis. Hence, the market can more easily make a transition from an emerging to a developed market.

With accelerated technological development, every industry is going through radical changes. Financial technology or FinTech represents new innovative solutions in the development of applications, processes, products, or even business models. Those innovative solutions are brought by artificial intelligence, Internet of Things, or big data and are related to the financial services industry. FinTech solutions are customer oriented, highly innovative, pioneering, and above all disruptive. FinTech applications can be related to payments, financing and investment activities, insurance, or advisory. Types of FinTech services include money transfer, peer-to-peer lending, trading platforms, credit scoring, etc. Among others, fuzzy logic can be successfully implemented for the credit scoring purposes (Latinovic et al. 2018b). FinTech technologies alter the financial landscape and will increase its efficiency. Fundraising and lending will change, due to the possibility of initial coin/token offering or crowdlending (Lee and Low 2018). However, the success of the crowd campaigns can vary depending on the fulfilment of the critical success factors.

If we look at the equity crowdfunding campaigns, those factors are, but are not limited to size of team that conducts the campaign, the number of backers of that campaign, and the amount that is set as a fundraising target (Latinovic and Bogojevic Arsic 2019). There is evidence that companies acquire successful start-ups involved with FinTech. That is evident, especially in the e-commerce sector. In that way, companies, for example, can include innovative payment methods into their business models. FinTech is not reserved solely for the financial services industry, but also for the different corporations. For example, Google invested in innovative solutions related to investments, payment and loans, trading, accounting, and analytic. E-commerce companies expand into FinTech arena and utilize social media companies to provide micro-credit, lending, crowdfunding, investment products, and more (Lee and Low 2018).

The brave new "digital" world could not function without blockchain technologies. Blockchain technologies enable digital assets to move from a sender to a recipient, and it allows us to know that the sender is no longer in a possession of that asset (Bogojevic Arsic and Latinovic 2018). Blockchain technologies can be very important for corporations, due to their value increasing potential. These technologies can reduce the costs of financing and enable companies to avoid intermediaries (Adhami et al. 2018).

Another important concept that emerged from the Industry 4.0 is the concept of digital currency. There are different types of currencies: tangible and digital. Governments issue fiat currencies. The first and most famous digital currency is the bitcoin. Bitcoin is a system for value transfer without a centralized authority. "Bitcoin" is a term for a technology, and a "bitcoin" is a term that represents a unit of digital currency. Cryptocurrency is a peer-to-peer programmable digital currency, which allows for online payments without an intermediary. Besides bitcoin, there are around 900 cryptocurrencies that trade regularly. Bitcoin is recognized as an asset for accounting purposes in Japan. Australia is also working on the cryptocurrency accounting standard. The token can be defined as a digital commodity. For example, Switzerland is well established in the Token domain, but bitcoin is widely used as well. Northern and other developed European countries recognize bitcoin as a payment instrument (Lee and Low 2018). More and more investors around the world adopt cryptocurrencies. Depending on the country of their origin, reasons for the increased interest in cryptocurrencies vary. Investors in emerging markets favor cryptocurrencies since they preserve value of their savings and help them with business transactions. In developed countries, increase in interest in cryptocurrencies comes from institutional investments (Chainalysis 2021). Private equity company investment managers are open to investing in cryptocurrencies for which there is a high degree of brand familiarity and trust in trading service providers, since there were known examples of pyramidal schemes and fraud. Furthermore, institutional investors that have a high tendency to innovativeness will have higher investment intention in cryptocurrencies (Sun et al. 2021).

Many companies worldwide invested and continue to invest funds into cryptocurrency. US-based tech company—Microstrategy is the company that

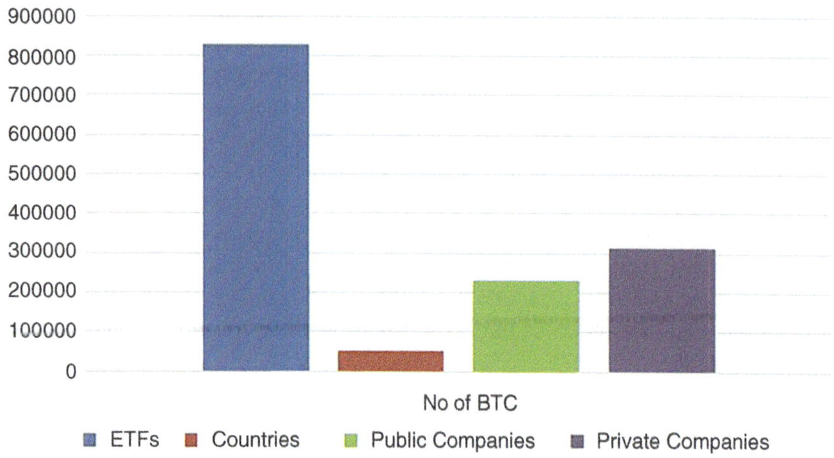

Fig. 1 Number of bitcoins held per different categories (Source: Own presentation, information derived from https://www.buybitcoinworldwide.com/treasuries/)

holds the most bitcoin globally[3] (Buy Bitcoin Worldwide 2022). Figure 1 displays the number of bitcoins that different kinds of organizations and governments have as their property, where ETFs have the highest stake (Buy Bitcoin Worldwide 2022). As we can see from Fig. 2, mainly countries situated in the USA invest in bitcoin (Buy Bitcoin Worldwide 2022). Public companies from Germany are the only European public companies that have substantial holdings of bitcoin. From that figure, we can see that among public companies with the highest bitcoin stakes, there are no public companies from Central and Eastern Europe.

However, CEE companies do operate with cryptocurrencies, but not in substantial amounts compared to the other world regions. For example, airBaltic a Latvian Airline Company that is majority owned by the Latvian government uses different cryptocurrencies. They started accepting payment in bitcoin for airline tickets in 2014, and recently they extended the range of acceptable cryptocurrencies (airBaltic 2021).[4] If we look at the percentage of the population that owns bitcoin, in Poland that is 2.5% and in the Czech Republic it is 2.08% (Triple A 2022).[5]

Initial Coin Offering (ICO) represents a way to raise capital. With ICO, liquid cryptocurrencies are exchanged for a token. Afterward, the token can be sold or switched for a product/service. Furthermore, ICO generates built-in customer base and positive network effect, and token mechanism provides a secondary market for the funders (Adhami et al. 2018). ICOs are open to investors, not yet highly regulated, and are of great significance for start-ups (Lee and Low 2018). For example, first ICO on the reward-based crowdfunding platform was successfully

[3] https://www.buybitcoinworldwide.com/treasuries/

[4] https://www.airbaltic.com/en/airbaltic-bitcoin-payments-extended-by-various-crypto-currencies

[5] https://triple-a.io/crypto-ownership-data/

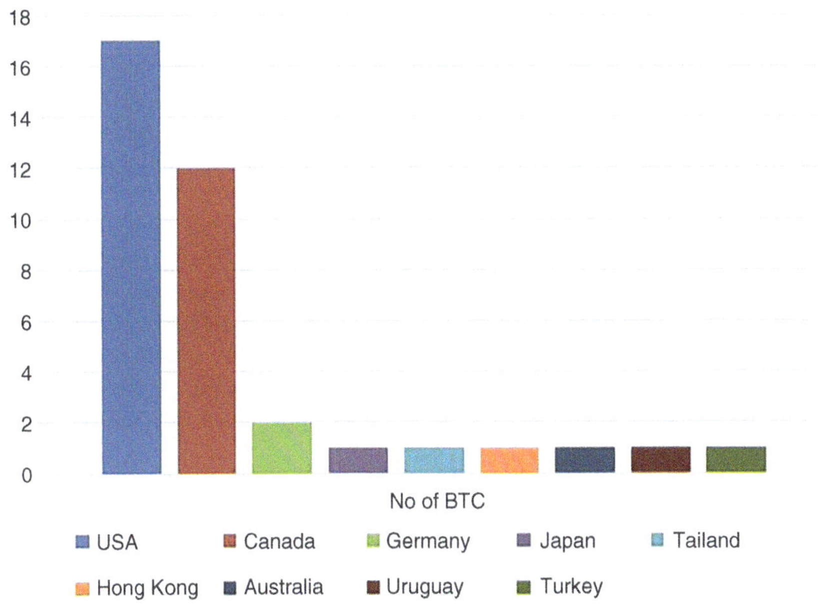

Fig. 2 Number of bitcoins held by public companies worldwide (Source: Own presentation, information derived from https://www.buybitcoinworldwide.com/treasuries/)

funded and it was related to a football league (the Fan-controlled Football League ICO from the Indiegogo) (Bogojevic Arsic and Latinovic 2018). ICOs in Central and Eastern Europe represent a 20% portion of the global ICO market (Carrol 2018).[6]

3 Value Creation Potential of "Crypto" Markets

3.1 Spillover, Investment and Trading of Different Asset Classes

Data from July 2020 show that there are around 5000 different cryptocurrencies (Aslanidis et al. 2021). If a company is looking to invest in cryptocurrencies or tokens, it is wise to know the properties of that alternative asset classes. Moreover, the intensity of the connection between different asset classes, and the direction of that connectedness is very important. If the linkage is not that strong, there is a potential for diversification (Latinovic et al. 2018a). The possibility of achieving a higher return at lower risk is every investor's dream. Companies that explore the

[6]https://irishtechnews.ie/central-and-eastern-europe-accounts-for-20-of-global-ico-market/

possibility of investing in one or more cryptocurrencies, should be aware of linkage and spillover in return and volatility between different asset classes.

If we look at the link between different cryptocurrencies, Aslanidis et al. (2021) find a strong market linkage between them. Cryptocurrencies are linked in return and volatility. When looking at the spillover between cryptocurrency returns, transmitted shocks have mainly short-term effects. Spillover in volatility is mainly created at low frequencies (Aslanidis et al. 2021).

Aharon and Demir (2022) examine the connectedness of the returns of various asset classes like non-fungible tokens (NFTs), equity, bonds, currencies, oil, Ethereum, and gold during the pandemic, and present evidence that they exhibit higher linkage. During normal times NFTs transmit systematic risk to some degree, but during times of crisis NFTs absorb risk. Generally, NFTs are not responsive to innovativeness in other asset classes. NFTs do not react even to the changes in Ethereum, which is perhaps not expected since they are quoted in its terms (Aharon and Demir 2022).

Umar et al. (2021) investigated whether there is a connection between cryptocurrencies and technology sector. Their results suggest that there is less integration between these two sectors, and therefore, there is an opportunity for diversification (Umar et al. 2021).

We focus on the connection between stock markets and cryptocurrency markets. Caffera (2022) find evidence that stock markets and cryptocurrencies are connected in terms of sentiments spread among investors, which suggests that investment strategies are influenced more by sentiments than price dynamic. Furthermore, there is evidence of return spillover and a weak volatility spillover from cryptocurrencies to "crypto" stocks. Evidence is more prominent when a company is more involved with blockchain technologies (Frankovic et al. 2022).

Diversification potential of certain assets is always crucial when considering their inclusion in the portfolio. Ma et al. (2020) find evidence that cryptocurrencies increase portfolio return, while decreasing volatility. These results are additionally amplified when there is no restriction regarding short sales. Furthermore, Ethereum shows better results in this respect compared to bitcoin.

Culjak et al. (2022), also find evidence of increased portfolio performance if cryptocurrencies are included. The novelty in this research is that cryptocurrencies are analyzed according to the sector and market capitalization. Sectors that are included in the study are financial, exchanges, and business services. Cryptocurrencies with lower market capitalization exhibit higher growth potential. Results show that a portfolio with a 20% weight in cryptocurrencies with lower market capitalization increases portfolio performance (Culjak et al. 2022).

There is some evidence that return of stock markets and cryptocurrency markets are related in a time of crisis, and that downside risk contagion between them can increase. Diversification benefits of cryptocurrencies apply to all markets globally, regardless of their financial system development. Ethereum is the most effective diversifier in the short run, but all the cryptocurrencies exhibit the same property in a long run. Furthermore, if investors have holdings in stocks and cryptocurrencies during the time of the crisis, position in cryptocurrencies should be short one (Jiang et al. 2021).

Moreover, if we look at the trading strategies, we can find evidence that momentum strategy outperforms the passive investment strategy. These results are true for both, stock markets and cryptocurrency markets. However, momentum trading cryptocurrencies exhibit higher risk-adjusted returns and lower downside risk compared to momentum trading on stock markets (Borgards 2021).

If we move from blockchain and cryptocurrencies to the token arena, we can find evidence that there is a potential for high returns if tokens are used for investing purposes. There is significant trading activity, user network growth and, especially, high return when the token is cross listed (Benedetti and Nikbakht 2021).

Based on the findings of the current research related to the return potential of different cryptocurrencies, NFTs and tokens, we can see that it would be wise for companies to invest in them.

3.2 Investor Reaction to the Corporate "Crypto" Events

Many top managers believe that blockchain technologies are value enhancing. Therefore, they are investing a large amount of capital on technology development, or they are implementing some type of these innovative technologies. However, it is important to determine do investors have the same point of view as executives regarding blockchain, and whether investors' preferences are region specific. Autore et al. (2021) find that credible blockchain announcement is connected to a higher announcement reaction and no reversal afterward. Chen et al. (2022) present evidence that blockchain announcements significantly increase the value of the listed companies.

Cahill et al. (2020) investigate investors' reaction associated with corporate announcements related to the blockchain. They find evidence that there is a positive abnormal return related to those types of announcements. The positive average abnormal return is higher with smaller companies than with the ones that have a large market capitalization. The effects are more pronounced with US companies and small-cap companies. Also, there is evidence that those returns are related to the performance of bitcoin. They conclude that investors might still not fully understand new disruptive technologies, and they consider blockchain and bitcoin to be the same terms (Cahill et al. 2020).

Akyildirim et al. (2020a) investigate how corporate name change when "crypto" terms are included influence corporate performance. They find that "crypto" name change has a negative impact on the company's short-term profitability. Also, following the quarter when the announcement is made there is a decrease in financial leverage. There are pricing premiums related to such name changes, and they can last up to 6 months after the announcement became known to the public. Following the price premiums, volatility also increases. Hence, investor perception shifts to different information flow and sources of information (Akyildirim et al. 2020a). Corporate name changes to "crypto" related terms are not the only type of the announcement that will trigger investors' reaction. Akyildirim et al. (2020b) find that blockchain announcements such as coin creation, offer price premium, but at the same time they are volatility increasing.

Current research findings suggest that investors agree with corporate decisions to include some type of "crypto" technologies in their business activities.

4 Case Studies

In this research, we are going to test investor reaction to the announcements that companies are "going crypto." By going "crypto" we assume all activities related to the FinTech, or inclusion of blockchain technologies into the company's business operations or investments into cryptocurrencies. In this research, we employ an event study methodology.

5 Methodology

Event study methodology is preferred methodology when one wants to study how a company's stock price acts around certain corporate events. Stock prices can change due to an important announcement, and depending on the news type effects can be short- or long-term (Kothari and Warner 2007). In order for us to be able to implement this methodology, we need to specify several dates. The event date is a day when an event of interest took place. Then, we look at the desired short- or long-term intervals and try to capture the significance of investors' reaction. To be able to determine the significance, we compare the real return that the stock exhibited in that interval and estimated one. Another set of dates we require for estimating returns is the estimation window.

Event date in this study is a trading date when corporation made an announcement that they are going "crypto." In this research, we implement several event windows, since we would like to test short-term ([−1; 1], [−3; 3]) and longer-term ([−10, 10], [−20, 20]) investors' reaction (Bouzzine and Lueg 2020). First, normal stock return is estimated using market model. After that abnormal return is calculated using formula (1), which represents the difference between the real return and the one calculated using market model:

$$A_{it} = R_{it} - (\beta_{0i} + \beta_{1i} R_{\mathrm{mt}}) \tag{1}$$

R_{it} is the rate of return of the company i on the day t, $\beta_{0\mathrm{i}}$ is the intercept term, $\beta_{1\mathrm{i}}$ represents the coefficient of the market index return on the return for the company i, R_{mt} is the rate of return on the local stock market index on the day t, and $\varepsilon_{\mathrm{it}}$ is an error term. In order for us to estimate normal return using market model, as estimation window is needed. We implement period of 220 trading days prior to the event till the 21 trading days before the event. In this study, we are going to analyze investor behavior related to the announcements of the companies listed on the Warsaw stock exchange and London stock exchange. Therefore, as a benchmark of the Warsaw stock exchange movement, we use WIG a major stock market index. The FTSE 100 is a representative of the market movement on the London Stock Exchange and is also used in calculations.

Afterward, abnormal returns are accumulated in the event window period, and cumulative abnormal return is calculated using formula (2). Its significance is determined with t-statistic (Cahill et al. 2020).

$$\mathrm{CAR}_i(t_1, t_2) = \sum_{t=t_1}^{t_2} \mathrm{AR}_{it} \tag{2}$$

6 CEE Public Companies Going "Crypto"

Companies from Central and Eastern Europe that are users, developers, or investors in blockchain technologies or cryptocurrencies are mainly private companies.[7] In order for us to find public companies and test investors' reaction to the different types of companies involved with these innovative technologies we use research and report issued by Digital Poland Foundation. They examined technological companies from CEE region and classified them into Digital Phoenixes, Digital Dragons, and Digital Wolves (Digital Poland 2021),[8] depending on their market value. Companies from those three categories are either public or backed by private investors (Recursive 2021).[9] However, the majority of them are still not listed on the stock exchanges. Therefore, our sample is rather small, which represents limitation of our study. However, due to large market capitalization of the sample companies, results of this study can be considered important.

Some of the companies from the Foundation report, like Bitdefender are planning to become public, but are not there yet. Bitdefender is a Romanian cybersecurity company that plans to go public in 2022. On December 13, 2021, they submitted documents needed for an IPO to the SEC (Bitdefender 2021; Mergermarket 2021).[10,11] For the sample of the tech public companies, manual search was

[7] Criteria related to users, developers and investors are done according to the Frankovic et al. (2022).

[8] https://digitalpoland.prowly.com/164485-phoenixes-dragons-and-wolves-meet-100-digital-champions-who-are-building-digital-economy-in-central-and-eastern-europe

[9] https://therecursive.com/which-are-the-cee-companies-with-the-highest-valuation/

[10] https://www.bitdefender.com/news/bitdefender-announces-confidential-submission-of-draft-registration-statement-to-sec-for-proposed-u-s-listing-4052.html

[11] https://info.mergermarket.com/bitdefender-eyes-2022-ipo-heels-uipath-sources/

Table 1 Company characteristics

Comp. name	Country of origin	Stock exch.	Market Cap.	Industry	Sector	News
Allegro	Poland	Warsaw	25.387B (PLN)	Internet retail	Consumer cyclical	Embraced blockchain Launched fintech payment (Allegro Pay)
CD Projekt	Poland	Warsaw	8.96B (PLN)	Electronic gaming and multimedia	Comunic. Services	Offers blockchain watch
Avast	Czech Republic	London	153.965B (CZK)	Software—Infrastructure	Technology	Acquisition of a blockchain company

Source: Data compiled from yahoo finance, https://tokeny.pl/en/allegro/; https://about.allegro.eu/news-releases/news-release-details/allegro-customers-love-allegro-pay-starting-now-its-available/; https://www.gameinformer.com/2021/12/02/this-pricey-cyberpunk-2077-watch-uses-blockchain-technology-to-prevent-counterfeiting; https://www.ledgerinsights.com/avast-acquires-second-blockchain-decentralized-identity-provider-securekey/

performed in order to find an announcement that the company "went crypto." Announcements were found on the companies' websites or other relevant portals. Some companies that belong to the sample, and that are publicly traded did not enter the crypto arena just yet. Therefore, when search did not yield any result that a public company announced that it is either a user or a developer or an investor, we did not include it in our analysis. In this research, we are going to test investors' reaction toward introduction of some type of "crypto" technologies into corporate strategy. Public companies from CEE region that introduced innovative changes in their businesses, and companies that we are going to analyze are two Polish companies and one company from Czech Republic. Their names and main characteristics are presented in Table 1.

6.1 Allegro (Poland)

Allegro is a Polish public company, listed on the Warsaw Stock Exchange. Allegro went public in October 2020 (Reuters 2020),[12] and its IPO was the largest one on this exchange. Allegro is a leading e-marketplace in Poland, with 13 million active buyers and 128,000 merchants. With approximately 21 million user visits per month, Allegro is among the 100 most visited websites in the world. Customers can buy primarily new products, from merchants, but from customers as well. Business to customers ("B2C") is their primary business model since customer to

[12] https://www.reuters.com/article/us-allegro-ipo-idUSKBN26X1P1

customer ("C2C") generates less than 4% of their revenue. In less than 1%, Allegro acts as the first party in the transactions. Products offered in the e-marketplace are from a wide range of categories. Furthermore, Allegro operates the website Ceneo, which is multi-category site comparison with 26 million users per month. In addition, Allegro runs a website for ticket sales—eBilet. Company generates profits from other related activities and consultancy services (Allegro 2020[13]).

An important milestone in Allegro's historical development happened in the year 2020, when Allegro acquired FinAi, a Polish FinTech company. The importance of this acquisition lies in acquiring the team of the FinAi. Their FinTech-related knowledge and capabilities such as machine learning, artificial intelligence, credit scoring and similar enabled Allegro to improve its business strategy. That acquisition empowered the launch of Allegro Pay. Allegro Pay is a proprietary consumer lending solution for buyers. The pilot launch of the FinTech financial service product, happened at the end of 2020 (Allegro 2020[14]). On September 8, 2021, Allegro Pay became available to everyone (Allegro 2021).[15] That is also, the first corporate announcement that we are going to test. Our aim is to determine do investors approve of innovative turns in corporate strategy. Hence, the content type of the first news is related to the FinTech.

Second news that is going to be included in the analysis relates to the announcement that Allegro turned to blockchain technology on March 25, 2022 (Tokeny 2022).[16] However, that information was not announced on the company's official website. Moreover, on March 24, 2022, the company announced what will be the closing day for the acquisitions of Mall Group A. S. and WE|DO CZ s.r.o. (Allegro 2022).[17] Since the blockchain news is not released on the official website, and there is an important announcement published on the corporate website the day prior to the blockchain announcement, we might expect to see investors' blockchain reaction blurred by the acquisition announcement. In Table 2, the results of the analysis are displayed. The investors' reaction is tracked in two short-term intervals and two longer-term intervals.

From Table 2, we can see that investors' reaction is solely short term. Although, investor sentiment is different depending on the news content. For the introduction of FinTech lending service, we can see that investors' reaction is negative immediately after the news spread to the web. Investors displayed negative reaction in the next 3 days, as well. Cumulative abnormal return in the 3-day period was −6.3%, and in the 7-day interval it reached −10%. Perhaps, a negative reaction was not in connection to FinTech, but rather the increased lending that it will enable. However,

---

[13] https://about.allegro.eu/static-files/e1c6f962-8152-4554-81a0-cd9751ede2c6

[14] https://about.allegro.eu/static-files/e1c6f962-8152-4554-81a0-cd9751ede2c6

[15] https://about.allegro.eu/news-releases/news-release-details/allegro-customers-love-allegro-pay-starting-now-its-available

[16] https://tokeny.pl/en/allegro/

[17] https://allegro.gcs-web.com/news-releases/news-release-details/title-setting-date-closing-acquisition-mall-group-and-wedo-cz

Table 2 Investors' reaction to the "crypto" news

Name	Date	R^2	[−1, 1] CAR	[−3, 3] CAR	[−10, 10] CAR	[−20, 20] CAR
Allegro	25.03.2022	0.211	0.0712*	0.1215*	−0.02	0.0584
	08.09.2021	0.105	−0.063*	−0.10*	−0.02	−0.034
CD Projekt	02.12.2021	0.106	0.0032	−0.030	0.157	0.3206*
Avast	24.03.2022	0.005	−0.003	−0.011	−0.15***	−0.177***

Source: own research. *, **, *** denote statistical significance at the 10%, 5%, and 1% level, respectively

in this instance reaction was immediate, but it does not last for a longer period of time. When we look at the investor reaction toward the adoption of blockchain technologies, we can observe that they react in short period of time, as well. Hence, we can see that investors exhibit immediate positive reaction toward adoption of innovative technologies. However, that news is mixed with the official announcement related to the acquisition closure, and therefore, the results might go in favor of the acquisition.

6.2 CD Projekt S. A. (Poland)

CD Projekt S. A. is a holding company and it conducts its operations within two business segments: CD PROJEKT RED and GOG.COM. CD PROJEKT RED is a business segment that is involved in the creation, licencing, and marketing of video games. They are globally known for the Witcher and Cyberpunk 2077 games. In addition, they are developing GWENT. Furthermore, fans can buy products through their online store (CD PROJEKT 2022[18]). GOG.COM is an independent digital game distribution platform. It offers customer support. It is connected to the local payment mechanisms and is available currently in 13 languages. CD Projekt S. A. is a public company, listed on the Warsaw Stock Exchange since January 2002 (Warsaw Stock Exchange 2022).[19]

CD Projekt already offers fans different game-related products, like accessories or clothes. On December 2021, they decided to do things a bit differently and they offered fans an item that is much more expensive and "crypto." Instead of a new mug, they offered players a watch that runs based on a blockchain technology (Guisao 2021; CD PROJEKT RED GEAR 2022).[20,21] Again, we test investors'

[18] https://www.cdprojekt.com/en/investors/regulatory-announcements/consolidated-report-for-q1-2022/

[19] https://www.gpw.pl/company-factsheet?isin=PLOPTTC00011

[20] https://www.gameinformer.com/2021/12/02/this-pricey-cyberpunk-2077-watch-uses-blockchain-technology-to-prevent-counterfeiting

[21] https://eu.gear.cdprojektred.com/t-2077-cyberpunk-2077-x-blonie-watch.html

reaction to the announcement that the company decided to go "crypto," and results can be seen in Table 2. News that a company is going to offer a wristwatch for the fans was first released on December 02, 2021. The news content of CD PROJEKT S. A. announcement is related to the blockchain. In this case, investors again, react positively to blockchain news. However, they need more time to process the announcement, and the results are significant in the longest time period, of the ones being tested.

6.3 AVAST (Czech Republic)

Avast is a consumer cybersecurity company with headquarters in Prague, Czech Republic. It offers products in two segments: consumer and corporate. Consumers have an option to pay directly for an Avast product. Avast free and paid products are based on artificial intelligence and machine learning and are used for security of devices, networks, and data. Furthermore, consumers can access Avast products indirectly through advertising or third-party software (Avast 2021[22]). Corporate customers buy Avast products in two ways, either directly or through Avast's partners. Corporate solutions range from network protection of one office to the protection of a global company. Avast went public in May, 2018 (London Stock Exchange 2018).[23] Although, Avast is a CEE country company it is listed on the Western Europe stock market. Avast made its debut on the London Stock Exchange in 2018 and two years later it became a constituent of the FTSE100 (Avast 2022),[24] which goes in support of Avast's persistent superior performance.

Another news that we are going to analyze relates to the blockchain announcement. Avast decided to make an acquisition of the blockchain company—SecureKey (Ledger Insights 2022),[25] and the news broke on March 24, 2022 (Ledger Insights 2022).[26] This type of business decision is not a novelty for Avast, since this is their second acquisition of a blockchain company. In Table 2, we can see that investors' reaction is significantly negative in two longer intervals. Global investors are trading on the London Stock Exchange, and their reaction to the acquisition of the blockchain provider is a negative one. This is not consistent with the previous results. However, the negative investors' reaction might be connected to the acquisition part of the announcement. Alternatively, we can conclude that investors in

[22] https://investors.avast.com/media/1908/avast-annual-report-2021.pdf

[23] https://www.lseg.com/markets-products-and-services/our-markets/london-stock-exchange/equities-markets/raising-equity-finance/market-open-ceremony/london-stock-exchange-welcomes-avast-main-market

[24] https://investors.avast.com/our-story/history/#page=1

[25] https://www.ledgerinsights.com/avast-acquires-second-blockchain-decentralized-identity-provider-securekey/

[26] https://www.ledgerinsights.com/avast-acquires-second-blockchain-decentralized-identity-provider-securekey/

emerging markets and more specifically in Poland (CEE country) are more prone to the adoption of innovative technologies compared to investors in developed countries. However, a number of companies and number of the related corporate announcements are rather small for us to be able to make a generalized conclusion. Further studies could investigate differences in investor reaction depending on the company's origin and its primary listing market. Furthermore, when blockchain announcement is mixed with a term acquisition, investors react differently in the emerging and developed markets. Again, further research should address this difference.

7 Conclusion

The financial landscape is changing due to innovations. However, legislation regarding innovative technologies is not uniform globally and investors do not exhibit the same level of enthusiasm in every region. Perhaps synchronized legislation regarding digital assets worldwide should be established, which will yield higher trust among investors and consequently to their higher involvement and acceptance. That in turn can be more stimulating for companies to incorporate "crypto" into their day-to-day operations.

To stay competitive, companies should adapt their strategies. Corporations can change its business strategy and pursue innovations in payments, lending, investing, credit scoring, etc. Based on the findings of the contemporary research related to the return and volatility spillover of different cryptocurrencies, we can see that it would be profitable for companies to invest in "crypto" assets. Cryptocurrencies of small market capitalization offer higher return possibilities. Furthermore, Ethereum proved to be a better alternative to bitcoin. Moreover, research show that investors approve of such corporate decisions.

We analyzed investor's reaction to the announcements that large tech companies from Poland and Czech Republic are going "crypto." Findings are mixed. Investors do not approve FinTech, and their reaction contributes to the negative CAR in the short run. Investors generally approve blockchain-related news, which is in accordance with previous studies (Autore et al. 2021; Cahill et al. 2020; Chen et al. 2022). However, their reaction is different depending on the financial market development. Furthermore, there is a difference in reaction in relation to the acquisition in an emerging and developed market. Further research should explore regional differences in investors' reaction.

However, these results must be taken with caution. First of all, we acknowledge that our sample is rather small which represent a limitation of our study. This is due to the fact that a very small number of tech companies, classified in the Foundation study is public. Moreover, just a modest number of those listed companies joined the disruption trend. However, market value and strength of the sampled companies are vast and therefore, investors' reactions to their "crypto" announcements can be taken as important. From Table 2, if we look at the R^2, we can see that its values are quite modest. This suggests that some other model, different from the market one is more suitable for return estimation. In the case of Allegro and CD PROJEKT S.A., which are Polish companies that are being traded on the Warsaw Stock Exchange this might be a necessity. Although these two companies are both of large market capitalization, they trade on the stock market of emerging countries. Therefore, a model that will include some additional explanatory variables might be more suitable. In that case, we might get more credible results. Perhaps, in years to come more tech startup's will grow and become public. That would allow us to study investors' preferences toward innovative technologies in more detail.

References

Adhami S, Giudici G, Martinazzi S (2018) Why do businesses go crypto? An empirical analysis of initial coin offerings. J Econ Bus 100:64–75. https://doi.org/10.1016/j.jeconbus.2018.04.001

Aharon DY, Demir E (2022) NFTs and asset class spillovers: lessons from the period around the COVID-19 pandemic. Financ Res Lett 47. https://doi.org/10.1016/j.frl.2021.102515

airBaltic (2021) airBaltic bitcoin payments extended by various crypto currencies. https://www.airbaltic.com/en/airbaltic-bitcoin-payments-extended-by-various-crypto-currencies. Accessed 26 July 2022

Akyildirim E, Corbet S, Sensoy A, Yarovaya L (2020a) The impact of blockchain related name changes on corporate performance. J Corp Financ 65:101759. https://doi.org/10.1016/j.jcorpfin.2020.101759

Akyildirim E, Corbet S, Cumming D, Lucey B, Sensoy A (2020b) Riding the wave of crypto-exuberance: the potential misusage of corporate blockchain announcements. Technol Forecast Soc 159:120191. https://doi.org/10.1016/j.techfore.2020.120191

Allegro (2020) Annual report of Allegro.EU S. A GROUP https://about.allegro.eu/static-files/e1c6f962-8152-4554-81a0-cd9751ede2c6. Accessed 29 July 2022

Allegro (2021) Allegro customers love Allegro Pay! Starting now its available to all. https://about.allegro.eu/news-releases/news-release-details/allegro-customers-love-allegro-pay-starting-now-its-available/. Accessed 28 July 2022

Allegro (2022) Setting the date of the closing of the acquisition of the Mall Group and WE|DO CZR s.r.o. https://allegro.gcs-web.com/news-releases/news-release-details/title-setting-date-closing-acquisition-mall-group-and-wedo-cz. Accessed 30 July 2022

Aslanidis N, Bariviera AF, Perez-Laborada A (2021) Are cryptocurrencies becoming more interconnected? Econ Lett 199:109725. https://doi.org/10.1016/j.econlet.2021.109725

Autore DM, Clarke N, Jiang D (2021) Blockchain speculation or value creation? Evidence from corporate investments. Financ Manage 50:727–746. https://doi.org/10.1111/fima.12336

Avast (2021) Avast plc annual report 2021. https://investors.avast.com/media/1908/avast-annual-report-2021.pdf. Accessed 30 July 2022

Avast (2022) History. https://investors.avast.com/our-story/history/#page=1. Accessed 30 July 2022

Benedetti H, Nikbakht E (2021) Returns and network growth of digital tokens after cross-listings. J Corp Financ 66:101853. https://doi.org/10.1016/j.jcorpfin.2020.101853

Bitdefender (2021) Bitdefender announces confidential submission of draft registration statement to the SEC for proposed US listing. https://www.bitdefender.com/news/bitdefender-announces-confidential-submission-of-draft-registration-statement-to-sec-for-proposed-u-s-listing-4052.html. Accessed 27 July 2022

Bogojevic Arsic V, Latinovic M (2018) Alternative online finance: crowdfunding and ICO In: Žarkić-Joksimović N, Marinković S (eds) XVI International symposium SymOrg 2018 – doing business in the digital age: challenges, approaches and solutions. Zlatibor, 07–10 June 2018: University of Belgrade, Faculty of Organizational Sciences, pp 480–484. ISBN: 978-86-7680-361-3

Borgards O (2021) Dynamic time series momentum of cryptocurrencies. N Am J Econ Financ 57: 101428. https://doi.org/10.1016/j.najef.2021.101428

Bouzzine YD, Lueg R (2020) The contagion effect of environmental violations: the case of Dieselgate in Germany. Buc Strat Env 29:3187–3202. https://doi.org/10.1002/bse.2566

Buy Bitcoin Worldwide (2022) Bitcoin Treasuries. Santa Fe. https://www.buybitcoinworldwide.com/treasuries/. Accessed 25 July 2022

Caffera R (2022) Sentiment spillover and price dynamics: information flow in the cryptocurrency and stock market. Physica A 593:126983. https://doi.org/10.1016/j.physa.2022.126983

Cahill D, Baur DG, Liu Z, Yang JW (2020) I am a blockchain too: how does the market respond to companies' interest in blockchain? J Bank Financ 113:105740. https://doi.org/10.1016/j.jbankfin.2020.105740

Carrol C (2018) Central and Eastern Europe accounts for 20% of global ICO market. https://irishtechnews.ie/central-and-eastern-europe-accounts-for-20-of-global-ico-market/. Accessed 25 July 2022

CD PROJEKT (2022) Consolidated report for Q1 2022. https://www.cdprojekt.com/en/investors/regulatory-announcements/consolidated-report-for-q1-2022/. Accessed 30 July 2022

CD PROJEKT RED GEAR (2022) T-2077 cyberpunk 2077 x Blonie watch. https://eu.gear.cdprojektred.com/t-2077-cyberpunk-2077-x-blonie-watch.html. Accessed 30 July 2022

Chainalysis (2021) The 2021 Geography of Cryptocurrency Report: Analysis of Geo-graphic Trends in Cryptocurrency Adoption and Usage. https://go.chainalysis.com/2021-geography-of-crypto.html. Accessed 15 Mar 2022

Chen K-H, Lai TL, Liu Q, Wang C (2022) Beyond the blockchain announcement: signaling credibility and market reaction. Int Rev Financ Anal 82:102209. https://doi.org/10.1016/j.irfa.2022.102209

Culjak M, Tomic B, Zikovic S (2022) Benefits of sectoral cryptocurrency portfolio optimization. Res Int Bus Financ 60:101615. https://doi.org/10.1016/j.ribaf.2022.101615

Digital Poland (2021) Phoenixes, dragons, and wolves. Meet 100 digital champions who are building digital economy in Central and Eastern Europe. https://digitalpoland.prowly.com/164485-phoenixes-dragons-and-wolves-meet-100-digital-champions-who-are-building-digital-economy-in-central-and-eastern-europe. Accessed 27 July 2022

Ferreira A, Sandner P (2021) EU search for regulatory answers to crypto assets and their place in the financial markets' infrastructure. Comput Law Secur Rev 43:105632. https://doi.org/10.1016/j.clsr.2021.105632

Frankovic J, Liu B, Suardi S (2022) On spillover effects between cryptocurrency-linked stocks and the cryptocurrency market: evidence from Australia. Glob Finance J 54:100642. https://doi.org/10.1016/j.gfj.2021.100642

Guisao J (2021) This pricey cyberpunk 2077 watch uses blockchain technology to pre-vent counterfeiting. https://www.gameinformer.com/2021/12/02/this-pricey-cyberpunk-2077-watch-uses-blockchain-technology-to-prevent-counterfeiting. Accessed 30 July 2022

Jebran K, Chen S, Ullah I, Mirza SS (2017) Does volatility spillover among stock markets varies from normal to turbulent periods? Evidence of emerging markets of Asia. J Financ Data Sci 3(1–4):20–30. https://doi.org/10.1016/j.jfds.2017.06.001

Jiang Y, Lie J, Wang J, Mu J (2021) Revisiting the roles of cryptocurrencies in stock markets: a quantile coherency perspective. Econ Model 95:21–34. https://doi.org/10.1016/j.econmod.2020.12.002

JP Morgan (2018) Blockchain and the Decentralization Revolution: A CFO's Guide to the potential implications of the distributed ledger technologies. https://www.jpmorgan.com/solutions/cib/investment-banking/corporate-finance-advisory/blockchain. Accessed 15 Mar 2022

Kothari SP, Warner JB (2007) Econometrics of event studies in. In: Bev E (ed) Hand-book of corporate finance: empirical corporate finance, vol 1, North-Holland, pp 4–22

Latinovic M, Bogojevic Arsic V (2019) Determinants of equity crowdfunding success. In: Proceedings of 5th IPMA SENET conference "challenges of growing Economies". Belgrade, 19–21 May 2019: International Project Management Association. https://doi.org/10.2991/senet-19.2019.24
Latinovic M, Milosevic N (2019) Income inequality and credit expansion in post-communist countries. Post-Communist Econ 31(1):106–122. https://doi.org/10.1080/14631377.2018.1443247
Latinovic M, Bogojevic Arsic V, Bulajic M (2018a) Volatility spillover effect in West-Ern Balkans. Acta Oecon 68(1):79–100. https://doi.org/10.1556/032.2018.68.1.4
Latinovic M, Dragovic I, Bogojevic Arsic V, Petrovic B (2018b) A fuzzy inference system for credit scoring using boolean consistent fuzzy logic. Int J Comput Int Sys 11(1):414–427. https://www.atlantis-press.com/journals/ijcis/25888773
Le DV, Tran TQ (2022) Does the private sector increase inequality? Evidence from a transitional country. Struct Change Econ D 62:451–466. https://doi.org/10.1016/j.strueco.2022.06.005
Ledger Insights (2022) Avast acquires second blockchain decentralized identity provider SecureKey. https://www.ledgerinsights.com/avast-acquires-second-blockchain-decentralized-identity-provider-securekey/. Accessed 30 July 2022
Lee DKC, Low L (2018) Inclusive FinTech: blockchain, cryptocurrency and ICO. World Scientific Publishing Co. Pte, Singapore
London Stock Exchange (2018) London stock exchange welcomes Avast to the main market. https://www.lseg.com/markets-products-and-services/our-markets/london-stock-exchange/equities-markets/raising-equity-finance/market-open-ceremony/london-stock-exchange-welcomes-avast-main-market. Accessed 30 July 2022
Ma Y, Ahmad F, Liu M, Wang Z (2020) Portfolio optimization in the era of digital financialization using cryptocurrencies. Technol Forecast Soc Change 161:120265. https://doi.org/10.1016/j.techfore.2020.120265
Mergermarket (2021) Bitdefender eyes on the 2022 IPO on the heels of the UiPath – sources. https://info.mergermarket.com/bitdefender-eyes-2022-ipo-heels-uipath-sources/. Accessed 27 July 2022
Mushtaq R, Bruneau C (2019) Microfinance, financial inclusion and ICT: implications for poverty and inequality. Technol Soc 59:101154. https://doi.org/10.1016/j.techsoc.2019.101154
Quiroz-Gutierrez M (2022) Crypto is fully banned in China and 8 other countries. https://fortune.com/2022/01/04/crypto-banned-china-other-countries/ Accessed 15 Sept 2022
Recursive (2021) Which are the CEE companies with the highest valuation. https://therecursive.com/which-are-the-cee-companies-with-the-highest-valuation/. Accessed 27 July 2022
Reuters (2020) Polish e-commerce company Allegro light's up Europe's IPO market. https://www.reuters.com/article/us-allegro-ipo-idUSKBN26X1P1. Accessed 30 July 2022
Schlecht L, Schneider S, Buchwald A (2021) The prospective value creation potential of Blockchain in business models: a delphi study. Technol Forecast Soc Change. 166:120601. https://doi.org/10.1016/j.techfore.2021.120601
Sun W, Tohirovich Dedahanov A, Shin HY, Li WP (2021) Factors affecting institutional investors to add cryptocurrency to asset portfolios. N Am J Econ Financ 58:101499. https://doi.org/10.1016/j.najef.2021.101499
Tokeny (2022) Blockchain technology in the e-commerce sector. Allegro. https://tokeny.pl/en/allegro/. Accessed 30 July 2022
Triple A (2022) Global crypto adoption. https://triple-a.io/crypto-ownership-data/. Accessed 15 Sept 2022
Umar Z, Trabelsi N, Alqahtani F (2021) Connectedness between cryptocurrency and technology sectors: international evidence. Inter Rev Econ Financ 71:910–922. https://doi.org/10.1016/j.iref.2020.10.021
Warsaw Stock Exchange (2022) CDPROJEKT (PLOPTTC00011). https://www.gpw.pl/company-factsheet?isin=PLOPTTC00011. Accessed 30 July 2022

The Future of Banking in FinTech Era: Decentralized and Embedded Finance

Sladjana Barjaktarović Rakočević and Nela Rakić

Abstract The main goal of this paper is to analyze the impact of FinTech innovations on financial services industry in South-East Europe. The paper summarizes existing knowledge of banking services in the FinTech era and pays special attention to decentralized and embedded finance. Qualitative exploratory research was conducted using in-depth semi-structured interviews. Participants were bankers selected based on their experiences in the banking sector. In this study, we identified the most important factors driving the success of FinTech innovations in the banking sector: legal framework, impact of FinTech innovations on financial market and regulators, protection of personal and institutional data, major changes that happened with the use of FinTech innovations, advantages and disadvantages of FinTech innovations, competition in terms of embedded finance, and decentralized finance. According to the study results, it is not clear whether the FinTech innovations will disrupt traditional ways of working in the banking sector or lead to improved modern ecosystems of financial services. The FinTech industry is attractive and promising, and financial sector will experience great changes in the future. Additionally, most of the participants think that banks and FinTech should cooperate and find solutions together—expertise in banks is enormous, and FinTech brings agility and flexibility.

Keywords Banking · Digital transformation · FinTech · Decentralized finance (DEFI) · Embedded finance

1 Introduction

Historically, organizations are driven by innovations. In this era, we are witnessing the highest level of innovations mankind is faced so far. Continuous innovation is of ultimate importance, but those innovations must be customer oriented, and should

S. B. Rakočević (✉) · N. Rakić
Faculty of Organizational Sciences, University of Belgrade, Belgrade, Serbia
e-mail: sladjana@fon.bg.ac.rs; nela.rakic@fon.bg.ac.rs

S. Benković et al. (eds.), *Digital Transformation of the Financial Industry*, Contributions to Finance and Accounting,
https://doi.org/10.1007/978-3-031-23269-5_6

create value both for the customer and for the business itself (Aslam et al. 2020). Any innovation is driven by the technology underneath and banking industry is one of the most innovative ones in the world (Zaleska and Kondraciuk 2019).

One of the most prominent innovative technologies is digital technologies. The use of those technologies led to digitalization and change in business models in all industries. Digitalization has been seen as the new, fourth industrial revolution. Digital technology has been changing social, economic, and financial perspectives in numerous ways. Brennen and Kreiss (2014) have explained digitalization as "the adoption or increase in use of digital or computer technology by an organization, industry, country, etc."

Milošević et al. (2018) have analyzed the literature on digitalization and found out that there are two main streams in research—one is focused on the usage of digital technologies on macro and micro levels, and the second one is covering a digital gap, focusing on the differences in the development of digital technologies.

Numerous studies have been conducted to reveal the impact that digital technologies have on economic and social development and growth. For instance, Evangelista et al. (2014) point out that digitalization may drive productivity and employment growth. Authors Heredia et al. (2022) have explored and proposed the role of leadership management in improving firm performance through digital capabilities and found out that digital capabilities are sufficient but not a necessary condition for firm's performance improving. Milošević et al. (2019) recommended a mechanism for top management involvement and knowledge sharing to enhance project performance in the banking sector.

Additionally, it has been shown that digital technologies influence all kinds of businesses. Financial services are in the epicenter of those changes and one of the business areas that are affected by those changes, however, they are also active participants that are pushing digitalization forward.

As other businesses, financial services industry is immersing into the field of digitalization. Digital transformation in the financial services industry, and specifically in banking, has been seen both as an outcome of customers' demand from one side and as the initiation from a bank itself as a perceived necessity due to heavy competition in the field.

Analyzing innovation in the banking sector Milosevic et al. (2021) concluded that better performance results are achieved with innovation agility and readiness than quality of innovation. This means that the influence of innovation speed is more effective for performance success than the effect of innovation quality.

In their research OECD (2020) conclude that banks will create customer-centric business models as a reaction to digital disruption in financial services generally.

According to Statista (2022) and their research performed among managers in global financial services institutions, two main challenges facing digital banking worldwide in 2021, were ensuring data security and ensuring cybersecurity across the network and infrastructure.

Industry of financial services belongs to one of the most dynamic and innovation-driven industries. This industry is considered to be an active innovator and creator of new technologies, especially continuous development and improvement of financial technologies (FinTech). On the other hand, banking industry is facing huge competition from non-financial players. Financial technologies and their applications are significantly disrupting financial services arena. FinTech is not a new term in the industry of financial services, but in the last decade, it brought immense changes to the field of financial services.

The main goal of this paper is to analyze the impact of FinTech innovations on financial services industry in South-East Europe. More precisely, the paper will summarize existing knowledge of banking services in the FinTech era, especially having in focus on decentralized and embedded finance. Additionally, the paper will reveal the current level of FinTech development in financial services, especially banking services, and propose a future progress of FinTech innovations in banking services in the countries from South-East Europe. Those countries are bank oriented, and it is challenging to analyze the implications of FinTech on financial services, especially banks, in those countries. The research will rely on 12 elements that the International Monetary Fund (IMF) and World Bank have prepared in the document called "Bali FinTech Agenda paper" from 2018. The purpose of the agenda is to give a framework for FinTech issues that countries should consider in their financial technologies' development and growth (International Monetary Fund; The World Bank 2018).

Attractiveness of FinTech leads to the most important factors driving the success of FinTech innovations in banking sector, particularly in emerging economies. In this study, we identified nine factors such as legal framework, impact of FinTech innovations on financial market and regulators, protection of personal and institutional data, major changes that happened with the use of FinTech innovations, advantages and disadvantages of FinTech innovations, competition in terms of embedded finance, and decentralized finance. The study used qualitative exploratory research. More precisely, 16 participants gave their opinion on FinTech innovations in banking sector through semi-structure interviews. Our results confirm that the FinTech industry is attractive and promising and that financial sector will experience great changes in future.

Paper structure comprises several parts: after the introduction, literature review has been presented with financial technologies innovations in financial services, especially banking, then special focus has been on decentralized financial DEFI and its influence on banking sector, and finally basics of embedded finance are presented. Next section includes research methodology and the description of the data obtained from the research. Results section presents findings from the undertaken research, and finally in the conclusion part authors summarize obtained findings, analyze implications and provide directions for the future study of the subject. Paper closes with a list of applied references.

2 Literature Review

2.1 Banking Industry and FinTech

Traditional financial services have been changed significantly and credits go to financial technologies. Involving digital technologies in financial services has created enhanced business opportunities. Possibilities and chances from FinTech are enormous. FinTech suggests entirely new ways of offering financial services and benefits go to consumers, financial services institutions, regulators, and governments. Altogether, in shortest, FinTech changed financial services helping them be less costly and much faster.

Financial industry has ever been an early adopter and intensive user of information and communication technologies, nevertheless FinTech, with new business models and new players, has created dramatical changes in this sector (Gomber et al. 2017).

In the past, information and communication technologies supported but also changed the financial industry. FinTech—financial technologies are one of the prominent areas of digital technologies and transformation. Financial technologies, as the name implies, relate to the usage of technologies to create new and upgraded financial services (Thakor 2019). FinTech has transformed financial services—created a new landscape and introduce new players who offer new, innovative services and products.

Authors Boot et al. (2021) have conducted research on two important dimensions of financial innovations—information and communications, both are being influenced by technological changes. This conclusion disturbed traditional banks in a sense that allowed new financial players to entry arena and offer new services much easier, without accessing balance sheet, for example, for payments or wealth management services.

Being a very broad term—FinTech covers various aspects from almost all areas of finance like payments, lending, investment, wealth management, personal finance, cryptocurrencies, and stock market. FinTech uses blockchain technologies, artificial intelligence (AI), and data science, to transform traditional financial services. FinTech makes access to financial services easier and encourages competition introducing new players into the financial services arena. New players are mainly FinTech start-ups, which act alone or allied with traditional financial institutions, but also non-financial tech and big data companies. Main threats for FinTech are dealing with potential financial risks and security issues for all participants, as well as regulatory concerns considering digital transformation of financial services.

Chen et al. (2019) proposed a very interesting, extensive typology of FinTech encompassing seven categories: cybersecurity, mobile transactions, data analytics, blockchain, peer-to-peer (P2P), robo-advising, and IoT. For every category, they gave a short explanation and main technologies it uses, as well as real-case examples.

Banking, as one of the important segments of financial service industry, is facing huge impact of FinTech. There is scientific research that have analyzed the evolution of relationships between banks and FinTech of Carbó-Valverde et al. (2021).

In their research, Bofondi and Gobbi (2017) discuss that FinTech stands as a serious challenge for traditional banking institutions.

Further, considering the competition between FinTech lending and incumbent banking services, authors Bejar et al. (2022) found out that FinTech impact is associated with lower net interest margins and defensive responses of banks regarding FinTech adoption, lowering of fees, and expansions into new markets, all of which are beneficial to customers.

Elsaid (2021) finds out that although FinTech companies have been taking some market share from banks, it is hard to believe that banks would be substituted by FinTech companies. It is more likely, as for now, that there will be strategic partnerships between banks and FinTech companies. That would bring advantages to both parties, banks will offer new services, or they will present new business models, and FinTech companies will enter the market and get a broader customer base. In Murinde et al. (2022) it has been confirmed that "it is unlikely that FinTech lenders will replace banks, perhaps because banks are developing their own FinTech platforms or working with FinTech start-ups." Navaretti et al. (2018) state that, to survive, banks will have to react, face rising competitive pressure, and adopt new strategies.

If we look at developed European markets such as German financial market, then from the research of Dorfleitner et al. (2017) we could see that "87% of the surveyed banks either currently cooperate with a FinTech business or are pursuing a partnership or cooperation with FinTech businesses in the future." However, even though banks are aware that cooperation with FinTech would speed up their innovative business models, they still hesitate and resist facing challenges of this cooperation (Drasch et al. 2018).

Open question is to grasp the level of impact FinTech has on incumbent financial institutions, predominantly banks. Siek and Sutanto (2019) have done research on this topic, particularly focusing on whether peer-to-peer (P2P) lending platforms, have disrupted banking services. They found out that considering P2P payments, FinTech start-ups significantly affected banks in the early period of adoption of FinTech. Nevertheless, according to their research (research done before COVID-19, prim. authors) it is not as emphasized as it used to be, since bank customers value safety reasons.

Several research analyzed the influence that COVID-19 had on FinTech usage and adoption, and that research found out positive influence FinTech innovations had on financial services and peoples' lives (Liu et al. 2020; Xu et al. 2021).

Questions regarding the cost efficiency of FinTech innovations have been posted in scientific research. Lee et al. (2021) have done research analyzing whether FinTech innovations have improved bank efficiency. They found twofold benefits of FinTech innovation for banks: the first one relates to improved cost efficiency and the second one implies improved technology used by banks.

Research by Chen et al. (2019) have just covered the technologies that are being leveraged in FinTech innovations and what benefits pertained technologies give to the innovators. They concluded that blockchain technology has been particularly valuable as an underlining technology.

Both FinTech firms and banks have advantages one over the other, banks have the advantage of large established consumer bases, more experience in dealing with regulators, and a broader set of product offerings. FinTech firms for their part, have the advantage of being less regulated, they are much flexible and not burdened with legacy IT systems (Stulz 2019).

Wonglimpiyarat (2017) has tried to develop a systematic innovation business model for the banks that can be used as a dynamic tool to track the progress and pattern of technology development and diffusion in the banking industry.

Authors Li et al. (2022) have researched the impact of FinTech innovations in banking and their risk-taking levels. They have concluded that if a bank improves the level of its FinTech innovations, then it, generally, reduces the level of risks it takes.

Authors Lien et al. (2020) considered that customers' intention to use FinTech services will influence banks' improvement in the quality of their FinTech services. Through their research authors suggested that banks should primarily focus on improving the usefulness of FinTech services to meet demand of all customer segments.

Hu et al. (2019) have suggested an improved technology acceptance model (TAM) that incorporates user innovativeness, government support, brand image, and perceived risk as determinants of trust to investigate how users adopt Fintech services. According to this research, to accept new technology, customers first start using it, under the influence of government, brand image and user characteristics, and then rate benefits and potential risks.

Ryu (2018) in his research has analyzed the potential benefits and risks of FinTech use, and for a better understanding of FinTech behavior, has divided users into two groups of early and late adopters. Study revealed that both benefits and risks significantly influence further continued use of FinTech services, but perceived benefits had a much stronger impact on FinTech usage decisions than the perceived risks. Considering two groups of users, study showed that early adopters mainly focus on the efficiency of financial transactions, while the late adopters request more financial gains through FinTech usage.

Once again, as with financial services industry generally, with a new, innovative FinTech landscape, regulators face challenges of setting the right level or balance of regulation—the one that will encourage innovations and preserve financial stability and protect consumers (Vives 2019).

FinTech has reshaped financial services industry and banking itself. Having in mind all the characteristics and benefits financial technology innovation has brought to financial services industry, both customers and financial institutions now expect adaptability and expeditious processes.

2.2 Decentralized Finance: DEFI and Embedded Finance

As mentioned before, financial industry has a long relationship with information, communication, and now digital technologies. Further improvements in those technologies, especially in the domain of digital technologies, have remodeled traditional financial services, markets, and regulations. Today, we can talk about DeFi—decentralized finance, because of the FinTech influence on the financial system. Basically, DeFi relates to blockchain technologies, and represents digital financial infrastructure that does not need any central regulator that approves financial transactions.

Decentralized financial services could have existed in merit to blockchain technology. A blockchain is basically a digital ledger of transactions that is duplicated and distributed across the entire network of computer systems on the blockchain (Euromoney 2022). System of recording transactions in a blockchain is very difficult or probably impossible to alter or misapply. Blockchain technology, as peer-to-peer network, allows participants to confirm transaction without a need for a central clearing authority (PWC 2022).

Banking sector gained several benefits from the revolutionary technology such as blockchain technology (Ramchandra et al. 2022).

Martino (2021) emphasizes that blockchain's distributed ledger technology (i.e., second-generation blockchain) provides an opportunity for the banking industry because it can enhance efficiency of the banking processes and enrich services that banks offer to their customers. All have a positive impact on banks' profitability. According to the same author, main banking areas that could benefit from adopting blockchain technology are lending, payment systems, trade finance, and capital markets.

Blockchain impact on financial services can be huge, as Fanning and Centers (2016) concluded, financial institutions could save costs of at least 20 billion US dollars annually in settlement, regulatory, and cross border payments.

Blockchain technologies, as mentioned before, enable decentralized finance to be applied. Grassi et al. (2022) stated that DeFi does not "eliminate financial intermediation, but enables it to be performed in new ways, where decentralization means that no single entity can hold too much power or monopoly." Same authors state that DeFi is an alternative financial system where anyone can access financial services like lending, investing, or insurance from any place.

With this model of financial services, question of regulations comes across. In that sense, authors Zetzsche et al. (2020) point out that DeFi needs regulation in order to achieve the objective of decentralization itself. Those authors think that DeFi offers an opportunity for the regulatory approach to be built into DeFi design and to decentralize both finance and its regulation.

DeFi has developed significantly in recent years, and consequently its growth brought some new risks. Authors Werner et al. (2021) emphasis that decentralised nature allows that any participant can create unaudited and maybe malicious smart contracts within DeFi system.

Although DeFi constructs financial intermediation as being more decentralized, innovative, and transparent, it still has to overcome numerous issues in order to reach its full potential (Chen and Bellavitis 2020). However, DeFi will mark future of financial innovation in financial services industry, and the main question is in what form and when it will lead to financial disintermediation.

Another challenge that banking institutions are facing due to digitalization of financial services is incorporated in embedded finance. This term refers to non-bank providers offering banking services like payments, lending, and deposits. Being very beneficial for both the customers and companies, it can be noticed that there is a switch from all types of companies, like telecommunications, retailers, big techs and software companies, car manufacturers, insurance providers, and logistics firms to launch embedded financial services (McKinsey 2021). For the consumers, this means that they receive financial services when they need them, without going to financial service institutions.

For the banks, this means they are going to stay aside, and lose profits, or they can actively participate in this process. Hensen and Kötting (2022) state that banks could "adopt this approach by embedding financial services into the products of non-bank companies, thus offering seamless processes and an increased level of convenience to their clients."

3 Methodology

In this study qualitative exploratory research was conducted using in-depth semi-structured interviews. A convenience sampling method was used to analyze the perceived future of banking services in the FinTech era. Therefore, participants were bankers selected based on their experiences in the banking sector. Sixteen participants were chosen aged between 30 and 55 years. The numbers of male and female participants were balanced to avoid gender bias.

The primary data collection process ended after data saturation was reached. Data saturation was reached when additional sampling was unnecessary because no new information related to the research question was obtained after the additional interviews. Open and manual coding is feasible for the code with a few interviews (Basit 2003), and this study has 16 interviewees. Data were analyzed using open and manual coding to ensure comprehensive analysis and interpretation (Saldana 2009).

The nine factors identified during the interviews were: legal framework, impact of FinTech innovations on financial market and regulators, protection of personal and institutional data, major changes that happened with the use of FinTech innovations, advantages and disadvantages of FinTech innovations, competition in terms of embedded finance, and decentralized finance.

Legal framework refers to the level of legal clarity and certainty regarding FinTech innovations. It is essential for trustful and long-term relationships between financial intermediaries and clients. Clear and predictable legal rules are important for technological change and they became one of the top priorities for FinTech innovations, especially in developing countries.

In order to reach social and economic *impact* it is necessary to build robust financial and data infrastructure.

Protection refers to the goal to safeguard the integrity of financial system through identifying, understanding, and mitigating all potential risks in terms of personal and institutional data (Murinde et al. 2022).

Major changes require strong institutional capacity and involvement of relevant ministries and agencies which lead to economic and financial development (Romānova and Kudinska 2016).

The main *advantages* of decentralization and disintermediation are open financial systems, reduction of transactional costs, and direct connection through peer-to-peer network (Navaretti et al. 2018; Chen et al. 2019).

Disadvantages are described as the main obstacles to successful adoption of FinTech innovations and main problems in terms of effectiveness and efficiency of regulation.

Competition between banks and other players in the market should be balanced and based on knowledge sharing and openness about different experiences and best practices. In this research competition refers to non-bank providers offering banking services like payments, lending, and deposits (Wullweber 2020).

DeFi—decentralized finance—relates to blockchain technologies, and represents a digital financial infrastructure that does not need any central regulator that approves financial transactions (Chen et al. 2019). DeFi creates new opportunities, encourages permissionless innovation, and facilitates open access (Chen et al. 2019). For the purpose of this research participants were asked about their expectations in terms of DeFi.

4 Results

This research aims to fill the gap in literature by uncovering empirical insights into FinTech innovations in banking sector. In terms of legal framework, people generally think that there is room for improvement. Participants point out that the main problem refers to legal frameworks which do not come as a necessity, but as an order. Law is too rigidly implemented, i.e., it is not always adapted to local specificities. Moreover, participants argue that it is often too late with adoption and implementation in the field.

Majority of participants think that it is not clear whether the FinTech innovations will disrupt traditional ways of working in the banking sector or lead to improved modern ecosystems of financial services. Nevertheless, it can be safely considered that FinTech will leave a big impact on the entire financial market.

Fintech innovations increase the need for strong frameworks to protect individual and institutional data. Three participants stated that the most important part of the bank–client relationship is trust in data protection. However, they point out that there is a long way to go until the standards of developed countries are reached in terms of data protection.

In terms of major changes that happened with the use of FinTech innovations, participants argue that innovative solutions will enable us to have available information in the so-called immediate response, which is the basis of any communication or business, especially for the young generations.

Additionally, participants point out that FinTech offers numerous benefits such as expanding access, reducing costs, and increasing transaction convenience. Moreover, FinTech innovations promote new business models and develop financial markets. However, being in line with market changes and developments may be challenging for regulatory authorities. Participants argue that inconsistent legal framework is not stimulating FinTech innovations in South-East Europe.

Only one participant thinks that banks should compete with other players in financial markets, especially in terms of talented, experienced employees that create new solutions. The participant thinks that banks very often lose hard-working employees because they do not support them and recognize the need for change and innovation. Others think that there is a space for synergy between banks and FinTech, and that they should cooperate and find solutions together—expertise in banks is enormous, and FinTech brings agility and flexibility.

Decentralized finance is still a fairly new term in the cryptocurrency and blockchain world. Participants believe that decentralized finance is the future, but they do not expect major changes in the next 10 years. They perceive financial markets as underdeveloped and unprepared for so many changes. However, having in mind that banks are large and not so agile systems where changes happen slowly, it is important to be focused on innovations and ensure a timely response. The interview results from open coding are shown in Table 1.

5 Conclusion

The main goal of this paper is to analyze the impact of FinTech innovations on financial services industry in South-East Europe. More precisely, the paper summarizes existing knowledge of banking services in the FinTech era, especially having in focus on decentralized and embedded finance.

The gap in the literature regarding FinTech innovations in the banking sector led us to apply a qualitative method to gather information from bankers. The nine factors identified during the interviews and perceived as important by bankers were: legal framework, impact of FinTech innovations on financial market and regulators, protection of personal and institutional data, major changes that happened with the use of FinTech innovations, advantages and disadvantages of FinTech innovations, competition in terms of embedded finance, and decentralized finance. In this study, we used in-depth semi-structured interviews. Participants were selected based on their experiences in the banking sector. Sixteen participants were chosen aged between 30 and 55 years.

Table 1 Interview results

Code	Description	Sample quotations
Legal framework	Legal framework refers to the level of legal clarity and certainty regarding FinTech innovations.	"I believe that the FinTech sector should have equal or stronger legal norms in relation to other parts of the financial system." "The legal framework is very rigid and only fully licensed banks can offer a complete set of financial services." "The problem is that legal frameworks do not come as a necessity, but as an order. Law is too rigidly implemented, i.e., it is not always adapted to local specificities; it is often too late with adoption and implementation in the field."
Impact	This variable refers to social and economic impact.	"It is very important to coordinate the regulator and 'practice' in order to avoid the complexity of the regulatory framework, which can significantly slow down business, or even devalue 'innovations'." "FinTech innovations have a positive effect on financial market since they initiate change and efficiency. They help traditional market participants to understand and accept trends, i.e., the need for business model changes. Moreover, FinTech innovation leads to the possibility of alternative investments." "The legal framework is being modernized and a better competitive atmosphere is being created. FinTech innovations lead to the development of the market."
Protection	Protection refers to the goal to safeguard the integrity of financial system through identifying, understanding and mitigating all potential risks in terms of personal and institutional data.	"Data protection is a big challenge even for large universal banks that can invest significant funds in this area, which implies that it is significantly more difficult for 'smaller entities' like FinTech companies." "It is necessary to implement the GDPR regulation, which enables the clear participation of data owners in the use of data."
Major changes	Major changes require strong institutional capacity and involvement of relevant ministries and agencies which lead to economic and financial development.	"FinTech should liberalize the financial sector and increase competition. Also, a very important role is education and greater orientation towards the client, greater transparency and

(continued)

Table 1 (continued)

Code	Description	Sample quotations
		better user experience." "FinTech innovations will change the structure of employees in the financial sector (more IT profile)."
Advantages	The main advantages of decentralization and disintermediation are open financial system, reduction of transactional costs, and direct connection through peer-to-peer network.	"Improving efficiency, availability of services, simple use of financial services, speeding up processes, getting to know clients and their financial habits and patterns of financial behavior; it is opportunity to optimize their processes and save time."
Disadvantages	Disadvantages are described as main obstacles to successful adoption of FinTech innovations and main problems in terms of effectiveness and efficiency of regulation.	"Slow implementation; still complicated customer identification system, limited customer support." "Possible loss of personal relationship with the client and lower level of loyalty." "Lack of understanding of complex banking processes, lack of recognition and trust."
DeFi	DeFi relates to blockchain technologies and represents digital financial infrastructure that does not need any central regulator that should approve financial transactions.	"With the development of technology, the process of decentralization will take place. I am not optimistic that something will significantly change in the next 10 years, but definitely the future is in decentralization and greater democratization of the financial sector." "I expect some 'upgrade' of the old model of the financial system."

The findings of this study are relevant to banking sector and FinTech firms that intend to innovate and ensure timely response to technological changes. Moreover, results are valuable for regulators in the financial market, especially for those who influence the development of legal framework.

However, our study has several limitations. The first limitation of this study is its methodology. Since interviews give us a unique chance to discuss and analyze the perception of bankers, their attitudes toward FinTech innovations and thoughts on embedded and decentralize finance, we started with qualitative research. In terms of future research, it would be interesting to test identified factors through international quantitative survey. Additionally, the study might be more captivating by using an experimental approach to collecting real-time data. Additionally, since this study is limited to examining the experiences of people who work in a banking sector, another possible area of future research is analyzing the perceptions of other players in the financial market. This would be very interesting, especially in terms of embedded and decentralized finance.

References

Aslam F, Aimin W, Li M, Ur Rehman K (2020) Innovation in the era of IoT and industry 5.0: absolute innovation management (AIM) framework. Information 11:1–24. https://doi.org/10.3390/info11020124

Basit T (2003) Manual or electronic? The role of coding in qualitative data analysis. Educ Res 45(2):143–154. https://doi.org/10.1080/0013188032000133548

Bejar P, Ishi K, Komatsuzaki T, Shibata I, Sin J, Tambunlertchai S (2022) Can Fintech Foster competition in the banking system in Latin America and the Caribbean? Latin Am J Central Bank 3(2):100061. https://doi.org/10.1016/j.latcb.2022.100061

Bofondi M, Gobbi G (2017) The big promise of Fintech. Series: European Economy - banks regulation and the real sector - FinTech and banks. Friends or Foes? (2):107–119. https://european-economy.eu/book/fintech-and-banks-friends-or-foes/

Boot A, Hoffmann P, Laeven L, Ratnovski L (2021) Fintech: what's old, what's new? J Financ Stab 53:100836. https://doi.org/10.1016/j.jfs.2020.100836

Brennen S, Kreiss D (2014) Digitalization and digitization. http://culturedigitally.org/2014/09/digitalization-and-digitization/. Retrieved 8.03.2022

Carbó-Valverde S, Cuadros-Solas PJ, Rodríguez-Fernández F (2021) FinTech and banking: an evolving relationship. In: King T, Stentella Lopes FS, Srivastav A, Williams J (eds) Disruptive technology in banking and finance. Palgrave studies in financial services technology. Palgrave Macmillan, Cham. https://doi.org/10.1007/978-3-030-81835-7_6

Chen AM, Wu Q, Yang B (2019) How valuable is FinTech innovation? Rev Financ Stud 32(5):2062–2106. https://doi.org/10.1093/rfs/hhy130

Chen Y, Bellavitis C (2020) Blockchain disruption and decentralized finance: the rise of decentralized business models. J Bus Ventur Insights 13:e00151. https://doi.org/10.1016/j.jbvi.2019.e00151

Dorfleitner G, Hornuf L, Schmitt M, Weber M (2017) The FinTech market in Germany. FinTech Germany 13–46. https://doi.org/10.1007/978-3-319-54666-7_4

Drasch BJ, Schweizer A, Urbach N (2018) Integrating the "troublemakers": a taxonomy for cooperation between banks and fintechs. J Econ Bus 100:26. https://doi.org/10.1016/j.jeconbus.2018.04.002

Elsaid HM (2021) A review of literature directions regarding the impact of fintech firms on the banking industry. Qual Res Financ Mark Vol. ahead-of-print No. ahead-of-print. https://doi.org/10.1108/QRFM-10-2020-0197. ISSN: 1755-4179

Euromoney (2022) Euromoney learning. https://www.euromoney.com/learning/blockchain-explained/what-is-blockchain. Retrieved 12.07.2022

Evangelista R, Guerrieri P, Meliciani V (2014) The economic impact of digital technologies in Europe. Econ Innov New Technol 23(8):802–824. https://doi.org/10.1080/10438599.2014.918438

Fanning K, Centers DP (2016) Blockchain and its coming impact on financial services. J Corporate Account Finance 27(5):53–57

Gomber P, Koch J-A, Siering M (2017) Digital finance and FinTech: current re-search and future research directions. J Bus Econ 87(5):537–580. https://doi.org/10.1007/s11573-017-0852-x

Grassi L, Lanfranchi D, Faes A, Renga FM (2022) Do we still need financial intermediation? The case of decentralized finance–DeFi. Qual Res Account Manag 19:323. https://doi.org/10.1108/QRAM-03-2021-0051

Hensen J, Kötting B (2022) From open banking to embedded finance: the essential factors for a successful digital transformation. J Dig Banking 6(4):308–318

Heredia J, Castillo-Vergara M, Geldes C, Gamarra FMC, Flores A, Heredia W (2022) How do digital capabilities affect firm performance? The mediating role of technological capabilities in the "new normal". J Innov Knowl 7(2):100171. https://doi.org/10.1016/j.jik.2022.100171

Hu Z, Ding S, Li S, Chen L, Yang S (2019) Adoption intention of fintech ser-vices for bank users: an empirical examination with an extended technology acceptance model. Symmetry 11(3):340. https://doi.org/10.3390/sym11030340

International Monetary Fund; World Bank (2018) The Bali Fintech agenda: Chapeau paper (English). World Bank Group, Washington, DC. http://documents.worldbank.org/curated/en/390701539097118625/The-Bali-Fintech-Agenda-Chapeau-Paper. Retrieved 12.03.2022

Lee C-C, Li X, Yu C-H, Zhao J (2021) Does fintech innovation improve bank efficiency? Evidence from China's banking industry. Int Rev Econ Financ 74:468–483. https://doi.org/10.1016/j.iref.2021.03.009

Li C, He S, Tian Y, Sun S, Ning L (2022) Does the bank's FinTech innovation reduce its risk-taking? Evidence from China's banking industry. J Innov Knowl 7(3):100219. https://doi.org/10.1016/j.jik.2022.100219

Lien NTK, Doan T-TT, Bui TN (2020) Fintech and banking: evidence from Vietnam. J Asian Finance, Econ Bus 7(9):419–426. https://doi.org/10.13106/JAFEB.2020.VOL7.NO9.419

Liu T, Pan B, Yin Z (2020) Pandemic, mobile payment, and household consumption: micro-evidence from China. Emerg Mark Financ Trade 56(10):2378–2389. https://doi.org/10.1080/1540496X.2020.1788539

Martino P (2021) Blockchain technology and the banking industry. In: Blockchain and banking. Palgrave Pivot, Cham, pp 33–52. https://doi.org/10.1007/978-3-030-70970-9_3

McKinsey&Company (2021) What the embedded-finance and banking-as-a-service trends mean for financial services. https://www.mckinsey.com/industries/financial-services/our-insights/banking-matters/what-the-embedded-finance-and-banking-as-a-service-trends-mean-for-financial-services. Retrieved 15.03.2022

Milošević N, Tošković O, Barjaktarović RS (2019) Does perceived top management involvement and knowledge sharing affect perceived project performance? Evidence from the banking sector. JEEMS J East Eur Manage Stud 24(2):259–279. https://doi.org/10.5771/0949-6181-2019-2-259

Milošević N, Dobrota M, Rakočević SB (2018) Digital economy in Europe: evaluation of countries' performances. Zbornik Radova Ekonomski Fakultet u Rije-ka 36(2):861–880. https://doi.org/10.18045/zbefri.2018.2.861

Milosevic N, Dobrota M, Dmitrovic V, Barjaktarovic Rakocevic S (2021) Managerial perception of human capital, innovations, and performance: evidence from banking industry. Eng Econ 32(5):446–458. https://doi.org/10.5755/J01.EE.32.5.26032

Murinde V, Rizopoulos E, Zachariadis M (2022) The impact of the FinTech revolution on the future of banking: opportunities and risks. Int Rev Financ Anal 81:102103. https://doi.org/10.1016/j.irfa.2022.102103

Navaretti GB, Calzolari G, Mansilla-Fernandez JM, Pozzolo AF (2018) Fintech and banking. Friends or foes? Available at SSRN: https://ssrn.com/abstract=3099337 or https://doi.org/10.2139/ssrn.3099337

OECD (2020) Digital disruption in banking and its impact on competition. http://www.oecd.org/daf/competition/digital-disruption-in-financial-markets.htm. Retrieved 15.06.2022

PWC (2022). https://www.pwc.com/us/en/industries/financial-services/fintech/bitcoin-blockchain-cryptocurrency.html. Retrieved 12.07.2022

Ramchandra MV, Kumar K, Sarkar A, Mukherjee SK, Agarwal K (2022) Assessment of the impact of blockchain technology in the banking industry. Materials Today: Proc 56:2221–2226. https://doi.org/10.1016/j.matpr.2021.11.554

Romānova I, Kudinska M (2016) Banking and Fintech: a challenge or opportunity? In: Contemporary issues in finance: current challenges from across Europe. Emerald Group Publishing Limited

Ryu H-S (2018) What makes users willing or hesitant to use Fintech?: the moderating effect of user type. Ind Manag Data Syst 118(3):541–569. https://doi.org/10.1108/imds-07-2017-0325

Saldana J (2009) An introduction to codes and coding. The coding manual for qualitative researchers, pp 3–21

Siek M, Sutanto A (2019) Impact analysis of Fintech on banking industry. 2019 international conference on information management and technology (ICIMTech). https://doi.org/10.1109/ICIMTech.2019.8843778

Statista, Statista Research Department (2022) Top challenges with digital banking worldwide 2021. https://www.statista.com/statistics/1292443/top-challenges-with-digital-banking-worldwide/. Retrieved 18.07.2022

Stulz RM (2019) FinTech, BigTech, and the future of banks. J Appl Corp Financ 31(4):86–97. https://doi.org/10.1111/jacf.12378

Thakor AV (2019) Fintech and banking: what do we know? J Financ Intermed 100833. https://doi.org/10.1016/j.jfi.2019.100833

Vives X (2019) Digital disruption in banking. Annu Rev Financ Econ 11(1):243–272. https://doi.org/10.1146/annurev-financial-100719-120854

Werner SM, Perez D, Gudgeon L, Klages-Mundt A, Harz D, Knottenbelt W (2021) SoK: decentralized finance (DeFi). arXiv preprint arXiv:2101.08778. https://doi.org/10.48550/arXiv.2101.08778

Wonglimpiyarat J (2017) FinTech banking industry: a systemic approach. Foresight 19(6): 590–603. https://doi.org/10.1108/fs-07-2017-0026

Wullweber J (2020) Embedded finance: the shadow banking system, sovereign power, and a new state–market hybridity. J Cult Econ 13(5):592–609. https://doi.org/10.1080/17530350.2020.1741015

Xu J, Gao M, Zhang Y (2021) The variations in individual consumption change and the substitution effect under the shock of COVID-19: evidence from payment system data in China. Growth Chang 52(2):990–1010. https://doi.org/10.1111/grow.12477

Zaleska M, Kondraciuk P (2019) Theory and practice of innovation development in the banking sector. Financ Sci 24(2):76–87. https://doi.org/10.15611/fins.2019.2.06

Zetzsche DA, Arner DW, Buckley RP (2020) Decentralized finance. J Financ Regul 6(2):172–203. https://doi.org/10.1093/jfr/fjaa010

Digital Transformation of the Serbian Car Insurance Industry: A Mixed-Method Approach

Nemanja Milanović, Miloš Milosavljević, and Nevenka Žarkić Joksimović

Abstract Although insurance industry is not seen as technology-driven industry by both scholars and practitioners, novel technologies are inevitably expected to reshape its landscape. As most of the extant studies examine startups in the context of the digitalization of the insurance industry, incumbent insurance companies have been left behind. The aim of this study is to fill this gap by examining the managers' perspective on the digitalization of the insurance industry. The particular goals of this study are to investigate and explore how executive managers of incumbent insurance companies see (1) the use of technology, (2) available resources for digitalization, and (3) main challenges and opportunities for the use of novel technologies. Qualitative by nature, the study examines the potential of the digitalization of car insurance using primary data collected through semi-structured questionnaires with the C-level managers of Serbian insurance companies. Even though the Serbian insurance industry significantly lags behind more developed and technologically advanced markets, the results indicate that the managers of insurance companies are aware of digital transformation trends in the industry and the inevitability of a partial or complete transition to innovative insurance models in the near future.

Keywords Insurtech · Car insurance · Usage-based insurance · Digital transformation · Resource-based view

1 Introduction

Insurance is not seen in both scholarly literature or practical publications as a dynamic or technology-driven industry (Milanović et al. 2021).This is mainly because insurance is considered as traditional, rigid, heavily regulated, and highly

---

N. Milanović (✉) · M. Milosavljević · N. Ž. Joksimović
Faculty of Organizational Sciences, University of Belgrade, Belgrade, Serbia
e-mail: nemanja.milanovic@fon.bg.ac.rs; milos.milosavljevic@fon.bg.ac.rs

S. Benković et al. (eds.), *Digital Transformation of the Financial Industry*, Contributions to Finance and Accounting,
https://doi.org/10.1007/978-3-031-23269-5_7

risk-aversive industry. Accordingly, the body of knowledge recognizes it as a laggard toward the acceptance of new technologies, particularly the technologies related to artificial intelligence (Riikkinen et al. 2018), blockchain (Kar and Navin 2021) or Internet of Things (Milanović et al. 2020; Eling and Kraft 2020). Nonetheless, novel technologies are inevitably expected to reshape the landscape of insurance industry primarily to counter the changing needs of customers (Bhardwaj 2021).

Using a well-suited combination of terms "insurance" and "technology," the term insurtech is created to describe innovative technologies used to improve business processes throughout the insurance value chain. The definition of insurtech is still amorphous. However, the majority of studies describe it as a complex ecosystem. Ricciardi (2018) provides the most comprehensive definition by implying that insurtech is "the ecosystem of focused, innovation-based companies (often startups) that generate value for clients and/or insurance incumbents by disrupting or solving problems across the insurance value chain through the engagement of technology by following a lean and user-centric approach."

Like most novel research areas, the insurtech phenomenon still lacks consistent and distinctive classification of its fundamental categories. On the other side, Cappiello (2020) delineates this ecosystem and provides a segmentation to:

- Digital brokers and online comparison portals.
- Customized insurance products, including P2P, on demand, and usage-based insurance.
- Insurance business processes optimization and automatization.

Widespread digitalization and rapidly evolving customer expectations severely affected each segment of the financial industry. Consequently, the insurance market has been overwhelmed with disruptive competitors led by insurtech and other tech startups. On account of their flexible business models, these startups are more agile than incumbent insurance companies in responding to customers' sophisticated expectations with provision of innovative, value-added insurance products. Striving to minimize financial and market losses caused by these new entrants, incumbent insurance companies are forced to find a suitable and efficient strategic response to evolved competitive environment and to improve each segment of their value chain.

As most of the extent studies examine startups in the context of the digitalization of the insurance industry, incumbent insurance companies have been left behind. Our aim is to fill this gap by examining the managers' perspective on the digitalization of the insurance industry. Our study is focused on the incumbent insurance companies, rather than small and disruptive insurtech startups. Particular goals of our study are to investigate and explore how executive managers of incumbent insurance companies see (1) the use of technology, (2) available resources for digitalization, and (3) main challenges and opportunities for the use of novel technologies throughout the value chains of their companies.

For the purpose of this paper, the potential of digitalization of car insurance companies is seen as a hardly mimicable resource. Thus, this study is based on a Resource-Based View. In order to gain an advantage in a highly competitive market, firms deploy various physical, human, and organizational resources and competences. A Resource-Based View posits that if these resources and capabilities are valuable, rare, and hard to imitate, they have the potential to unlock a strategic advantage on the marketplace (Kozlenkova et al. 2014). Following these suppositions of the Resource-Based View, this study investigates the availability of both tangible and intangible resources required for the digital transformation of the insurance industry in Serbia.

This study is qualitative by nature. To examine the potential of the digitalization of car insurance we collected primary data from the C-level managers of Serbian insurance companies. A semi-structured questionnaire was specifically developed to address the aim of our study and collect in-depth responses. In total, the questionnaire consisted of seven broad inquiries. The first three inquiries were focused on the perception and the method of reaction toward the digitalization trends of insurers in Serbia. The second group of inquiries was focused on potential and resource adequacy for the digital transformation of Serbian insurers (strategies, business models, key drivers, and barriers for the digital transformation).

In total, we collected responses from nine executives (out of 11 companies operating in the Serbian car insurance market). The data analysis of the collected data was conducted following the principles of Wolcott (1994). The data processing was conducted in Nvivo version 12. This tool is frequently used in qualitative studies, particularly those related to the transformation of financial services (see Chang et al. 2020; Van Looy 2021).

To the best of authors' knowledge, a study of this kind has never been conducted before. A number of studies address the digitalization in the insurance industry as a whole from a rather theoretical perspective (Eling and Lehmann 2018). Other studies emphasize the digital agendas of the insurance companies and awareness of insurers toward the acceptance of novel technologies (Bohnert et al. 2019) or the approaches that incumbent insurance companies use to adopt new technologies (Pisoni 2020). However, our study takes a specific look on managerial perspective of digital transformation capabilities, resources, and needs. Moreover, we provide evidence from a highly underinsured market.

The additional added value of this qualitative in-depth study is its geographical context. Serbian car insurance industry has not been vastly explored. An important reason for Serbia not being a focal point of scholarly interest, is evidently low total insurance premium and car insurance as the only mandatory form of insurance. Also, car insurance is viewed as a traditional and saturated segment of the insurance industry.

The remainder of this paper is organized as follows. Section 2 reviews the concurrent literature and explains the digital transformation of the value chains in car insurance industry. This section of the paper also illustrated the Resource-Based View as a conceptual background for the research. Section 3 elaborates on the qualitative approach used in the study, by explaining the variables, interview design, sampling procedure, and data processing. Section 4 delineates the results of the study. Section 5 contextualizes the results by explaining the key findings, contributions, implications, limitations and further recommendations, as well as by presenting the concluding remarks.

2 Background

2.1 Digital Transformation of Incumbent Insurance Companies

The formulation of the digital transformation strategy has been vastly elaborated topic in both theory and practice in the last few decades. Nonetheless, it is still hard to find a unique and comprehensive definition or guidelines for the effective digital transformation. For the purpose of this chapter, an approach developed by Hess et al. (2016) might be the most appropriate. Among others, this study suggests that, independently from the industry background or the type of organization, the framework for the strategic answer to the changes in the external environment should encompass four key dimensions:

- The level of application of technology in the organization resulting from its attitude toward technological development (or, put simply, from its abilities and approach to research and exploitation of modern technologies).
- Transformation based on modern technologies is aimed at changes in the way of creating and delivering value.
- A prerequisite for the efficient exploitation of modern technologies is structural changes in the form of modifying the organizational structure, IT infrastructure, and human resources.
- The financial context of transformation implies the financial pressures of the accelerated development of technologies on the organization's operations and the possibility of internal/external financing of transformation initiatives and projects.

When looked through the lens of insurance-specific digital transformation, a number of papers have dissected this phenomenon. For instance, general transformative features were elaborated in Eling and Lehmann (2018). Transformative capabilities of insurance companies have been explored by Stoeckli et al. (2018). Finally, the effects of digital transformation on financial and nonfinancial performances have been empirically tested in a number of publications (Weill 1992; Liang et al. 2010). It is, however, evident that these studies primarily focus on new businesses and startups, thus neglecting the incumbent insurance companies.

A paucity of concurrent studies has examined the topic of insurance digitalization from a broader perspective, including the industry-wide analysis (Eling and Lehmann 2018). Some of them emphasized the digital agendas of traditional insurance companies and the need for the implementation of modern technologies (Bohnert et al. 2019). Others put accent on the accelerated adoption of existing technologies in the age-old industry of insurance (Pisoni 2020). The focal point of these studies are managerial structures of insurance incumbents.

2.2 *Resource-Based View of Digital Transformation in Insurance*

Corporate resources are seldom considered as a paramount factor that causes disruptive innovation and consequently increases the competitive advantage (Breidbach et al. 2020). This, however, is not a mere supposition, since a number of studies confirm that the whole fintech revolution is based on superior resources (Jaber and Issa 2022). Empirical evidence indicates that these superior resources even attract more investments in fintech, thus additionally driving the development of fintech companies (Bömer and Schwienbacher 2018).

The argumentation that resources are the most influential factor that drives success (in terms of this paper—digital transformation) is a line of reasoning of a so-called Resource-Based View (RBV). The term itself is firstly mentioned by Wernerfelt (1984). Wernnefelt claims that resources are everything that creates strengths of the company, and that hard-to-imitate resources have potential to create strategic competitive advantage. The profound popularization of this approach is a work of Jay Barney (1991). Barney also categorizes the main resources that drive competitive advantage into three distinct groups:

- Physical resources: Equipment, technology, location, and access to raw materials.
- Human resources: Training, experience, access to information, proactive management, and operational structures.
- Organizational resources: Organizational structure, systems for planning, control and coordination, formal and informal reporting channels, informal relations within the organization, and relations with the external environment.

According to proponents of the Resource-Based View, unique skills, capabilities, and other resources that differentiate an organization from its competitors are the primary source of its success and competitive advantage. These resources are especially important when observed through the trend of widespread digitization that has given birth to new participants in the insurance market in the form of insurtech startups. Their flexible business models make them more agile in responding to sophisticated user demands. Accordingly, these startups have the potential to deliver greater value to owners and users compared to their incumbent counterparts.

In an effort to limit the losses caused by the entry of new competitors, traditional insurance companies are forced to find an adequate strategic response to the new circumstances and to improve practically every segment of the value chain. Transformative power of incumbent insurance companies is somewhat inadequate "since they still have to devote the bulk of their resources to maintaining existing processes and attending the existing business" (Albrecher et al. 2019). It turns out that "old" insurance companies suffer from the "incumbent's curse." This term is developed from various anecdotes and experiences that "never has any leader pioneered the industry in the next stage" (Chandy and Tellis 2000). Crittenden et al. (2019) claim that "incumbent firms are too strongly committed to current operating models, organizational structures, and routinized behaviors that inhibit them from embracing new technologies."

3 Methodology

3.1 Research Instrument

This study used a qualitative research framework. The main instrument of the qualitative research was a standardized open-ended interview. This approach is considered as effective and the most frequently used technique in qualitative research (Rapley 2001).

Respondents are asked identical questions and provided with complete freedom regarding the scope, detail, and quality of the answers given. Thus, they are given the opportunity to answer questions in accordance with their personal beliefs and professional experience. On one hand, contrary to surveys and similar methods in which respondents are viewed exclusively as a source of data, in an open interview the interviewees are collaborators. On the other hand, this research method is often criticized for the difficult coding of collected data (Creswell 2007). As for the complexity of the phenomena researched in this paper, the structured open interview was chosen as the most appropriate research method.

The questionnaire consisted of seven open-ended questions categorized into two groups. The first group of questions analyzed the perception of digitalization and the way in which the insurance company responds to the global trend of insurtech. The second group of questions is aimed at collecting evidence of the required resources of a specific insurance company needed to ignite and facilitate digital transformation. The detailed structure of the questionnaire is given in Table 1.

The collected answers were analyzed following Wolcott's (1994) guidelines for the transformation of qualitative data: (1) description—keep the originality of the original data; (2) analysis—organize the data so that it is possible to identify key constructs and their interrelationships, and (3) interpretation—draw meaningful conclusions that correspond to the specific context of the conducted research.

3.2 Sampling Procedure

The research was conducted in February 2022. Due to the objective limitations caused by the COVID-19 virus pandemic, the interviews with respondents were

Table 1 The structure of inquiries from the questionnaire

No	Inquiry
PART A: Insurtech and the application of novel technologies in the insurance industry	
A01	To survive in the conditions of growing entropy brought about by the so-called Fourth Industrial Revolution, insurance companies heavily rely on modern technologies. At the center of this strategic turn is the aspiration toward a better understanding of the modern business environment and accompanying risks, both for economy and for insurance companies. In this context, the phenomenon called "insurtech" has been unavoidable in the last few years. The term refers to the application of innovative technologies to automate and improve business processes throughout the entire value chain in the insurance industry. How would you define the attitude of your insurance company toward this trend?
A02	Broadly speaking, initiatives in the insurtech and digital transformation field are applied through different internal and external channels. Which channel do you see as the dominant in your company?
PART B: Innovative business models in car insurance—Usage-based insurance (UBI)	
B01	Do you find that consumers are ready to accept and adopt novel technologies such as UBI?
B02	UBI models such as PAYD (Pay-As-You-Drive) or PHYD (Pay-How-You-Drive) have been receiving more and more intention in the last few years. UBI models "provide a strong motivation for drivers to improve their driving behaviour, differentiate their travel behaviour and reduce their degree of exposure by receiving feedback and monitoring their driving preferences and performance, which would result in crash risk reduction both totally and individually" (Tselentis et al. 2017). Their technological basis consists of telematics systems in vehicles and adjustment of the amount of the premium to the individual insured, depending on the way he drives and the degree of real exposure to risk. Have you been considering similar initiatives in your insurance company on the motor third-party liability insurance market in the Republic of Serbia?
B03	Does your insurance company have adequate capacities for the application of telematics systems and the implementation of a usage-based insurance model? (a) Technological infrastructure (b) Human resources and expertise (c) Organizational resources
B04	What factors do you see as the key drivers of the transformation of motor third-party liability insurance toward a usage-based insurance model?
B05	What factors do you consider to be the key constraints of the transformation of motor third-party liability insurance toward a usage-based insurance model?

conducted electronically, with the technical support of the Serbian Association of Insurers.

To address the purpose of this study, we first isolated the total population of non-life insurances in Serbia that offer car insurance. In total, 11 insurance companies offer such products to customer. The list is given in Table 2. The table also displays the main financial characteristics of the listed insurance companies.

In the next phase, we created a list of key informants from these companies. This step was carried out with the support of the Serbian Association of Insurers. When identifying the key respondents, the recommendations of the Association were taken into account, considering the wide range of work it performs, expert knowledge of the insurance industry, and the fact that its members are all insurance companies that provide mandatory traffic insurance services. Accordingly, among the

Table 2 The list of non-life insurance companies in Serbia that offer car insurance and the main financials in million RSD

No.	Company name	Assets (2021)	Total premium (2021)
1	AMS osiguranje a.d.o. Beograd	8.165	4.646
2	DDOR Novi Sad a.d.o. Novi Sad	23.713	13.948
3	DUNAV osiguranje a.d.o. Beograd	60.773	31.578
4	GENERALI osiguranje Srbija a.d.o.	74.708	23.396
5	GLOBOS osiguranje a.d.o. Beograd	4.751	4.167
6	GRAWE osiguranje a.d.o. Beograd	37.213	4.796
7	MILENIJUM osiguranje a.d.o. Beograd	6.741	3.622
8	SAVA neživotno osiguranje a.d.o. Beograd	4.618	2.719
9	TRIGLAV osiguranje a.d.o. Beograd	11.643	8.147
10	UNIQA neživotno osiguranje a.d.o. Beograd	6.755	4.220
11	WIENER STÄDTISCHE osiguranje a.d.o. Beograd	48.339	13.518

Source: NBS (2021)

representatives of the management structures of the insurance companies, those who, based on their work experience and expert knowledge in the field of motor third-party liability insurance and its transformation, as well as direct participation in making strategic decisions, were considered adequate interlocutors on the topic of resource base and readiness of insurance companies for the transformation of motor third-party liability insurance services based on modern technologies. The list composed of company CEOs, except when the company has an executive (C-level manager) dedicated solely to digital transformation. The questionnaire was distributed to 11 managers, and 9 of them correctly fulfilled the answers. The responses were coded with $OD_{1\text{-}n}$ to preserve the anonymity of the interviewees.

3.3 Data Processing

After the data was gathered, it was entered into the software package QSR International's Nvivo 12 (2018 edition). This software allows a researcher to perform transcript analysis, text coding and interpretation, content analysis, network analysis, discourse analysis, and application of Grounded Theory methodology.

This tool is widely used in previous studies that use a qualitative or mixed-method research approach. Particularly important are examples of its use in studies dealing with the application of modern technologies in the transformation of financial services (for example, Chang et al. 2020; Van Looy 2021). From the wide set of functionalities provided by this software, the greatest contribution to the interpretation of the conducted interviews was obtained from the module called "codes." It is an interview encoding function that works as follows. First, text versions of the interviews are prepared and added to the appropriate folder. Second, the researcher, based on the analysis of available literature, professional experience, and personal observations, creates appropriate codes for which the term "nodes" is used in the Nvivo environment. A single code represents a theme, thought, attitude, or interpretation that the researcher wishes to identify in the respondents' responses. Finally, by activating a code, the representation of the topic represented by that code is quantitatively and/or visually identified.

4 Results

This chapter presents the results of the qualitative research, which are divided into two segments. The first segment presents the main conclusions of the analysis of answers to questions related to insurtech and the application of modern technologies in the insurance industry. The second segment consists of questions about the possibilities of implementing innovative models of motor third-party liability insurance in the Republic of Serbia. The collected responses were analyzed using the Nvivo 12 software tool.

4.1 General Attitudes Toward Insurtech

In this subsection, we analyzed general trends in insurance digitalization. Table 3 displays the findings of segment A questions (responses to inquiries 1 and 2).

The results of the analysis reveal that all respondents agreed that insurance companies in the Republic of Serbia are aware of the strategic importance of transforming motor third-party liability insurance services based on modern technologies. Although this qualitative research showed certain differences in the level of awareness and the intensity of reaction, none of the respondents consider their insurance company to be completely indifferent to the insurtech trend. There is a noticeable consensus around the position that insurance companies in the Republic

Table 3 Segment A—Insurtech and application of modern technology in insurance

Q	Code	*f*	Interviewee
Question A01	Active research of potential solutions and their applicability in the insurance company.	6	OD1, OD3, OD4, OD6, OD7, OD9
	Intensive development and/or investment in innovative solutions.	2	OD2, OD5
	Passive observation of the market and competition.	1	OD8
Question A02	Localization of solutions developed at the level of the corporation group (i.e., headquarters).	7	OD2, OD4, OD5, OD6, OD7, OD8, OD9
	"In-house" development of solutions.	6	OD2, OD4, OD5, OD6, OD8, OD9
	Partnership with existing fintech/insurtech startups.	3	0D1, OD2, OD3

of Serbia have evolved enough to overcome the status of passive observers of technological transformation in other sectors of the financial industry. The majority of respondents, 6 out of 9, believe that the insurance companies they manage actively research and analyze possible solutions and their applicability. Two respondents believe that their insurance companies have gone a step further than their competitors and that they are considering existing resources and capacities for more intensive development and investment in innovative solutions. In contrast to them, only one respondent (OD8) positions his insurance company in the category of passive observers.

Afterward, we analyzed the strategies and actions for the implementation of digital transformation of insurance companies. The interviewees pointed out that insurance companies in the Republic of Serbia rely to the greatest extent on adapting the solutions that have already been developed in mother companies. The dominance of this approach is more understandable if one takes into account the fact that most insurance companies in the Republic of Serbia are foreign-owned and operate as part of international insurance groups (multinational corporations). Accordingly, digital transformation is imported through multinational patterns of technology diffusion. Consequently, it can be expected that the strategies for innovating and transforming insurance services are firstly adopted and implemented at the group level, and only then are they transferred to hierarchically lower organizational units, i.e. local markets. This opinion is shared by 7 out of 9 respondents.

The study results indicate that insurance companies in Serbia independently develop and implement solutions based on modern technologies that are less demanding and generally more operational than strategic by nature. A noteworthy consensus is created around the importance of local development teams, internal capacities, and "in-house" development of tech-based solutions. Primarily, attention is drawn to their contribution to the field of adapting generic strategies adopted at the group level to the specific characteristics and requirements of the insurance market in Serbia.

The respondents were aware that competition in the insurance market is becoming fiercer. The paradigm shift toward digitalization at the global level paves the way for the 'local battles' in Serbia. As an indication of this finding, we isolated the mentioning of the term "insurtech" for more than 40 times in total. However, only three respondents explicitly singled out cooperation with startups as a good practice for the transformation of motor third-party liability insurance.

Surprisingly, none of the interviewees mentioned acquisitions of startups as a strategic alternative for digital transformation. It might be speculative to claim that this strategy has not been utilized or even considered, since the insurance market in Serbia is still in a developing phase, which is reflected in the financial and organizational capacities of insurance companies to implement the aforementioned strategies. Other causes can be found in the limitations of financial markets and accompanying regulations, and in the (under)development of the startup ecosystem in the Republic of Serbia and the region.

4.2 *Attitudes Toward the Digitalization of Car Insurance*

In this subsection, we analyzed innovative car insurance models. Table 4 summarizes the findings from the interviews.

B01: As for the readiness of customers (current and prospective policyholders in motor third-party liability insurance), interviewees generally find them ready for novelties, particularly the digitalization of insurance services. However, this is marked as a possibility since 7 out of 9 interviewees claim that certain preconditions need to be met first. Through a more profound analysis, key preconditions have been isolated. Among them, the level of technological and financial literacy of users,

Table 4 Segment B—Innovative car insurance models

Q	Code	*f*		Interviewee
Question B01	Customers are prepared for the acceptance if necessary prerequisites are met.	7		OD1, OD3, OD4, OD5, OD6, OD7, OD9
	Customers are completely unprepared for innovations in the field of UBI.	1		OD8
	The insured are fully prepared, without special limitations and/or preconditions.	1		OD2
Q B02	There is currently no initiative to provide usage-based insurance services in the company.	9		All interviewees
Question B03	The insurance company has adequate technological infrastructure.	Yes	7	OD2–7, OD9
		No	2	OD1, OD8
	The insurance company has adequate human resources and expertise.	Yes	8	OD1–7, OD9
		No	1	OD8
	The insurance company has adequate organizational resources.	Yes	7	OD2–7, OD9
		No	2	OD1, OD8
Question B04	A change in the needs and expectations of customers	9		All interviewees
	The pace of the development of novel technologies in other industries.	6		OD1, OD2, OD4, OD5, OD7, OD8
	Readiness of customers to accept telematic devices in vehicles.	6		OD1, OD2, OD3, OD5, OD7, OD9
	Differentiation in the competitive position.	4		OD4, OD5, OD6, OD8
Question B05	Regulatory burdens.	9		All interviewees
	Pressures in data privacy.	7		OD1, OD2, OD4, OD5, OD6, OD7, OD9
	Unlucrative solutions for the company.	6		OD2, OD3, OD5, OD6, OD8, OD9
	Technological backwardness of the company.	3		OD1, OD6, OD7
	Lack of interest of the customer and lack of understanding of the concept of UBI.	2		OD4, OD6,
	Unclear benefits for the customer.	2		OD2, OD9

transparently communicated financial compensation for participation in innovative programs and data privacy management should be highlighted.

B02: In the conducted qualitative research, usage-based insurance models (Usage Based Insurance—UBI) follow the Pay-As-You-Drive and Pay-How-You-Drive principles. These systems are based on: (1) telematics devices integrated or added to vehicles and (2) adjustment of the individual premium, depending on the way policyholders drive and the degree of the real exposure to his/her risk (Arumugam and Bhargavi 2019). Question B02 in the interview investigates whether insurance companies offer such services (or at least plan any similar initiatives) in Serbia. The interviewees stated that novel models in car insurance (in specific PAYD and PHYD) have not been implemented by any insurance company in Serbia. This comes as a surprise, since "[d]rivers with adequate driving behavior are preferred as policyholders" (Nedić et al. 2014).

Interviewees find external factors to be the most important in limiting the further development of UBI models. Individually, insurance companies do not have capacities to either affect or change the environment. The main external factor isolated as an obstacle is regulation. This finding should be taken into account with limitations and professional skepticism. Other studies confirm that insurance companies in Serbia, rather than regulator, should extensively work on the "technological modernization, creation of products attractive to the growing middle class and development of new sales channels and methods" (Knežević and Đurić 2019).

B03: To assess the resource base of insurance companies, interviewees were asked about the technology infrastructure, human resources, and organizational capacities for the implementation of novel business models in car insurance.

The results indicate that interviewees generally consider the technology infrastructure of their insurance companies as sufficient for any further development of processes and services. Nonetheless, they highlight that this is only potential, and that this potential is somewhat passivized by the regulator. The results showed that 7 out of 9 respondents expressed confidence that their insurance companies have the appropriate IT infrastructure that can be adjusted in the short term for the transition to a new usage-based insurance model. However, it must not be ignored that this type of research carries a high risk of subjectivity in the answers, which is why the results should be considered with a research reserve. Only two respondents explicitly expressed skepticism on this issue. Namely, respondents OD1 and OD8 suggested that the available software and hardware capacities are absolutely sufficient for the current level of digitization of operations, but that they would not be able to support the complication of the data management process required by the transition to the new premium calculation system.

As for the human resources and professional expertise, interviewees were consistent in claiming that insurance companies have adequate knowledge and skills required for the digital transformation and implementation of UBI models. Only one respondent (OD8) believes that his insurance company has professional and productive staff for the successful functioning of the existing insurance system, but that the transition to innovative models requires additional time to adapt employees and improve their knowledge and skills. Despite the noticeable optimism on this issue, the respondents presented a number of challenges in the field of human resources management. Some of them are related to changes in the way of working due to the pandemic and the current situation in the market of IT experts and other personnel with specific technological knowledge.

As for the organizational resources, interviewees confirmed that these capacities are adequate and allow for the implementation of novel solutions. In general, they find organizational culture and value system in the company to be supporting for the innovations, even though they recognize rigidness compared to some other industries. When it comes to the organizational structure, 5 interviewees claimed that their company has a special organizational unit dedicated to the projects of digital transformation.

B04: Interviewees were asked to assess the needs of customers and their willingness to accept UBI-based solutions in car insurance. Respondents were unequivocal in supporting the claim that customers are paramount drivers of digital transformation, and their needs can be singled out as the most important driver for any paradigm shifts. In this section, respondents were particularly interested in providing opportunities and use cases for customer-driven changes, such as the novelties in travel and health insurance.

Other than customer-driven change, interviewees claimed that technology itself induces changes. Finally, four interviewees mentioned competitive differentiations and market pressure as an important factor that shapes customers' willingness to embrace novel technologies.

B05: When it comes to the limitations related to the digital transformation directed toward the implementation of UBI models, interviewees were focused on regulatory environment as an obstacle. Two factors were emphasized in particular: low liberalization of the insurance market and pricing of insurance products. Since the supervision of the insurance market is a full responsibility of the National Bank of Serbia (Zarkovic et al. 2012), any faster changes and purposeful adjustments of the system are highly unlike the cause of events.

According to the criterion of representation in the answers, the next limitation in importance refers to the challenges of protecting the privacy of the insured's personal data, which was highlighted by 7 out of 9 respondents. Although previous research has repeatedly confirmed the thesis that users in various industries, including the insurance industry, are ready to give up their privacy for some financial compensation, this does not lessen the pressure on insurance companies to reduce the possibility of misuse of personal data to an absolute minimum. On the other hand, in order for insurance companies to be able to guarantee complete security and data protection, significant investments are needed in the construction of IT infrastructure according to high-security standards and adaptation of organizational procedures to regulations governing this area, such as GDPR.

The third most significant obstacle pointed out by six participants in the research refers to the current financial unprofitability of such initiatives for insurance companies in the Republic of Serbia. It should be noted that the respondents agree that the existing regulations and conditions on the auto liability insurance market call into question the financial profitability of the potential transformation toward usage-based insurance. As the main culprit, the respondents single out the current structure of the premium, that is, the defined amount of the technical reserve.

Other than the above mentioned, interviewees emphasized low technology development of the insurance industry and economy, lack of interest of customers, and general illiteracy when it comes to insurance products.

5 Discussion and Conclusions

In this section, we contextualize the study results by elaborating on key findings, contributions, and twofold implications (for scholars and practitioners).

5.1 *Key Findings and Contributions*

The results of the research indicate that the managers of insurance companies are aware of the disruptive potential of modern technologies in the field of transformation of motor third-party liability insurance services. This result confirms the potential of the insurtech disruption in general, as indicated in other studies (Che et al. 2021). The study results indicate that in the last few years, insurance companies have left the role of passive observers of the transformation in other sectors of the financial industry and are actively researching and analyzing the possibilities of innovating "age-old" insurance models using modern technologies.

As for the strategies for the development of technology-based solutions, companies most often rely on the localization of solutions developed at the level of their parent group, which should not be surprising if their ownership structure is taken into account. This is in line with the well-documented findings of the effect of technology spillover and technology dependency in multinational corporations (Eapen et al. 2019). On the other hand, simpler solutions that are more operational and less strategic in nature are created by local development teams.

The research indicated that managers of insurance companies believe that customers are in principle ready to participate in innovative insurance programs. This is in line with the findings that report on customer readiness for innovation in insurance both globally (Hu et al. 2019; de Andrés-Sánchez et al. 2021) and in Serbia (Milanović et al. 2020). To make this possible, certain precondition need to be met. Some of them are the appropriate level of financial and technological literacy of the insured, a more transparent exchange of information and guaranteeing the protection of personal data.

Furthermore, according to the research participants' knowledge so far, there is currently no transition from a traditional to a usage-based insurance model. Although there are similar initiatives and concrete solutions in the region (Husnjak et al. 2015), respondents believe that more significant developments are possible only after harmonization of national regulatory frameworks with more developed markets such as, for example, Italy (Carfora et al. 2019).

The key part of the interview is related to the examination of the resource base of the examined insurance companies in the context of their strength for the digital transformation toward usage-based insurance. The respondents were also unanimous in claiming that Serbian insurance sector has sufficient internal resources (human, organizational, technological, and financial) for the transition toward tech-based insurance regime.

Nonetheless, the main barrier is the market regulation—as it became rigid and obsolete. Regulation has been recognized as a barrier in other studies as well (Wilamowicz 2019; Manes 2020).

Apart from the limitations of a regulatory nature, the respondents also emphasized two additional barriers to the development of an appropriate car insurance ecosystem in Serbia: (1) the importance of data privacy concerns and (2) possible financial cost-benefit ratio of investment into novel technologies. As for the first one, data privacy in car insurance has been vividly discussed in other studies as well, and it seems that a unified approach to this problem is still far from conceptualization, let alone any implementation. As for the second one, other studies also infer that not all the technology advancements are 'value-adding' ones (Takeda and Ito 2021).

Even though the insurance industry in Serbia lags significantly behind more developed and technologically advanced markets in the area of transformation of motor third-party liability insurance services, the managers of insurance companies are aware of global trends in the industry and the inevitability of a partial or complete transition to innovative insurance models in the near future. In this context, as the key drivers of this transformation, the respondents identified the changed needs and expectations of the insured as a consequence of the technological revolution and the pandemic of the COVID-19 virus and the trend of accelerated development of new technologies in other industries.

5.2 *Implications*

This study has twofold implications loosely grouped as directions for: (1) for researchers and (2) for practitioners.

For researchers, it provides an opportunity to further enrich the existing knowledge fund on the adoption of novel technologies to transform motor third-party liability insurance. The study identifies the key drivers and limitations of future development in this direction. The study is theoretically based on the resource-based approach, which many authorities consider one of the most well-known theories or approaches in the field of modern management. Thus, the list of areas in which the approach is applied has been expanded with an example from the field of insurance, i.e., its digital transformation. The research is of a qualitative type and is based on data collected through an open structured interview. Accordingly, it is based on a novel research instrument for examining the attitudes of the top management of insurance companies toward the trend of insurtech and the possibilities of innovating the traditional motor third-party liability insurance model.

As for practitioners, the research results contribute to the demystification of the insurtech phenomenon and provide insight into the current trends in the motor third-party liability insurance market in Serbia. Although the research included the perspective of one of the numerous stakeholders, i.e., the point of view of managers of insurance companies, the key findings can serve other stakeholders as well. For example, part of the results related to the key limitations of the future development and implementation of innovative initiatives may draw the attention of the regulator to the necessity of harmonizing with the regulations of more developed and technologically advanced markets where usage-based insurance models have already been introduced.

5.3 Limitations and Further Recommendations

This study has a number of downsides that might affect the generalizability of the findings. They can be broadly categorized as: (1) conceptual, (2) methodological, and (3) geographical.

First, the conceptual limitation of this study is the resource-based foundation. Although it is one of the most influential and most frequently cited theories in the field of management, the approach has been exposed to numerous criticisms since its inception. Given that this is an extremely complex and extensive topic, the shortcomings of the resource-based approach will not be discussed in detail here. One of the more comprehensive criticisms of the approach can be found in the study Resource-based competition: 3 schools of thought and 13 criticisms (El Shafeey and Trott 2014). Follow-up studies should be conceptually developed around some newer lines of reasoning, such as the Resource Fit Approach or a more practically oriented methodology for defining the technological innovation strategy of the renowned consulting company Booz Allen Hamilton.

Second, this study has methodological imperfections. Since the study reports on the findings of small-scale sample, it has the limitations typical to all qualitative methods. Also, it is common sense to ask the question of to what extent the respondents were objective when giving answers, given that the majority of questions related directly to the insurance companies they manage. The recommendation for future research of this type is to use focus groups that would also include experts belonging to other stakeholders, such as representatives of insurtech startups, academia, and regulatory authorities. These stakeholders could develop a discussion, examine different views on the same issue and contribute to a deeper understanding of the complex phenomenon of transformation based on modern technologies.

Third, this study is geographically constrained. Representatives of insurance companies from Serbia were interviewed. It has been pointed out several times in this paper that this market falls behind the more developed European markets in terms of a myriad of parameters. On one side, this study contributes to the expansion of the modest body of knowledge related to the digital transformation of motor third-party liability insurance. On the other side, any wider applicability of the obtained conclusions to more developed markets could be nothing else but judicious speculation. Some of the subsequent studies should have a comparative nature and expand the sample to managers of insurance companies operating in similar markets, and potentially to international experts who have significantly more practical experience in this area.

5.4 Concluding Remarks

Insurance industry functions on the century-old principles. Rigid regulation brought about a number of positive effects, especially when it comes to the trust between the interested parties. Nonetheless, rigid regulation became an obstacle to technology-induced changes. In today's changing environment, inflexibility and sluggishness have indirectly made it difficult to preserve the adopted values in insurance, such as mutual trust, solidarity, transparency, fairness, and ensuring economic security. Even in the twenty-first century, traditional insurance models have not completely freed themselves from earlier shortcomings and problems, such as vulnerability to fraudulent actions, overly complicated procedures, time and resource inefficiency in processing compensation claims, insufficiently precise definition of the risk profile and determination of the premium amount based strictly on these profiles, and others.

This study emphasizes the importance of disruptive power of technology in changing the landscape of the insurance industry. As the technological base develops, insurance business models and operations are expected to develop as well. The results of this paper unambiguously show that there is an evident awareness among insurance executives of the necessity of transforming the existing conventional motor third-party liability insurance system. At the same time, the presence of a complete consensus that regulatory restrictions and an illiberal market are the main obstacles to the concretization of transformation in the direction of usage-based insurance should raise the awareness of regulatory authorities about the need to harmonize legal and other relevant frameworks with examples of good practice from more innovative and developed insurance markets.

References

Albrecher H, Bommier A, Filipović D et al (2019) Insurance: models, digitalization, and data science. Eur Actuar J 9(2):349–360

Arumugam S, Bhargavi R (2019) A survey on driving behavior analysis in usage based insurance using big data. J Big Data 6(1):1–21

Barney J (1991) Firm resources and sustained competitive advantage. J Manag 17(1):99–120

Bhardwaj G (2021) Analysis of digitization, IOT and block chain in Bancassurance. In: 2021 International conference on technological advancements and innovations (ICTAI), pp 506–509
Bohnert A, Fritzsche A, Gregor S (2019) Digital agendas in the insurance industry: the importance of comprehensive approaches. Geneva Papers Risk Insurance-Issues Pract 44(1):1–19
Bömer M, Schwienbacher A (2018) Resource-based perspective of VC investments in FinTech. Available at SSRN 3312793
Breidbach CF, Keating BW, Lim C (2020) Fintech: research directions to explore the digital transformation of financial service systems. J Serv Theory Pract 30(1):79–102
Cappiello A (2020) The technological disruption of insurance industry: a review. Int J Bus Soc Sci 11(1):1–11
Carfora MF, Martinelli F, Mercaldo F et al (2019) A "pay-how-you-drive" car insurance approach through cluster analysis. Soft Comput 23(9):2863–2875
Chandy RK, Tellis GJ (2000) The incumbent's curse? Incumbency, size, and radical product innovation. J Mark 64(3):1–17
Chang V, Baudier P, Zhang H et al (2020) How Blockchain can impact financial services – the overview, challenges and recommendations from expert interviewees. Technol Forecast Soc Chang 158:120166. https://doi.org/10.1016/j.techfore.2020.120166
Che X, Liebenberg A, Xu J (2021) Usage-based insurance—impact on insurers and potential implications for InsurTech. North Am Actuarial J 1–28
Creswell JW (2007) Qualitative inquiry & research design: choosing among five approaches, 2nd edn. Sage, Thousand Oaks, CA
Crittenden AB, Crittenden VL, Crittenden WF (2019) The digitalization triumvirate: how incumbents survive. Bus Horiz 62(2):259–266
De Andrés-Sánchez J, González-Vila Puchades L, Arias-Oliva M (2021) Factors influencing policyholders' acceptance of life settlements: a technology acceptance model. The Geneva papers on risk and insurance-issues and practice, pp 1–27
Eapen A, Yeo J, Sasidharan S (2019) Finance constraints and technology spillovers from foreign to domestic firms. Econ Model 76:50–62
El Shafeey T, Trott P (2014) Resource-based competition: three schools of thought and thirteen criticisms. Eur Bus Rev
Eling M, Kraft M (2020) The impact of telematics on the insurability of risks. J Risk Financ 21(2): 77–109
Eling M, Lehmann M (2018) The impact of digitalization on the insurance value chain and the insurability of risks. Geneva Papers Risk Insurance-Issues Pract 43(3):359–396
Hess T, Matt C, Benlian A et al (2016) Options for formulating a digital transformation strategy. MIS Q Exec 15(2)
Hu Z, Ding S, Li S et al (2019) Adoption intention of fintech services for bank users: an empirical examination with an extended technology acceptance model. Symmetry 11(3):340
Husnjak S, Peraković D, Forenbacher I et al (2015) Telematics system in usage based motor insurance. Proc Eng 100:816–825
Jaber J, Issa H (2022) Disruptive innovation in the middle eastern FinTech sector: resource-based view. Int J Technol Hum Interact (IJTHI) 18(1):1–21
Kar AK, Navin L (2021) Diffusion of blockchain in insurance industry: an analysis through the review of academic and trade literature. Telematics Inform 58:101532
Knežević M, Đurić Z (2019) Some aspects of insurance development in Serbia. Ekonomika 65(2): 39–49
Kozlenkova IV, Samaha SA, Palmatier RW (2014) Resource-based theory in marketing. J Acad Mark Sci 42(1):1–21
Liang T, You J, Liu C (2010) A resource-based perspective on information technology and firm performance: a meta analysis. Ind Manag Data Syst 110(8):1138–1158. https://doi.org/10.1108/02635571011077807
Manes P (2020) Legal challenges in the realm of InsurTech. Eur Bus Law Rev 31(1):129

Milanović N, Milosavljevic M, Benković S et al (2020) An acceptance approach for novel technologies in car insurance. Sustainability 12(24):10331
Milanović N, Milosavljevic M, Joksimovic NZ (2021) The emergence of insurtech: a bibliometric survey. In: Book of proceedings of the economic and social development conference, pp 1124–1133
NBS (2021) Insurance sector in Serbia - annual report 2021. Belgrade: National Bank of Serbia. https://nbs.rs/sr/finansijske-institucije/osiguranje/poslovanje/. Accessed 18 June 2022
Nedić A, Nedić N, Stevanović I et al (2014) Review of vehicle telematics usage based insurance: contribution to sustainable insurance strategy. J Appl Eng Sci 12(2):165–169
Pisoni G (2020) Going digital: case study of an Italian insurance company. J Bus Strateg 42(2): 106–115
Rapley TJ (2001) The art(fulness) of open-ended interviewing: some considerations on analysing interviews. Qual Res 1(3):303–323. https://doi.org/10.1177/146879410100100303
Ricciardi V (2018) InsurTech definition as its own manifesto. The INSURTECH book: the insurance technology handbook for investors, entrepreneurs and Fintech visionaries: 6–8
Riikkinen M, Saarijärvi H, Sarlin P et al (2018) Using artificial intelligence to create value in insurance. Int J Bank Mark 36:1145
Stoeckli E, Dremel C, Uebernickel F (2018) Exploring characteristics and transformational capabilities of InsurTech innovations to understand insurance value creation in a digital world. Electron Mark 28(3):287–305
Takeda A, Ito Y (2021) A review of FinTech research. Int J Technol Manag 86(1):67–88
Tselentis DI, Yannis G, Vlahogianni EI (2017) Innovative motor insurance schemes: a review of current practices and emerging challenges. Accid Anal Prev 98:139–148
Van Looy A (2021) A quantitative and qualitative study of the link between business process management and digital innovation. Inf Manag 58(2):103413. https://doi.org/10.1016/j.im.2020.103413
Weill P (1992) The relationship between investment in information technology and firm performance: a study of the valve manufacturing sector. Inf Syst Res 3(4):307–333
Wernerfelt B (1984) A resource-based view of the firm. Strateg Manag J 5(2):171–180
Wilamowicz A (2019) The great FinTech disruption: InsurTech. Bank Finance Law Rev 34(2): 215–238
Wolcott HF (1994) Transforming qualitative data: description, analysis, and interpretation. Sage
Zarkovic N, Lisov M, Dragan M (2012) National bank as insurance supervisor in Serbia as a developing country. Afr J Bus Manag 6(8):2816–2824

InsurTech: New Competition to Traditional Insurers and Impact on the Economic Growth

Vladimir Njegomir and Jelena Demko-Rihter

Abstract Innovation, especially in the field of technology, is a key driver of competitiveness, economic growth, and prosperity. Contemporary technological changes, primarily information, and communication, are gradually transforming the economy and society, creating new ways of working and new types of jobs. These changes become challenges for insurance companies, which are conservative in terms of adopting innovations. Digitization has the ability to completely transform the insurance industry with the aim of realizing numerous benefits for the insurers and reinsurers, but also for the insured and for the economy. The aim of the paper is to analyze the importance of InsurTech as a new competition to traditional insurers and its impact on the economic growth. Given that the insurance sector contributes to the economic growth, data from the EU27 member states (for the year 2021) indicate economic recovery reflected in the GDP growth in comparison to pre-pandemic year 2019 and rebound of total insurance premiums.

Keywords Competition · Digitization · Economic growth · Insurance · InsurTech

1 Introduction

The simplest and most widespread form of risk management in modern society is insurance. Insurance and reinsurance play the most important role in minimizing the total risk and its atomization. Insurance companies through their basic functions of risk insurance and institutional investment have a positive effect on the economic growth (Njegomir and Stojic 2010).

V. Njegomir
Faculty of Law and Business Studies, Union University, Novi Sad, Serbia
e-mail: vladimir.njegomir@flv.edu.rs

J. Demko-Rihter (✉)
Faculty of Technical Sciences, Department of Industrial Engineering and Management, University of Novi Sad, Novi Sad, Serbia
e-mail: jciric@uns.ac.rs

S. Benković et al. (eds.), *Digital Transformation of the Financial Industry*, Contributions to Finance and Accounting,
https://doi.org/10.1007/978-3-031-23269-5_8

Table 1 The impact of digitization on the value chain of insurance companies

Product development	Big Data facilitates the collection of new behavioral data that enables personalization
	Telematics devices enable the reduction of related risks but create new risks, such as cyber risks
Sale and distribution	The platforms contain numerous offers and enable comprehensive comparation and selection for potential customers
	Techno insurance start-ups enter the insurance market
Actuarial science	Instant information and Big Data enable predictive analytics and evaluation
	More detailed segmentation is possible thanks to high processing power
Compensation claims	Telematics devices enable more accurate assessment of damage and reduce fraud
	Technology reduces processing time of compensation claims

Source: Cappielo A (2018) Technology and the insurance industry: reconfiguring the competitive landscape, Pisa, Italy, p. 12

Innovation, especially in the field of technology, is a crucial driver of competitiveness, economic growth, and prosperity. Contemporary technological changes are gradually transforming the economy and society, creating new ways of working and new types of jobs. These changes present challenges for insurance companies, which are conservative in terms of developing and adopting innovations.

The key importance of the paper is the analysis of the InsurTech trend which does not necessarily arise within the framework of traditional insurance companies. The aim of the paper is to analyze the importance of InsurTech as a new competition to traditional insurers and its impact on the economic growth.

To achieve the set goal, we gave an overview of the application of digitization in insurance where we included the latest trends in the application of information technology (IT). Then, we pointed out the different meanings of the term InsurTech, trends in the development of InsurTech competition in traditional insurance industry, and then the contribution of InsurTech to the economic growth. For this research, we used available secondary sources of data.

2 The Review of Digitization Trends in Insurance

The innovations of insurance companies are predominantly incremental in nature and focused on the development of insurance services, processes, marketing, and organization of the operations of insurance companies (Njegomir and Demko-Rihter 2013). The development of IT, as well as other challenges, such as endangering insurability, have enforced insurance companies to innovate their operations in order to survive. The number of data processed by information systems is greater than ever. This enables the correct determination of premiums, risks, and damages. In summary, the impact of digitization on the development of insurance is shown in Table 1.

Analysis by Bain and Google shows that a typical insurer in Germany that implemented these technologies could increase revenue by up to 28% over a 5-year period, reduce costs of compensation claims by up to 19%, and reduce administration costs by up to 72%.

Next, we focus on the most important and dominant trends in information and communication technologies related to insurance industry, which are also applied by InsurTechs: big data, predictive analytics, blockchain technologies, Internet of Things (IoT), telematics, use of drones and satellites (Njegomir et al. 2021).

Predictive analytics is specially developed based on the potential of IT that have enabled "Big data" management. Big data are groups of data that are so large or complex that could not be processed by traditional application software.

A particularly important role of "Big data" and predictive analytics is the prevention of insurance fraud. In order to reduce the mistakes of humans, big data and predictive analytics can identify discrepancies between insureds, third parties involved in compensation claims, and even social media and online activity of insureds. Fraudulent claims that cost the worldwide insurance industry an additional 10% of total sum of compensation claims can be identified simply and quickly. The insurance company could improve its market position by reducing the volume of compensation claims.

Big data improves the consumer experience, i.e., the satisfaction of the insureds. Big data enables insurance companies to respond to client requests more simply and quickly. Big data analytics enables insurance agents and brokers to identify discrepancies in insurance policies and make more relevant offers. Also, big data enables the adequate application of the risk management model (Njegomir and Ciric 2012), which additionally supports the adequate determination of premiums and capital for risk coverage. This allows insurers to add value to their services. Although the engagement of the employees of the insurance company is crucial for customer relationship management, big data and predictive analytics enable a fully understanding of the insureds, their behavior, needs, and expectations, which is of key importance for improving relations with them.

The IoT refers to the connection of billions of devices around the world equipped with sensors and software connected to the Internet to collect and share data. IoT provides numerous opportunities for insurance companies. The emergence of "smart homes" allows insurers more effective application of risk management techniques. For example, intelligent sensors can monitor the flow of water through pipes to prevent damage that may occur due to leaking water pipes. Similar technology can be used to control the possibility of fire or flood or burglary in households and firms. IoT enables better identification of risks and reduction of damages, making insurance more efficient both for the insurance companies and the insureds (Masic 2014). By better identification of risks, insurance companies can reduce their losses after a realization of insured events and offer some clients a lower insurance premium that corresponds to a lower risk. The IoT improves the business of insurers by reducing costs, improving the consumer experience as well as improving the efficiency of risk acceptance in insurance coverage.

Sensors and telematics devices have the potential for widespread insurance applications in different types of insurance: (1) real-time driver behavior information in motor vehicle insurance, (2) smart applications, including thermostats and security alarms, in home insurance, (3) monitoring of fitness devices in life and health insurances, (4) warehouse monitors and for fleet or truck fleet management in the case of commercial insurances. "The 21st Century Insurance Company" was the first to use GPS technology to enable parents to determine the exact location of the cars and driving characteristics of their teenage children. Also, with the "*Pay As You Drive*" model, which is based on the application of a GPS drive tracking device that measures mileage and driving time, Siemens has enabled insurance companies to offer insurance premiums that reflect individual behavior of drivers (their clients) and to resolve compensation claims in a more reliable way. Insurance companies that provide health insurance services are investing efforts in developing similar devices or ways of obtaining useful information from already existing devices that enable monitoring of the insured, which is referred to as the "*Pay As You Live*" model. If insureds use devices, such as smart watches and the like, which monitor their physical activity or exercises, they can get more favorable insurance conditions.

In order to improve the acceptance of risks in insurance, as well as the process of compensation for damages covered by insurance, drones, and satellite technologies, are increasingly being used. In terms of processing of compensation claims, drones and satellites can perform many tasks instead of employees in insurance companies. A remote assessment of damages can significantly reduce the time of processing claims.

Blockchain technology has the potential for numerous applications in finance, such as bond issuance based on cryptocurrencies or in insurance. According to Pavlovic (2018) the greatest potential for the application of blockchain technology in insurance is found in the following: microinsurance, payment of compensation claims, fight against fraud, reinsurance, smart contracts, undertake of standard and specific risks, and insurance of specific property.

3 Insurtech: The Concept, Differences, and New Competition to Traditional Insurance

New market players use technology better than traditional financial market participants. They enter these markets and bring their innovative and opportunity-driven strengths to these markets. They change the way how traditional players in banking and insurance industry compete, and bring other changes, too.

FinTech companies mainly emerged as start-ups, affecting disruptions in banking markets. These companies operate at lower costs compared to traditional banks, have fewer employees, base their business on IT and capital, and widespread business, thanks to the use of modern IT systems and ATMs that replace branches, as well as innovative services delivered in a real time.

InsurTech is part of a broader trend of applying IT in financial services known as FinTech, which emerged in the first decade of the twenty-first century. InsurTech covers various terms, from the broad concept of digitization and the application of IT in the business of insurance companies to the designation of new competition to insurance companies that originate from the IT sector and enter insurance sector. For example, McKinsey & Company (2017) in a report about InsurTech states that it is about technology-driven companies that enter the insurance industry, taking advantage of the application of new technologies and providing insurance coverage for customers who prefer to use IT in providing insurance services. Also, according to Allied Market Research, InsurTech refers to the technology applied in the creation, distribution, and administration of the insurance coverage.

In the report on the application of IT and innovations in the insurance industry, OECD (2017) states that InsurTech is a term used to describe new technologies with the potential to introduce innovations in the insurance industry and to influence regulatory practices related to insurance markets.

Thanks to the development of IT, insurance companies can better manage their risk exposures. According to Gencer (2022) InsurTech implies the use of emerging technologies in the insurance industry, which usually includes: replacement of manual processes aimed at more efficient operations, better risk assessment and providing improved service to insureds, leading to increased consumer satisfaction and, to greater loyalty of the insureds. InsurTech companies provide IT solutions to traditional insurers, but also offer insurance services directly to consumers. According to the broader definition, InsurTech, includes all technologies that enable innovations in insurance, such as artificial intelligence, chatbots, and advanced predictive analytics.

The appearance of new competition in the insurance industry is relatively limited due to the necessary capital requirements legally determined in Serbia and, defined by the minimum capital requirement in the European Union. However, competition also emerges outside the insurance industry, mainly from the financial market, banks, and recently from technological giants and internet insurance companies. Certain segments of InsurTech, such as sales via mobile phones, use of social networks or interactive sites, big data, artificial intelligence, the IoT, and cloud computing are also applied by traditional insurance companies. A typical example of InsurTech application is Amazon.com, as the world leader in the sale of products and, more recently, services via the Internet. Amazon employs around 400,000 workers worldwide and provides warranty services for the goods sold. In addition, Amazon plans to offer global insurance for the products it sells. These jobs are currently under development within Amazon, but realization can be expected soon. Google also tried to offer a motor vehicle insurance through Google Compare, but failed due to a lack of understanding of the specifics of insurance. The difficulties or limitations of the business model of traditional insurance companies include (Zhong An and KPMG 2019): the homogeneity of insurance services that do not meet the needs of insureds, the possibility of control of collaborative channels, the high costs of acquiring insurance, the profitability of providing insurance services is low, while the long-term development is limited. Because of homogenized services insurance industry should focus more on closer cooperation with customers in order to meet their needs. Insurance companies still base their business on traditional sales channels: banks, brokers, third-party online platforms, or insurance intermediaries. This leads to an increase in insurance acquisition costs. Finally, traditional insurance companies operate with a low profitability rate based on the providing insurance services. They realize an additional return as institutional investors. Low profitability limits the long-term development of insurance companies.

InsurTech companies represent a market risk for traditional insurance companies. They have full control over distribution, IT contributes to cost reduction, higher profitability, and greater satisfaction of insureds, which encourages the growth and development of InsurTechs. Their agile business model and digital innovation provide significantly greater opportunities for growth and profitability.

InsurTechs act on the market in a fundamentally different way compared to traditional insurance companies (McKinsey & Company 2017). Simpler IT solutions and operations followed by digital expertise aimed at maximizing value for customers is the key to the success of InsurTechs, their above-average returns and satisfied customers.

In terms of taking risks in insurance coverage, InsurTechs apply technologies such as effective data collection, data and document processing, IoT, and natural language processing to automate the interpretation of complex and large data sets in a short period (Gencer 2022). These results are more reliable and enable faster risk assessment, which leads to lower insurance premiums.

When it comes to processing compensation claims, the most important thing is the speed of the insurer's response after submitting the claim. Claims processing is the most transparent aspect of an insurer's operations and the segment of business that insureds are most interested in, when purchasing insurance coverage. The application of IT facilitates processing of documents, paying compensation and, at the same time preventing fraudulent claims, which is also a significant advantage of InsurTechs. Thanks to the application of IT and cost optimization, InsurTechs are able to offer the market customized insurance policies, such as "pay-as-you-drive."

Barriers for InsurTechs to enter the insurance market have been significantly reduced in some countries. In Australia, Singapore, and the UK InsurTechs are encouraged to test their innovative business models on specific customer segments without compliance with the full regulatory frameworks which are mandatory for traditional insurance companies. As in the case of FinTechs, InsurTechs disseminate innovation in the insurance industry, thus creating a competitive threat for traditional insurers, but also opportunities for cooperation in a changing market. Expectations of customers (insureds) about instant digital transactions through digital channels are becoming standard in all industries, and thanks to the pandemic (Njegomir and Demko-Rihter 2021) and development of InsurTechs it applies to the insurance industry, too.

Unlike FinTech in banking, the initial focus of InsurTech was on the retail segment (75% of the business), while the rest was in the commercial sector (McKinsey & Company 2017). Considering that Millennials and Z generation have taken precedence over the baby boomers, the offer via mobile channels and

Table 2 The role of InsurTechs by type of insurance and along the value chain of each type of insurance

Type of insurance	Service development (%)	Marketing (%)	Distribution (%)	Premium calculation (%)	Claims (%)	Total (%)
Property and casualty	8	4	17	10	7	46
Health insurance	5	3	11	8	6	33
Life insurance	3	2	9	5	2	21

Source: McKinsey Panorama Insurtech Database, according to Insurtech—the threat that inspires, McKinsey & Company, March, 2017, p. 4

online offers marked a significant success. Millennials and Z generation are less loyal to companies and consider financial services replaceable, as long as they satisfy their individual needs. They prefer the use of digital channels, active 24/7 and online transactions without direct interaction with the institution, which enables information about the insurance premium or compensation claims. InsurTechs also bring innovations in commercial insurance, which is especially important for small and medium-sized enterprises (SMEs).

Finally, when it comes to the target insurance types of InsurTechs, 46% is non-life insurance, 33% is health insurance, and the rest (21%) is life insurance. The share of InsurTechs by type and along the value chain is shown in Table 2.

As can be seen from Table 2, InsurTechs primarily target pure risk, i.e., property, health, and liability insurance. As the table shows, along the insurance value chain, InsurTechs focus on distribution and premium calculation.

Considering InsureTechs deals by business lines in Europe in 2021, a similar insight can be obtained. InsureTechs innovations are more directed in Property&Causalty risks (40%), Commercial lines (21%), and Enterprise Software (19%), while Life (13%) and Health insurance (7%) were lagging.[1]

4 Trends of Insurtech as a New Competition

The value of the global insurance industry is about a staggering US$4 trillion (McKinsey & Company 2017). However, the insurance industry has had relatively modest growth in the regions where InsurTechs have the highest penetration—in Western Europe and North America. In these regions, only the four-year growth in the field of health insurance significantly exceeds the growth of the gross domestic product (GDP), while the development of non-life and life insurance is below the

[1] https://tech.eu/2022/01/19/the-numbers-are-in-2021-was-a-banner-year-for-insurtech-in-europe. Accessed Sep 05, 2022.

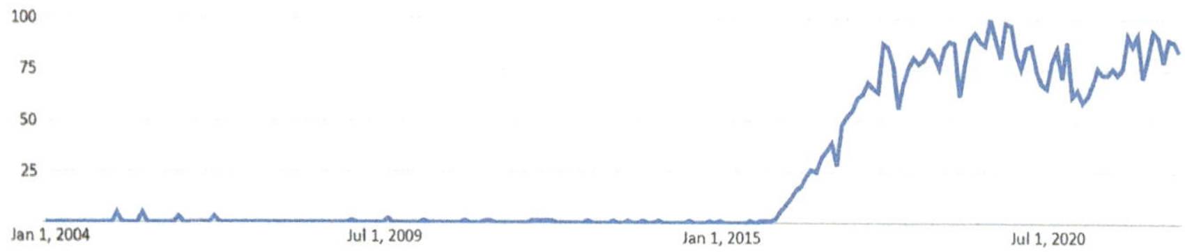

Fig. 1 Interest for InsurTech in the period 2004–2022 (Source: Google Trends, InsurTech: https://trends.google.com/trends/explore?date=all&q=insurtech Accessed Jun 19, 2022)

growth rate of the GDP (McKinsey & Company 2017). Although the InsurTech business model is still in the development phase, InsurTechs already have a significant impact on the overall insurance industry.

Successful InsurTechs are Brolly, Cover, So-sure, ZhongAn, and others. Apart from the developed markets of the USA and Great Britain, the significant market for the development of these companies is China. Chinese investors place immense capital into insurance technology. In 2016, there were 173 newly launched InsurTechs in China. ZhongAn is the first such company on the Chinese market, and in 2017 it provided additional capital of US$1.5 billion for development and became the largest technoinsurance company in the world. The emergence of technoinsurance disrupts the traditional insurance industry. In the case of ZhongAn, the key contribution was from the initial founder of Ant Financial, an affiliate of Alibaba, which enables the world's largest digital payments platform. Ant Financials' strength and technology have enabled the rapid development of ZhongAn's e-sale of insurance services.

As can be seen in Fig. 1, interest in InsurTech has existed before but has been especially present since 2015, with an increase in interest during the COVID-19 pandemic, after a temporary decline in late 2019 and early 2020.

According to a survey by PricewaterhouseCoopers (2017) on the insurance industry, as many as 94% of industry leaders find ways to improve risk assessment and customer relationships by applying digital technologies. The size of the market for InsurTech has grown rapidly in recent years, in the USA, for example, in 2016 it was a market worth US$0.25 billion, in 2021 it was worth US$3.85 billion, while in 2022 it was worth US$5.45 billion. Expectations are that from 2022 to 2030, it will grow at a rate of 51.7%, reaching US$152.43 billion.

The COVID-19 pandemic has forced organizations from different sectors to reduce office work. As a result, many industries adopted innovations and digital technologies at a faster rate. Global investments in InsurTech increased by more than 12% in the Q2 of 2020, despite a significant global economic slowdown (Deloitte 2020). Overall, 2021 saw a flood of fintech innovation capital and, by the end of Q3 2021, global fintech funding reached US$94.7 billion (with 3549 deals), almost double 2020s full-year total (Global FinTech trends 2022). According to Insurtech Global Outlook 2022 InsurTech development continued in 2021, despite the pandemic, but partly thanks to the global recovery. Globally, 2021 was without any doubt a booming year for InsurTechs, with global investments reaching $10 billion, passing 2020s total of $6 billion. InsurTechs attract large investments, not only insurers, reinsurers, and technology companies, but also from other investors. In terms of investor type, Venture Capital's presence is 5 times larger than that of companies in the insurance industry.

According to Insurtech Global Outlook 2022, the largest percentage of investments in InsurTech were investments in health insurance and cross insurance lines, while in 2021 the participation of commercial lines and motor vehicle insurance increased, and at the same time investments in household insurance decreased. In the last decade, the largest investments in InsurTechs were in the marketing and distribution, design and development of insurance services, as well as in the policy administration, collection, and disbursement (Insurtech Global Outlook 2022).

The largest investments in InsurTech were marked in North America, but the share of transactions in Europe was also increasing in the observed period.

Total investments of 92 deals of European InsurTechs was around 2.5 bilion euros in 2021. It is almost twice in comparison to 2019 and 2020 together. Average deal size increased from 8 million euros (2020) to 28 million euros (2021). According to the number of deals, the largest end most important InsurTech ecosystems are the UK (33%), France (20%), and Germany (17%) and around 30% of all deals number emerged in other European countries. Regarding total funding, 87% is in Germany, 78% in France, and 59% in the UK. Considering deals along the value chain, the majority of deals was directed to the distribution (57%), then to product (14%), underwriting (10%), claims (8%), and full-stuck (11%). It might be expected having in mind that InsurTechs mostly focus on distribution.

An increasing number of InsurTech companies can be expected as a challenge to traditional insurance companies that have to improve their offer in order to gain a competitive advantage over easily available and more cost-effective insurance services provided by InsurTech.

Technologies such as telematics and the IoT have enabled the development of new insurance services in motor insurance, home insurance, and health insurance. InsurTech companies have attracted new customers with selective discounts based on the insureds' behavior that minimizes different risks and the usage of smart devices (e.g., fire detectors with autonomous signals to emergency services). If the insured suffered a traffic accident, taken and sent a photo of the car damage is valid for the payment of compensation claim. Software installed in the car enables estimation of damage, which significantly speed up the damage processing and payment of the claim, but also eliminate intentional damages, i.e., insurance fraud. Benefits for insureds include lower insurance premiums and faster processing of claims.

In light of technological changes, consumers prefer a unique product or service, media, and sales, i.e., individually customized marketing (concept of mass customization and personalization). InsurTechs are able to offer mass customization of insurance services by duration, amount of premium, covered risk, etc., unlike traditional insurance companies. Also, the COVID-19 pandemic emphasized the role of digitized product and service, which has sparked the development of InsurTech. The analysis of the Swiss Re group points out the same, that the goal of digital transformation is to enable insurers and reinsurers, as well as InsurTechs, to create customized risk protection for the changing needs of customers.

In addition to the numerous positive effects of InsurTechs and digitization in the insurance industry in general, which include cost savings based on the reduction of claims and administration costs, increased efficiency, improved competitiveness, better fulfilment of the requirements of insureds, government, rating agencies, more precise determination of insurance premiums and better risk and capital management, digitization also has negative aspects. The negative aspects of digitization for traditional insurance companies include increased investment in training people and purchasing hardware and software that should support the implementation of digitization, a greater risk of copying a business model based on digitization, as well as the emergence of new competition in the form of InsurTech, greater exposure to risks, primarily cyber risk, the possibility of making wrong decisions in analytics based only on digital data processing, the resistance of certain segments of insurers, especially the elderly, as well as problems in managing relations with them due to the absence of personal contact in sales based on IT.

Certainly, the biggest negative aspect of the digitization of traditional insurers is the exposure to increased risk. Based on the application of IT so far and the manifestation of risks, we believe that the first place in terms of importance belongs to computer fraud, damaged systems and data, and violations of privacy, i.e., cyber risk. The importance of cyber risk is also indicated by the Convention on Cybercrime, signed in Budapest in 2001, which defines illegal access, illegal interruption, data and system interference, device abuse, computer-related falsification, fraud, child pornography, and misuse of intellectual property rights, as criminal activities.

According to Deloitte cyberattacks are growing exponentially with insurers' efforts to implement digital channels to develop stronger relations with insureds, offer new insurance services and expand the share in their clients' financial portfolios. Changes toward greater participation of IT in the operations of insurers, require increasing investments and highly integrated platforms such as agency portals, filling out policies, and submitting compensation claims online. Although investments in digitization provide strategic advantage, they expose insurers to higher cyber risk.

Ernst & Young surveyed a sample of 1755 insurance company executives on how insurance companies manage cyber risk exposures (Ernst & Young 2017). As many as 55% of insurers outsource to experts the assessment of cyber risk exposure, 59% of insurers emphasize that budget constraint are key barriers to the contribution of information security to improving the functioning and value of the organization. Asked about the focus of the information system security function, 11% of insurers indicated that this function is directed to devices connected to the IoT, 7% to focus on advanced machine learning or artificial intelligence, 5% to robotic processes, and 4% to blockchain and cryptocurrencies. About 49% of surveyed insurers have detected significant cyberattacks on their organization, even 71% of respondents do not think that it is very likely that their organization could detect a sophisticated attack, 59% think that there is no adequate management support, 83% indicate that the discovery of the cyberattack on the organization would most likely contribute to increasing the budget for information security, 19% of insurers could not assess the financial impact of cyberattacks on their key customers, 11% of respondents believe that their level of exposure to cyberattacks is sufficient, 56% of respondents see criminal syndicates as the most likely source of cyberattacks, while 82% believe that the most common cause of cyberattacks is employee negligence.

Insurance companies and InsurTechs have to be able to manage these risks in an adequate way. Identifying these risks implies the establishment and continuous monitoring and revision of management and administrative procedures, internal and external security measures, which can be ensured by obtaining information through the application of system testing, interviewing employees, and reviewing documentation.

5 Contribution of Insurtech to the Economic Growth

Back in the 1980s, a new growth theory or endogenous growth theory was developed to identify gaps in the explanation of economic growth factors. This theory implies that investments and growth of one sector in the economy can provide positive externalities to other sectors. Of these theories, special importance is given to the financial sector, firstly the banking sector and then the insurance sector.

Numerous literature sources emphasize indirect contribution of insurance to economic growth (Rejda 2005; Skipper and Kwon 2007; Dorfman 2008; Haiss and Sumegi 2008). Attention is directed to issues of growth and development of insurance, through the size of the premium per capita as well as the share of premium in GDP (Skipper and Kwon 2007). Research into the role of insurance companies as institutional investors, i.e., the function of accumulation and efficient allocation of capital, is usually carried out in a broader context, such as research of the impact of insurance on economic growth (Ward and Zurbruegg 2000; Webb et al. 2002; Arena 2008; Adams et al. 2009).

In researches on the impact of insurance on economic growth in the region of the former Yugoslavia (Njegomir and Stojic 2010), was found that the gross insurance premium per capita has a significant influence on economic growth, with a statistical significance level of 10%. This means that insurers, as providers of insurance coverage and claims compensation, have a positive impact on the economic growth. Also, the investment function of insurance companies has a positive effect on economic growth with a statistical significance level of 5%. Insurance contributes positively to economic growth through risk protection and additionally through the institutional investments of insurance companies. Also, it was determined that the indirect economic protection against risk provided by insurance and institutional investment have a positive impact on economic dynamism, which is related to economic growth (Njegomir and Demko-Rihter 2015).

Experience from developed countries indicates that insurance companies are the largest employers, investors, and the largest taxpayers, thus making a significant contribution to economic growth. For example, in the USA, insurance and reinsurance companies employ 2.9 million people, and related activities, such as brokers, agents, appraisers, employ additional 27,000 workers (Insurance Information Institute). In the USA, in 2020, non-life insurers had a total investment of US$2 trillion, while life insurers had investments of US$4.7 billion and US$3 billion on separate accounts, where the investment risk is borne by the insureds. Thus, total investments in the USA amounted to US$9700 billion. Insurance companies have been the largest institutional investors in Europe (European Capital Markets Institute 2020). For example, in 2020, the total investments of insurance companies reached EUR 10.6 trillion, which roughly represents about 61.1% of the total GDP of all countries of the European Union together. Insurers' total investment portfolio in the EU27 member states increased 4.1% in the fourth quarter of 2021 to 9.7 trillion euros (Insurance Europe 2022).

Institutional investment of insurance companies contributes to the improvement of economic activities, and the development of financial markets. They indirectly affect the development of entrepreneurial activities because the development of economic activities strengthens the entrepreneurial activities, SMEs to develop new products and technologies and to place them on the market. The effect of insurance development on the economic growth of a country is indirect because it depends on the performance of the investment of insurers (Lee et al. 2018). Also, through the development of financial markets, possibilities of financing economic activities increase by increasing available capital and lowering its price. They are also important for individual insureds, who are safer thanks to the insurer's adequate investment policy, and insurance companies can offer lower insurance premiums.

Insurance has traditionally been viewed as an instrument of indirect economic compensation of individuals, businesses, and state institutions for damages that occur after the realization of harmful events, covered by insurance contracts. However, in post-COVID-19 conditions, insurance increasingly gets the role of supporting the economy and becomes a key tool for managing social risks, as well as a financial instrument for entrepreneurs. InsurTechs support development of economies at the national and global levels, especially in distribution, customer service, and claims management (Manta et al. 2021). According to Insurance Europe (2022) preliminary figures for 2021 of the GDP of EU27 member states marked strong year-on-year growth of 5.4% in the pandemic year, thanks to the emergence of vaccines, increased household consumption, and national and European economic recovery plans. But at the same time rising energy prices, supply chain disruptions, and other factors increased inflation rate, reaching new maximum. Inflation impacts the insurance industry in different aspects. Higher inflation rate increases claims costs which could be rolled over to higher insurance premiums. Health insurance is considerably sensitive to the higher inflation rate due to increased medical expenses. Life insurance is the most hit by high inflation, while in aggravated economic conditions it might reduce the people's ability to purchase life insurance coverage. In such economic circumstances, some people decide to reduce their long-term savings. Figures for 2021 showed that recovery of European economies contributed to the increase of total insurance premiums, compared to pre-pandemic year 2019.

The preliminary figures showed that different markets marked positive growth in health and P&C premiums in 2021. It has to be noticed that these lines are highly exposed to inflation, and this growth of premiums could also be caused by overall rising costs.

Global economic slowdown caused by different economic, geopolitical, pandemic, and other factors directly affects the insurance industry. If economy slows, demand for insurance also slows and market becomes more competitive. In a recession, return on investments of insurance companies in the financial market, decreases. They have to find new investment opportunities in order to retain the returns on investments.[2]

InsurTech rapidly develops and disrupts the traditional business model of insurance companies. InsurTech creates opportunities as well as challenges for traditional insurance companies. The opportunities offered by InsurTech are particularly significant for developing countries with significant gaps in insurance protection. This gap exists due to low insurance penetration, i.e., a small share of insurance premiums in the GDP, which together with insurance density (the insurance premium per capita), represents a measure of development in a certain country, usually yearly. New business models and the application of IT are key to closing the protection gap, which represents the key development implication of InsurTech on economic growth, given that insurance penetration is directly positively related to the economic growth. The penetration of insurance in developing countries is lower than in developed countries. Empirical data show that insurance begins to develop especially in developing countries when GDP per capita reaches US$5000. The following rule is valid for the relationship between insurance penetration and GDP: 1% growth in insurance penetration is usually associated with a 2% growth in GDP (Holiday 2019).

In addition to insurance penetration, two additional indicators are used as a measure of the development of insurance industry: insurance coverage of catastrophic events and health risks and costs. In developing countries, there is insufficient coverage of disaster and health insurance. Although certain discrepancies also occur in developed countries, the biggest insurance protection gap occurs in developing countries. At the same time, 58% of catastrophic events happen in developing countries, where only 26% are covered by insurance (Holiday 2019). Considering the health system, there is an insurance protection gap, which is reflected in the large payment for health services by individuals, especially in countries with medium-low income.

Most of the InsurTechs and insurers that have embraced digitization operate in North America, Western Europe, and the developed region of Asia. In countries like China or India, mobile banking is established and relatively widely accepted, especially in China. In developing countries, insurance is a less known financial service and usually not adequately understood, such as in Western European

[2]https://www.spixii.com/blog/the-economy-is-slowing-down-what-does-it-mean-for-insurance-companies. Accessed Sep 05, 2022.

countries, North America, and Japan. Similarly, as in Serbia, insureds are either not enough familiar with the characteristics of insurance, or not well educated about the importance of insurance, or perceive insurance as an expense and not an investment. InsurTechs are able to improve the trust of the population in the insurance and provide education, which would contribute to the improvement of insureds' satisfaction and would attract new customers.

InsurTechs ignore market barriers and reduce insurance market concentration, allowing insureds a more affordable insurance service, which indirectly leads to increased competition, increased efficiency in the insurance market, and economic growth. In addition to the usual contribution to economic growth, through risk protection and indirect economic protection as well as by investing surplus reserves, InsurTech contributes to economic growth through lower insurance premiums and greater competitiveness.

Through higher efficiency and competitiveness, InsurTech enables lower insurance premiums in their offer, as well as in the offer of traditional insurers. The above is particularly significant for the price-sensitive insurance markets, such as Serbia and other countries in the region. InsurTech enables more affordable insurance services, thanks to increased efficiency and reduced costs of administration, insurance fraud, and claims compensation. We believe that InsurTech would especially develop in the Serbian insurance market where customers are particularly sensitive to the insurance premium, which would have an additional impact on greater coverage of insurance and thus support economic growth.

InsurTechs are able to offer a customer-centric approach thanks to the application of IT. The customer-centric approach is possible thanks to the use of digital interaction, artificial intelligence, and big data, which additionally enables the customized offer and provides insurance coverage for shorter periods, compared to the standard coverage of 1 year. The mass customization of services enabled by InsurTech provides a better relationship with customers and their satisfaction, which finally affects higher sales, higher market share, and higher profitability (Njegomir et al. 2021).

InsurTech enables shortening the period of insurance coverage, i.e., the insurance contract. This means that the owner of the bike can contract insurance while lending the bike to a friend, or insure a laptop during the travel. Short-term insurance policies have always existed for some types of insurance such as travel health insurance, but the role of digital technologies has enabled their more practical and cost-effective application, as well as increasing premiums for those situations where insurance would not exist, which also contributes to economic growth.

6 Conclusion

Digitization as the application of IT in various aspects of operations of insurance companies and/or new competition, brings advantages, but also new risks and challenges. In addition to the numerous positive effects of digitization in insurance, which include cost savings based on the reduction of claims and administration costs, higher efficiency and competitiveness, better fulfilment of requirements of insureds, government, rating agencies, more accurate calculation of insurance premiums, and better risk and capital management, digitization also has negative aspects.

The negative aspects of digitization include an increasing need for investing in the education of employees and purchase of hardware and software that supports the digitization processes, a greater risk of copying a business model based on digitization and the emergence of new competition (InsurTechs), higher exposure to cyber risks, the possibility of making wrong decision based only on digital data processing and analytics, the resistance of elderly population as consumers.

We focused the research on InsurTech, which conceptually has several different meanings. We explained why InsurTech represents new competition to traditional insurance companies.

There are a growing trend of digitization and technological changes, a rising interest in InsurTech and increasing investments in InsurTech. Pandemic conditions together with InsurTech have particularly emphasized the importance of the "digital customer." Apart from the greater use of IT, customers or potential insureds are more inclined to a personalized approach, which requires mass customization of the insurance service. Insurers appear in the role of investors in InsurTech companies, although the participation of venture capital is even five times higher. In addition to InsurTechs as new competition, traditional insurers are seeking to form partnerships with them to improve efficiency of marketing and distribution. InsurTech includes companies that provide insurance services as well as distribution of insurance services and software services to existing, traditional insurance companies. InsurTech companies are estimated to grow at a rate of 51.7% between 2022 and 2030. The COVID-19 pandemic had a big impact on growth, which can be seen in the growth of investments in InsurTech.

Numerous studies have confirmed the positive relationship between insurance and economic growth. Research also indicate that the risk acceptance in insurance coverage and indirect financial protection against potential damages with the institutional investment of insurance companies have a positive effect on the economic growth. Bearing in mind the above and InsurTech as a new competition that brings new capital to the insurance market and thus the possibility of increased acceptance to insurance coverage, we conclude that InsurTechs also contribute to the economic growth. The special contribution of InsurTechs is that they, as a new competition, contribute to the improvement of operations of traditional insurance companies with the aim of increasing competitiveness and a greater contribution to the economic growth. Also, the opportunities of InsurTechs are particularly significant in developing markets where exists a significant gap in the provided insurance coverage due to low insurance penetration. This has significant implications given that is confirmed that insurance penetration has a direct positive relationship to the economic growth. InsurTechs as well as new technologies in insurance companies are important for closing the existing gap in these markets.

InsurTechs by providing insurance services improve the financial stability of families and companies, encourage competition, develop commerce, reduce public expenditures needed for claims compensation programs, facilitate the prevention of claims and increase liquidity, considering that they appear as supplementary or new providers of insurance services together with traditional insurance companies.

The main limitation of our research is the lack of quantitative data which could prove causality of Insurtech and economic growth expressed through the GDP. InsurTechs still do not operate in the Serbian insurance market and this is a limitation for our research, and testing their influence on the economic growth. Our future research depends on emerging start-ups in the Serbian insurance ecosystem, interested in the InsurTech operations, as a new competition to existing traditional insurers.

References

Adams M, Andersson J, Andersson L-F, Lindmark M (2009) Commercial banking, insurance and economic growth in Sweden between 1830 and 1998. Account Bus Financ Hist 19(1):21–38

Allied Market Research Global. InsurTech Market, Opportunities and Forecast, 2021–2030. https://www.alliedmarketresearch.com/insurtech-market-A12373. Accessed 28 Mar 2022

Arena M (2008) Does insurance market activity promote economic growth? A cross-country study for industrialized and developing countries. J Risk Insurance 75(4):921–946

Bain & Company Digitalization in Insurance. The Multibillion Dollar Opportunity. https://www.bain.com/insights/digitalization-in-insurance. Accessed 10 Mar 2022

Boston Consulting Group (2022) The funding streak in Insurtech continues, June 08

Cappielo A (2018) Technology and the insurance industry: reconfiguring the competitive landscape. Pisa

Deloitte Center for Financial Services, Deloitte Development LLC (2020) COVID-19 pandemic shifts InsurTech investment priorities, Hermitage, TN

Deloitte, Global Cyber Executive Briefing, Insurance. https://www2.deloitte.com/be/en/pages/risk/articles/insurance.html. Accessed 05 Apr 2022

Dorfman MS (2008) Introduction to risk management and insurance. Pearson Education, Upper Saddle River, NJ

Ernst & Young (2017) Governing cyber risks in financial institutions. www.ey.com/gl/en/industries/financial-services/ey-governing-cyber-risks-financial-service

European Capital Markets Institute (2020) Asset allocation in Europe: reality vs. expectations. Task Force Report, April. https://wwwcepseu/wp-content/uploads/2020/04/TFAA_Final-Report_ECMIpdf. Accessed 12 May 2022

Gencer G (2022) In-depth guide to Insurtech: Trends & Technologies of 2022. AIMultiple, Tallinn

Global Fintech Trends in 2022, Linklaters. https://www.linklaters.com/en/insights/blogs/fintechlinks/2022/january/fintech-global-trends-2022#:~:text=Overall%2C%202021%20saw%20a%20flood,%245.9%20billion%20in%20Q3%202021. Accessed 17 Mar 2022

Haiss P, Sumegi K (2008) The relationship between insurance and economic growth in Europe: a theoretical and empirical analysis. Empirica 35(4):405–431

Holiday S (2019) How Insurtech can close the protection gap in emerging markets. EMCompass Notes

https://tech.eu/2022/01/19/the-numbers-are-in-2021-was-a-banner-year-for-insurtech-in-europe. Accessed 12 Sep 2022

https://www.bcg.com/publications/2022/insurance-tech-funding-streak-continues

https://www.insuranceeurope.eu/publications/2674/european-insurance-preliminary-figures-2021/download/Preliminary+figures%202021.pdf. Accessed 05 Sep 2022

https://www.spixii.com/blog/the-economy-is-slowing-down-what-does-it-mean-for-insurance-companies. Accessed 05 Sep 2022

Insurance Europe (2022) Statistics. Brussels. https://www.insuranceeurope.eu/statistics. Accessed 10 May 2022

Insurance Information Institute A Firm Foundation: How Insurance Supports the Economy. https://www.iii.org/publications/a-firm-foundation-how-insurance-supports-the-economy/introduction/insurance-industry-at-a-glance Accessed 10 May 2022

Insurtech Global Outlook (2022) NTT DATA Corporation. Koto City, Tokyo

Insurtech Market Size, Share & Trends Analysis Report by Type (Auto, Business, Health, Home, Specialty, Travel) (2022) By Service (Consulting, Support & Maintenance, Managed Services), By Technology, By End Use, By Region, And Segment Fore-casts, 2022–2030, Report ID: GVR-4-68038-093-4, Grand View Research, San Francisco

Lee HS, Yong ZJ, Lim QM (2018) Insurance development and economic growth. Financ Statistical J 1. https://doi.org/10.24294/fsj.v1i4.1057

Manta O, Militaru I, Croitoru L (2021) Financial instruments InsurTech on the financial market in the current global context. SSRN Electron J.

Masic N (2014) Internet stvari – nova digitalna pomoc osigurateljima. Svijet osiguranja, Tectus, Zagreb

McKinsey & Company (2017) Insurtech—the threat that inspire. Panorama Insurtech Database

McKinsey How top tech trends will transform insurance. https://www.mckinsey.com/industries/financial-services/our-insights/how-top-tech-trends-will-transform-insurance. Accessed 11 Mar 2022

Njegomir V, Ciric J (2012) Risk modeling in the insurance industry. Strat Manage 17(1):53–60

Njegomir V, Demko-Rihter J (2013) Innovations of insurance companies and investment funds. Management 18(68):59–68

Njegomir V, Demko-Rihter J (2015) Insurance companies as driving forces of economic dynamics. In: Losonc A, Ivanisevic A (eds) Institutional assumptions about so-cio-economic dynamics in east and Central Europe: proceedings. University of Novi Sad, Faculty of technical sciences, Novi Sad, pp 147–159

Njegomir V, Demko-Rihter J (2021) The impact of covid-19 on the business of insurers and reinsurers. Econ Themes 59(4):445–459

Njegomir V, Demko-Rihter J, Bojanic T (2021) Disruptive technologies in the operation of insurance industry. Tehnicki Vjesnik 28(5):1797–1805

Njegomir V, Stojic D (2010) Does insurance promote economic growth: the evidence from ex-Yugoslavia region. Econ Thought Pract 19(1):31–48

OECD (2017) Technology and innovation in the insurance sector

Pavlovic B (2018) Potencijal veci od rudarenja Bitcoina. Svet osiguranja 10:48–49

PricewaterhouseCoopers (2017) Redrawing the lines: FinTech's growing influence on financial services. Global FinTech Report, London

Rejda GE (2005) Principles of risk management and insurance. Pearson Education, Upper Saddle River, NJ

Skipper HD, Kwon WJ (2007) Risk management and insurance: perspectives in a global economy. Blackwell Publishing, Oxford

Smartphones Shape Habits in Europe. https://www.warc.com/newsandopinion/news/smartphones_shape_habits_in_europe/30470. Accessed 05 Mar 2022

SSRN: https://ssrn.com/abstract=3801096 or https://doi.org/10.2139/ssrn.3801096

Swiss Re. How digitalisation brings customers closer https://www.swissre.com/risk-knowledge/risk-perspectives-blog/digitalisation-brings-customers-closer.html. Accessed 05 Apr 2022

Ward D, Zurbruegg R (2000) Does insurance promote economic growth? Evidence from OECD countries. J Risk Insurance 67(4):489–506

Webb I, Grace MF, Skipper HD (2002) The effect of banking and insurance on the growth of capital and output. Center for Risk Management and Insurance Working Paper 02-1

Zhong An Fintech Institute and KPMG CHINA Insurance Service (2019) InsurTech: Infrastructure for New Insurance

Customers' Intention in Terms of Using Mobile Banking Services in Serbia

Zenaida Šabotić, Semir Vehapi, and Ahmedin Lekpek

Abstract The research subject of this paper is the intention to use mobile banking services by banking clients in Serbia. The aim of the research is to analyze the influence of the factors included in the TAM model on the intention to use mobile banking by banking clients in Serbia. The research used an extended TAM model, which includes: perceived usefulness, perceived ease of use, perceived risk, trust, social influence, lifestyle, and perceived self-efficacy. The data used in the research were collected by surveying banking clients in Serbia and processed through correlation and regression analysis. The correlation analysis showed that there is mostly a positive and statistically significant linear correlation between the variables of the used model. Only perceived risk has a statistically significant but negative correlation with all other variables. The univariate correlation analysis showed that perceived usefulness, perceived ease of use, trust, social influence, lifestyle, and perceived self-efficacy have a positive influence on the intention to use mobile banking, while the impact of perceived risk is negative. On the other hand, using multivariate regression analysis, perceived usefulness, lifestyle, and social impact were singled out as significant predictor variables.

Keywords Mobile banking · Technology acceptance model · Intention of using · Serbia

1 Introduction

The dynamic technological development we have witnessed in the last few decades has significantly influenced the reshaping of lifestyles and the way people satisfy their needs and carry out work. The increasing availability and quality of Internet connection contributed in particular to this, which encouraged significant changes in

Z. Šabotić (✉) · S. Vehapi · A. Lekpek
State University of Novi Pazar, Novi Pazar, Serbia
e-mail: zsabotic@np.ac.rs; svehapi@np.ac.rs; alekpek@np.ac.rs

S. Benković et al. (eds.), *Digital Transformation of the Financial Industry*,
Contributions to Finance and Accounting,
https://doi.org/10.1007/978-3-031-23269-5_9

the habits and expectations of the average consumer. The modern consumer is not characterized by patience but by the expectation that one can access most of the services one uses easily and at any time, which a high-quality Internet connection has made possible. Even the banking sector could not remain immune to the aforementioned changes. The need for banking mediation is reduced by strengthening non-banking financial institutions and the emergence of innovative digital financial instruments, such as cryptocurrencies (Lekpek 2021). There was an emergence of revolutionary thinking that "banking is essential to a modern economy, banks are not" (Tan and Teo 2000, cited in Akturan and Tezcan 2012). In order to survive in such a turbulent environment, banks had to drastically change the process of creation and the way of providing services to clients (Luarn and Lin 2005). Mobile banking has emerged in line with the banks' desire to meet the clients' demands for constant availability of banking services. Mobile banking is the process of accessing banking services through mobile telecommunication devices (Dahlberg et al. 2008 cited in Yuan et al. 2016). It is a natural result of the evolution of electronic banking and has shown its superiority concerning other e-banking forms (Püschel et al. 2010). Mobile telephony is globally the most widely represented telecommunication platform, available even in countries with insufficiently developed technological infrastructure (Singh and Srivastava 2018). Banks are enabled to reach those individuals for whom access to banking services was previously difficult or non-existent by developing a mobile banking system whose services can be used through numerous mobile devices. It is estimated that the number of users of mobile banking services in developing countries has increased by almost 17 times in the last few years (Ho et al. 2020). Due to mobile banking, banks can significantly improve their profitability and business efficiency. This is a contribution of the aforementioned growth of their services user base, as well as a significant reduction in the cost of providing banking services (Jebarajakirthy and Shankar 2021). On the other hand, bank clients are enabled to use banking services, such as bank account management, money transfer, and borrowing, in a much more efficient and secure way (Gu et al. 2009; Oliveira et al. 2014). However, the challenges of effective mobile banking implementation should not be overlooked either. Firstly, the development of mobile banking requires significant investments in modern IT systems (Oliveira et al. 2014). Secondly, a considerable number of users of banking services still consider mobile banking insufficiently secure (Munoz-Leiva et al. 2017). This is the main reason why, despite the expansive growth achieved over the last few years, the mobile banking market has not yet realized its full potential (Tan and Lau 2016). Consequently, banks must also invest in the development of security systems that should protect the bank and users of mobile banking services from potential abuses. Mobile banking is also experiencing expansion in Serbia. According to the data presented by the National Bank of Serbia, the number of transactions carried out through mobile banking in 2021 compared to 2020 increased by 32.20% (NBS 2021). Several factors contributed to such trends: the high level of use of mobile telephony services in Serbia; the dominance of banks in majority foreign ownership, as a result of which the business practices of parent banks, operating in economically and technologically advanced societies, are implemented in all subsidiary banks; growth of financial literacy and awareness of banking clients in Serbia about the possibilities offered by mobile banking; and the need for physical distance and conducting as many transactions remotely as possible, imposed by the onset of the COVID-19 pandemic. Following the growing importance of mobile banking, the research subject of this paper is the intention to use mobile banking services by banking clients in Serbia. The aim of the research is to analyze the influence of the factors included in the TAM model on the intention to use mobile banking by banking clients in Serbia. Numerous authors have dealt with consumer behavior within various sectors in Serbia, most often in the food industry and mobile commerce (Giraud et al. 2013; Vehapi and Doličanin 2016; Kalinić and Marinković 2016; Grubor and Đokić 2016; Marinković and Kalinić 2017; Liébana-Cabanillas et al. 2017; Kalinić et al. 2019; Mitić and Vehapi 2021; Vehapi and Šabotić 2021), while a small number of them were engaged in researching consumer behavior in the mobile banking sector (Pavlović and Savić 2017; Lukić et al. 2019; Vehapi et al. 2021). Therefore, determining the key factors influencing consumers' intention to use mobile banking services in Serbia will contribute to a better understanding of consumer behavior in this growing sector. The structure of the paper is as follows: at the beginning, a literature review was performed, then the research methodology was presented, followed by a presentation of the obtained results, results analysis, and conclusion.

2 Literature Review

The motivation and willingness of consumers to use mobile banking services largely determine the success of implementing this modern distribution channel of banking services. Many researchers have examined the factors influencing consumers' intention to adopt mobile banking and start using the services it offers. In Portugal, it has been noticed that performance expectancy, initial trust, technology characteristics, and task technology fit are the most significant determinants of behavioral intentions, and behavioral intention, together with facilitating conditions, directly affects the mobile banking adoption (Oliveira et al. 2014). While favorable intention encourages consumers to adopt mobile banking, attitude mainly determines the intention to use mobile banking applications (Talukder et al. 2014; Munoz-Leiva et al. 2017). Akturan and Tezcan (2012) in their study prove that perceived usefulness, perceived social risk, perceived performance risk, and perceived benefit are key factors that influence the attitudes of younger consumers toward mobile banking, and that attitude leads to intentions to use mobile banking. Chitungo and Munongo (2013) conclude that perceived ease of use, perceived usefulness, relative advantages, personal innovativeness, and social norms significantly influence the user's attitude toward mobile banking, which influences intention toward mobile banking. The same study finds that perceived risk and cost negatively affect mobile banking adoption. A review of 55 relevant publications reveals that in addition to attitude, compatibility with lifestyle and perceived usefulness are significant drivers of intention to adopt mobile banking services in developed and developing countries (Shaikh and Karjaluoto 2015). Alalwan et al. (2016a, 2017) in two separate studies examined the key factors influencing Jordanian bank customers' intention to adopt mobile banking. In the first study, it was determined that Jordanian customers' behavioral intention was significantly influenced by perceived usefulness, perceived ease of use, and perceived risk, while the second study identified performance expectancy, effort expectancy, hedonic motivation, price value, and trust as key factors. Koksal (2016) reveals the fundamental factors that separate consumers with a high intention to adopt mobile banking from other consumers in Lebanon. Factors identified include perceived compatibility, trialability, perceived usefulness, perceived ease of use, perceived credibility, and trust. A recent survey conducted in Lebanon among banking customers shows that digital literacy, resistance to change, perceived risk, perceived ease of use, and perceived usefulness significantly influence user attitudes toward mobile banking adoption, while awareness and compatibility have no statistically significant impact (Elhajjar and Ouaida 2020). Riquelme and Rios (2010) tested the factors influencing mobile banking adoption among current Internet banking users in Singapore and showed that perceived usefulness, social norms, and perception of risk directly influence mobile banking adoption intention, while relative advantage and perceived ease of use influence indirectly through perceived usefulness. Priya et al. (2018) found that the determinants of mobile banking adoption among younger Indian consumers were perceived usefulness, perceived ease of use, perceived credibility, structural assurance, while perceived risk did not show a significant impact on the behavioral intention to use these services. A very interesting study in India was conducted by Chawla and Joshi (2017). They used five factors for cluster analysis that influence user perception of mobile banking—ease of use, convenience, efficiency, trust, and lifestyle. Analyzing the above factors, the authors formed three clusters of consumers who differ in terms of attitude and intention toward mobile banking: technology adoption leaders (TA leaders), technology adoption followers (TA followers), and those who lag behind in technology adoption (TA laggards). In the same study, it was assessed that the included clusters differ in terms of age in such a way that technology adoption leaders (TA leaders) are primarily younger users who are inclined to accept new innovations, while those who lag behind in technology adoption (TA laggards) are mainly older users who show doubt and greater resistance in adopting new innovations. Another extensive study was conducted among banking customers in India by Singh and Srivastava (2018) and they found that security, computer self-efficacy, perceived ease of use, and perceived financial cost had influenced consumers' intention to use mobile banking. Hanafizadeh et al. (2014) examined the impact of eight variables on the adoption of mobile banking in Iran. The research results show that perceived usefulness, perceived ease of use, compatibility with lifestyle, perceived credibility, and trust positively influence, while perceived risk, perceived cost, and need for interaction negatively influence the adoption of mobile banking. Makanyeza (2017) surveyed banking customers in Zimbabwe and found that perceived usefulness, perceived self-efficacy, social influence, relative advantage, and perceived compatibility had a positive influence, while perceived risk negatively influenced consumers' intention to adopt mobile banking services. Tan and Lau (2016) examined Malaysian Generation Y consumers' intention to adopt mobile banking services, and based on the results, they concluded that performance expectancy was the strongest predictor of intention to adopt these services, followed by effort expectancy, perceived risk, and social impact. According to Farah et al. (2018), significant predictors of intention to adopt mobile banking in Pakistan are perceived value, performance expectancy, habit, social influence, effort expectancy, hedonic motivation, perceived risk, and trust. Van et al. (2021) investigated consumers of one of the largest joint-stock commercial banks in Vietnam came to the result that trust, perceived ease of use, and perceived usefulness had been positively related to the intention to use mobile banking, while perceived risk had been negatively related to this intention. Based on an empirical study conducted in North Macedonia, Mijoska Belsoska et al. (2020) found that performance expectancy, effort expectancy, facilitating conditions, perceived risk, and bank's reputation determined consumers' intention to use mobile banking services, while social influence had no significant effect on their intention to use these services. Mortimer et al. (2015) investigated motivational factors toward mobile banking in two countries—Thailand and Australia. Research findings indicate that perceived risk, perceived usefulness, and social influence are the main determinants of mobile banking adoption in Australia, while in Thailand, perceived ease of use, perceived usefulness, and perceived risk play an important role in determining user behavior. Comparing three different consumer segments (Egyptian consumers living in Egypt, Egyptian consumers living in the U.S., and American consumers in the U.S.), Hassan and Wood (2020) identify factors that directly influence the intention to use mobile banking services: perceived usefulness, trust, and social influence. Both of the aforementioned studies show that national culture influences consumers' intention to adopt mobile banking. Several studies have investigated the factors influencing customers' refusal to use mobile banking services. Laforet and Li (2005) researched the market status of mobile banking in China and concluded that the main barriers to the adoption of mobile banking were the lack of awareness and understanding of the benefits provided by mobile banking. Based on a survey of non-users of mobile banking in Ghana, Iddris (2013) states the following as the main reasons for refusing to use mobile banking: (1) mobile banking requires knowledge and learning; (2) mobile banking attract additional costs; (3) poor telecommunication network; and (4) consumer preference for traditional means of banking. It was determined that the influence of the observed factors differed depending on the respondents' income level, age, and marital status.

3 The Hypotheses Development and Research Framework

Previous studies have applied various conceptual frameworks and models to study mobile banking adoption (Souiden et al. 2021): technology of acceptance model (TAM) as a dominant theoretical model, followed by unified theory of acceptance and usage of technology (UTAUT/UTAUT 2), diffusion of innovation (DOI), and task technology fit (TTF). This research starts from the TAM model taking into account "its reported reliability and validity in measuring the acceptance of numerous innovative technologies within a variety of societies and cultures" (Hassan and Wood 2020, p. 4). According to the TAM model, the two key determinants of mobile banking adoption are perceived usefulness and perceived ease of use (Davis 1989). The TAM model in this study was extended by including five more determinants of intention to use mobile banking services: perceived risk, trust, social influence, lifestyle, and perceived self-efficacy. Perceived ease of use is the degree to which a person believes they could use mobile banking with a minimum of effort (Davis 1989, p. 320). If mobile banking services are easy to use, it will relieve consumers of fatigue and simplify their way of using these services (Priya et al. 2018, pp. 746–748). Numerous studies have confirmed the positive relationship between perceived ease of use and intention to use mobile banking services (Luarn and Lin 2005; Gu et al. 2009; Hanafizadeh et al. 2014; Talukder et al. 2014; Mortimer et al. 2015; Koksal 2016; Alalwan et al. 2016a; Singh and Srivastava 2018). Therefore, if consumers perceive mobile banking services as easy to use, they are more likely to adopt them. Based on the above, the following hypothesis can be formulated:

H1: Perceived ease of use positively affects consumers' intention to use mobile banking services.

Perceived usefulness refers to the degree to which a person believes using a mobile banking system would improve his or her work performance (Davis 1989, p. 320). People use mobile banking because they believe it is useful for their banking transactions, and this usefulness is primarily reflected in lower costs and time savings (Priya et al. 2018, p. 746). Other studies also found a positive influence of perceived usefulness on consumers' intention to use mobile banking services (Luarn and Lin 2005; Riquelme and Rios 2010; Koenig-Lewis et al. 2010; Talukder et al. 2014; Mortimer et al. 2015; Alalwan et al. 2016a; Makanyeza 2017; Hassan and Wood 2020; Elhajjar and Ouaida 2020). Accordingly, the following hypothesis is put forward:

H2: Perceived usefulness positively affects consumers' intention to use mobile banking services.

The risk in mobile banking is even higher "because mobility increases the threat of security violations" (Riquelme and Rios 2010, p. 331), and security is the most important factor that motivates consumers to adopt mobile banking (Laforet and Li 2005). Mobile banking users are mostly afraid of financial fraud, loss of PIN code, the appearance of many hackers, and loss of the mobile device (Priya et al. 2018, p. 749). A review of relevant studies indicates that perceived risk is negatively related to the intention to use mobile banking services (Mortimer et al. 2015; Alalwan et al. 2016a; Tan and Lau 2016; Makanyeza 2017; Munoz-Leiva et al. 2017; Van et al. 2021). Accordingly, the following hypothesis can be formulated:

H3: Perceived risk negatively affects consumers' intention to use mobile banking services.

Trust is defined "as the subjective probability with which customers believe that a particular transaction occurs in a manner consistent with their confident expectations" (Koksal 2016, p. 334). Non-adopters of mobile banking claim that initial trust significantly influenced their intention to use mobile banking services (Chiu et al. 2017). Several more studies state trust as one of the strongest drivers of consumers' intention to use m-banking (Hanafizadeh et al. 2014; Koksal 2016; Alalwan et al. 2017; Farah et al. 2018; Van et al. 2021). Starting from the above, the following hypothesis is put forward:

H4: Trust has a positive effect on consumers' intention to use mobile banking services.

Social influence is defined as the degree to which an individual cares about other people's opinions about whether he or she should use mobile banking services (Venkatesh et al. 2003, p. 451). Previous studies have shown an association between social influence and intention to use mobile banking (Amin et al. 2008; Riquelme and Rios 2010; Tan and Lau 2016; Farah et al. 2018; Hassan and Wood 2020). Therefore, individuals are likely to adopt mobile banking services if they are encouraged to do so by important people in their lives, which points to the following hypothesis:

H5: Social influence has a positive effect on consumers' intention to use mobile banking services.

Perceived self-efficacy can be defined "as the judgment of one's ability to use mobile banking" (Koksal 2016, p. 334). Several studies confirm a positive relationship between perceived self-efficacy and consumers' intention to use mobile banking (Luarn and Lin 2005; Makanyeza 2017; Singh and Srivastava 2018). The compatibility of mobile banking services with the consumer's lifestyle is another important factor that encourages the use of these services (Koenig-Lewis et al. 2010; Chemingui and Ben Iallouna 2013; Hanafizadeh et al. 2014). The same conclusion is reached by Lin (2011), who states that consumers who find mobile banking to fit their lifestyle enjoy performing m-banking transactions. Consumers are more likely to adopt mobile banking if they believe they have the skills needed to use these services and if the mobile banking services are compatible with their lifestyle. Accordingly, the following hypotheses are derived:

H6: Perceived self-efficacy has a positive effect on consumers' intention to use mobile banking services.

H7: Lifestyle has a positive influence on consumers' intention to use mobile banking services.

Figure 1 presents a conceptual model that examines the impact of perceived ease of use, perceived usefulness, perceived risk, trust, social influence, lifestyle, and perceived self-efficacy on consumers' intention to use mobile banking services. A

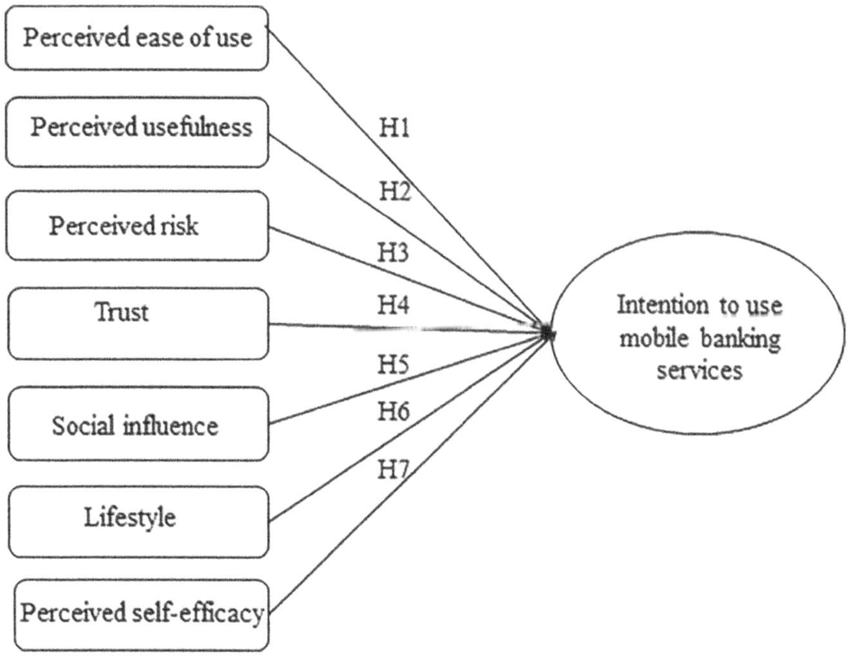

Fig. 1 Conceptual model

better understanding of these relationships helps banks retain existing and attract new customers and achieve a competitive advantage in the markets they serve.

4 Research Methodology

The study presented in this paper is based on findings obtained in quantitative research using the survey technique. A structured questionnaire, divided into three parts, was used as an instrument. The first part includes four questions that reveal habits regarding the use of mobile banking services, with the first question being a filter question separating the group of mobile banking users from those who have never used this type of service. The second part consists of 36 statements (items) measured on a five-point Likert scale that refer to the observed variables of mobile banking (1—I do not agree at all, 5—I completely agree). Items from this part of the questionnaire are grouped into seven variables and have been taken from earlier research (Table 1). The second part of the questionnaire includes five questions related to the respondents' demographic characteristics (gender, age, education, work status, and monthly income).

The research was conducted on a convenient sample, and banking clients from Serbia participated in the survey. In order to enable the participation of different

Table 1 Constructs, items, and source

Construct/source	Items
Perceived ease of use (Davis 1989; Chawla and Joshi 2018)	It is easy for me to learn to use mobile banking services
	Instructions for using mobile banking are easy to follow
	Interacting with mobile banking does not require much mental effort
	It is easy to become adept at using mobile banking services
Perceived usefulness (Davis 1989; Hassan and Wood 2020)	I can manage my banking activities much more efficiently by using mobile banking
	Using mobile banking improves my performance in doing banking transactions
	Using mobile banking allows me to complete my banking activities faster
	Mobile banking is more suitable for banking transactions than other channels of distribution of banking services
	Overall, I find mobile banking services very useful
Perceived risk (Featherman and Pavlou 2003; Martins et al. 2014)	Using mobile banking exposes my bank account to potential fraud
	Using mobile banking puts my privacy at risk
	The security systems built into the mobile banking system are not strong enough to protect my bank account
	I feel that I will waste time if I switch to mobile banking
	Using mobile banking can negatively affect other people's opinions of me
	Using mobile banking does not fit into my personal concept or personal image
	Using mobile banking exposes me to overall risk
Trust (Chawla and Joshi 2018)	I find mobile banking to be reliable
	Mobile banking sites take into account the interests of users
	My bank provides secure mobile banking
	Mobile banking sites do not disclose my personal information
Social influence (Venkatesh et al. 2003, 2012)	People important to me think that I should use mobile banking services
	People who influence my behavior think that I should use mobile banking services
	My bank supports the use of mobile banking services
Lifestyle (Chawla and Joshi 2018)	Mobile banking is compatible with my lifestyle
	Embracing mobile banking fits perfectly with the way I want to manage my banking activities

(continued)

Table 1 (continued)

Construct/source	Items
	Embracing mobile banking fits well with my work style
	I consider mobile banking to be compatible with my profession
Perceived self-efficacy (Compeau and Higgins 1995; Alalwan et al. 2016b)	I could complete a transaction using mobile banking without anyone's help
	I could complete the transaction using mobile banking with someone's help if needed
	I could complete the transaction using mobile banking if there is a built-in help feature
	I could complete a transaction using mobile banking even though I have never used such a system before
Intention of use (Venkatesh et al. 2012; Anouze and Alamro 2020)	I intend to use mobile banking in the future
	I will try to always use mobile banking in my daily life
	I plan to use mobile banking more often in the future
	I will recommend others to use mobile banking
	I am satisfied with the benefits of using mobile banking

groups of respondents and increase the participation rate, the questionnaire was published online (Google Survey Form) and distributed through various social media channels and e-mail. The survey was carried out in two intervals, from May 15 to June 5, 2021, and from January 25 to February 4, 2022. The final sample included 223 respondents, whose demographic characteristics are shown in Table 2. The results presented in the following part of the paper were obtained on the basis of descriptive statistics, correlation analysis, regression analysis, and cluster analysis.

Out of the total number of participants (223), 142 (63.68%) use mobile banking services, while 81 (36.32%) do not use mobile banking services. Regarding the sample structure, 85 participants (38.1%) were male, and 138 (69.1%) were female. Taking into account the age structure of the respondents, the majority of participants were younger than 27 years—78 (35%), followed by respondents between 28 and 43 years old—66 (29.6%), then 60 (26.9%) of respondents were between 44 and 57 years old. In our sample, 16 (7.2%) respondents were between 58 and 77 years old, and 3 (1.3%) participants were older than 78. The educational structure of the respondents was such that the majority of respondents were highly educated—114 (51%), of which 42 respondents (18.8%) have completed basic studies, 17 respondents (38%) have completed master's studies, and 34 (15.2%) have completed Ph.D. studies. 95 (42.6%) respondents completed high school, and 14 (6.3%) finished university. Respondents were predominantly permanently employed—110 (49.3%), followed by respondents who are students—69 (30.9%), temporarily employed—29 (13%), retired—9 (4%), and unemployed—6 (2.7%).

Table 2 Demographic structure of the sample

Characteristics of respondents		Number of respondents	% of respondents
Total		223	100
Gender	Male	85	38.1
	Female	138	61.9
Year of birth	Between 1925 and 1945	3	1.3
	Between 1945 and 1964	16	7.2
	Between 1965 and 1978	60	26.9
	Between 1979 and 1994	66	29.6
	Between 1995 and 2012	78	35.0
Education	High School	95	42.6
	Higher School (3 years)	14	6.3
	Bachelor's degree (4 years or more)	42	18.8
	Master's degree	38	17.0
	Ph.D. degree	34	15.2
Work status	Full-time job	110	49.3
	Temporarily employed	29	13.0
	Unemployed	6	2.7
	Pupil/student	69	30.9
	Pensioner	9	4.0

5 Research Results

Out of the total number of respondents (223), 142 of them (63.7%) use mobile banking services, while 81 of them (36.3%) do not use mobile banking services. Of the 25 banks operating in Serbia, the largest number of respondents use the services of Unicredit banka—30 (13.5%), followed by Banka Intesa—25 (11.2%), Komercijalna banka—23 (10.3%), AIK banka—10 (4.5%), and Raiffeisen banka—10 (4.5%). Regarding the length of time of using mobile banking, the largest number of respondents, 54 (38%), have used mobile banking services between 1 and 4 years, while the number of respondents who are new users of these services, i.e., they have used them for less than a year, the same as the number of respondents who have used mobile banking services between 4 and 8 years, which is 36 (25.4%). There were 16 (11.3%) respondents who have used mobile banking for more than 8 years. As for the frequency of using mobile banking services, the largest number of users, 115 (80.8%), use mobile banking services within a month, with 39 (27.5%) of them using these services once a month, followed by respondents who use the services once a week—38 (26.5%), once in 3–4 days—19 (13.4%), almost every day—17 (12%), and several times a day 2 of them (1.4%). Other respondents use mobile banking services somewhat less frequently, 12 of them (8.5%) once in three months, 4 of them (2.8%) once in six months, and 11 of them (7.7%) once a year. During the research, it was ensured that the measuring scale had been reliable, that is, that there was an internal consistency of the scale. The internal consistency of the

Table 3 Reliability analysis

Variables	The Cronbach's alpha coefficient value
Perceived ease of use	0.769
Perceived usefulness	0.874
Perceived risk	0.850
Trust	0.794
Social influence	0.710
Lifestyle	0.875
Perceived self-efficacy	0.659
Intention of use	0.900

statements used to measure the research variables was evaluated by looking at the value of the Cronbach's alpha coefficient. The value of this coefficient ranges from 0 to 1, whereby all values above 0.70 are considered acceptable (Pallant 2011). The Cronbach's alpha coefficient values for all variables that make up the conceptual model vary from 0.659 to 0.900 (Table 3). The obtained values show that almost all variables in the research, except for the variable perceived self-efficacy, whose Cronbach's alpha coefficient value is at the threshold level, have high reliability, i.e. they are measured through internally consistent findings.

Correlation analysis was conducted to determine whether there was a relationship between the variables of the baseline model and establish the relationship's direction and strength. In this case, the relationship was investigated using the Pearson coefficient, whose value from 0.1 to 0.29 indicates a weak correlation, from 0.30 to 0.49 to a moderate one, while a value from 0.50 to 1.0 indicates a strong correlation (Pallant 2011). The attached Table 4 shows that only between perceived self-efficacy and perceived risk, there is no statistically significant linear correlation ($p = 0.645$). The strongest degree of linear correlation exists between the variables perceived usefulness and lifestyle ($r = 0.747$, $p < 0.0005$), as well as between the variables lifestyle and intention to use ($r = 0.741$, $p < 0.0005$). Perceived risk has a statistically significant but negative correlation with all other variables. The weakest but statistically significant correlation ($r = 0.185$, $p = 0.028$) was confirmed between the variables trust and perceived self-efficacy.

In order to determine the degree and direction of the relationship between the dependent (intention to use—y) and independent variables (perceived ease of use—x_1, perceived usefulness—x_2, perceived risk—x_3, trust—x_4, social influence—x_5, lifestyle—x_6, and perceived self-efficacy—x_7), univariate and multivariate regression analysis is conducted. Using regression analysis makes it possible to determine the connection between dependent and independent variables, as well as how changes in independent variables (as predictors) affect changes in the dependent (categorical) variable (Marinković et al. 2018). Univariate linear regression showed that perceived ease of use was significantly related to intention to use mobile banking services. Coefficient B is 0.534, which means that every increase in ease of use leads to an increase in intention to use by 0.534. As $F = 34.227$, $p < 0.0005$, this linear model significantly predicts the values of the dependent variable of intention to use.

Table 4 Correlation matrix

	Perceived ease of use	Perceived usefulness	Perceived risk	Trust	Social influence	Lifestyle	Perceived self-efficacy	Intention of use
Perceived ease of use		0.577**	−0.286**	0.275**	0.338**	0.424**	0.242**	0.443**
Perceived usefulness			−0.492**	0.425**	0.368**	0.747**	0.308**	0.746**
Perceived risk				−0.436**	−0.251**	0.410**	−0.039	−0.414**
Trust					0.476**	0.397**	0.185*	0.434**
Social influence						0.480**	0.332**	0.477**
Lifestyle							0.365**	0.741**
Perceived self-efficacy								0.364**

* Correlation is significant at the 0.01, * Correlation is significant at the 0.05 level

Table 5 Univariate regression for the dependent variable of intention to use mobile banking services

Independent variables	R^2	p	Model
Perceived usefulness	0.557	<0.0005	$y = 0.636 + 0.846x_2$
Perceived risk	0.172	<0.0005	$y = 5.254 - 0.380x_3$
Trust	0.188	<0.0005	$y = 2.781 + 0.425x_4$
Social influence	0.228	<0.0005	$y = 2.833 + 0.409x_5$
Lifestyle	0.549	<0.0005	$y = 1.510 + 0.685x_6$
Perceived self-efficacy	0.132	<0.0005	$y = 3.191 + 0.317x_7$

Table 6 Cluster analysis

Statement	Cluster 1	Cluster 2
I intend to use mobile banking in the future.	3.43	4.97
I will recommend others to use mobile banking.	3.45	4.89
I am satisfied with the benefits of using mobile banking.	3.63	4.85
I will try to always use mobile banking in my daily life.	3.25	4.81
I plan to use mobile banking more often in the future.	3.30	4.80

R^2 is 0.196, which means that the model explains 19.6% of the variance of intention to use. The model for the dependent variable is: $y = 2.082 + 0.534x_1$. That confirms the first research hypothesis. Similarly, from Table 5, the connection of a variable intention to use with other independent variables is interpreted, confirming all other research hypotheses.

Using multivariate regression analysis, the stepwise method, three independent variables are kept as significant predictor variables in the model: perceived usefulness, lifestyle, and social influence ($p < 0.0005$). The regression model is:

$$y = 0.353 + 0.490 \times \text{Perceived usefulness} + 0.131 \times \text{Social influence} + 0.319 \times \text{Lifestyle} \quad (1)$$

and describes 65.1% of the variability of intention to use ($R^2 = 0.651$) through changes in these variables, with the condition of multicollinearity being met (Variance Inflation Factor—VIF value is less than 5).

Finally, by applying cluster analysis, respondents were grouped according to the similarity of the ratings they gave to the variable of intention to use. Based on the cluster analysis results, two clusters can be identified, which are formed according to the homogeneity of the responses regarding the intention to use mobile banking. The results are given in Table 6.

Thirty-eight respondents belong to the first cluster, while 96 belong to the second cluster. Based on these data, our sample confirmed a great homogeneity in respondents' answers and their classification into two clusters that included almost all respondents who use mobile banking services (a total of 8 respondents were not in these two clusters). Based on the average answers of the respondents about the intention to use mobile banking in the first cluster, we can characterize this cluster as a segment of probable users of mobile banking services, to whom the benefits of using should be brought closer, either through educational workshops or through familiarization with greater possibilities of its use, outside of the range they are currently using. As far as the specific structure of respondents in the first cluster is concerned, it is dominated by female (63.2%), respondents with completed high school education (60.5%), born in the period 1994–2012 (47.4%), of which 44.7% are permanently employed, and the same number are students. The second cluster consists of respondents with the strongest intentions to use mobile banking services. In this cluster, too, female are more represented (55.2%). At the same time, the difference is present in the educational structure—the largest number of respondents have higher education (68.8% of respondents, of which 24% have completed bachelor studies, 23% have completed doctoral studies, and 19.8% have completed master's studies). The largest number of respondents were born in the period 1979–1994 year (35.4%), followed by respondents born in the period from 1965 to 1978 (32.3%). The largest number of respondents who belong to the second cluster are permanently employed (58.3%).

6 Conclusion

Modern business processes and life habits are largely shaped under the influence of advanced technology, which has become ubiquitous in the private and business life. Consequently, banks are forced to develop electronic distribution channels to make their services more accessible to clients. Among the mentioned distribution channels, mobile banking has been singled out as the most effective, which perfectly fits the modern consumer's expectations that the necessary services are constantly available. Due to the widespread infrastructure that enables the unhindered use of mobile telephony, mobile banking has become the most accessible platform for using banking services worldwide. This has partially alleviated the large gap in the availability of banking services between developed and developing countries. Mobile banking is increasingly prevalent in Serbia, thanks to smart mobile devices, efficient mobile banking applications developed by banks, and the need to conduct as many transactions as possible online, imposed both by the modern lifestyle and the emergence of the COVID-19 pandemic. One of the most important questions regarding mobile banking for providers of the mentioned service and researchers is the intention of bank clients to use mobile banking services and the factors that influence that intention. This paper has analyzed the intention of using mobile banking services by banking clients in Serbia. In the sample, the most represented respondents were female, born after 1995, with completed high school, and a full-time job. Among the respondents, 2/3 started to use mobile banking services relatively recently. Starting from the determinants of the use of mobile banking covered by the TAM model and the application of correlation and regression analysis, the paper reached the following results. Correlation analysis shows that there is mostly a positive and statistically significant linear correlation between the variables of the used model. However, only perceived risk has a statistically significant but negative correlation with all other variables. Considering the influence of certain variables of the used model on the intention to use mobile banking services, the univariate correlation analysis showed that perceived usefulness, perceived ease of use, trust, social influence, lifestyle, and perceived self-efficacy have a positive influence on the intention to use mobile banking. In contrast, the impact of perceived risk is negative. On the other hand, using multivariate regression analysis, perceived usefulness, lifestyle, and social impact were singled out as significant predictor variables. The research was completed with the application of cluster analysis, through which the respondents were grouped into two clusters according to the homogeneity of the given answers. Based on the conducted cluster analysis, it is concluded that the strongest intentions to use mobile banking services are shown by female respondents born in the period 1979–1994, with higher education degree and permanent employment. This study is equally useful for both practitioners and theorists because it provides a deeper insight into consumer behavior in mobile banking in developing countries. Based on the identified determinants, the obtained research results can help commercial banks formulate appropriate strategies for reducing resistance to mobile banking and increasing the adoption rate of mobile banking services in Serbia. The limitations of the conducted research include a relatively small and suitable sample and the non-use of moderator variables. Recommendations for future research are to expand the sample used, use newer research models in mobile banking such as UTAUT or UTAUT 2, and include moderate variables.

References

Akturan U, Tezcan N (2012) Mobile banking adoption of the youth market: perceptions and intentions. Mark Intell Plan 30(4):444–459. https://doi.org/10.1108/02634501211231928

Alalwan AA, Dwivedi YK, Rana NPP, Williams MD (2016a) Consumer adoption of mobile banking in Jordan: examining the role of useful-ness, ease of use, perceived risk and self-efficacy. J Enterp Inf Manag 29(1):118–139. https://doi.org/10.1108/JEIM-04-2015-0035

Alalwan AA, Dwivedi YK, Rana NP, Simintiras AC (2016b) Jordanian consumers' adoption of telebanking: influence of perceived useful-ness, trust and self-efficacy. Int J Bank Mark 34(5): 690–709. https://doi.org/10.1108/IJBM-06-2015-0093

Alalwan AA, Dwivedi YK, Rana NP (2017) Factors influencing adoption of mobile banking by Jordanian bank customers: extending UTAUT2 with trust. Int J Inf Manag 37(3):99–110. https://doi.org/10.1016/j.ijinfomgt.2017.01.002

Amin H, Rizal M, Hamid A, Lada S, Anis Z (2008) The adoption of mobile banking in Malaysia: the case of Bank Islam Malaysia Berhad (BIMB). Int J Bus Soc 9(2):43–53

Anouze ALM, Alamro AS (2020) Factors affecting intention to use e-banking in Jordan. Int J Bank Mark 38(1):86–112. https://doi.org/10.1108/IJBM-10-2018-0271

Chawla D, Joshi H (2017) Consumer perspectives about mobile banking adoption in India-a cluster analysis. Int J Bank Mark 35(4):616–636. https://doi.org/10.1108/IJBM-03-2016-0037

Chawla D, Joshi H (2018) The moderating effect of demographic variables on mobile banking adoption: an empirical investigation. Glob Bus Rev 19(3):90–113. https://doi.org/10.1177/0972150918757883

Chemingui H, Ben Iallouna H (2013) Resistance, motivations, trust and intention to use mobile financial services. Int J Bank Mark 31(7):574–592. https://doi.org/10.1108/IJBM-12-2012-0124

Chitungo S, Munongo S (2013) Extending the technology acceptance model to mobile banking adoption in rural Zimbabwe. J Bus Adm Educ 3(1):51–79

Chiu JL, Bool NC, Chiu CL (2017) Challenges and factors influencing initial trust and behavioral intention to use mobile banking services in the Philippines. Asia Pac J Innov Entrepreneur 11(2):246–278. https://doi.org/10.1108/APJIE-08-2017-029

Compeau D, Higgins C (1995) Application of social cognitive theory to training for computer skills. Inf Syst Res 6(2):118–143. https://doi.org/10.1287/isre.6.2.118

Dahlberg T, Mallat N, Ondrus J, Zmijewska A (2008) Past, present and future of mobile payments research: a literature review. Electron Commer Res Appl 7(2):165–181. https://doi.org/10.1016/j.elerap.2007.02.001

Davis FD (1989) Perceived usefulness, perceived ease of use, and user acceptance of information technology. MIS Q 13(3):319–340. https://doi.org/10.2307/249008

Elhajjar S, Ouaida F (2020) An analysis of factors affecting mobile bank-ing adoption. Int J Bank Mark 38(2):352–367. https://doi.org/10.1108/IJBM-02-2019-0055

Farah MF, Hasni MJS, Abbas AK (2018) Mobile-banking adoption: empirical evidence from the banking sector in Pakistan. Int J Bank Mark 36(7):1386–1413. https://doi.org/10.1108/IJBM-10-2017-0215

Featherman MS, Pavlou PA (2003) Predicting e-services adoption: a perceived risk facets perspective. Int J Hum-Comput Stud 59(4):451–474. https://doi.org/10.1016/S1071-5819(03)00111-3

Giraud G, Amblard C, Thiel E, Zaouche-Laniau M, Stojanović Ž, Pohar J, Butigan R, Cvetković M, Mugosa B, Kendrovski V, Mora C, Barjolle D (2013) A cross-cultural segmentation of western Balkan consumers: focus on preferences toward traditional fresh cow cheese. J Sci Food Agric 93(14):3464–3472. https://doi.org/10.1002/jsfa.6350

Grubor A, Djokić N (2016) Organic food consumer profile in the Republic of Serbia. Br Food J 118(1):164–182. https://doi.org/10.1108/BFJ-06-2015-0225

Gu JC, Lee SC, Suh YH (2009) Determinants of behavioral intention to mobile banking. Expert Syst Appl 36(9):11605–11616. https://doi.org/10.1016/j.eswa.2009.03.024

Hanafizadeh P, Behboudi M, Koshksaray A, Tabar M (2014) Mobile-banking adoption by Iranian bank clients. Telematics Inform 31(1):62–78. https://doi.org/10.1016/j.tele.2012.11.001

Hassan HE, Wood VR (2020) Does country culture influence consumers' perceptions toward mobile banking? A comparison between Egypt and the United States. Telematics Inform 46: 101312. https://doi.org/10.1016/j.tele.2019.101312

Ho JC, Wu CG, Lee CS, Pham TTT (2020) Factors affecting the behavioral intention to adopt mobile banking: an international comparison. Technol Soc 63:101360. https://doi.org/10.1016/j.techsoc.2020.101360

Iddris F (2013) Barriers to adoption of mobile banking: evidence from Ghana. Int J Acad Res Bus Soc Sci 3(7):356–370. https://doi.org/10.6007/IJARBSS/v3-i7/59

Jebarajakirthy C, Shankar A (2021) Impact of online convenience on mobile banking adoption intention: a moderated mediation approach. J Retail Consum Serv 58:102323. https://doi.org/10.1016/j.jretconser.2020.102323

Kalinić Z, Marinković V (2016) Determinants of users' intention to adopt mcommerce: an empirical analysis. IseB 14(2):367–387. https://doi.org/10.1007/s10257-015-0287-2

Kalinić Z, Marinković V, Đorđević A, Liébana-Cabanillas F (2019) What drives customer satisfaction and word of mouth in mobile commerce services? A UTAUT2- based analytical approach. J Enterp Inf Manag 33(1):71–94. https://doi.org/10.1108/JEIM-05-2019-0136

Koenig-Lewis N, Palmer A, Moll A (2010) Predicting young consumers' take up of m-banking services. Int J Bank Mark 28(5):410–432. https://doi.org/10.1108/02652321011064917

Koksal MH (2016) The intentions of Lebanese consumers to adopt mo-bile banking. Int J Bank Mark 34(3):327–346. https://doi.org/10.1108/IJBM-03-2015-0025

Laforet S, Li X (2005) Consumers' attitudes towards online and mobile banking in China. Int J Bank Mark 23(5):362–380. https://doi.org/10.1108/02652320510629250

Lekpek A (2021) Cryptocurrencies in the Islamic financial system viewed through the prism of Shariah law. Anali Pravnog fakulteta u Beogradu 69(2):371–388. https://doi.org/10.51204/Anali_PFBU_21204A

Liébana-Cabanillas F, Marinković V, Kalinić Z (2017) A SEM-neural network approach for predicting antecedents of m-commerce acceptance. Int J Inf Manag 37(2):14–24. https://doi.org/10.1016/j.ijinfomgt.2016.10.008

Lin H (2011) An empirical investigation of mobile banking adoption: the effect of innovation attributes and knowledge-based trust. Int J Inf Manag 31(3):252–260. https://doi.org/10.1016/j.ijinfomgt.2010.07.006

Luarn P, Lin HH (2005) Toward an understanding of the behavioral intention to use mobile banking. Comput Hum Behav 21(6):873–891. https://doi.org/10.1016/j.chb.2004.03.003

Lukić V, Čolić L, Prica I (2019) Perspectives and adoption of mobile banking in Serbia: the case of young adults. Ekonomika preduzeća 67(5–6):334–344. https://doi.org/10.5937/EKOPRE1906334L

Makanyeza C (2017) Determinants of consumers' intention to adopt m-banking services in Zimbabwe. Int J Bank Mark 35(6):997–1017. https://doi.org/10.1108/IJBM-07-2016-0099

Marinković V, Kalinić Z (2017) Antecedents of customer satisfaction in mobile commerce: exploring the moderating effect of customization. Online Inf Rev 41(2):138–154. https://doi.org/10.1108/OIR-11-2015-0364

Marinković S, Šabotić Z, Banković D (2018) EU enlargement: does eco-nomics of regional integration matter? Zbornik radova Ekonomskog fakulteta u Rijeci: časopis za ekonomsku teoriju i praksu 36(2):881–904. https://doi.org/10.18045/zbefri.2018.2.881

Martins C, Oliveira T, Popovič A (2014) Understanding the internet banking adoption: a unified theory of acceptance and use of technology and perceived risk application. Int J Inf Manag 34(1):1–13. https://doi.org/10.1016/j.ijinfomgt.2013.06.002

Mijoska Belsoska M, Trpkova-Nesterovska M, Treneska Blagoeva K (2020) Predicting consumer intention to use mobile banking services in North Macedonia. Int J Multidiscipl Bus Sci 6(10): 5–12

Mitić S, Vehapi S (2021) Food choice motives of generation Z in Serbia. Econ Agric 68(1): 127–140. https://doi.org/10.5937/ekoPolj2101127M

Mortimer G, Neale L, Hasan SFE, Dunphy B (2015) Investigating the factors influencing the adoption of m-banking: a cross cultural study. Int J Bank Mark 33(4):545–570. https://doi.org/10.1108/IJBM-07-2014-0100

Munoz-Leiva F, Climent-Climent S, Liébana-Cabanillas F (2017) Determinants of intention to use the mobile banking apps: an extension of the classic TAM model. Spanish J Market - ESIC 21(1):25–38. https://doi.org/10.1016/j.sjme.2016.12.001

NBS (2021) Nastavlja se rast korišćenja savremenih oblika plaćanja. https://nbs.rs/sr/scripts/showcontent/index.html?id=17582

Oliveira T, Faria M, Thomas MA, Popovic A (2014) Extending the understanding of mobile banking adoption: when UTAUT meets TTF and ITM. Int J Inf Manag 34(5):689–703. https://doi.org/10.1016/j.ijinfomgt.2014.06.004

Pallant J (2011) SPSS survival manual: a step by step guide to data analysis using the SPSS program. Allen & Unwin, Berkshire

Pavlović G, Savić J (2017) Determinants of the intentions of consumers in terms of using mobile banking services. Mark Theory 48(2):96–106. https://doi.org/10.5937/Markt1702096P

Priya R, Gandhi AV, Shaikh A (2018) Mobile banking adoption in an emerging economy: an empirical analysis of young Indian consumers. BIJ 25(2):743–762. https://doi.org/10.1108/BIJ-01-2016-0009

Püschel J, Mazzon JA, Hernandez JMC (2010) Mobile banking: proposition of an integrated adoption intention framework. Int J Bank Mark 28(5):389–409. https://doi.org/10.1108/02652321011064908

Riquelme HE, Rios RE (2010) The moderating effect of gender in the adoption of mobile banking. Int J Bank Mark 28(5):328–341. https://doi.org/10.1108/02652321011064872

Shaikh A, Karjaluoto H (2015) Mobile banking adoption: a literature review. Telematics Inform 32(1):129–142. https://doi.org/10.1016/j.tele.2014.05.003

Singh S, Srivastava RK (2018) Predicting the intention to use mobile banking in India. Int J Bank Mark 36(2):357–378. https://doi.org/10.1108/IJBM-12-2016-0186

Souiden N, Ladhari R, Chaouali W (2021) Mobile banking adoption: a systematic review. Int J Bank Mark 39(2):214–241. https://doi.org/10.1108/IJBM-04-2020-0182

Talukder M, Quazi A, Sathye M (2014) Mobile phone banking usage behavior: an Australian perspective. Austral Acc Bus Financ J 8(4):83–104. https://doi.org/10.14453/aabfj.v8i4.6

Tan E, Lau LJ (2016) Behavioural intention to adopt mobile banking among the millennial generation. Young Consum 17(1):18–31. https://doi.org/10.1108/YC-07-2015-00537

Tan M, Teo TS (2000) Factors influencing the adoption of internet banking. J Assoc Inf Syst 1(1): 1–42

Van HN, Pham L, Williamson S, Chan CY, Thang TD, Nam VX (2021) Explaining intention to use mobile banking: integrating perceived risk and trust into the technology acceptance model. Int J Appl Decis Sci 14(1):55–80. https://doi.org/10.1504/IJADS.2021.112933

Vehapi S, Doličanin E (2016) Consumers behavior on organic food: evidence from the republic of Serbia. Econ Agric 63(3):871–889. https://doi.org/10.5937/ekoPolj1603871V

Vehapi S, Šabotić Z (2021) Willingness of generation Z consumers to pay more for organic food in Serbia. Mark Theory 52(4):247–258. https://doi.org/10.5937/mkng2104247V

Vehapi S, Šabotić Z, Lekpek A (2021) Determinants of the bank clients satisfaction with the internet banking services in Serbia. Mark Theory 52(2):83–94. https://doi.org/10.5937/mkng2102083V

Venkatesh V, Morris MG, Davis GB, Davis FD (2003) User acceptance of information technology: toward a unified view. MIS Q 27(3):425–478. https://doi.org/10.2307/30036540

Venkatesh V, Thong JYL, Xu X (2012) Consumer acceptance and use of information technology: extending the unified theory of acceptance and use of technology. MIS Q 36(1):157–178. https://doi.org/10.2307/41410412

Yuan S, Liu Y, Yao R, Liu J (2016) An investigation of users' continuance intention towards mobile banking in China. Inf Dev 32(1):20–34. https://doi.org/10.1177/0266666914522140

New Ways of Providing Public Services: Platforms of Service Provision and the Role of Artificial Intelligence: In the Light of the Development of the Hungarian Public Administration

István Hoffman and András Bencsik

Abstract Platforms became important ecosystems in the economic life after the end of the twentieth century. In order to operate more efficiently, platforms as an ecosystem and technology are now widely applied by the different national public administration systems. However, platforms are mainly used by the central administration; the municipalities started to build their own systems. There are several limitations of the application of the platforms in public administration—the majority of them are linked to a lack of resources and expertise. Platforms can be even tools of a latent, 'stealth' centralisation, mainly because of the required access to the central data systems. It should be emphasised that the platforms—especially in the business (private) sector—are linked to artificial intelligence (AI) tools. However, compared to the business sector, the government sector has several specialties by which the application of AI is influenced. Therefore, these specialties and the possibilities of the use of AI by the Hungarian public administration are reviewed in our chapter.

Keywords Platforms · Platform services · Administrative platforms · AI and administration · Hungarian administration

---

I. Hoffman (✉)
Faculty of Law; Department of Administrative Law, Eötvös Loránd University, Budapest, Hungary

Centre for Social Sciences, Institute for Legal Studies, Budapest, Hungary

Faculty of Law and Administration, Department of International Public Law, Maria Curie-Skłodowska University, Lublin, Poland
e-mail: hoffman.istvan@ajk.elte.hu; hoffman.istvan@tk.mta.hu

A. Bencsik
Faculty of Law; Department of Administrative Law, Eötvös Loránd University, Budapest, Hungary

Faculty of Law, Department of Financial Law, Károli Gáspár University of the Reformed Church in Hungary, Budapest, Hungary

S. Benković et al. (eds.), *Digital Transformation of the Financial Industry*,
Contributions to Finance and Accounting,
https://doi.org/10.1007/978-3-031-23269-5_10

1 Introduction

First of all, it should be emphasised that social systems have been transformed by the ICT revolution. This extremely rapid transformation has also brought significant changes to the economy, perhaps most notably in the last decade with the widespread adoption of platforms. Platforms can be approached from several angles: firstly, as a specific product development outcome, secondly, as a specific technological strategy, and thirdly, as an industrial economic phenomenon (Baldwin and Woodard 2009). Platforms can be examined from the perspective of market theory, technology management, and strategic management. However, platforms can also be analysed as a specific network, typically connected to the Internet, and as a specific system or as ecosystem. Platforms are interpreted by the market theory approaches as network interfaces connecting different groups and as systems that create value through a common architecture. The ability of the platforms to produce content and/or functionality is emphasised by the technology management approach. Similarly, these interpretations highlight that, on the other hand, they are standardised ecosystems which are highly interconnected and systemised. Corporate operation of the platforms as networks and systems of processes that create value is emphasised by the strategic management interpretations (Hein et al. 2020). These platforms that are most familiar to the general public are systems connected to the provision of services, including various entertainment platforms and systems (e.g. Netflix, HBO Max, Spotify), systems in the tourism sector (booking.com, Airbnb), and some personal service solutions (e.g. Uber, Taxify—now Bolt). However, the role of platforms is much broader than that: in fact, modern corporate governance relies extensively on these solutions, which can be easily adapted to your own corporate processes and to other companies' systems because they are standardised. Taking into account the impact and results of platforms in economic life, the administrative systems also have started to use platform-like solutions relatively early, at the turn of the millennium (Kim et al. 2022).

The aim of our chapter is to analyse the transformations of public service provision based on the digitalisation and platformisation. The theoretical and technical framework of these transformations has been examined by the chapter, the major field of public service provision which is impacted by the platforms, and last but not least, the impact of the transformation on the modern ecosystems and economics has been analysed.

2 Methods

The approach of the chapter has been mainly based on the approach of the administrative sciences. The theoretical framework of the platforms has been examined by the introductory part, as a framework of the analysis. This analysis was based on the methods of the management studies (Yablonski 2018).

As part of the analysis of the framework of public service platforms has been based on the methods of jurisprudence because the regulatory environment of this phenomena has been analysed. Our chapter focuses on the analysis of the regulation, and it focuses on the analysis of the legal norms, soft law documents, and partly the policy papers. Because the issues have a limited judicial practice, therefore, the judgements are just narrowly reviewed by our chapter (Evans et al. 2015). Secondly, the major fields of public service provisions have been examined by our chapter. Because the national legal systems are different, even in the European Union, our paper focuses on the analysis of a national—primarily the Hungarian—legislation and partly the legislation and regulation of the European Union (Bogdandy 2012). Thus, the regulatory issues have been part of the examination, but—as we have mentioned earlier—even the policy issues of these public services and platforms of them, and similarly the major economic data have been analysed. The data analysis is based on the review of the official statistical data, especially the data of the Eurostat.

Similarly, the social impacts of these changes have been part of the examination. The role of the AI and the technical possibilities have been analysed as well. The regulatory issues of the AI in the field of administrative tasks and public services are analysed by the chapter. The analysis on social impact is based on the brief examination of the quantitative statistical data. Similarly, social data provided by the national statistical offices are used by our review. Therefore, the chapter has not only a jurisprudential approach, but it has had a mixed, administrative methodology.

The 'platformisation' of the public services can be interpreted as a new phenomenon; the regulation and the statistical date offers limited information about it. However, this transformation has been analysed detailed by the literature, especially the literature on administrative and management sciences, and partly by jurisprudence. Therefore, it is important to review the major statements and results of the literature on the topic. Our chapter is significantly based on the analysis of the literature.

The major challenges and results of the transformations have been summarised by the chapter. Because this analysis focuses on the impact of these trends on economics, we would like to analyse the available and comparable economic data. The primary impact of the reforms on the government sector has been analysed by the chapter as well.

3 Hypotheses

The services of the business sector have been transformed by the introduction of the platforms, by which a new more effective and resilient ecosystem has been evolved. Platforms can be examined from the perspective of market theory, technology management, and strategic management. Public service provision—not only the traditional administrative services but even those services which are organised or performed by public bodies (e.g. health care, social care, education)—has been transformed by the establishment of platforms (Kim et al. 2022). The ecosystem of the services has become more centralised because of the centralised nature of the platforms. However, the accountability of these services has increased, and the platforms offer a better possibility for the co-creation of these services, because the citizens are better informed, and they have access to that information which was formerly closed to them. The better accountability and the enhanced co-creation resulted increased the trust in these services. As part of the digitalisation and platformisation of the public services, the role of the artificial intelligence (AI) has increased as well (Kostrubiec 2022). It is emphasised by the literature that consumer protection of services (including public services) can be an important field where AI could be applied because of the neutral nature of artificial intelligence (Zawiślak-Białek 2022). It is mentioned that administrative decision-making is now not a field of the AI; however, the business platforms are partly based on AI solutions. Therefore, it has potential as well (Agarwal 2018).

Not only the traditional government services—such as e-administration and the e-decision-making—have been analysed by our chapter. The chapter examines the different public services which are provided by public companies, or which are controlled and supervised by public bodies (e.g. electricity, district heating). However, our analysis focuses on the platforms of the traditional universal services (human services), especially the platformisation of the health care, education, and social care services. It should be emphasised that the digitalisation and platformisation of these services have been increased by the impact of the COVID-19 pandemic.

If we look at the local level, it should be emphasised that the platforms have also been introduced in local government, but their wider use has been hampered by several factors, notably resource constraints, and they have become more important in metropolitan administrations. The 'smart city' projects are partially based on public service provision platforms, as an example of the influence on metropolitan administration. The (municipal) platforms, and in particular their link to central systems, also serve as a new centralisation factor: their use can contribute to the centralisation of public administration. Because 'smart city' projects are impacted by different AI solutions, this part of the analysis focuses on the application of AI in metropolitan administration as well.

Therefore, this new ecosystem can be considered as a Janus-faced one: in one part the centralisation of the systems has been increased, but the flexibility and resilience of these services have been strengthened by the enhanced access to information and by the improved possibility of the participation of the citizens.

These tendencies can be observed in the modern countries. These tendencies will be analysed by the examination of the Hungarian public administration and its socio-economic environment.

4 Evolvement and Development of Platforms in the Hungarian Public Administration

It is undeniable that the digital revolution has now reached the public administration systems. E-government brings many benefits. For example, customers are not tied to office hours, they do not have to meet officials, and they have easier access to information and a range of tools to help the administrative staffs make their decisions (Bowman and Kearney 2016). E-government is an umbrella term: in the literature it is used to describe government innovation and government information and services. The goal of e-government is often defined as paperless offices, meaning that electronic administration transforms paper-based processes into electronic processes (Wohlers 2010). E-government creates many ways for governments and citizens to communicate with each other. As a result, customers have become actors in the administrative system. Therefore, e-government can be interpreted as a tool for economic development. Simplified procedures and automation of decision-making can speed up procedures, which in turn can lead to a reduction in administrative costs. Taking into account the impact and results of platforms in economic life, some public administration systems started to adopt platform-like solutions relatively early, at the turn of the millennium (Ansell and Miura 2020). In the Hungarian public administration, several e-government systems have also emerged that ultimately fit the various descriptions of platforms: thus, the general government electronic administration system, the so-called (Administrative) Client Gateway, and its associated Central Identification Agent can clearly be interpreted as such a specific network and ecosystem.

If we look at the development of Hungarian systems, it could be highlighted that platform-like solutions have been firstly developed in the field of financial administration, mainly in the area of public revenue management. One of the first of these systems, which was later integrated into the Client Gateway portal, was the eBev (e-Declaration, eDec) system which, in addition to filing and electronic administration, soon had an electronic payment interface. Thus, it could be interpreted as one of the first Hungarian administrative platforms (Hoffman and Cseh 2020). Later on, several administrative sectors followed this pattern, firstly those which have been related to public revenues, such as social security and construction administration (EKÁER) systems. Various platforms have also been developed in other areas of traditional public administration. Thus, since 2011, the 'Robocop' *(Robotzsaru)* system in the police administration can be considered as such a platform-like solution (Horvayné Fehér and Munk 2011).

Platform-like solutions have also appeared in property register systems, including the electronic land registry system and the vehicle registry system as well. The range of these administrative platforms has been steadily expanding in recent years. These platforms were essentially related to administrative public authority functions, they were linked to the traditional administrative activities of public authorities, including the enforcement of public authority, and, to some extent, the supervision activities of the public authorities.

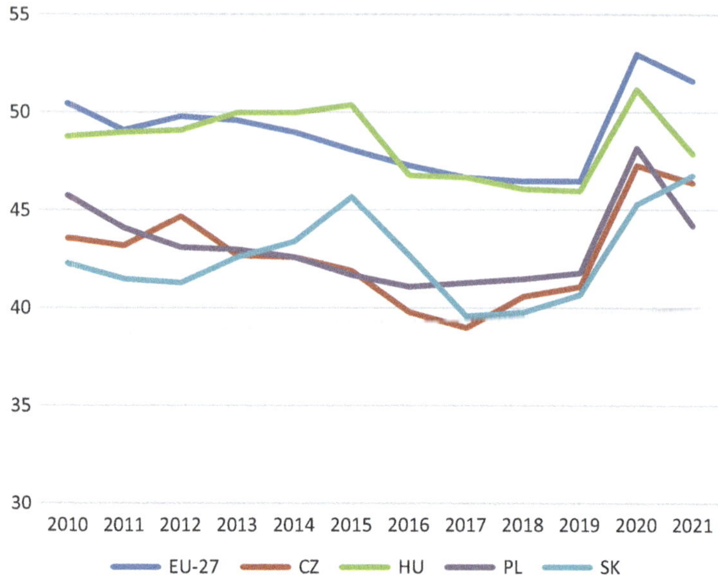

Fig. 1 General government expenditures—Visegrád Countries and EU-27 (in the share of GDP) from 2010 to 2021 (Source: Eurostat)

Public administrations also provide a wide range of public services. Given that economic platforms have been particularly successful in the area of services, it makes sense that these solutions have also been introduced in the area of public services in the various public administrations (Ansell and Miura 2020). These platforms for service information and administration have also appeared in public services organised by the Hungarian public administration. These services have a significant role in Hungary. Hungary follows the continental pattern (Stiglitz 2020; Kuhlmann and Wollmann 2019) of the modern economies: the government sector is important part of the national economy in Hungary. The share of the government sector in the gross domestic product is the highest among the Visegrád Countries (Czech Republic, Hungary, Poland, and Slovakia) (see Fig. 1).

Public services have a significant role among government expenditures. However, the share of the human public service (especially the social care and health expenditures) in the GDP is lower than the European average; it can be considered as significant (see Fig. 2).

Thus, platform-like solutions have already emerged in the services provided by social security and, in particular, in health services, since the turn of the millennium. These systems have been adapted several times, and the services they provide and the data they handle have been continuously extended. By the mid-2010s, this had resulted in the emergence of a single space, the Electronic Health Care Space (EHCS) *(Elektronikus Egészségügyi Szolgáltató Tér, EESZT)*. The development of EHCS has not only increased access to data but also strengthened the potential of telemedicine, thus highlighting that it can also lead to changes in healthcare delivery.

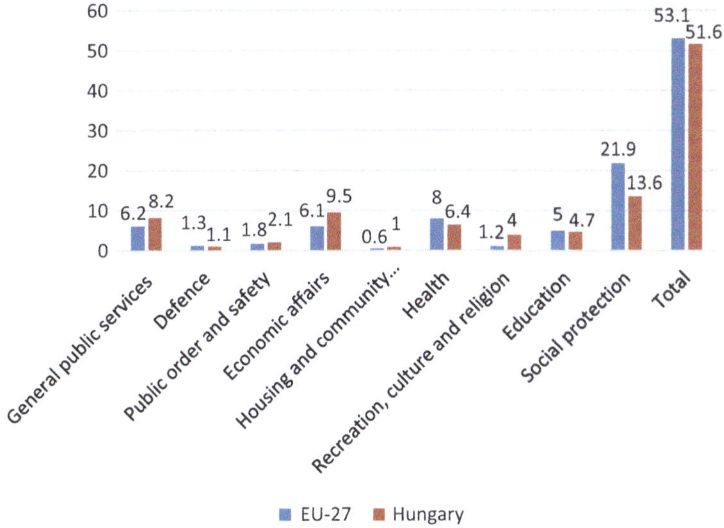

Fig. 2 Government functions in EU-27 and in Hungary in 2020 (share of the GDP in precent) (Source: Eurostat)

The role of EHCS as a platform and tool for telemedicine has been particularly valued in the context of the COVID-19 pandemic over the last 2 years (Győrffy et al. 2020). Similarly, the COVID-19 pandemic has brought to the fore platforms in the field of education. The first platforms to emerge in higher education administration at the turn of the millennium were Electronic Education System (*Elektronikus Tanulmányi Rendszer, ETR*) and Neptun, with the associated platforms being linked and developed by individual higher education institutions in the same period to internationally available platforms for education, such as Coospace, Canvas, and Moodle, and the integration of tools for e-conferencing and classroom solutions (especially MS Teams, Webex, and Zoom). The importance of e-learning became prominent in the context of the restrictions and digital curriculum imposed by the COVID-19. In the second semester of the academic year 2019/20 and for most of the academic year 2020/21, the use of these platforms has significantly shaped the teaching work in the Hungarian higher education institutions. Similarly, during the 2010s, the use of the management and collaboration platform, the so-called *KRÉTAsystem* and the associated Digital Collaboration Space (DCS), which was developed in public education, increased significantly during the COVID-19 epidemic.

Although the use of platforms in public administration has also increased significantly in recent years, the personal nature of administration and the public services requires a wide range of face-to-face personal interactions. Thus, the use of platforms cannot, on the whole, replace the entire public service provision and management (Van Mart et al. 2019). In addition to the personal dimension, other factors that hinder the uptake of these tools are also present in the digital delivery of local authorities. As will be discussed later, the fragmented nature of the local government system in Hungary means that the capacity of models that are necessarily smaller than state administration systems and based on the autonomy of local communities is much more finite, and the development of such a system requires significant financial and human capital—both IT and sector-specific expertise (Milosavljević et al. 2017). The role of platforms in local government administration is therefore very limited, and they are mainly used by larger municipalities. In any case, the use of these tools is already very much in evidence in these municipalities. Since the turn of the millennium, these larger municipalities have also started to use platform-based solutions for their new types of service organisation, thanks to the smart cities concept. In other words, platforms seem to have become a phenomenon specific to metropolitan municipalities (Anttiroiko et al. 2014).

As we have mentioned earlier, artificial intelligence is applied widely by platforms (Ullah et al. 2018). Therefore, the analysis of the role of the platform requires the examination of the role of the artificial intelligence.

5 The Role of Artificial Intelligence in Public Administration

5.1 Starting Points and Theoretical Framework

The public administration (including its organisational structure, its operational mechanisms, and its staffing framework) does not (or cannot) remain unchanged and cannot be independent of the trends of the contemporary world, and thus it can be said that public administration is constantly in flux. One of the greatest challenges of our time is digitalisation in the broadest sense, which has required a reorganisation of both the public administration's approach to citizens and its infrastructure in all the countries of the world. I should be emphasised that however inevitable the emergence of the digital explosion in the public sector may be, experience to date—especially in the Central Eastern European (CEE) region—does not necessarily suggest that it is a complete success story. The reasons for this include the difficulty of taking organisational and procedural aspects into account at the same time, the slow and costly process of building infrastructure, and the general resistance to change (especially in human resources), which is also a classic barrier to innovation.

For the sake of completeness, however, the authors of this chapter cannot fail to highlight the undisputed virtues of optimal digitisation of public administration, which are also relevant to our study. The leading foreign literature is unanimous in the view that the use of proven digital tools can have a pull effect, which can legitimise the use of new technological tools in new sectors not previously affected by digitisation. This effect is reinforced by the fact that standardised platforms and other digital solutions from the competitive sector can be easily transferred to public administrations, within certain scope and under certain conditions. In fact, this intermediary interactive online value creation is a phenomenon also known in the 'traditional' offline economy, which generally operates on the technology and infrastructure of a business. On the other hand, it should also be stressed that technological tools can be used to a greater extent to achieve and reinforce the objectives declared as goals to be achieved by national and EU public administration policy (e.g. customer focus, efficiency, and subsidiarity), particularly with regard to the activities of public authorities and the organisation of public services. In this context, we would like to refer to the indicators of the so-called DESI (Digital Economy and Society Index), which ranks the countries of the Central and Eastern Europe in the bottom third of the scale, in particular in terms of the efficiency of public services. According to the index, Hungary ranks 23rd, Slovakia 24th, Poland 25th, and the Czech Republic 18th, with slightly better indicators (DESI 2022).

5.2 *Types of Public Administration and the Potential of AI*

In the context of the core activities of public administration, the relevant organisational law doctrine distinguishes between types of activities of a public authority nature, activities deriving from a position of organisational or proprietary power, and so-called non-public power activities (Fazekas 2015; Maurer and Waldhoff 2020). Because of the limitations of this chapter, only the core activities which are relevant to AI (such as strategy formulation, organisation of internal processes, information to customers, and substantive administration) and the scope of application of AI technologies linked to them are analysed by it.

As a starting point, it should be noted that policymaking can be understood more as part of governmental activity, despite the fact that planning itself has a specific legal basis in administrative law, and that management activity can be understood within an institution (and thus not in a public authority aspect). There are AI-based tools which can be used to support these activities (e.g. digitalisation of impact assessment, use of chatbots, use of machine vision, or speech understanding), but we will not focus on these in our study, and will therefore focus on technologies that can be used in interactions between customers (citizens) and public administration. In terms of substantive administration, there are two major issues that fundamentally determine the reality of the application of AI. On the one hand, a distinction must be drawn between administrative procedures initiated ex officio and those initiated at the request of the client, since these procedures are carried out by public administrations according to different logics, both in terms of perception (see initiation of the procedure) and clarification of the facts (see preparation of the decision). At this point, it can be concluded that in Hungary—basically in the field of financial administration—there are technologies that work for both types of procedure, but these are sector-specific solutions, all of which have a 'teething problem'.

The Hungarian State Treasury uses the Téba application (Budai 2016), which is an OPA-based IT framework for the automation of certain normative family support procedures that can be applied for, but the shortcoming of the application is that its explanation (justification) function is currently underused. The National Tax and Customs Administration uses several AI-based programmes, of which Eskort is an expert system supporting ex officio VAT audits, which was introduced by the tax administration in 1999. Its strength is that it has a meaningful explanatory function, but its drawback is that it is only capable of drawing one-step conclusions (Fejes and Futó 2021).

The other fundamental issue in relation to public authority action is the discretionary power of the public administration: in this respect, it is useful to differentiate between cases that should be decided in favour of normative regulation and those that require discretion. The former refers to the issuance of so-called legally binding acts, where the public authority can only take one type of legal decision, given the facts and the rules, and this way of applying the law can be easily modelled and thus supported by artificial intelligence (Fejes and Futó 2021). Discretion essentially refers to an attitude of law enforcement where, due to the looser nature of the legal regime, the authority is left to its discretion to choose between several lawful decisions (e.g. determining the exact amount of the fine between a minimum and a maximum, choosing the enforcement method) (Maurer and Waldhoff 2020). By its nature, modelling this decision-making pattern requires a combination of machine learning and expert systems, as well as explicitly big data processing and data mining.

Related to this problem is the 'production' of substantive decisions using artificial intelligence, which is in its infancy in Hungarian law. The reasons for this may include the lack of a horizontal perspective and the inadequacy of the infrastructure in its present state, but some in the literature argue that the obligation of the public administration to give reasons for its decisions prevents automation (Fejes and Futó 2021). In addition to the fact that this approach is suitable for reassuring the legislator, the authors of this study dispute this idea for two reasons: firstly, as indicated in connection with the NAV Eskort, it is IT soluble to develop an explanatory function, and secondly, the forms applied intensively in the public administration can easily be used to digitise the justification, so there is no reason to turn away from planning further developments on this basis.

5.3 Challenges and Responses in the Relationship Between Public Administrations and Artificial Intelligence

IT solutions (also) used in AI-based public administrations have shown varying degrees of effectiveness in different developed countries. Looking at examples from abroad, it can be highlighted that both machine learning and the use of expert systems are not alien at international level, with the Anglo-Saxon countries in particular leading the way in this field. Machine learning is the basis for the OPSI and BIT technologies, among others, which have been in existence since 2017, while examples of successful use of expert systems can be found in the UK (ESI), Australia (IVAG), New Zealand (CSLC), and the US (e-HASP2).

In addition to the need to keep up with technological advances, it is also evident that the challenges of recent years (e.g. pandemics, war, restrictions on fundamental rights) have forced public administrations to proactively exploit these existing infrastructures. An example of this in the Hungarian documentary administration is the effort to reinforce the so-called customer call kiosks in the district offices with artificial intelligence, which, at least according to plans, will in the near future enable the online initiation and issuance of documents of a decision nature (e.g. identity card, proof of address, driving licence, passport) without the involvement of human beings.

The other aspiration that pervades the domestic related legislation is to use artificial intelligence as (one of) the means to shorten the administrative time. To illustrate this, one can cite the automatic decision-making institutionalised by the former Administrative Procedure Act and further developed by the Act CL of 2016 on the Code of General Administrative Procedure (hereinafter CGAP). The basic idea is that a decision is taken or communicated within 24 h of the initiation of the procedure, provided that the facts are clear and the necessary information is available to the authority. It should be mentioned that the sectoral legislation was originally modelled on ex officio procedures for certain traffic offences, but was later extended to procedures on request and to other sectors (e.g. certain family allowances, the issue of an inauthentic title deed). The scope of this chapter does not allow for a comprehensive evaluation of this legal instrument established by the CGAP, so we would just like to add that—according to the conceptual coordinate system of the GDPR regulation—this cannot be considered as a real automated decision, since under the current regulation, the human factor is required to intervene approvingly to reach the actual decision (Wachter et al. 2018). Similarly, this legal instrument cannot be considered as a pure application of artificial intelligence, even though the nature of the legislative act (i.e. the issuing of a legally binding act) would allow for the application of full automatism.

Finally, we would like to emphasise, in addition to the classical public authority activities, there is also the possibility of using AI in the context of public service organisation (once the guaranteed framework is in place). Examples of possible sectors include the organisation of public transport (which could be based on the operating mechanisms of Uber's existing platform) and the linking of so-called basic registers with administrative planning (e.g. birth registers could be used to draw automated conclusions from the number of children born in a municipality in order to plan the number of places in nurseries and kindergartens).

As a conclusion, the benefits of digitalisation of public administration (in this context, the use of artificial intelligence) in terms of increasing efficiency or reducing administrative costs are undisputed, but it should also be stressed that bringing the administrative location closer to the citizen has not resulted in the decentralisation of tasks and competences. On the contrary, the digitalisation of public administration has reinforced the principle of centralisation, so that the cautious rise of AI in Hungary can be identified with the process of centralisation.

6 'No Country for Municipalities': Platforms as a New Tool of Centralisation?

6.1 Fragmented Municipal System as a Framework of the Municipal Platforms

The Hungarian public administration system was highly decentralised before the 2011/2013 reforms. After the democratic transition, a radically fragmented and very autonomous system of local government emerged (see Fig. 3).

The majority of local administrative tasks were the responsibilities of local governments, and local government officials also played an important role in state (central) administration activities through delegated central administration tasks as well. The issue of e-government in the Hungarian municipal system has become a significant element of Hungarian strategies and service delivery. In Hungary, the development of e-local government has been partly linked to 'bottom-up' initiatives, especially in the case of large municipalities, but has been characterised by top-bottom implementation. After the 2010 reforms, the former highly decentralised Hungarian public administration system—by transferring a large number of local government tasks to the responsibility of the central government and its agencies—was significantly centralised. Even the Hungarian municipal administration has been concentrated, because the village municipalities with less than 2000 inhabitants have

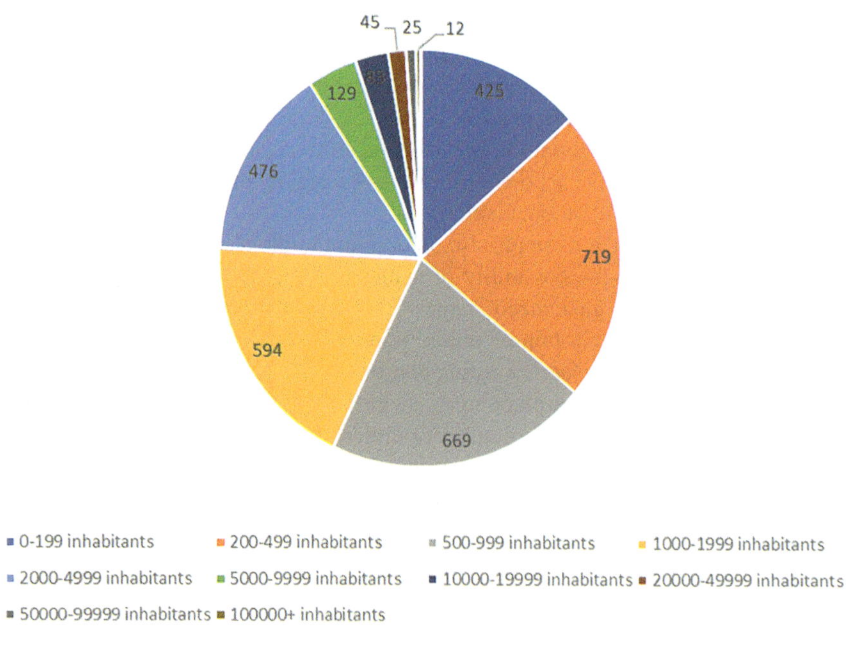

Fig. 3 Number of Hungarian municipalities (including the district municipalities of Budapest Capital City) (January 2021) (Source: Hungarian Central Statistical office—www.ksh.hu)

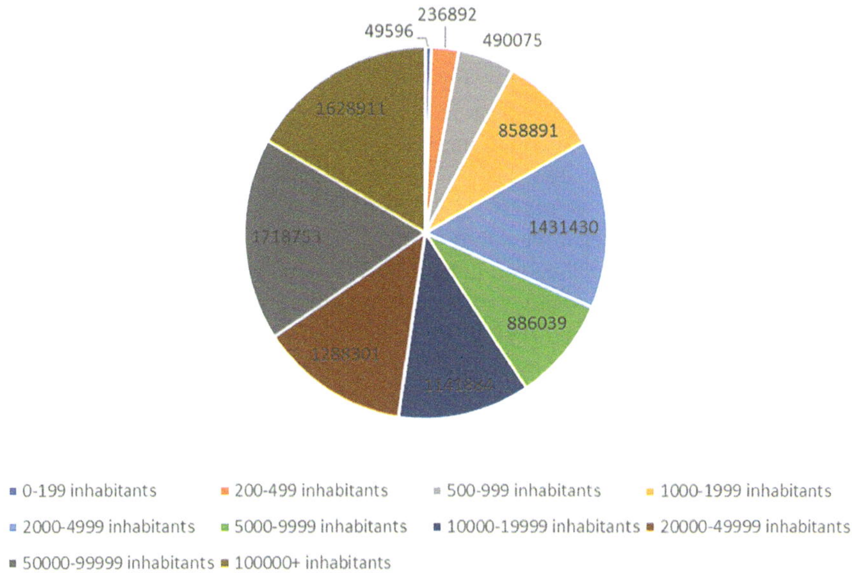

Fig. 4 Population of Hungarian municipalities (including the district municipalities of Budapest Capital City) (January 2021) (Source: Hungarian Central Statistical office—www.ksh.hu)

Table 1 Number of municipalities and municipal offices in Hungary (2019)

Number of municipalities in Hungary	Number of independent municipal offices (offices of the mayors)	Number of joint municipal offices	Number of municipalities which participate in joint municipal offices
3153	521	749	2632

Source: Hungarian Central Statistical office—www.ksh.hu

been forced to establish joint municipal offices (town municipalities and village municipalities with more than 2000 inhabitants can be the seats of the joint municipal offices; thus, they can participate in this cooperation) (Hoffman et al. 2016) (Fig. 4 and Table 1).

Municipalities have developed a new model of municipal e-government following new administrative and fiscal procedural rules, as municipalities are required to provide a fully electronic administrative platform in the field of local taxes. These changes have also had an impact on municipal e-services.

The new service and e-government system built after 2013/14 was based on the prominent role of the financial administration. The electronification of large public registers also took place after 2010. This included the Act I of 2010 on civil registry procedures (which entered into force on 1 January 2014) by which ultimately one of the most important basic public registers has been transformed to an electronic one. As we have indicated, platforms have also been created for the significant public service systems. In the area of basic health care, which has remained a municipal responsibility, the above-mentioned EESZT, and in the field of basic social services, basic child welfare services and specialised municipal services for the elderly, the Social Sector Portal *(Szociális Ágazati Portál)*, can be interpreted as a specific platform-like solution. However, the fragmentation of the system persisted after the centralisation reforms: on the one hand, the different registers operated as separate platforms, partly due to data protection and partly due to the use of traditional administrative solutions. Thus, the interconnection between them was severely limited by this legal regulatory context and administrative traditions.

As it has been mentioned above, larger (urban) municipalities are one of the few municipalities worldwide where platforms have traditionally played a more important role (Lytras and Visvizi 2018). In Hungary, this trend has also prevailed: from the 1990s onwards, the larger municipalities in Hungary—typically the districts of Budapest and the towns with county rights—began to develop their own platforms and electronic administrative systems to increase administrative efficiency. As with the development of public administration, this was first seen in financial administration. A kind of zero step in the development of local government platforms was the emergence of local government electronic accounting systems. Initially, there was no single platform, and the larger municipalities began to develop their own accounting systems, based on systems developed by market players and in line with public finance rules. The 'first generation' of municipal platforms was the development of these accounting systems to automate local taxation. In fact, these larger municipalities developed specific systems for the management of local government revenues, which were classified as local taxation platforms. These developments were mostly carried out by the larger municipalities themselves, with the involvement of a partner in the implementation of the accounting system, and initially typically used their own authentication systems, with little or no interoperability. Later on, in particular with the spread of electronic tax administration solutions and the widespread use of centralised client-gate identification, municipal systems were also made available with a unified and centralised client-gate identification system. However, significant differences remained between local administration platforms in view of the different developments. The mandatory introduction of the application service provider (ASP) system, operated by the Hungarian State Treasury, marked a new turning point in the evolution of local government platforms for public administration. This system, which allows the financial management of municipalities to be monitored in real time, also brought about a reform of the previous administrative and accounting systems. The ASP, which can be understood as a platform, will be progressively implemented by all local authorities from 1 July 2016. The system provides a single accounting and related administrative interface. In view of the rollout of the ASP system, the former separate platforms of the municipalities were adapted to the centralised systems, with some of the previous improvements becoming unusable and those that could be integrated into the centralised systems being maintained (Hoffman and Karpiuk 2022).

In addition to the municipal tasks as public authorities, Hungarian municipalities have introduced smart city solutions, especially in the field of transport services. Some of them have developed their own platforms, in particular for the use of local public transport (e.g. Budapest Transport Centre's—BKK—Courier system on which the 'Budapest GO' platform is based) and for monitoring and paying for parking in public spaces. These solutions were partly based on in-house developments, but centralisation has also been introduced in this area. On the one hand, in the case of public parking services, the development of the national mobile payment system was a particular point of convergence, as the systems had to be interconnected with it. On the other hand, a more subtle, soft form of centralisation of smart city solutions has been the creation of national data centres and the provision of professional solutions (e.g. Lechner Knowledge Centre). Unlike international trends (Lytras and Visvizi 2018), where smart city solutions are increasingly being applied in the field of public human public services, the Hungarian smart city solutions are just partially applied for health, social, and education services. The reason of this difference is that these services have been significantly nationalised and centralised, thus limiting the role of municipalities. Another reason is that national regimes which can communicate with municipal systems and provide meaningful services to the beneficiaries only started to be extensively developed by the end of the 2010s. A third reason could be that there has not been a significant demand for smart solutions from the users of these services, because of the lack of the digital competences of the Hungarian population. From the 2010s onwards, these processes began to extend beyond the larger (urban) municipalities—and in Hungarian terms, beyond the municipalities with county rights: public administration platforms and some smart solutions, typically for transport services, were also adopted by some medium-sized municipalities (larger districts or municipalities with a population of more than 20,000–25,000 inhabitants). The presence of digital solutions and platforms among municipalities is particularly low. Thus, even in a national context, platforms are perceived as a municipal issue (Henk 2018).

Closing Remarks
Even public administrations and the provision of public services have been impacted by the evolvement of platforms. Platforms have been widely used by the public service systems as well. AI is applied for the management of platforms. The platformisation of the public service provision enhanced the accountability of the public service provision, and therefore, even the trust in these systems has been increased. But the platforms as ecosystems are mainly centrally managed, and therefore new forms of administration have been evolved during the last decade: platforms became the tools of 'silent' centralisation as well.

6.2 *Platforms and Municipal Governance: Towards a New Type of Centralisation?*

Centralisation and decentralisation have taken different forms, but two main trends have emerged in the various reforms affecting municipal administration. The first form has been typical of the Western and Northern European states, where various reforms have been partly top-down and aimed primarily at modernising systems. In the field of local public services, these states were more reliant on local government systems; the various reforms were primarily aimed at transforming the economy of scale of municipalities. Although these reforms also sought to create larger local and regional units, they were carried out within the local government system. Therefore, they could be interpreted mainly as concentration and not centralisation of local governance (Pálné Kovács 2019). The trends towards integration and concentration were further reinforced by the changing municipal framework at the turn of the millennium, in particular the increasing urbanisation trends. The emerging housing crisis in large cities, with affordable housing being pushed to the periphery of large cities, and the resulting intensification of suburbanisation, posed challenges that could not be adequately addressed by traditional municipal spatial structures, as service units extended well beyond the administrative boundaries of municipalities. In order to manage these units, a variety of solutions have been adopted: either merged units or specific forms of compulsory inter-municipal cooperation. Local government concentration, for example merging of municipal units and the development of inter-municipal associations, has posed additional challenges, particularly in the field of public human services. Municipal human service systems must therefore provide services to a relatively uniform standard. This has created a particular tension in these systems. Given the wide range of local government functions, both in education-cultural and in welfare public services, a specific latent 'stealth' centralisation has emerged, whereby the freedom of local communities to organise services has been eroded through the regulation of various service standards, typically not by law but by ordinance and in many cases by soft law. Alongside 'stealth' centralisation, a trend has emerged since the 2000s in some decentralisation solutions in Northern and Western European countries, which the literature refers to as 'cynical decentralisation'. In this case, the primary aim of reform was not to strengthen welfare functions, but was in fact to shift responsibility, as additional resources were not provided for increasing tasks, or were provided inadequately (Pálné 2019).

The emergence of municipal platforms can be interpreted as a part of this latent centralisation process. They can be seen as a specific twenty-first century form of 'stealth' centralisation. With the widespread use of ICT and the emergence of the information society, information and data related to public services are becoming increasingly important. In the majority of modern states, these data systems and platforms are generally organised at central level (Tomlinson 2019). Since without this data, the new types of public service organisation solutions for municipalities cannot be implemented or can only be implemented to a limited extent. The ownership of data and access to them have also led to a 'soft' centralisation in these states, which is only indirectly perceived at first sight, but it is a very real one. As we have mentioned above, this soft centralisation—albeit on a smaller scale, because of the extensive direct centralisation of the 2010s—has also been present in the Hungarian local government system, especially in larger urban municipalities. Indeed, smart city solutions inevitably entail data requirements, which central systems can provide. However, access to data also implies adaptation to central platforms, and local systems must be interoperable with central systems. This necessarily implies adaptation to the interface and logic of the central systems. This allows the central government and its agencies to have a significant influence on the local service provision through the design of its own data systems, without seeming to interfere. A unified data management and processing system also reinforces the centralisation of an administration; it makes the system more centralised, even if this is not, or only barely, noticeable at first sight.

7 Concluding Remarks

Even public administrations and the provision of public services have been impacted by the evolvement of platforms. Platforms have been widely used by the public service systems as well. AI is applied for the management of platforms. The platformisation of the public service provision enhanced the accountability of the public service provision, and therefore, even the trust in these systems has been increased. The application of AI has been started and strengthened by the establishment of platforms, but the use of it can be considered as a limited one. Platforms as ecosystems are mainly centrally managed, and therefore, new forms of administration have been evolved during the last decade: platforms became the tools of 'silent' centralisation as well.

Acknowledgements This research was supported by the project '*Resilience of the legal system in the post-Covid society: Risks and opportunities*' (principal investigator: Fruzsina Gárdos-Orosz), by the project NKFIH OTKA FK 138965 (principal investigator Kitti Mezei), and by the Cost Action CA20123 *Intergovernmental Coordination from Local to European Governance*.

References

Agarwal PK (2018) Public administration challenges in the world of AI and bots. PAR Public Adm Rev 78(6):917–921. https://doi.org/10.1111/puar.12979

Ansell C, Miura S (2020) Can the power of platforms be harnessed for governance? Public Adm 98(1):261–276. https://doi.org/10.1111/padm.12636

Anttiroiko A-V, Valkama P, Bailey SJ (2014) Smart cities in the new service economy: building platforms for smart services. AI & Soc 29:323–334. https://doi.org/10.1007/s00146-013-0464-0)

Baldwin CY, Woodard CJ (2009) The architecture of platforms: a unified view. In: Gawer A (ed) Platforms, markets and innovation. Edward Elgar, Cheltenham and Northampton, pp 19–44

Bogdandy A v (2012) National legal science in the European legal area. A manifesto. Revista Espanola de Derecho Constitutional 32(94):13–28

Bowman A, Kearney RC (2016) State and local government. Wadsworth, Boston

Budai BB (2016) E-közigazgatás az ügyfélszolgálatban. NKE VTKI, Budapest

DESI (2022) https://digital-strategy.ec.europa.eu/en/policies/desi (31.07.2022)

Evans MC, Cates CL, McIntosh WV (2015) The reality of jurisprudence(?): Interpretive methods in the opinions of justices Antonin Scalia and Stephen Breyer. Justice Syst J 36(1):20–48. https://doi.org/10.1080/0098261X.2014.969853

Fazekas M (ed) (2015) Közigazgatási jog. Általános rész I, ELTE Eötvös Kiadó, Budapest

Fejes E, Futó I (2021) Artificial intelligence in public administration - supporting substantive administration. Financ Rev 1:23–51. https://doi.org/10.35551/PFQ_2021_s_1_2

Győrffy Z, Békási S, Szathmári-Mészáros N, Németh O (2020) A telemedicina lehetőségei a COVID–19-pandémia kapcsán a nemzetközi és a magyarországi tapaszta-latok és ajánlások tükrében. Orv Hetil 161(24):986–989

Hein A, Schreieck M, Riasanow T, Setzke DS, Wiesche M, Böhm M, Krcmar H (2020) Digital platform ecosystems. Electron Mark 30:87–98. https://doi.org/10.1007/s12525-019-00377-4

Henk T (2018) Okosváros-megoldások Magyarországon. In: Gy S (ed) Az okos város (Smart City). Dialóg Campus, Budapest, pp 217–240

Hoffman I, Cseh KB (2020) E-administration, cybersecurity and municipalities – the challenges of cybersecurity issues for the municipalities in Hungary. Cybersecur Law 2(2):199–211

Hoffman I, Karpiuk M (2022) E-administration in polish and Hungarian municipalities – a comparative analysis of the regulatory issues. Lex localis – J Local Self-Governments 20(3): 617–640. https://doi.org/10.4335/20.3.617-640(2022)

Hoffman I, Rozsnyai K, Fazekas J (2016) Concentrating or centralising public services? The changing roles of the Hungarian inter-municipal associations in the last decades. Lex localis – J Local Self-Governments 14(3):451–471. https://doi.org/10.4335/14.3.451-471(2016)

Horvayné Fehér J, Munk S (2011) A rendőrségi informatikai hálózat fogalma, rendel-tetése. Hadmérnök 6(2):217–226

Kim S, Andersen KN, Lee J (2022) Platform government in the era of smart technology. PAR Public Adm Rev 82(2):362–368. https://doi.org/10.1111/puar.13422

Kostrubiec J (2022) Cybersecurity system in Poland. Selected legal issues. In: Karpiuk M, Kostrubiec J (eds) The public dimension of cybersecurity. Lex Localis Press, Maribor, pp 7–18

Kuhlmann S, Wollmann H (2019) Introduction to comparative public administration. Administrative Systems and Reforms in Europe. Edward Elgar, Cheltenham

Lytras MD, Visvizi A (2018) Who uses Smart City services and what to make of it: toward interdisciplinary smart cities research. Sustainabilty 10(6):1998–2013. https://doi.org/10.3390/su10061998

Maurer H, Waldhoff C (2020) Allgemeines Verwaltungsrecht. C. H. Beck, München

Milosavljević M, Mianović N, Benković S (2017) Waiting for Godot: testing transparency, responsiveness and interactivity of Serbian local governments. Lex localis – J Local Self-governments 15(3):513–528. https://doi.org/10.4335/15.3.513-528%20(2017)

Pálné Kovács I (2019) A középszintű kormányzás helyzete és perspektívái Magyarországon, Budapest, Dialóg Campus

Stiglitz JE (2020) Rewriting the rules of the European economy. An agenda for growth and shared prosperity. W. W. Norton and Company, New York

Tomlinson R (2019) The failure to learn from others: vertical fiscal imbalance, centralisation and Australia's metropolitan knowledge deficit. Aust J Public Adm 78(2):213–226. https://doi.org/10.1111/1467-8500.12387)

Ullah F, Sepasgozar SME, Changxin W (2018) A systematic review of smart real estate technology: drivers of, and barriers to, the use of digital disruptive technologies and online platforms. Sustainability 10(9). https://doi.org/10.3390/su10093142

Van Mart M, Alexandru R, XioaHao W, Cheol L (2019) Operationalizing the definition of e-leadership: identifying the elements of e-leadership. Int Rev Adm Sci 85(1):80–97. https://doi.org/10.1177/0020852316681446

Wachter S, Mittelstadt B, Russell C (2018) Counterfactual explanations without opening the black box: automated decisions and the GDPR. Harv J Law Technol 31(8):461–464. https://jolt.law.harvard.edu/assets/articlePDFs/v31/Counterfactual-Explanations-without-Opening-the-Black-Box-Sandra-Wachter-et-al.pdf (31/07/2022)

Wohlers TE (2010) Local E-government sophistication in the United States. In: Scholl HJ (ed) E-government: information, technology and transformation. Routledge, London, pp 89–106

Yablonski S (2018) A multidimensional framework for digital platform innovation and management: from business to technological platforms. Syst Res Behav Sci 35(4):485–501. https://doi.org/10.1002/sres.2544

Zawiślak-Białek A (2022) Digitisation in the profession of attorney-at-law and the security of customer E-service. Cybersecur Law 4(1):297–308

Preventing the Abuse of the FinTech Sector for Money Laundering and Fiscal Fraud in Terms of Polish Law: Legal Measures and Postulates of Normative Changes

Jarosław Kostrubiec

Abstract The aim of the chapter is to analyse measures against the abuse of the FinTech sector for the purpose of money laundering and fiscal fraud. The FinTech sector is developing dynamically in Poland. However, entities undertaking modern financial activities suffer from the problem of the lack of completeness and clarity of law. Despite the normative gaps, the FinTech sector in Poland stands out from other European Union countries. The main method used in the study is the formal-dogmatic method. This method includes, first of all, logical interpretation, as well as analysis, argumentation, and hermeneutics. The study showed that significant normative changes in the Polish legal system are necessary. First, it is necessary to adopt a law regulating the financial information system. This law should properly implement EU law. The EU legislator therefore proposes to establish centralised automatic mechanisms such as registers or data retrieval systems in all Member States. Essentially, the national legislator should also include the FinTech sector within the scope of this act. Secondly, the current anti-money laundering and fiscal fraud measures should be adapted to the dynamically changing financial market.

Keywords FinTech · Money laundering · Fiscal fraud · Financial regulation

1 Introduction

The Polish Financial Supervision Authority is taking steps to strengthen the modern financial services sector. One of the forms of support for innovative enterprises from the modern financial services sector is issuing individual interpretations of legal provisions. A request for an interpretation issued by the Financial Supervision Authority may only apply to products and services that are aimed at developing

J. Kostrubiec (✉)
Faculty of Law and Administration, Maria Curie-Skłodowska University (Lublin), Lublin, Poland
e-mail: jaroslaw.kostrubiec@mail.umcs.pl

S. Benković et al. (eds.), *Digital Transformation of the Financial Industry*, Contributions to Finance and Accounting,
https://doi.org/10.1007/978-3-031-23269-5_11

innovation in the financial market. However, the development of the FinTech sector generates problems related to the protection of these entities against the use of their activities to commit money laundering and fiscal crimes (Zavoli & King 2021). Present state of affairs negatively affects the condition of public finances as well as the security of legal transactions (Bajda 2021: 41–42).

The main goal of the chapter is to examine the regulations of Polish law and assess whether they adequately prevent the abuse of the FinTech sector for money laundering and fiscal fraud. These regulations, in principle, should enable early detection of events leading to money laundering and fiscal fraud. The study is to verify the thesis that the regulations of Polish law do not allow for effectively counteracting the use of the FinTech sector for money laundering and fiscal fraud.

2 Methodology and Sources of Law

The presented research goals require the use of appropriate research methods. The main method used in the study will be the formal-dogmatic method. This method includes, first of all, logical interpretation, as well as analysis, argumentation, and hermeneutics. The research conducted on the basis of the formal-dogmatic method allowed for the critique of the applicable law and for proposing *de lege lata* and *de lege ferenda* conclusions.

The norms of Polish law were analysed, including, in particular, the standards resulting from the Act of March 1, 2018, on Anti-Money Laundering and Counter-Financing of Terrorism (hereinafter: the AML Act). It is one of the legal acts regulating instruments aimed at constructing a special regime for dealing with money in circulation. The purpose of this law is to prevent the use of the financial system for money laundering or terrorist financing. In the provisions of the AML Act, the regulation of EU directives, including in particular the AML IV Directive and the AML V Directive, was implemented, fighting financial crime as well as ensuring greater corporate transparency (Silva 2019: 60–64; Gerbrands et al. 2022).

In addition, the analysis of the Act of August 29, 1997—Tax Ordinance was performed. This act regulates the measures to counteract fiscal fraud. Limitation of fiscal fraud is to be achieved by the obligation to audit and identify cashless cash settlements made by entrepreneurs and other profit-making entities. Therefore, the Head of the National Tax Administration was equipped with related competences with an analysis of the risk of using certain financial market institutions to commit fiscal fraud and applying measures to counteract them in the form of account blockages. Two types of bank account blockage can be distinguished depending on its duration, i.e. short- and long-term blockade of a qualified entity's account. The first type of account hold is made for a maximum period of 72 h. Then, the Head of the National Tax Administration is entitled to extend the period of blocking the account of a qualified entity for a specified period, but not longer than 3 months.

3 Hypotheses

Research in the field of counteracting the abuse of the FinTech sector for money laundering and fiscal frauds allowed for the adoption of several research conclusions. It should be signalled that advances in technology and communication have made it easy to conceal and shift funds anywhere in the world in a global interconnected financial system, creating quickly and easily more cover companies in different countries, making it increasingly difficult to track down such measures.

The FinTech sector is particularly exposed to exploitation for money laundering and fiscal fraud. Polish law regulations are not adapted to the dynamically changing digital environment. An example of a problem may be transactions performed with the use of virtual currencies, which are not sufficiently monitored by state administration bodies. Likewise, measures to reduce the risk of money laundering and fiscal fraud related to anonymous prepaid instruments are not sufficient.

A significant problem of Polish legislation is also the lack of implementation of EU directives regarding the financial information system. Delayed access by state authorities to information on the identity of holders of bank and payment accounts and safe deposit boxes, especially anonymous accounts and boxes, makes it difficult to detect money laundering and anti-terrorism transfers. Data enabling the identification of bank and payment accounts and safe deposit boxes belonging to the same person are fragmented and therefore unavailable to state authorities in a timely manner, including the so-called financial intelligence units.

4 Legal Institutions Against Money Laundering

The catalogue of legal institutions provided for in Polish law to prevent money laundering is provided for in the AML Act (Kędzierski 2021; Szafrański 2021). This Act, within the scope of its regulation, implements the Directive (EU) 2015/849 of the European Parliament and of the Council of 20 May 2015 on the prevention of the use of the financial system for the purposes of money laundering or terrorist financing, amending Regulation (EU) No 648/2012 of the European Parliament and of the Council, and repealing Directive 2005/60/EC of the European Parliament and of the Council and Commission Directive 2006/70/EC (Text with EEA relevance), OJ L 141, 5.6.2015, p. 73–117. Act of March 1, 2018, on counteracting money laundering and terrorist financing also serves to apply, among other things, Regulation (EC) No 1889/2005 of the European Parliament and of the Council of 26 October 2005 on controls of cash entering or leaving the Community & Regulation (EU) 2015/847 of the European Parliament and of the Council of 20 May 2015 on information accompanying transfers of funds and repealing Regulation (EC) No 1781/2006 (Text with EEA relevance).

Institutions which are obliged to recognise the risk of money laundering and document the recognised risk in the Polish legal order include in particular (Article

2 (1) (1–25) of the AML Act): (1) national banks, branches of foreign banks, branches of credit institutions, financial institutions, and their branches; (2) cooperative savings and credit associations and the National Co-operative Savings and Credit Fund; (3) national payment institutions, national electronic money institutions, branches of EU payment institutions, branches of EU and foreign electronic money institutions, small payment institutions, payment service bureaus, and settlement agents; (4) investment firms and custodian banks; (5) foreign legal persons conducting brokerage activities on the territory of the Republic of Poland; (6) companies operating a regulated market - to the extent to which they operate an auction platform; (7) investment funds, alternative investment companies, investment fund companies, managers of alternative investment companies, branches of management companies, and branches of European Union managers located on the territory of the Republic of Poland; (8) insurance companies; (9) insurance intermediaries; (10) the National Depository for Securities; (11) entrepreneurs conducting exchange activities; (12) entities engaged in the business of providing services of (a) exchange between virtual currencies and means of payment, (b) exchange between virtual currencies, (c) intermediation in exchange between virtual currencies and means of payment and exchange between virtual currencies, (d) maintaining accounts in the form of an electronic set of identification data providing authorised persons with the ability to use units of virtual currencies; (13) notaries to the extent of certain activities performed in the form of a notarial deed; (14) advocates, attorneys at law, foreign lawyers, and tax advisers to the extent to which they provide legal assistance or tax advisory activities to the client; (15) tax advisers to the extent of certain tax advisory activities and chartered accountants; (16) entrepreneurs whose main business activity is the provision of services consisting in the preparation of returns, keeping of tax books, providing advice, opinions, or explanations on tax or customs law; (17) entrepreneurs providing services consisting, inter alia, in acting or enabling another person to act as trustee of a trust created by a legal transaction or in acting or enabling another person to act as a person exercising rights over shares for an entity other than a company listed on a regulated market subject to disclosure requirements under European Union law or subject to equivalent international standards; (18) entities conducting activity within the scope of provision of accounting services; (19) real estate agents; (20) postal operators; (21) entities conducting activity within the scope of games of chance, pari-mutuel betting, card games, and slot machine games; (22) foundations and associations to the extent to which they accept or make payments in cash of a value equal to or exceeding the equivalent of 10,000 €; (23) entrepreneurs to the extent to which they accept or make payments for goods in cash of a value equal to or exceeding the equivalent of 10,000 €; (24) entrepreneurs to the extent to which they conduct business activity consisting in providing safe deposit boxes and branches of foreign entrepreneurs conducting such activity in the territory of the Republic of Poland; (25) entrepreneurs within the scope of transactions of a value equal to or exceeding the equivalent of 10,000 €, conducting business activity consisting in storing, trading, or acting as intermediaries in trading in works of art, collector's items, and antiques; and (26) lending institutions.

Entities referred to in Polish law as "institutions" obliged to identify the risk of money laundering and document the identified risk in this respect are obliged to apply certain financial security measures to their clients. A financial security measure is a legally prescribed behaviour of an obliged institution towards a customer or a person who carries out an occasional transaction, performed in situations provided for by the law, the aim of which is to reduce the risk of money laundering or terrorist financing caused by the customer or the occasional transaction (Obczyński 2020).

In the Polish legal system, there is a principle of absolute application of financial security measures (Nowakowski 2020). Specified institutions are required, in the first place, to document the identified risk of money laundering that is related to a business relationship or an occasional transaction, as well as its assessment, taking into account a number of factors. In particular, the legislator has identified those factors that relate to the following: the type of customer; the geographical area; the purpose of the account; the type of products, services, and means of distribution; the level of assets deposited by the customer or the value of the transactions carried out; and the purpose, regularity, or duration of the business relationship (Article 33 (3) of the AML Act). In assessing risk, obliged institutions may take into account the applicable national risk assessment (https://www.gov.pl/web/finanse/krajowa-ocena-ryzyka-prania-pieniedzy-oraz-finansowania-terroryzmu. Accessed 1 Aug 2022) or the European Commission's report provided for in Article 6(1)–(3) of the Directive (EU) 2015/849 of the European Parliament and of the Council of 20 May 2015. It should be emphasised that a proper assessment of the risk of money laundering is a necessary condition for the application of appropriate financial security measures.

The Polish legislator has defined a catalogue of situations, the occurrence of which gives rise to the obligation to apply financial security measures (Article 35 (1) of the AML Act). These include (1) the establishment of economic relations; (2) the carrying out of an occasional transaction of the equivalent of 15,000 € or more; (3) the carrying out of an occasional transaction that constitutes a cash transfer of an amount exceeding the equivalent of 1000 €; (4) the carrying out of an occasional transaction using virtual currency of the equivalent of 1000 € or more; (5) the carrying out of an occasional cash transaction of the equivalent of 10,000 € or more; (6) placing bets and receiving winnings of the equivalent of 2000 € or more; (7) suspicion of money laundering or terrorist financing; and (8) doubts about the veracity or completeness of customer identification data obtained to date. Authorised institutions are also obliged to apply financial security measures to those customers with whom they have a business relationship, however, when there has been a change in the established nature or circumstances of the business relationship, as well as when there has been a change in the previously established data concerning the customer or the beneficial owner. The application of financial security measures depends on the level of risk of the customer and is based on the principle of a risk-based approach, i.e. risks understood on an individual basis.

Basic financial security measures include (Article 34 (1) of the AML Act: (1) identification of the client and verification of his or her identity; (2) identification of the beneficial owner; (3) assessment of the purpose and intended nature of the business relationship; and (4) monitoring of the business relationship.

The identification of the client and the verification of his or her identity consists of establishing, in the case of an individual, the name, nationality, the General Electronic System of Population Registration ("PESEL") number, and the country of birth, which in practice makes it possible to determine the client's level of risk. Where no "PESEL" number has been assigned, the date of birth must be provided. The "PESEL" number register is the basic register in Poland from which, among other things, the date of birth and gender can be read. It contains information on Polish citizens and foreigners who have been assigned such a number. Identification of a customer and verification of his or her identity also requires establishing the series and number of the document confirming the identity of a natural person. Polish regulations do not define the concept of a natural person's identity document. However, in particular an identity card, a passport, and, in the case of foreigners, additionally a residence card, a Polish identity document, and a document confirming possession of a permit for tolerated stay should be considered as such documents (Article 226 of the Act of 12 December 2013 on foreigners, consolidated text Journal of Laws 2021, item 2354, as amended). A driver's licence or an official identity card is not considered to be identity documents (Kapica 2020). Problems in using the financial security measure of customer identification and verification of customer identity may arise in the absence of physical contact between clients and institutions. In this situation, the verification of the customer's identity should take place using the electronic identification means referred to in Regulation (EU) No 910/2014 of the European Parliament and of the Council (Regulation (EU) No 910/2014 of the European Parliament and of the Council of 23 July 2014 on electronic identification and trust services for electronic transactions in the internal market and repealing Directive 1999/93/EC, OJ L 257, 28.8.2014: 73–114). If it is not possible to use means of electronic identification, according to the opinion of the Polish Financial Supervision Authority, the bank should consider the use of so-called enhanced financial security measures, including video verification, which may possibly be carried out with the simultaneous use of biometric methods (Polish Financial Supervision Authority's Position Paper of 5 June 2019 on client identification and identity verification in banks and branches of credit institutions based on the video verification method, https://www.knf.gov.pl/knf/pl/komponenty/img/Stanowisko_UKNF_dot_identyfikacji_klienta_i_weryfikacji_jego_tozsamosci_w_bankach_oraz_oddzialach_instytucji_kredytowych_w_oparciu_o_metode_wideoweryfikacji_66066.pdf. Accessed 1 Aug 2022). In addition, the identification of the customer consists in determining the customer's residential address or (business) name, tax identification number, and the address of the principal place of business in the case of a natural person who carries on a business activity (Article 36 (1) of the AML Act).

In the case of a legal entity or an organisational unit without legal personality, the identification of the customer consists firstly in establishing the name (business name), its organisational form, and the address of its registered office or business address. In addition, the identification of these entities consists in determining the tax identification number and, if there is no such number, in determining the country of registration, the name of the relevant register, and the number and date of registration. The institution obliged to apply financial security measures should also establish the name and surname and the General Electronic Population Registration System ("PESEL") number of the person who represents the legal person or organisational unit without legal personality in question. According to the position of the Polish Financial Supervision Authority, to verify the identity of an institutional client (a natural person conducting a business activity, a legal person, or an organisational unit without legal personality) or a person authorised to act on behalf of a client, which is done without their physical presence, the obliged entity should consider using various verification materials from reliable and independent sources. An additional security measure may be to carry out the first transaction by means of a bank transfer from the client's account, which is held at another institution, to an entity that verifies the client's identity. According to the opinion of the Polish Financial Supervision Authority, this measure should not be regarded as the primary means of verifying the client's identity. The data can only serve as an auxiliary means of verifying the client's identity (position of the Polish Financial Supervision Authority on the identification of an institutional client and verification of its identity in the financial sector under the supervision of the Polish Financial Supervision Authority based on the video verification method, https://www.knf.gov.pl/knf/pl/komponenty/img/Stanowisko_UKNF_dot_wideoweryfikacji_klientow_instytucjonalnych.pdf. Accessed 1 Aug 2022).

The second basic financial security measure is the identification of the beneficial owner. In this case, this measure involves both taking reasonable steps to verify the identity of the beneficial owner and establishing ownership and control where the client is a legal person, an organisational unit without legal personality, or a trust. The obligation to apply this measure is absolute. Therefore, if an entity refuses to provide information on its beneficial owners, citing the obligation of professional secrecy (e.g. an investment fund manager), this does not relieve the institution concerned of its obligation to identify the beneficial owner. In such a situation, the institution may not establish a business relationship or terminates it. Furthermore, the obliged entity may also not carry out an occasional transaction or a transaction through a bank account (Article 41 (1) of the AML Act).

The third basic measure of financial security in Polish law is the assessment of the purpose and intended nature of the business relationship. The institution making such an assessment should rely on the full knowledge it has of the client, including its products, services, or transactions. The purpose and intended nature of the business relationship with the client derives in particular from the characteristics of the product purchased by the client or the transactions planned by the client, which is particularly evident in the case of insurance products or investments made through investment funds (Kapica 2020).

Monitoring of the business relationship is the fourth fundamental financial security measure. Ongoing monitoring of a client's business relationship should mainly involve an analysis of the transactions carried out in the business relationship to ensure that these transactions are consistent with the obliged institution's knowledge of the client, the nature and extent of the client's business, and the money laundering and terrorist financing risks associated with that client. Secondly, the monitoring of the client's business relationship consists of investigating the source of the assets at the client's disposal, where this is justified by specific circumstances. Thirdly, monitoring the client's business relationship involves ensuring that the documents, data, or information in the client's possession that relate to the business relationship is kept up to date (Esoimeme 2021).

It should be emphasised that the Polish legislator has created an open catalogue of obligations related to the process of monitoring business relations (Article 34 (1) (4) of the AML Act). Therefore, obliged entities may undertake other activities for the purpose of monitoring business relations, which should serve to enable the institution to detect potential cases of money laundering. It should be emphasised that the application of this financial security measure is an ongoing process. The provisions of Polish law oblige the institutions concerned to monitor economic relations on an ongoing basis, i.e. continuously. The idea is that the institutions should be able to notify the General Inspector of Financial Information, who, in addition to the minister responsible for public finance, is the administrative body competent in anti-money laundering matters (Article 10 of the AML Act), if they have a reasonable suspicion that a specific transaction or specific assets may be related to money laundering. If the General Inspector of Financial Information considers that a transaction may be related to money laundering, he or she shall forward a request to the institution concerned to stop the transaction or block the account for a period of up to 96 h. Upon receipt of this request, the transaction is stopped or the account is blocked (Article 86 (5) of the AML Act).

5 Legal Institutions for the Countering the Use of the Finance Sector for Fiscal Fraud

The regulation concerning measures to prevent the use of the financial sector for fiscal fraud was introduced in Section IIIB of the Tax Ordinance Act under the amendment of 24 November 2017 (Act of 24 November 2017 amending certain act in order to counter the use of the finance sector for tax fraud, Journal of Laws of 2017, item 2491. The regulation on the measures to counter the use of the finance sector for tax fraud purposes became effective on 13 January 2018). These rules were to reduce the so-called tax gap, i.e. the difference between the potential and the actual value of earned taxable income, caused by tax fraud (Article 119zg (9) of the Tax Ordinance). These rules are intended to allow early detection of events that may result in tax fraud and to freeze the funds thus obtained held in an account with a domestic bank or credit account. This renders it impossible or significantly difficult to transfer these funds from the accounts in question.

As types of tax fraud, the legislature lists tax offences, including tax evasion, operating a business under someone else's name, failure to issue an invoice or bill contrary to an obligation to do so, or misleading the competent authority by providing information contrary to the actual state of affairs or concealing the actual state of affairs. As a result of such misconduct, the State Treasury is exposed to the risk of making an undue refund of a payable tax amount. The category of tax fraud also includes the offences referred to in Article 270a § 1 and § 2, Article 271a § 1 and 2, and Article 277a § 1 of the Criminal Code, i.e. the offences of document forgery or false certification involving a document in the form of an invoice. Moreover, tax fraud includes crimes referred to in Article 258 § 1–3 of the Criminal Code, i.e. taking part in an organised group or organisation aimed at committing the above-mentioned crimes.

A measure to limit tax fraud is the obligation to investigate and the identify non-cash transactions made by undertakings and other profit-making entities. Therefore, the Head of the National Revenue Administration has been endowed with powers to analyse the risk of certain financial market institutions being used to commit tax fraud and to take measures against it in the form of a bank account freeze. Pursuant to the provisions of Chapter IIIB of the Tax Ordinance, two types of bank account freeze can be distinguished depending on its duration, i.e. short-term and long-term freeze of the bank account of a qualified entity. The first type of bank account freeze is established for a maximum period of 72 h (Article 119zv § 1 of the Tax Ordinance). The Head of the National Revenue Administration is then entitled to prolong the period of freeze of the bank account of a qualified entity for a specific period not exceeding 3 months (Article 119zw § 1 of the Tax Ordinance).

The provisions of the Act—Tax Ordinance apply to accounts kept by domestic banks and branches of credit institutions and branches of foreign banks, as well as credit unions (Article 119zg (1) of the Tax Ordinance). However, this is only about the accounts specified in Article 119zg (5) of the Act, i.e. clearing accounts, fixed-term deposit accounts and VAT accounts, and the account of a member of a credit union which is a qualified entity. Therefore, the scope of application of the Act—Tax Ordinance does not cover accounts that can be kept for entities which do not pursue profit-making activities, such as savings accounts, personal accounts, and fixed-term deposit accounts (Article 49 (3) of the Banking Law). Fixed-term deposit accounts were added to the catalogue of qualified entity accounts on 1 July 2019. As noted in the literature, this change was forced by the use of overnight deposits. In practice, the account of an overnight deposit used to be opened during working day afternoon hours and lasted until morning hours of the next working day (Mikos-Sitek 2019). Non-cash settlements can also be performed by payment institutions, as they are entitled to provide payment services. On the other hand, pursuant to Article 3(1) of the Act on payment services, payment services are defined as an activity involving, inter alia, the execution of payment transactions, including the transfer of funds to a payment account of the user's provider or another provider by performing direct debit or wire transfer services and using a payment card or a similar payment instrument. In view of the above, the catalogue of entities to whom the provisions on countering the use of the finance sector for tax frauds apply should be supplemented, as a proposal for the law to be amended, with payment institutions, as it has not been done so far (Opinion of the Legislative Council to the President of the Council of Ministers of 10 May 2017 on the draft law amending certain laws to counteract the use of the financial sector for fiscal fraud, RL-0303–16/17, Przegląd Legislacyjny 2019(3): 81).

The performance of duties by the Head of the National Revenue Administration is supported by the clearing house ICT system (System Teleinformatyczny Izby Rozliczeniowej, STIR). Three purposes of the operation of the system in question can be deduced from the provision of Article 119zha § 1of the Tax Ordinance. Firstly, the STIR system is used to receive and process data in order to establish the indicator of risk of the use of the financial sector for tax fraud. Secondly, the system allows data and information on the risk indicator to be transmitted to the Central Tax Data Register and to the ICT systems of banks and credit unions. Thirdly, the ICT system of the clearing house intermediates in the transmission of data, information, and requests between the Head of the National Revenue Administration and banks and credit unions. According to Article 119zk § 1 of the Tax Ordinance, the transmission of data, information, and requests between the clearing systems of banks and credit unions and the ICT system of the clearing house and the Central Tax Data Register shall be carried out automatically and immediately via the ICT system of the clearing house.

6 Conclusions

The study showed that significant normative changes in the Polish legal system are necessary. First, it is necessary to adopt a law regulating the financial information system. This law should properly implement EU law. The EU legislator therefore proposes to establish centralised automatic mechanisms such as registers or data retrieval systems in all Member States. These mechanisms are intended to allow timely information on the identity of holders of bank and payment accounts and safe deposit boxes, their proxy holders, and their beneficial owners. The content of the directive constitutes that Member States are obliged to ensure the complete confidentiality of the information obtained. Essentially, the national legislator should also include the FinTech sector within the scope of this act.

Secondly, the current anti-money laundering and fiscal fraud measures should be adapted to the dynamically changing financial market. Sometimes the Polish legislator imposes certain obligations on banks and cooperative credit unions, forgetting, for example, payment institutions and other sub-entities classified as FinTech.

References

Bajda K (2021) Criminological and forensic aspects of selected areas of organized crime in Poland. Studia Iuridica Lublinensia 30(4):33–47. https://doi.org/10.17951/sil.2021.30.4.33-47

Esoimeme E (2021) The Pandora papers: how anti-money laundering procedures and controls should have flagged $300 million earlier. SSRN Electron J. https://doi.org/10.2139/ssrn.3978080

Gerbrands P, Unger B, Getzner M, Ferwerda J (2022) The effect of anti-money laundering policies: an empirical network analysis. EPJ Data Sci 11(1):1–33. https://doi.org/10.1140/epjds/s13688-022-00328-8

Kapica W (ed) (2020) Przeciwdziałanie praniu pieniędzy oraz finansowaniu terroryzmu. Komentarz, Wolters Kluwer, Warszawa

Kędzierski M (2021) Notariusz jako instytucja obowiązana w rozumieniu ustawy o przeciwdziałaniu praniu pieniędzy oraz finansowaniu terroryzmu (omówienie niektórych zagadnień). Stud Prawnicze KUL 1:165–195. https://doi.org/10.31743/sp.10633

Mikos-Sitek M (2019) Rachunek podmiotu kwalifikowanego. Nius 8 January 2019

Nowakowski M (2020) FINTECH - technologia, finanse, regulacje. Praktyczny przewodnik dla sektora innowacji finansowych, [FINTECH - technology, finance, regulations. A practical guide for the financial innovation sector], Warsaw

Obczyński R (2020) Komentarz do art. 34. In: Kapica W (ed) Przeciwdziałanie praniu pieniędzy oraz finansowaniu terroryzmu. Komentarz, Wolters Kluwer, Warszawa

Silva PG (2019) Recent developments in EU legislation on anti-money laundering and terrorist financing. New J Eur Crim Law 10(1):57–67. https://doi.org/10.1177/2032284419840442

Szafrański W (2021) New regulations to counteract money laundering in the trading of works of art. Between the implementation of AMLD V and the systemic solution. Santander Art Cult Law Rev 1(7):61–82. https://doi.org/10.4467/2450050XSNR.21.006.14595

Zavoli I, King C (2021) The challenges of implementing anti-money laundering regulation: an empirical analysis. Mod Law Rev 84(4):740–771. https://doi.org/10.1111/1468-2230.12628

Digital Payment Systems: State and Perspectives

Božidar Radenković, Marijana Despotović-Zrakić, and Aleksandra Labus

Abstract This chapter strives to provide a comprehensive overview of current digital payment systems and point out their key opportunities, benefits, and constraints. We will discuss the following methods and channels for digital payment: credit cards, online credits, vouchers, different types of P2P, recurring payments, social pay, micro payments, and others. We will address the importance and role of mobile technologies and services in mobile commerce. Opportunities and challenges in harnessing modern technologies such as blockchain and artificial intelligence in the context of digital payments will be discussed. For each of the listed concepts, we will discuss pros and cons as well as applications and challenges. Further, we will explore the role of those concepts in real e-commerce ecosystems. In addition, we will discuss changes in digital payment systems caused by global pandemic and perspectives in post Covid-19 era.

Keywords Digital payment systems · Mobile payment · e-business ecosystems

1 Introduction

Modern e-business ecosystems encompass a wide corpus of concepts, subsystems, technologies, relations, and roles (Senyo et al. 2019; Kolagar et al. 2022). Providing seamless infrastructure and environment not only for all these components but for all the stakeholders, particularly end-users, becomes more and more challenging. Managing cash flow and the associated value transfers is at the core of every business. The digital payment system is considered the backbone of an e-business system and one of its most crucial components (Ferrari 2022). The emergence of digital transactions has disrupted the payments market (Jonker et al. 2022). Advances in technology, connected with the high growing demand for digital payment methods,

B. Radenković · M. Despotović-Zrakić · A. Labus (✉)
Faculty of Organizational Sciences, University of Belgrade, Belgrade, Serbia
e-mail: boza@elab.rs; maja@elab.rs; aleksandra@elab.rs

S. Benković et al. (eds.), *Digital Transformation of the Financial Industry*, Contributions to Finance and Accounting,
https://doi.org/10.1007/978-3-031-23269-5_12

are increasingly reshaping the way payments are made in e-business ecosystems. Digital payment mechanisms can lead to improved business outcomes by automating processes, shortening time, reducing errors, and allowing for greater control of payment processes.

Numerous studies have been published in recent years on digital payments due to the rapid expansion of payment systems, as well as the complexities of the factors that influence their adoption and use (Jonker et al. 2022; Arvidsson 2019; Visconti-Caparrós and Campos-Blázquez 2021). Digital payment can be defined as a transfer of money or digital currency from one (digital) account to another using digital payment technologies (Visconti-Caparrós and Campos-Blázquez 2021). Digitization of payments was a huge step toward easy, convenient, fast, and secure payment.

The goal of this article is to discuss the main drivers of digital payment globally, trends in fintech, and the roles of digital payments in e-business ecosystems. We will investigate the role of digital payment methods on the innovation of different parts of business models. In addition, the goal is to point out trends and directions in digital payment systems with a special focus on employing cutting-edge technologies and concepts, such as advanced big data, blockchain, and AI in the fintech. The study is intended to be a good starting point for an understanding of the current state and perspective of digital payments.

2 Digital Payment Methods

Payment cards, e-banking, and mobile payment instruments have provided broad corpus of ways to pay for any kind of service or product (Brown et al. 2022).

In addition, recent innovations to merchant payment infrastructure and consumer payment instruments further fueled the usage of both common and disruptive payment methods (Visconti-Caparrós and Campos-Blázquez 2021; Brown et al. 2022).

A digital payment "is the transfer of value from one payment account to another where both the payer and the payee use a digital device such as a mobile phone, computer, or a credit, debit, or prepaid card" (Khaitan and Joshi 2022).

In the common digital payment system, there are three roles (Fig. 1):

- Buyer (payer)
- Seller (payee)
- Payment processor

Numerous researchers have tried to make taxonomies of digital payment methods, focusing on various characteristics. However, the fast development of new payment methods makes it hard to develop a comprehensive taxonomy. In further text, we present the selected digital payment methods.

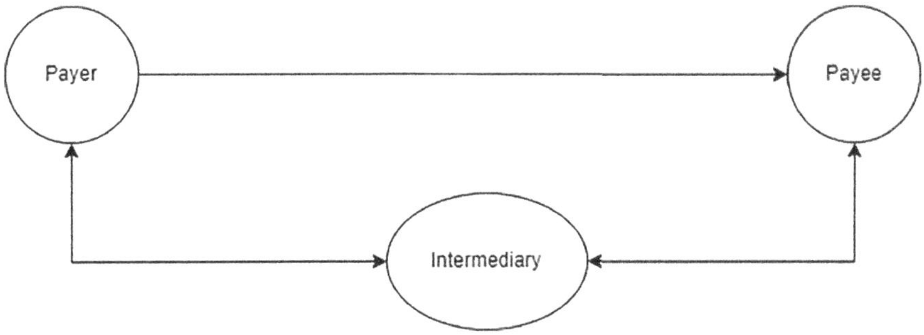

Fig. 1 Roles in the digital payment system

2.1 Debit and Credit Cards

A payment card is a non-cash payment instrument and an instrument for withdrawing cash from the card issuer or through an ATM. That is a small piece of plastic that contains some means of identification (signature or image), which allows the person to whom the card is addressed to use it for the stated purposes.

- Payment cards can be divided into three groups: credit cards, debit cards, prepaid cards.
- Credit cards contain a certain credit limit that the consumer can use when buying goods or withdrawing cash.
- A debit card allows the owner to directly debit his bank account. The owner of this card does not have a free credit period after the purchase.
- Prepaid cards contain a computer chip into which the amount of money is "inserted" from the cardholder's account or by cash collection from him.

A typical credit card transaction takes place as follows:

- The merchant calculates the value of the purchased goods and asks the customer to pay.
- The customer gives the merchant a credit/debit card.
- The merchant swipes the credit/debit card through the POS terminal. The value of the sold goods is entered manually, or taken from the cash register.
- The merchant submits credit/debit card information and the value of the purchased goods to his business bank, with a request for authorization.
- The merchant bank then processes the transaction, forwarding the authorization request to the credit/debit card-issuing bank. The credit/debit card number identifies the type of card, the issuing bank, and the cardholder's account.
- The bank issuing the credit/debit card authorizes the transaction and generates an authorization code. This code is sent back to the business bank. The card-issuing bank reserves money on the cardholder's account in an amount equivalent to the value of the purchased goods.

- The merchant bank processes the transaction and then sends an approval or rejection code to the merchant's POS terminal.
- The invoice is printed by the POS terminal or cash register.

Although, the traditional digital payment habits based on credit or debit cards are being replaced by new innovative formats of mobile instant payment among end-users (Brown et al. 2022), several researches pointed out the credit cards are still being predominant within many markets, particularly in developing countries (Yuan et al. 2021).

2.2 Online Credits

Online credits could be defined as issuing consumer loans online by financial intermediaries (Xia et al. 2021). This method is booming, particularly within e-commerce and in developing countries. For instance, Chinese online consumer lending issued 6.9 trillion RMB in 2018. Accordingly, it has a huge role in "inclusive finance and promotes household consumption in China" (Li et al. 2020).

In addition, new ways of online credits are to appear within the emerging markets, such as P2P lending via special marketplaces (Freedman and Jin 2017).

However, credit risk in online consumer lending is still a major concern; "partially due to low-quality borrowers online consumer lending typically suffers from higher credit risk than similar businesses in the conventional banking system" (Xia et al. 2021).

2.3 Vouchers/Coupons

From the very first appearances, vouchers have been popular and convenient way of payment. A voucher refers to a document, such as a coupon or ticket, that is redeemable for some good or service. Similar instruments are coupons, gift cards, tickets with promotional codes, etc. (Besharat et al. 2021; Li et al. 2021). They are employed in e-commerce and hospitality industries.

Further, this type of digital payment can bring a plethora of side benefits to both customers and merchants: loyalty, brand awareness, promotion, CRM in general, a good addition to omnichannel strategies, etc.

2.4 P2P Payments

Peer-to-peer (P2P) payments are person-to-person money transactions made between individuals (payer and payee) without a traditional or formal intermediary, such as banks. The role of intermediary is implemented within a P2P payment application, usually integrated and set up on a particular mobile device or used via web browser/mobile app. Each user in the P2P application has their own account used for sending and receiving money. These accounts can be linked to bank accounts of P2P users.

The number and value of P2P payments has been growing significantly, due to the increased need for mobile payments before and during COVID-19 pandemic (Belanche et al. 2022; Greene et al. 2022).

P2P payments can be made using paper (cash, checks, money order) or electronic methods (credit card, debit card, PayPal, Venmo, Zelle) (Greene et al. 2022).

The COVID-19 pandemic has accelerated the adoption of mobile payments to the extent that P2P systems today, in several contexts are in front of cards and cash for everyday purchases (Belanche et al. 2022). According to Apptopia,[1] the most downloaded P2P payment apps are PayPal, Google Pay, Alipay.

2.5 *Social Pay*

Similar to other people's activities, payments are intensively moving toward different kinds of mobile platforms (Hew 2017). The so-called social payments and activities on those platforms are changing from simple text message transfers to social computing platforms such as Apple Pay or Uber that connect network members (Acker and Murthy 2020). Mobile payment services support "social practices, digital communication, and commerce with social features found in social media platforms" (Acker and Murthy 2020). Social payment apps can be employed for buying goods, services, different kind of payments, and other chargeable things (Acker and Murthy 2020).

Figure 2 shows an example of a social payment app.

2.6 *Micropayments*

Micropayment as a small payment that is not profitable to process through common payment such as credit card due to the fact that processing fee of credit card may be higher than the value of the micropayment transactions. The high frequency of micropayment transactions further demands the need for low transaction cost (Tan and Tan 2012).

Due to the potential applications, many research results about micropayment schemes design and their performance enhancement have been published in the past few years (Yen et al. 2014).

[1] https://blog.apptopia.com/-most-downloaded-p2p-payment-apps-in-the-world-h1-2021

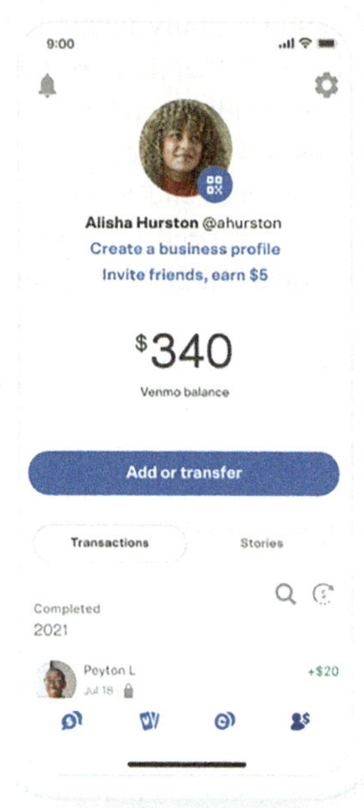

Fig. 2 Social payment app example (https://techcrunch.com/2021/07/20/venmo-removes-its-global-public-feed-in-a-significant-app-redesign/) (image credits: Venmo)

Figure 3 presents an example of a micro payment application.

2.7 *Mobile Payments*

Mobile payment can be described as a service that enable users to initiate, authorize, and complete financial transactions using a mobile device (Ahn and Nam 2022).

This type of payment is often referred to as "mobile wallet, contactless payment, or proximity payment, which is one prominent type of mobile payments" (Jung et al. 2020). Mobile payments imply consumers to possess a mobile phone/mobile devices that serve as a storage of payment information from credit or debit cards to complete a transaction. Most important types of mobile payments include: mobile proximity payments, mobile peer-to-peer payments, and mobile in-app payments (Ahn and Nam 2022). Today, mobile payments have become a multifunctional application tool that integrates shopping, food and takeaway, social networking, financial management, living expenses, and transportation expenses and many others (Zhao et al. 2022).

Mobile payments offer plethora of benefits to all the stakeholders (Jung et al. 2020). The adoption of contactless payment methods rocketed up during the pandemic (Ahn and Nam 2022; Daragmeh et al. 2021).

The following mobile payment technologies and concepts will be discussed: NFC, Sound waves, mobile wallets, QR, SMS, direct carrier billing, mobile apps.

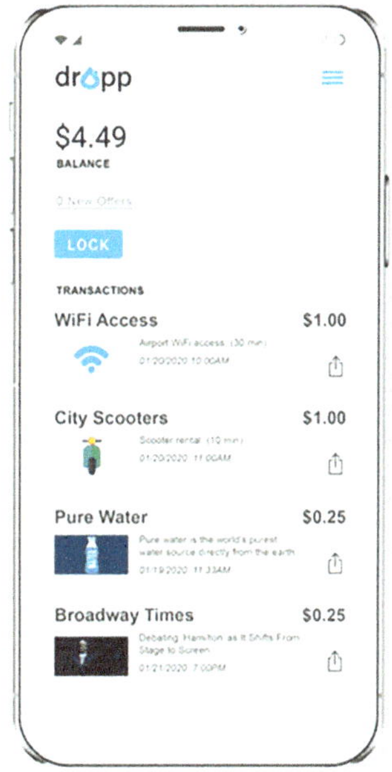

Fig. 3 An example of a micropayment application (Image credits: Dropp.cc, https://dropp.cc/)

2.8 NFC

Simply, NFC mobile payment implements near-field communication technology to establish a connection between the two devices. Using NFC technology, just by moving the cell phone to the store's POS device, which both have NFC technology, the user can pay for his or her payment (Tafti et al. 2021).

NFC has huge number of usages in the real world. Although main use cases include healthcare, transportation, and access control, the key application of NFC is in the field of mobile payment and contactless payment (Tafti et al. 2021).

2.9 Mobile Wallets

Digital wallets are methods for performing payments electronically, i.e. transferring funds between traditional banking accounts or electronic money deposit accounts. In the case the digital account is set up on mobile devices (e.g., smartphones, tablets) it is referred to as a mobile wallet (León 2021).

Mobile payments can foster the provision of payment services both person-to-person transfers and government-to-person transfers as well as buying goods and services (Bezovski 2016).

Figure 4 presents an application of a mobile wallet app.

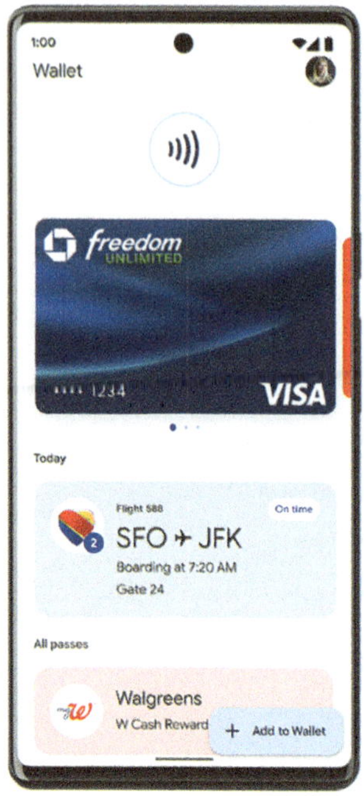

Fig. 4 An example of a mobile wallet app (https://www.yourwallet.app/)

2.10 Sound Waves

Sound Based Payment technology is a kind of contactless payments through sound waves. The idea behind the technology is to enable various devices such as smartphones, feature phones, card swipe machines, and point-of-sale devices (Kumar 2019).

ToneTag is considered one of the first-of-its-kind technology using sound waves to complete digital payments (ToneTag 2022). ToneTag's technology employs the mobile device's speaker and microphone as the medium to communicate with the PoS to make payments, similar to Bluetooth technology. The merchant authorize their identity through sound waves, while buyer gets a pop-up for the transaction to take place (ToneTag 2022). The transaction is completed within a couple of seconds.

2.11 QR

Basically, QR codes are 2D matrix images that can be easily displayed physically on printed media or digitally on a screen (Yan et al. 2021; Peng et al. 2019). Their popularity is due to their fast readability and storage capacity. There are a big number of applications from "product tracking and identification to entertainment, advertising, encryption, and payment" and many others.

2.12 SMS

Unexpectedly, despite omnipresent digitalization, the short message service (SMS), a text-based mobile communication, is still a popular and effective tool for delivering information from one person to another and payment as well (Sharma et al. 2021). Further, although there are many different payment methods and ways of message exchange, SMS has become a trusted platform for payment (Sharma et al. 2021).

2.13 Direct Carrier Billing

Main idea behind Direct Carrier Billing is to enable users to buy digital products from third-party vendors without need to employ their bank cards. The only thing a consumer needs are a mobile device and a SIM card.

3 The Role of Emerging Technologies in Digital Payment Systems

3.1 Blockchain Technologies and Digital Payments

Although the initial idea of blockchain was directed toward digital currencies, it is now employed into various fields, including payments. Decentralized payment systems, such as Bitcoin, were designed with the idea of avoiding intermediaries and enabling real-time validation of transactions. They represent the most mature blockchain applications. Bitcoin system provides pseudo-anonymity, having in mind that information about transactions, such as amount, origin and destination addresses are publicly available on the network, can be deanonymized and linked to real-world identities.

Zerocash was designed as version of Bitcoin that provides a higher level of privacy-preserving. With Zerocash, users can perform P2P payments, but the transactions do not reveal origin, destination, or the amount of payment.

Another privacy-enhanced cryptocurrency is Monero. Monero can be considered as a fully fungible electronic cash system that allows payments to and from anywhere in the world.

One of the blockchain-based payment platforms with corresponding cryptocurrency is Ripple. Ripple is an open-source protocol designed to enable fast and cheap transactions. The platform has its currency XRP used for all transactions, but other custom currencies can be developed as well. Other networks for

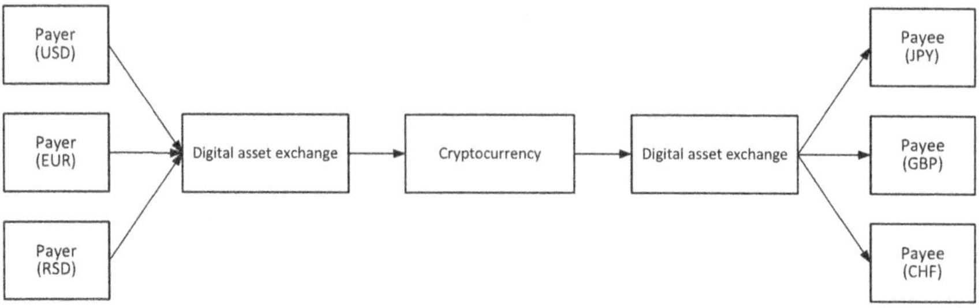

Fig. 5 A blockchain system for international fund transfer

similar purposes are being developed, such as Stellar. All of them are based on the idea to create a decentralized network that enables individuals and institutions seamless sending, receiving, and trading digital representations of all forms of money.

Although the area of digital currencies is booming, and researchers and practitioners show a great interest, fully decentralized and anonymous payment systems have not yet been fully developed (Lin et al. 2020). There is also a lot of work being done in the regulation of cryptocurrencies, where in most cases they are treated as commodity, and not as actual payment methods.

Lately, blockchain technologies have been considered in the context of inter-bank payment systems. Financial institutions are striving to find more efficient, secure, and decentralized systems that would replace traditional RTGS with improved confidentiality, instruction settlement finality, liquidity saving mechanism, and more efficient methods of gridlock resolution (Wang et al. 2018). Figure 5 illustrates the concept of a blockchain-based system that enables fast transfer of funds worldwide, providing businesses with a near real-time liquidity. All transactions are recorded and data can easily be obtained for auditing purposes.

3.2 *Artificial Intelligence for Digital Payments*

AI is a multidisciplinary technology, one with the capability of integrating cognition, machine learning, emotion recognition, human–computer interaction, data storage, and decision-making (Lu 2019).

AI provides a plethora of opportunities in the area of digital payment systems (Lu 2019). Main categories of cases are depicted in Table 1.

Table 1 AI applications in digital payment systems

Category	Description
Fraud prevention	It helps in assessing abnormal and out-of-order activities
Chatbots	Adopting chatbots to enhance customer engagement while ensuring greater financial inclusion (Mogaji et al. 2021)
Authentication	Synergy of AI and biometrics are driving next-generation authentication (Brostoff 2019)
Financial management	Personal financial management is one of the most significant developments of AI
Advisory services	The technologies are beneficial in understanding and making financial decisions
Risk assessment	The technologies have taken the place of humans, analyze the large volume of data, and examined the associated risks
Tasks automatization	Majority of activities in digital payments can be orchestrated and performed using AI services and apps (Lu 2019)
Trading	Machines and technologies have the power to observe patterns and to predict

4 Discussion and Implications

FinTech stimulates the development of the digital economy by promoting technological innovation (Chen et al. 2022; Daud et al. 2022).

The Global FinTech Adoption Index cited that the FinTech adoption rate grew from 16% in 2015 and consumer usage now exceeds two-thirds (64%) of available FinTech startups (Karim et al. 2022). Even before the COVID-19 pandemic, world was moving to FinTech, which fostered development of digital payments and other technology-driven transactions (Global FinTech adoption index 2019). Fintech will be among key drivers of digital payment ecosystems in future.

The main trends and topics we expect to be of the key importance within digital payment ecosystems for next decade are:

- Buy now, pay later
- Impact of blockchain and cryptocurrencies will constantly increase
- Open banking
- Embedded finance
- Green payments
- Metaverse
- Social commerce
- Mobile apps
- Contactless payment
- Omnichannel
- AI will be commonly used in digital payment systems
- P2P payments

Table 2 Research implications

Group	Implications
Practitioners	*Infrastructure and services providers* – Easy to use services and infrastructure – Integrations among ecosystem components – Partnerships and value networks – Innovations of different parts of business models – Harness pervasive technologies – Adoption dynamics is market-specific
	Merchants – Payment should be integral part of seamless customer journey – Try to be early adopters – Provide corpus of payment methods in must have – M-commerce – Partnerships and value co-creation
Academia	– Interdisciplinarity – Strong relations with practice – Empower students to work on fintech innovations
Government	– Blockchain has to be recognized as important part of digital business ecosystems – Cross-border payments are becoming more and more significant – Open banking should be fostered via infrastructure and laws – Strategies and laws that support and enhance innovation – Focus on education for all the stakeholders, particularly merchants, customers, and politicians – Crowdsourcing and citizens' participation

4.1 Implications

The main implications for government, academia, and practitioners who deal with digital payments are presented in Table 2.

5 Conclusion

The paper aimed to provide a brief overview of the modern digital payment method, instruments, and models. The main idea was to foster awareness regarding the possibilities and opportunities of employing newest technologies in digital payment. Numerous research and examples listed in the paper prove that this area have skyrocketed, particularly during the pandemic. On the other hand, many challenges and obstacles are to appear as well. The role of academia has always been of the high importance for both innovation and education in this area. Further, interdisciplinary and establishing synergy among all the stakeholders is the only way to maximize the outcomes of digital payment ecosystems.

Future research will be directed toward the concepts of acceptance of various digital payment systems, with respect to local contexts, as well as to their integration with smart retail (Đurđević et al. 2022) and crowdsourcing systems (Staletić et al. 2020).

References

Acker A, Murthy D (2020) What is Venmo? A descriptive analysis of social features in the mobile payment platform. Telematics Inform 52:101429

Ahn SY, Nam Y (2022) Does mobile payment use lead to overspending? The moderating role of financial knowledge. Comput Hum Behav 134:107319

Arvidsson N (2019) Building a cashless society: the Swedish route to the future of cash payments. Springer Nature

Belanche D, Guinalíu M, Albás P (2022) Customer adoption of p2p mobile payment systems: the role of perceived risk. Telematics Inform 72:101851

Besharat A, Nardini G, Roggeveen AL (2021) Online daily coupons: understanding how prepayment impacts spending at redemption. J Bus Res 127:364–372

Bezovski Z (2016) The future of the mobile payment as electronic payment system. Eur J Bus Manage 8(8):127–132

Brostoff G (2019) How AI and biometrics are driving next-generation authentication. Biometric Technol Today 2019(6):7–9

Brown M, Hentschel N, Mettler H, Stix H (2022) The convenience of electronic payments and consumer cash demand. J Monet Econ 130:86

Chen X, Teng L, Chen W (2022) How does FinTech affect the development of the digital economy? Evidence from China. North Am J Econ Finance 61:101697

Daragmeh A, Lentner C, Sági J (2021) FinTech payments in the era of COVID-19: factors influencing behavioral intentions of "generation X" in Hungary to use mobile payment. J Behav Exp Financ 32:100574

Daud SNM, Khalid A, Azman-Saini WNW (2022) FinTech and financial stability: threat or opportunity? Financ Res Lett 47:102667

Đurđević N, Labus A, Barać D, Radenković M, Despotović-Zrakić M (2022) An approach to assessing shopper acceptance of Beacon triggered promotions in smart retail. Sustainability 14(6):3256

Ferrari MV (2022) The platformisation of digital payments: the fabrication of consumer interest in the EU FinTech agenda. Comput Law Security Rev 45:105687

Freedman S, Jin GZ (2017) The information value of online social networks: lessons from peer-to-peer lending. Int J Ind Organ 51:185–222

Global FinTech adoption index 2019 (2019) EY https://assets.ey.com/content/dam/ey-sites/ey-com/en_gl/topics/banking-and-capital-markets/ey-global-fintech-adoption-index.pdf. Accessed 5 Aug 2022

Greene C, Prescott B, Shy O (2022) How people pay each other: data, theory, and calibrations. J Behav Exp Econ 96:101788

Hew JJ (2017) Hall of fame for mobile commerce and its applications: a bibliometric evaluation of a decade and a half (2000–2015). Telematics Inform 34(1):43–66

Jonker N, van der Cruijsen C, Bijlsma M, Bolt W (2022) Pandemic payment patterns. J Bank Financ 143:106593

Jung JH, Kwon E, Kim DH (2020) Mobile payment service usage: US consumers' motivations and intentions. Comput Hum Behav Rep 1:100008

Karim S, Naz F, Naeem MA, Vigne SA (2022) Is FinTech providing effective solutions to small and medium enterprises (SMEs) in ASEAN countries? Econ Anal Policy 75:335

Khaitan P, Joshi A (2022) What is a digital payment and how does it work? https://www.forbes.com/advisor/in/banking/what-is-a-digital-payment-and-how-does-it-work/. Accessed 5 Aug 2022

Kolagar M, Parida V, Sjödin D (2022) Ecosystem transformation for digital servitization: a systematic review, integrative framework, and future research agenda. J Bus Res 146:176–200

Kumar A (2019) The significance of soundwave technology-based payments. https://www.entrepreneur.com/article/342435. Accessed 5 Aug 2022

León C (2021) The adoption of a mobile payment system: the user perspective. Latin Am J Central Banking 2(4):100042
Li J, Wu Y, Xiao JJ (2020) The impact of digital finance on household consumption: evidence from China. Econ Model 86:317–326
Li Z, Yang W, Jin HS, Wang D (2021) Omnichannel retailing operations with coupon promotions. J Retail Consum Serv 58:102324
Lin C, He D, Huang X, Khan MK, Choo KKR (2020) DCAP: a secure and efficient decentralized conditional anonymous payment system based on blockchain. IEEE Trans Inf Forensics Security 15:2440–2452
Lu Y (2019) Artificial intelligence: a survey on evolution, models, applications and future trends. J Manage Anal 6(1):1–29
Mogaji E, Balakrishnan J, Nwoba AC, Nguyen NP (2021) Emerging-market consumers' interactions with banking chatbots. Telematics Inform 65:101711
Peng H, Lu L, Liu L, Sharf A, Chen B (2019) Fabricating QR codes on 3D objects using self-shadows. Comput Aided Des 114:91–100
Senyo PK, Liu K, Effah J (2019) Digital business ecosystem: literature review and a framework for future research. Int J Inf Manag 47:52–64
Sharma A, Dwivedi YK, Arya V, Siddiqui MQ (2021) Does SMS advertising still have relevance to increase consumer purchase intention? A hybrid PLS-SEM-neural network modelling approach. Comput Hum Behav 124:106919
Staletić N, Labus A, Bogdanović Z, Despotović-Zrakić M, Radenković B (2020) Citizens' readiness to crowdsource smart city services: a developing country perspective. Cities 107:102883
Tafti FSM, Mohammadi S, Babagoli M (2021) A new NFC mobile payment protocol using improved GSM based authentication. J Inf Security Appl 62:102997
Tan WK, Tan YJ (2012) Transformation of smart-card-based single-purpose e-micropayment scheme to multi-purpose scheme: a case study. Expert Syst Appl 39(3):2306–2313
ToneTag (2022) https://www.tonetag.com/. Accessed 5 Aug 2022
Visconti-Caparrós JM, Campos-Blázquez JR (2021) The development of alternate payment methods and their impact on customer behavior: the Bizum case in Spain. Technol Forecast Soc Chang 121330
Wang X, Xu X, Feagan L, Huang S, Jiao L, Zhao W (2018) Inter-bank payment system on enterprise blockchain platform. In: 2018 IEEE 11th international conference on CLOUD computing (CLOUD). IEEE, pp 614–621
Xia Y, Li Y, He L, Xu Y, Meng Y (2021) Incorporating multilevel macroeconomic variables into credit scoring for online consumer lending. Electron Commer Res Appl 49:101095
Yan LY, Tan GWH, Loh XM, Hew JJ, Ooi KB (2021) QR code and mobile payment: the disruptive forces in retail. J Retail Consum Serv 58:102300
Yen SM, Lin HC, Chen YC, Hung JJ, Wu JM (2014) PayStar: a denomination flexible micropayment scheme. Inf Sci 259:160–169
Yuan Y, Rong Z, Xu N, Lu Y (2021) Credit cards and small business dynamics: evidence from China. Pac Basin Financ J 67:101570
Zhao C, Wu Y, Guo J (2022) Mobile payment and Chinese rural household consumption. China Econ Rev 71:101719

Leveraging Open Banking: Challenges and Opportunities

Darko Vasić, Dušan Barać, and Miloš Radenković

Abstract The main goal of this research is to examine the application of innovative open banking models and services through the lens of the end users. Many countries have already started the process of writing regulations for open banking and its assorted services. These regulations are often written before the technology is entirely embraced by its intended users, and for this reason acceptance studies are of crucial importance in ascertaining the user expectations and the intended scope of their use. For this purpose, we present an UTAUT-2 based acceptance study which deals with user acceptance of open banking coupled with other notable technologies such as blockchain. By enabling open banking through the blockchain, many benefits could be achieved, primarily when dealing with trust and privacy of user data. These benefits are expected to play an influential part in raising the acceptance levels of open banking as a whole. Through the analysis of the model, we have identified several notable influential factors that can play a large part in the behavioral intention of users, and as such can be used as a guideline for the development of new and innovative open banking services.

Keywords Open banking · Banking as a service · Fintech · Blockchain

1 Introduction

The financial industry business models have historically been converging toward more rigid structures. This rigidness of doing business was mostly due to value chains of banks, where the creation, packaging, and distribution of products would be confined to their own personal ecosystems. As a result, these business models are

---

D. Vasić · D. Barać (✉)
Faculty of organizational sciences, University of Belgrade, Belgrade, Serbia
e-mail: dusan@elab.rs

M. Radenković
School of Computing, Union University, Belgrade, Serbia

S. Benković et al. (eds.), *Digital Transformation of the Financial Industry*,
Contributions to Finance and Accounting,
https://doi.org/10.1007/978-3-031-23269-5_13

monolithic, linear, and vertically integrated. Recently with the advent of digitalization, these business models are starting to change, vertical integrations are torn down, and banking value chains are becoming increasingly fragmented (Ramdani et al. 2020). The traditional idea of a banking product is further broken down into microproducts or services which can be bundled with external services to form a product ideally suited to the client's needs (Polasik et al. 2020).

Open banking offers its users many conveniences, but as it is often the case with such conveniences they bring into focus privacy concerns, and concerns for the security of customers' funds. These concerns must be addressed as open access can lead to unlawful and unauthorized access of malicious third parties. The two main issues that must be overcome for any open banking platform are security and privacy of data. Recently, considerable strides have been made in solving these issues by the application of the blockchain technology.

Blockchain is a distributed database, made up of smaller separate databases called blocks which are linked to each other. These linked blocks make up a chain, and the links in this chain are made through cryptography. Every block contains a hash value (digital fingerprint), which allows it to link itself to the chain. Besides its own hash value, the blocks also contain the hash values of the previous blocks in the chain. All of these hash values are then used as a seed for generating the hash value whenever a new block is linked. The result of this process is that any change to the contents of any block will result in an invalidation of the hash which warns the network of the attempt. This inability to change the data contained in the blockchain is what keeps it secure.

The research part of this chapter is carried out with the goal of ascertaining the trust and interest for open banking services among the potential clients. The study aims to analyze the readiness for adoption of open banking services based on clients' perception of conveniences and services provided. Likewise, a research was carried out to ascertain how the use of blockchain in open banking influences the client's perception of data security and privacy.

The primary tool for gathering data in this study was a survey based on the UTAUT2 model, which is primarily used for consumer acceptance studies of new technologies. The survey consisted of 40 questions, containing 5 demographic questions, with the rest being based around their attitudes, opinions, and understandings of Open banking and blockchain. All of the questions in the survey had to conform to certain UTAUT2 construct, the relevant constructs identified for this study are: performance expectancy, effort expectancy, social influence, facilitating conditions, price value, and habit.

The participants of this study were 146 users of banking services of various demographic background, most of the participants were 20–30 years old, since they are expected to be more keen on accepting new technologies.

In order to ascertain the dependencies and relations between the defined constructs and behavior intention, the PLS-SEM method was used. This method allows us to develop a model which explains the connections between the defined constructs and expected behavior of clients. SmartPLS 3.0 software suite was used to analyze the results.

The results show that the most influential factor in the behavioral intention is performance expectancy, while the effects of facilitating conditions and price value are insignificant. The variables effort expectancy, habits, and social influence play a significant role in user behavioral intention.

2 Open Banking

2.1 Key Concepts, Definitions, and Standards

Open Banking as a concept first appears in 2015 when the European parliament passed the PSD2 (Second Payment Service Directive) (Kinoti 2020). The main goal of this directive was to encourage innovations, competitiveness, and transparency of financial markets of Europe (National Transpositions by Member State Concerning: Directive (EU) 2015/2366 of the European Parliament and of the Council of 25 November 2015). The key component of this directive is the requirement for all banks to collaborate with third-party providers, by offering them access to the clients' accounts. Naturally, this access must be first approved by the client. This access to client data through a provided API is considered to be the cornerstone of Open Banking (Farrow 2020; Brodsky and Oakes 2017).

The main contribution of Open Banking as a whole is the emergence of new services which are regulated under PSD2 directive. These services are: PISP (Payment Initiation Service Providers) and AISP (Account Information Service Provider). The regulations imposed by PSD2 serves to make payments within Europe safer and to encourage innovations in the banking sector (Ozcan and Zachariadis 2021; Nanaeva et al. 2021). Open banking likewise allows for easier access of user data kept by banks and other related companies through the use of shared APIs (Nanaeva et al. 2021; Brodsky and Oakes 2017).

This easier access of user data, under agreed upon terms, allows third parties such as other banks, non-banking financial institutions to provide users with new and innovative services. These services often allow for better networking and unification of financial data in order to improve the quality of service. Likewise, this access to user data can be used for other purposes such as client credit risk analysis, this analysis can then be made visible to the client in return for allowing them access to their data (Fig. 1).

2.2 Banking-as-a-Service (BaaS)

The term Banking-as-a-Service (BaaS) is often used interchangeably with open banking since both heavily rely on sharing of data with third parties (Atabey and Berber 2021). Despite the apparent similarities, there is a distinction between what is shared. With open banking, user data and other financial data are shared via open

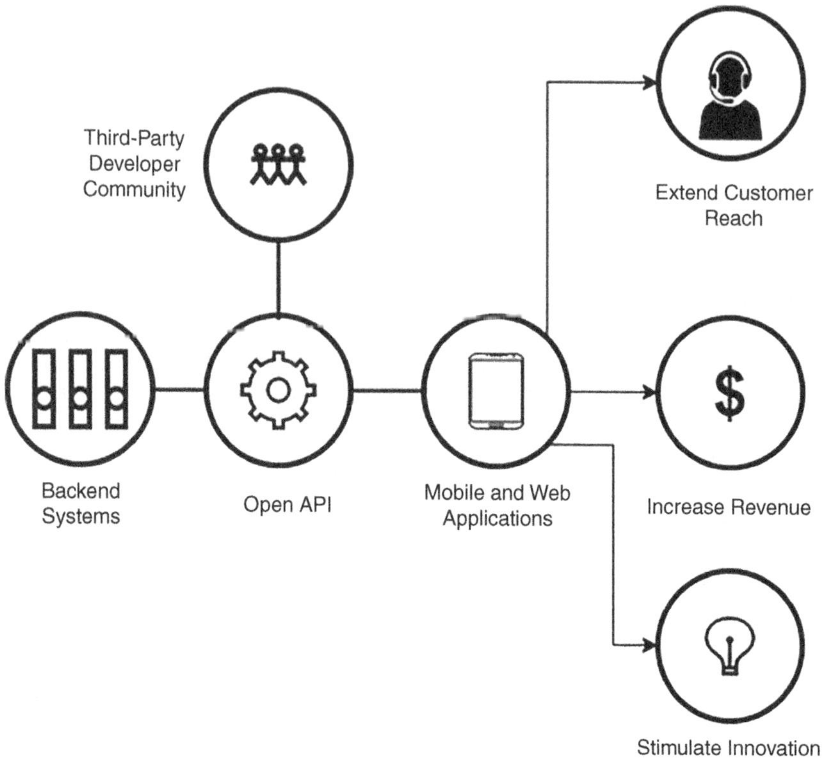

Fig. 1 Illustration of open banking

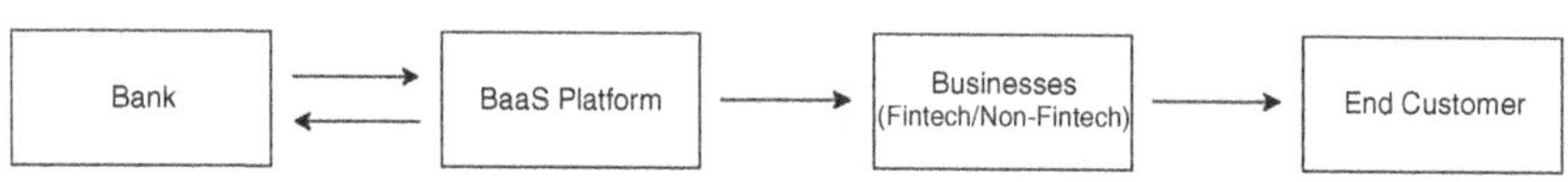

Fig. 2 BaaS players

APIs (Premchand and Choudhry 2018). On the other hand, BaaS allows access to certain banking services such as payments, loans, etc. There are three main users within the BaaS ecosystem:

1. Banks, both traditional and neobanks (digital banks that provide both cheaper and more specialized services)
2. Banking-as-a-Service Platform
3. Fintech or a company that wants to offer fintech services in their products (Padmanabhan 2021) (Fig. 2).

2.3 New Business Models and Examples Based on Open Banking

United Kingdom was the first country to adopt open banking in 2016, by making sure that banks provided start-up companies with data on their clients. By September 2019, the number of companies offering financial services enabled by these changes has grown to 143. These companies and their applications offer a wide range of services such as personal finance, consumer credits, small business support.

Hong Kong and Australia have taken a regulatory approach to open banking. Hong Kong introduced the national framework for APIs in 2018, rolled out in four phases. The first phase includes the regulations for sharing of information and services, while the fourth includes handling of sensitive transactional data.

Open Banking in Australia is regulated by the national law on consumer rights, which guarantees that users are the ones who choose who can access their data.

USA, Japan, India, Singapore, South Korea, and Nigeria have taken a market approach to open banking. In the market approach, banks, fintech, and service providers are the ones making data-exchange frameworks in lieu of government regulations.

Open banking is expected to speed up financial services, in particular the application and approval of credit or any other service which requires access to large amount of user data kept in disparate ecosystems. Clients will also see benefits in the form of being aware of services available to them, and saving them time with credit applications. This increased user awareness has given rise to new functionalities such as "Buy now and Pay later," with the largest platform for this service being Klarna (Nielsnon 2021). Some of the services that Klarna offers are: Direct payment, delayed payment, and paying through installments. Klarna offers an API called XS2A, which allows access to 4300 banks in 14 European markets, where fintech companies can develop test and deploy their services and products. This multitude of options allows clients higher conversions and profits. Clients are also allowed access to international markets and their payments are in line with national laws and regulations. Klarna likewise offers an open banking service which allows third-party providers and traders to access account details of their customers and to start transactions on their own.

3 Employing Blockchain in Open Banking

Blockchain is a distributed database made up of smaller interlinked databases called blocks (Bogdanović et al. 2019). These blocks contain transaction data, timestamp and its unique hash value. The blocks are linked in such a way that any retroactive change to transactions is not possible (Frizzo-Barker et al. 2020). These links are formed via cryptography, allowing any retroactive changes to be easily detected and stopped by inspecting the blocks hash value which contains the hash value of the

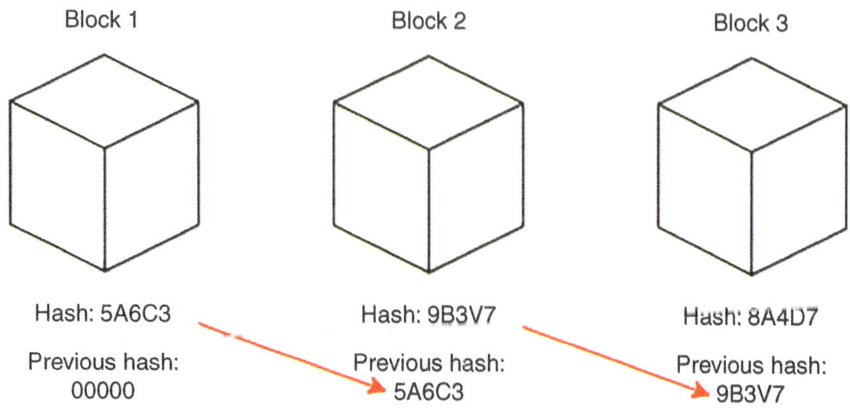

Fig. 3 The structure of blockchain

previous block. These attributes make blockchain a highly secure architecture (Mohanta et al. 2019) (Fig. 3).

Blockchain allows for the founding of a new digital financial ecosystem by linking its ledger to banking APIs. Through this platform third parties can securely communicate with banks and access their data without direct access to banking systems. Likewise users can rely on the platform to provide secure transactions between them in a trustless environment. Platform can also be used as a common data store, where actors across many industries can rely on services such as loans, investment packages, pension plans, etc.

Since blockchain is based on a distributed ledger, it allows for a categorization and hierarchical management of data within the blocks. Data within the blocks can easily be classified as either private, bank-owned, third-party usage data, or public data. Access and discovery of this data can further be controlled via smart contracts in order to minimize security risks. Privacy can further be improved by allocating a unique digital ID for accessing the banking ecosystems, without revealing personal information to third parties. In addition to this ID, blockchain can also enforce privacy policies, the result of these policies is that access to user data is adequately protected while also offering the users themselves full control and knowledge on how their data is used (Dong et al. 2020).

Smart contracts are distributed applications that allow for automated conduct of business within the blockchain (Lucas 2019). Smart contracts in their essence act as simple contracts that can be triggered upon predefined conditions, for example upon the arrival of goods, automatically transfer bitcoins to certain account. Smart contracts themselves are stored within the blockchain. Today smart contracts are also used as a basis for transfer of cryptocurrency and digital tokens, such as ERC-30 and ERC721 tokens that are themselves smart contracts. While having the same characteristics of simplified business contracts, smart contracts are not themselves legally binding like regular contracts. While there are initiatives to make smart contracts legally binding, there are many difficulties such as the definitions of smart contracts,

Table 1 Comparison of traditional and smart contracts

Traditional contracts	Smart contracts
1–3 days	Minutes
Manual remittance	Automatic remittance
Escrow necessary	Escrow may not be necessary
Expensive	Fraction of the cost
Physical presence (wet signature)	Virtual presence (digital signature)

which must differentiate it in some way from regular computer applications. From Table 1, we can see the benefits of smart contracts when compared to regular contracts.

4 Methodology

4.1 Research Context

For the purpose of this study an evaluation was performed in the form of an acceptance study for open banking. Besides the usual things that might affect the acceptance of new technologies special attention was paid to privacy of personal data and access to it by open banking service providers. Since blockchain is expected to play an important role in the future of open banking, participants were queried on how blockchain might affect their attitudes on data privacy.

4.2 Research Questions

For the purpose of forming a survey a UTAUT2 model was used (Venkatesh et al. 2012). In order for UTAUT2 to be applicable all survey questions had to be categorized in certain UTAUT2 constructs. The constructs that were identified for the purpose of this acceptance study are: performance expectancy (PE), effort expectancy (EE), social influence (SE), facilitating conditions (FC), price value (PV), and habit (HAB) (Fig. 4).

Six research hypotheses were defined:

H1: Performance expectancy of users has a positive impact on acceptance of open banking services.

H2: Effort expectancy of users has a positive impact on acceptance of open banking services.

H3: Social influence has a positive impact on acceptance of open banking services.

H4: Facilitating conditions of open banking services has a positive impact on their acceptance.

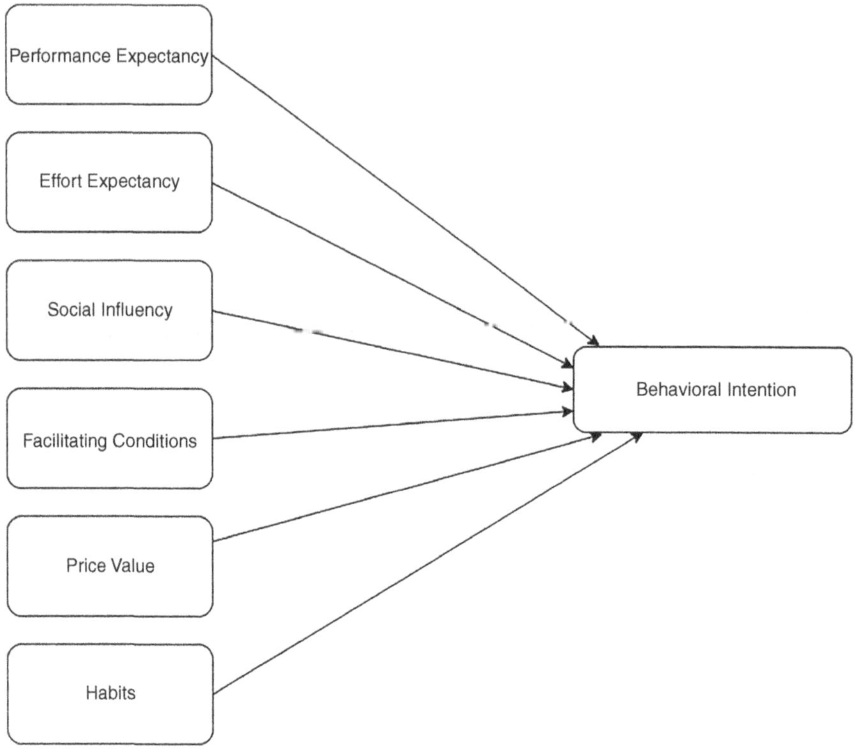

Fig. 4 The modified UTAUT2 model in the context of research

H5: Price value of services has a positive impact on user acceptance.
H6: User habits has a positive impact on acceptance of open banking services.

4.3 Instruments

All the necessary data for completing an acceptance study were gathered through a survey. Questions were formulated through the UTAUT2 model in the context of user readiness and acceptance of open banking services. The survey consisted of 40 questions, of which five were demographic in nature and the rest were used to ascertain user readiness and attitude toward open banking. The answers the participants provided were done through a 1–5 Likert scale.

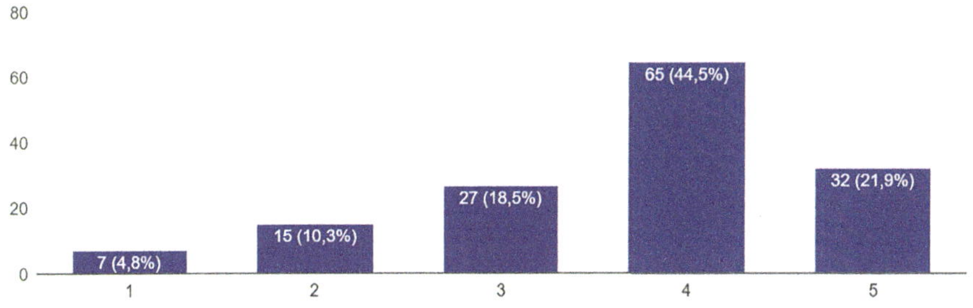

Fig. 5 The distribution of respondents according to how much trust they have in their bank

4.4 Research Sample

The focus group for this study were the people who already had a bank account, and were active users of banking services. Most of the participants were young people, and as such are expected to be more open to new technologies. The survey was taken by 146 participants with different demographic backgrounds, with most participants being between the ages of 20 and 25. Besides age, employment status and education were also provided. As a baseline for comparison purposes, the first question was on a scale of 1–5, how much they trust that their bank of choice won't abuse their data. The results of this question can be seen on Fig. 5.

5 Results

In order to ascertain the effect that UTAUT2 constructs have on the behavioral intention on open banking and blockchain, a detailed analysis needed to be performed, for this purpose PLS-SEM method was used, alongside the SmartPLS 3.0 software (Hair et al. 2021; Ringle et al. 2014, 2015). UTAUT2 constructs are regarded as latent variables and have survey questions attached to them. The effect of these variables on the behavioral intention (BI) has been analyzed. Variables such as age, gender, status, and education are moderating variables which can further influence the constructs, but not the behavioral intention. Since the majority of the participants are students or recently employed young people, the effect of these moderating variables will be disregarded.

Through the formed model, via the PLS-SEM method three algorithms were ran: PLS algorithm, blindfolding, and bootstrapping. The results of the PLS method can be seen on Fig. 6. Evaluation of the model was done in two phases: evaluation of model for measuring latent variables and evaluation of the structural model (Hair et al. 2013; Gudergan et al. 2008).

Assessment of reliability and validity of the measurement model is presented in Table 2.

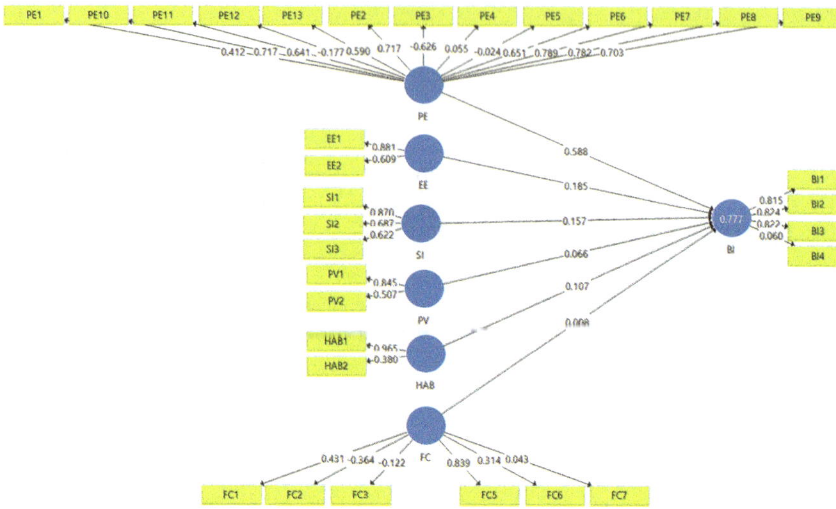

Fig. 6 The result of applying the PLS algorithm

In literature it is acceptable if a variable explains at least 50% of the variance of the indicator, or in different terms if the loading parameter is larger than the square root of the allowed value (0.707). In the model validity table, we can see that some of the values are smaller than 0.707 and are discarded due to not explaining enough variance.

Positive correlation between indicators is measured through AVE (Average Variance Extracted) and is expected to be above 0.5. As before some of the variables and in particular those falling in the categories of expected effort, price value and facilitating conditions exhibit positive correlation.

Composite reliability is the parameter used for grading internal consistency and acceptable values fall between 0.7 and 0.95. And we can see that some variables from Price Value, Habit, and Facilitating conditions for not fall within this range.

Table 3 shows cross-loading values. As can be seen from Table 3, not all cross-loading parameters for each variable are highest for their UTAUT2 construct. If this value is higher, it means that the connection between the indicator and the variable is stronger than between the indicator and other variables.

Fornell–Larcker criterion for validity of the model was also calculated, and it compares the correlation of latent constructs and the square root of average variance extracted AVE. This can be seen on Table 4.

Fornell–Larcker should tell is if latent constructs can explain the variance of their own construct better than the variance of any other construct. The only notable exception that can be seen from the table is the connection between BI and PE, where the there is a notable difference of 0.138.

The relationship between variables was also analyzed with path coefficients of the structured model. The values of path coefficients can be seen on Fig. 7. Values that are around +1 show high positive connection and are always statistically significant,

Table 2 Evaluation of validity of the latent variables measurement model

Variable	Indicator	Loadings	Composite reliability	AVE
Behavioral intention	BI1	0.815	0.762	0.505
	BI2	0.824		
	BI3	0.822		
	BI4	0.060		
Performance expectancy	PE1	0.412	0.764	0.349
	PE2	0.717		
	PE3	−0.626		
	PE4	0.055		
	PE5	−0.024		
	PE6	0.651		
	PE7	0.789		
	PE8	0.782		
	PE9	0.703		
	PE10	0.717		
	PE11	0.641		
	PE12	−0.177		
	PE13	0.590		
Effort expectancy	EE1	0.881	0.723	0.574
	EE2	0.609		
Social influence	SI1	0.870	0.774	0.539
	SI2	0.687		
	SI3	0.622		
Price value	PV1	0.845	0.640	0.486
	PV2	0.507		
Habits	HAB1	0.965	0.662	0.538
	HAB2	0.380		
Facilitating conditions	FC1	0.431	0.211	0.190
	FC2	−0.364		
	FC3	−0.122		
	FC5	0.839		
	FC6	0.314		
	FC7	0.043		

if the value is around 0 then there is no significant influence, while values around −1 show strong negative connection. From the values we can see that the most influential variables on behavioral intention is performance expectancy. While price value and facilitating conditions show practically no connection.

R^2 was used to grade the predictive accuracy of the model, with the value of 0.777, which is considered to be acceptable for acceptance studies. For a more accurate predictive accuracy, blindfolding technique was used and Q^2 was calculated to be 0.362. For values of Q^2 with the values higher than 0.35 or higher are

Table 3 Assessment of model validity—cross loadings values

	BI	EE	FC	HAB	PE	PV	SI
BI1	**0.815**	0.593	0.224	0.333	0.647	0.346	0.461
BI2	**0.824**	0.457	0.299	0.251	0.702	0.312	0.458
BI3	**0.822**	0.366	0.268	0.316	0.737	0.322	0.705
BI4	**0.06**	0.144	0.092	0.076	0.031	0.068	−0.082
EE1	0.528	**0.881**	0.213	0.234	0.438	0.117	0.287
EE2	0.315	**0.609**	0.255	0.094	0.335	0.019	0.264
FC1	0.119	0.059	**0.431**	0.105	0.088	−0.048	0.047
FC2	−0.105	−0.068	**−0.364**	−0.113	−0.091	−0.033	−0.066
FC3	0.053	−0.066	**−0.122**	−0.114	−0.003	0.085	0.037
FC5	0.263	0.26	**0.839**	0.151	0.33	0.155	0.167
FC6	0.053	0.067	**0.314**	0.129	0.062	−0.081	−0.083
FC7	−0.083	−0.086	**0.043**	−0.001	−0.048	−0.029	−0.082
HAB1	0.366	0.266	0.237	**0.965**	0.298	0.194	0.237
HAB2	0.104	−0.058	0.049	**0.38**	0.002	0.017	0.146
PE1	0.294	0.232	0.148	0.045	**0.412**	0.111	0.242
PE10	0.537	0.271	0.192	0.129	**0.717**	0.322	0.504
PE11	0.467	0.303	0.302	0.179	**0.641**	0.277	0.34
PE12	−0.109	−0.239	−0.196	−0.08	**−0.177**	−0.043	−0.032
PE13	0.48	0.258	0.161	0.107	**0.59**	0.27	0.444
PE2	0.589	0.305	0.111	0.178	**0.717**	0.354	0.557
PE3	−0.534	−0.307	−0.176	−0.206	**−0.626**	−0.193	−0.406
PE4	−0.043	0.113	−0.004	0.089	**0.055**	−0.038	0.115
PE5	−0.003	−0.055	−0.083	−0.156	**−0.024**	−0.043	0.089
PE6	0.585	0.499	0.371	0.146	**0.651**	0.218	0.407
PE7	0.777	0.408	0.296	0.229	**0.789**	0.369	0.532
PE8	0.658	0.469	0.274	0.282	**0.782**	0.362	0.503
PE9	0.619	0.304	0.233	0.279	**0.703**	0.377	0.51
PV1	0.335	0.054	0.042	0.124	0.338	**0.845**	0.124
PV2	0.208	0.106	0.113	0.147	0.274	**0.507**	0.233
SI1	0.669	0.312	0.188	0.255	0.633	0.219	**0.87**
SI2	0.362	0.288	0.121	0.16	0.47	0.173	**0.687**
SI3	0.323	0.172	0.027	0.12	0.308	0.095	**0.622**

Table 4 Assessment of model validity—Fornell–Larcker criterion

	BI	EE	FC	HAB	PE	PV	SI
BI	**0.711**						
EE	0.576	**0.757**					
FC	0.324	0.294	**0.435**				
HAB	0.368	0.233	0.234	**0.734**			
PE	0.849	0.512	0.346	0.278	**0.591**		
PV	0.4	0.103	0.097	0.185	0.439	**0.697**	
SI	0.662	0.357	0.173	0.259	0.671	0.232	**0.734**

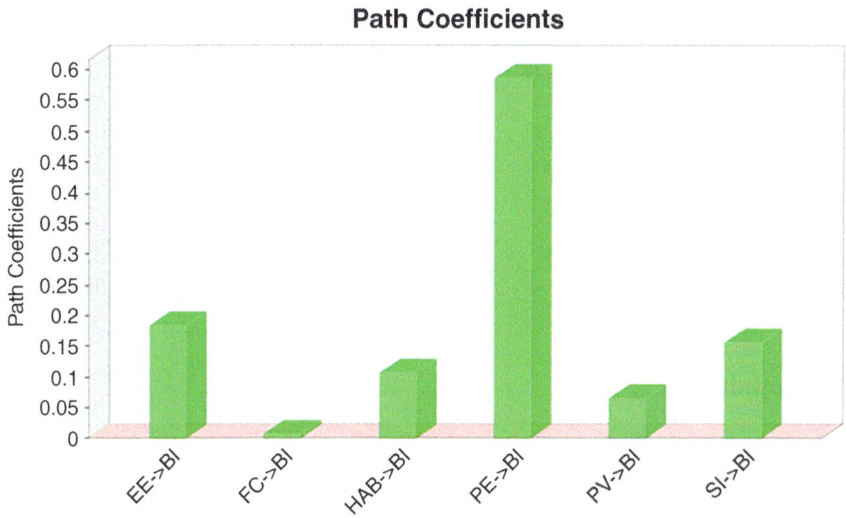

Fig. 7 Path coefficients

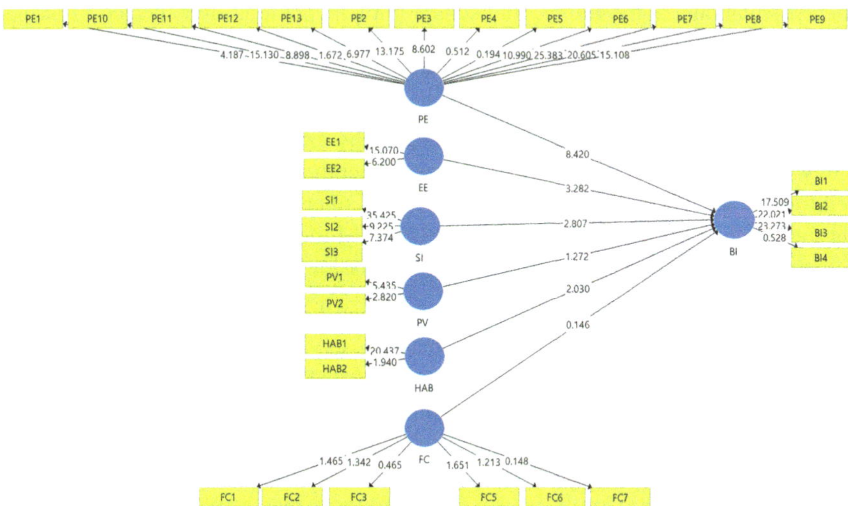

Fig. 8 Results of the bootstrapping method

considered to be highly accurate. A more detailed analysis on the significance was performed via *bootstrapping* with 500 samples with 5% significance (Fig. 8).

Results of the bootstrapping method can be seen in Table 5.

Variables with the p value of less than 0.05 are considered to be significant. Results suggest that the effort expectancy, habit, performance expectancy, and social influence have a significant effect on behavioral intention.

Table 5 Results of the bootstrapping method

	Original sample	Average value of sample	Standard deviation	T statistic	Significance
EE → BI	0.185	0.183	0.056	3.282	0.001
FC → BI	0.008	0.017	0.052	0.146	0.884
HAB → BI	0.107	0.100	0.053	2.030	0.043
PE → BI	0.588	0.586	0.070	8.42	0.000
PV → BI	0.066	0.064	0.052	1.272	0.204
SI → BI	0.157	0.158	0.056	2.807	0.005

6 Conclusion

Many countries have already started the process of writing regulations for open banking and its assorted services. In the future it would be reasonable to assume that the financial service industry will rely on shared data and infrastructure and will make such services commonplace for their users. Banks and financial institutions that realize these opportunities granted by open banking are expected to have a market advantage in the future. Blockchain implementations are expected to further improve open banking platforms, by offering secure tailor-made services to the clients, which is bound to make banking services more accessible.

The research conducted in this paper had the goal of seeing how acceptance of open banking based on blockchain is influenced by various factors. Furthermore, the study aims to see how much further these acceptance rates can be improved by reinforcing the perceived beneficial aspects of open banking. The data gathered through a survey was analyzed with the PLS-SEM method which led to a multitude of conclusions. The main conclusions and discussion of the results are:

- Performance expectancy is the main construct that influences behavioral intention. When developing various open banking services, the main effort should be directed to achieving good performance and satisfying user needs.
- Effort expectancy, habit, and social influence also have a significant effect on behavioral intention. The users are expecting to be provided with services that are easy to learn and use, and they are likely to use the services that have become the part of routine. The significance of social influence may come from the popularity of blockchain technologies.
- It is interesting that the perceived value has not been confirmed as an important factor. This may be due to the fact that users are not yet aware of the possible values that blockchain-based open banking services can bring.

Future research will be directed to providing more detailed recommendations for the design of blockchain-based open banking services, as well as to analyzing the interest of potential users for specific open banking services. It is needed to investigate how the new business models and services will fit into the existing entities and enable them business continuity (Labus et al. 2020), as well as to find out how they can be integrated into modern smart environments (Bogdanović et al. 2021).

References

Atabey A, Berber LK (2021) Open banking & banking-as-a-service (BaaS): a delicate turnout for the banking sector. Global Privacy Law Rev 2(1)

Bogdanović Z, Radenković B, Despotović-Zrakić M, Barać D, Labus A, Naumović T (2019) Blockchain technologies: current state and perspectives, Druga međunarodna naučna konferencija o digitalnoj ekonomiji DIEC 2019, Tuzla, BIH

Bogdanović Z, Labus A, Radenković M, Popović S, Mitrović S, Despotović-Zrakić M (2021) A Blockchain-based loyalty program for a Smart City. In: World conference on information systems and technologies. Springer, Cham, pp 360–370

Brodsky L, Oakes L (2017) Data sharing and open banking, vol 1097. McKinsey & Company, p 1105

Dong C, Wang Z, Chen S, Xiang Y (2020) BBM: a blockchain-based model for open banking via self-sovereign identity. In: International conference on blockchain. Springer, Cham, pp 61–75

Farrow GS (2020) An application programming interface model for open banking ecosystems. J Payments Strat Syst 14(1):75–91

Frizzo-Barker J, Chow-White PA, Adams PR, Mentanko J, Ha D, Green S (2020) Blockchain as a disruptive technology for business: a systematic review. Int J Inf Manag 51:102029

Gudergan SP, Ringle CM, Wende S, Will A (2008) Confirmatory tetrad analysis in PLS path modeling. J Bus Res 61(12):1238–1249

Hair JF, Ringle CM, Sarstedt M (2013) Partial least squares structural equation modeling: rigorous applications, better results and higher acceptance. Long Range Plann 46(1–2):1–12

Hair JF, Hult GTM, Ringle CM, Sarstedt M (2021) A primer on partial least squares structural equation modeling (PLS-SEM). Sage

Kinoti E (2020) The future of finance: open banking and blockchain synthesis. Taken from: https://medium.com/beyondhype/the-future-of-finance-open-banking-and-blockchain-synthesis-44861612187a

Labus M, Despotović-Zrakić M, Bogdanović Z, Barać D, Popović S (2020) Adaptive e-business continuity management: evidence from the financial sector. Comput Sci Inf Syst 17(2):553–580

Lucas M (2019) What's a smart contract (and how does it work)? Taken from: https://www.computerworld.com/article/3412140/whats-a-smart-contract-and-how-does-it-work.html

Mohanta BK, Jena D, Panda SS, Sobhanayak S (2019) Blockchain technology: a survey on applications and security privacy challenges. Internet of Things 8:100107

Nanaeva Z, Aysan AF, Shirazi NS (2021) Open banking in Europe: the effect of the revised payment services directive on Solarisbank and Insha. J Payments Strat Syst 15(4):432–444

National Transpositions by Member State Concerning: Directive (EU) 2015/2366 of the European Parliament and of the Council of 25 November 2015 on Payment Services in the Internal Market, Amending Directives 2002/65/EC, 2009/110/EC and 2013/36/EU and Regul [WWW Document]. https://eur-lex.europa.eu/legal-content/EN/NIM/?uri=CELEX:32015L2366

Nielsnon S (2021) The 5 best use cases of open banking. Taken from: https://subaio.com/the-5-best-use-cases-of-open-banking/

Ozcan P, Zachariadis M (2021) Open banking as a catalyst for industry transformation: lessons learned from implementing PSD2 in Europe. SWIFT institute working paper no. 2017-006. https://doi.org/10.2139/ssrn.3984857

Padmanabhan A (2021) Explained: neobanks the next evolution of banking. Taken from: https://economictimes.indiatimes.com/tech/trendspotting/explained-neobanks-the-next-evolution-of-banking/articleshow/86836735.cms

Polasik M, Huterska A, Iftikhar R, Mikula Š (2020) The impact of payment services directive 2 on the PayTech sector development in Europe. J Econ Behav Organ 178:385–401
Premchand A, Choudhry A (2018) Open banking & APIs for transformation in banking. In: 2018 international conference on communication, computing and internet of things (IC3IoT). IEEE, pp 25–29
Ramdani B, Rothwell B, Boukrami E (2020) Open banking: the emergence of new digital business models. Int J Innov Technol Manag 17(05):2050033
Ringle CM, Smith D, Reams R (2014) Partial least squares structural equation modeling (PLS-SEM): a useful tool for family business researchers. J Fam Bus Strateg 5(1):105–115
Ringle C, Wende S, Becker JM (2015) SmartPLS 3
Venkatesh V, Thong JY, Xu X (2012) Consumer acceptance and use of information technology: extending the unified theory of acceptance and use of technology. MIS Q 36(1):157–178

FinTech Innovations as Disruptor of the Traditional Financial Industry

Dino Arnaut and Damir Bećirović

Abstract The COVID-19 pandemic has led to a sudden jump in the digitization of financial services. Today, the financial sector is the target of disruptive action by a number of FinTech companies that are innovating and changing financial services. Since 1995, the term disruptive innovation has become widely used to describe the way of operating and market conquest of many, primarily technological, start-up companies that have achieved global success. This chapter goal is to give a clearer view of the way FinTech companies are changing the financial industry and how FinTech innovations are disrupting financial markets and tend to eliminate existing established financial companies. FinTech companies offer services that reach neglected market segments and were initially perceived as a small threat to established companies. A significant market share is taken by fully digitalized financial institutions that offer products and services that provide high level of satisfaction and low costs. Although traditional financial companies try to keep pace with technological changes by introducing new digital services, the entry of global technology brands into the financial services market further complicates their position. Traditional financial companies tend to develop a collaboration strategy with FinTech companies to bridge the technology gap and survive in the market.

Keywords FinTech · Disruptive innovation · Digital disruption · Financial industry · Start-ups

1 Introduction

In order to be able to understand, in general, how FinTech innovations are changing the financial industry nowadays, it is necessary at the beginning of this chapter to explain the concepts of the financial system and financial industry (sector), their

D. Arnaut (✉) · D. Bećirović
International Business and Information Academy Tuzla, Tuzla, Bosnia and Herzegovina
e-mail: dino@ipi-akademija.ba; direktor@ipi-akademija.ba

S. Benković et al. (eds.), *Digital Transformation of the Financial Industry*, Contributions to Finance and Accounting,
https://doi.org/10.1007/978-3-031-23269-5_14

structure, and their role and significance in relation to overall economic development. Without understanding the financial system and the financial industry, it is difficult to talk about the disruptive changes taking place in this sector. We will consider the concepts of the financial system and financial sector as unique although it should be noted that there are authors who make distinction between them. Therefore, Schmidt and Tyrell (2003) state the financial sector denotes a narrower concept. They define the financial sector as that part or sector of the economy that offers and provides financial services to the other sectors of the economy. It consists of the central bank, other banks, non-financial institutions, organized financial markets, and the regulator and supervisory institutions. The broader concept is related to the term financial system which can be defined as the interaction between the supply of and the demand for financial resources and the other finance-related services. In order to understand easier the functioning of the financial sector and respecting the fact that the focus of this chapter is not on a subtle consideration of the financial sector, we will use the term financial system to denote the financial sector. According to Van Horn (1978), the purpose of financial markets is to efficiently allocate savings in the economy to end-users, either for investment in real assets or for consumption. The financial system can be defined as the set of institutions (markets and intermediaries) through which households, companies, and governments obtain funds for their activities and invest their savings (Hartmann et al. 2003). According to Levine (2005), the functions of the financial system that support the aforementioned transformation of savings into investments include: ex ante creation of information about real investments and capital allocation, monitoring investments and exert corporate governance after providing finance, facilitating the exchange of goods and services, i.e. the trading, diversification, and management of risk, mobilization, and pool savings.

The fundamental importance of the financial system essentially derives from its basic function, which is that it connects entities that require financial resources with entities that dispose of excess financial resources. The financial system exists to enable a more efficient and effective reallocation of financial resources, which are as scarce as any other resource. If economics can be seen as a science that deals with the efficient and effective management of scarce resources, finance can be seen as a part of the economy that deals with efficient and effective management over financial resources.

A well-developed financial system basically plays a central role in economic activities and economic development. If the economic subjects who save were the same ones who deal with the creation of capital, the economy could exist and progress even without a financial system. However, in the modern economy, the number of investments of the economic sector exceeds their total savings. On the other hand, the household sector has total savings greater than total investments (Van Horn 1978). Financial intermediation enables the reallocation of financial resources towards those entities that seek to carry out some business activities, yet do not have enough capital available. On the other hand, entities with excess capital that do not want to carry out their own business activities in this way invest their capital by using other entities. The financial system is not just a neutral intermediary in the process of reallocation of financial assets between entities with surplus and deficit of capital. It ensures that those who borrow money do so in the most productive way, which contributes to overall economic development. The financial system of a country consists of banks, the central bank, insurance companies, capital and money markets, investment and pension funds, and regulatory bodies.

The advantages and disadvantages of financial systems based on banks in relation to market systems are the subject of discussions and analyses by economists. In financial systems in which the basis of the system is made up of banks, such as Germany and Japan, banks play a leading role in mobilizing savings, distributing capital, monitoring investment decisions of corporate managers, and providing mechanisms for risk management. In market financial systems such as England and the USA, securities markets share a central place with banks in terms of transferring social savings to companies, conducting corporate control, and facilitating risk management (Demirguc-Kunt and Levine 1999). Bank-centric financial systems offer stability and long-term financing of companies, while on the other hand, due to the very nature of the source of banks' financial potential, they are not suitable for financing start-up companies in new industries. On the other hand, market financial systems offer higher volatility, but also stronger support for new companies.

In terms of the financial system, COVID-19 pandemic brought that financial services have experienced an accelerated digitalization worldwide. This fact has significant implications for the direction to which the financial industry will head in the future. Even traditionally distrustful clients, in the absence of another alternative, switched to digital financial services. Nowadays, the banking sector is already going through significant digital disruptions that mean a complete transformation of the way it provides services to clients. Not only did digital innovations lead to the provision of services such as mobile payments, online deposits, or the application of artificial intelligence in the process of credit analysis and data processing, digitalization completely changes the traditional organization of work by enabling work from home for employees in the financial system.

At this point we come to the concept of neobanks or digital banks, as financial institutions that provide their services exclusively online via digital platforms without any need for a physical location or physical contacts with clients. This is a step up from digital services provided by traditional banks. This is a completely new concept in the banking industry which is believed to have a bright future especially as it targets the new digital native generation. Although some of these banks, such as Chime, Monzo, or Revolut, are already recognizable global brands, the emergence of new banks and the growth of existing ones can be expected based on the growing demand for digital banking services from younger consumers, as well as the growing trust of older clients in digital banking services. In addition, leading technology companies such as Amazon, Apple, or Google are entering the financial services industry by leaps and bounds, and thanks to the development of artificial intelligence, and based on a huge amount of information about potential clients, they can provide significant improvements in terms of risk assessment. This opens up a huge opportunity for attracting those demographic categories that have not been well served in traditional banking until now. First of all, this refers to the growing population of contract workers or freelancers, which represents a significant market considering that this form of employment is becoming more and more popular.

Trends in capital markets, in addition to digitalization, development of infrastructure for quality data management based on AI (artificial intelligence), also include the creation of new models of capital mobilization and collection through this market. Special purpose acquisition companies (SPACs) appeared as an alternative to the traditional Initial Public Offering (IPO). Many companies turn to SPACs in the process of rising capital through the stock market. SPACs can represent a more efficient way to reduce the costs, risks, and deadlines associated with going public than a traditional IPO. It is also necessary to mention the use of blockchain technology and the tokenization of assets as trends whose potential has not yet been fully realized.

All these changes are the result of the development of technology and the increase in the number of FinTech companies that appear as an alternative to traditional players on the financial market. How much they will change the classical way of functioning of the financial system in the future also depends on the reaction of regulatory and supervisory bodies. Financial markets function on the principles of trust and security, and it is important to find a balance between innovative solutions and the preservation of these principles. In the context of security and trust in the financial system in the future, it is necessary to pay great attention to the issue of cyber security and protection of personal data.

2 Fintech Innovations

The idea of FinTech is relatively new. According to Arner et al. (2015), it began in the first half of the nineteenth century with the invention of the telegraph and the successful building of the first transatlantic cable. These two technological advancements laid the groundwork for the late 1800s financial globalization. It can be challenging to imagine an unconnected world where information moves over regions and continents with tremendous difficulty in the Internet of Things era.

One of the first industries to use computers was the banking sector. A bank received the first mainframe created for commercial usage. Computers were utilized by banks themselves to improve and streamline legacy procedures.

Since the first mortgage was granted in the eleventh century, banks have created a strong but complex business model that has essentially not changed for decades. This model, which endured throughout time, maintained stability as a result of slowly shifting clients (De Jonghe 2010). The traditional banking model was barely altered during the most evolutionary technological disruption, the Internet boom between 1984 and 2007. Banks were still able to generate sustainable returns on their equity at that time. The old financial banking paradigm was heavily contested during this time by new market entrants who attempted to disrupt it with new digital currencies, payment options, etc. Over 450 of these new arrivals worldwide did not survive. Only five competitors persisted, and they did nothing more than supplement the existing banking model with new services (Abreu and Brunnermeier 2003; Brunnermeier 2009; McKinsey and Company 2016).

The ATM was the first invention to demonstrate the close relationship between finance and technology. It made it possible for people to conduct financial transactions over an electronic communications device. ATM enabled financial institutions to make significant financial savings by replacing human labour with automation in their interactions with clients. Since that time, the connections between financial services and technology have weakened.

According to Arner et al. (2015), 1987 was a turning point for the FinTech business. It is based on the famous Oliver Stone's film *Wall Street*, showing an investment banker using an early mobile phone and the *Black Monday* stock market collapse. The so-called program trading, a computerized style of trading that involves the execution of a basket of stocks at pre-determined conditions, is one of the known causes of the crash, which began in Hong Kong and quickly moved to Europe and the USA. In essence, when share prices cross certain criteria, a computer program buys and sells the shares. This disaster brought attention to the regulators to the close connections and risks between finance and technology.

The transition from analogue to digital technologies for the financial services sector began in the 1990s. This decade was distinguished by the growth of the World Wide Web and the initial Internet banking trials from Wells Fargo in the USA and ING in Europe. Additionally, the fax and email/instant messaging technologies that eventually replaced the telegraph improved global connections and created the foundation for greater business ties.

In order to promote and nurture technology collaboration with outsiders, Citicorp started a project in the 1990s. FinTech was its colloquial term, and its full name was *Financial Services Technology Consortium*. This term's definition has evolved in modern times. It no longer designates a particular project or company. It is a large category that also includes firms that offer technology-based proposition values that have the potential to enable, improve, and in some circumstances, potentially disrupt financial services. Therefore, the term *FinTech* refers to start-ups, the application of cutting-edge financial technologies by traditional financial institutions, and joint ventures between start-ups and established businesses.

Nowadays, the term *FinTech* refers to businesses that offer financial services using cutting-edge modern technologies. In a broader context, FinTech is understood as a new market that combines finance and technology (Arner et al. 2015) and replaces conventional financial structures with modern technology-based procedures (Hochstein 2015). Knewtson and Rosenbaum (2020) study provided a description of each FinTech subindustry as well as an organization for the FinTech sector based on these definitions.

The fast expansion of FinTech globally has drawn more and more attention. Third-party payments, money market funds, insurance products, risk management, authentication, and peer-to-peer (P2P) lending are all part of the developing financial services sector known as FinTech (Barberis 2014). The number of FinTech companies rose after the 2008 economic crisis, with a market size compound annual growth rate between 2008 and 2013 of 27%. From 920 million dollars in 2008 to 2.97 billion dollars in 2013, global investment in FinTech has tripled (Hwang 2014). After 2013, the market size for FinTech increased dramatically, going from $4 billion in 2013 to $12.2 billion in 2014 (McKinsey and Company 2016). In ten years, it had grown to $55.3 billion (Accenture 2020). The FinTech surge is more disruptive than the Internet boom for a variety of reasons. First, due to banks' detrimental influence during the financial crisis, client trust and loyalty towards the old banking system declined. Second, it became easier and more common to access financial services. Physical interaction with banks has become less useful as a result of connectivity and the expanded possibilities of mobile devices. Third, a younger generation that was raised with cutting-edge mobile technologies is more adaptable (McKinsey and Company 2016). Fourth, unlike during the Internet boom, new players are now having an impact on the whole financial industry (PWC 2016).

It is critical to recognize the FinTech evolution's three primary eras (Arner et al. 2015). Although closely connected to technology from around 1866 to 1967, the financial services sector remained essentially an analogue one, at least in the eyes of the general public, and where FinTech was at its version 1.0.

Since 1967, the transition of the financial system from an analogue to a digital business has been accelerated by the development of digital technologies for communications and transaction processing. Financial services had become increasingly globalized and digitalized by 1987, at least in industrialized countries. Up until 2008, FinTech 2.0 was in full swing. The traditional, regulated financial services sector dominated the financial technology endeavours throughout this time. It provided financial services and products using technology.

A new stage has started since 2008, a FinTech 3.0. Financial products and services became directly offered to businesses and consumers by established digital companies as well as novelty start-ups.

Industry 4.0, which is ongoing, envisions a stronger connectivity between actual and virtual industrial machines (Schlechtendahl et al. 2015). Manufacturing has benefited greatly from computerization, which has made it possible to collect, integrate, and analyse data on a scale never before possible. Similar to that, one could envision a FinTech 4.0 stage. At this level, there will be a closer connection between FinTech businesses and FinTech activities within traditional financial institutions. Technically speaking, that would mean systematizing technological solutions, and practically speaking, it would mean incorporating FinTech projects into the current financial system.

Threats could exist in the FinTech 4.0 world. Fintech start-ups will develop more connections with traditional service providers as their numbers and sophistication rise. Systems' interfaces are a frequent source of cyber vulnerabilities. To assist prevent this, during the product development process, interconnections between digital financial systems should be subject to extremely rigorous scrutiny, including penetration testing, including by people who can take a blank slate, comprehensive perspective of the aggregated system.

Two crucial factors, investments and market size have grown in the FinTech business. The two aspects are related to one another. The market size will certainly grow if banks and financial institutions spend more in cutting-edge technologies. The end consequence, or, in other words, the long-term payback and the return on investment of those investments is not clear and needs to be examined.

According to Venture Scanner (2021), FinTech business venture investments increased to $89 billion in 2021 which is more than double from the previous high from 2018. Also, there were 168 FinTech exits which was a new high point.

From a global viewpoint, the consulting firm Ernst & Young (EY 2016b) rated the most important FinTech ecosystems. It defined four fundamental characteristics of ecosystems, to which *solutions* must be added as a fifth characteristic (Nicoletti 2017):

1. *Demand*—the demand from customers across corporations, individuals, and financial organizations
2. *Talent*—the accessibility of financial services, technology, and entrepreneurial skills and talents
3. *Capital*—the availability of funding for new start-ups and internal projects
4. *Policy*—the government's initiatives for innovation, taxation, and regulations.
5. *Solutions*—the introduction of novel products, services, technologies, and procedures

A business ecosystem is an economic community that is maintained by a foundation of cooperating businesses and individuals. Customers purchase goods and services from the economic community because they are valuable to them. In addition to these entities, there are suppliers, lead producers, rivals, and other stakeholders. They jointly develop their positions and skills through time and frequently follow the guidelines established by one or more centralized companies. The companies in these positions may change over time, but the community values the ecosystem leader's role because it enables members to work towards common goals, coordinate their investments, and fill jobs that are mutually beneficial (Moore 1996).

The components of a FinTech ecosystem should be understood, starting with the subsystems linked to the stakeholders and the five key ecosystem traits (see Fig. 1). The demand attribute is the outcome of the collaborations that have been established between consumers, financial institutions, businesses, and governments. The talent attribute is dependent on academic institutions, financial institutions, and firms run by entrepreneurs in industries that have a strong correlation to financial technology. There are three basic groups of investors that influence the capital attribute. Angel investors, often known as business angels, are individuals who make investments in start-ups and early-stage businesses in exchange for stock ownership stakes. Investors in venture capital, also known as VC investors, fund or capitalize growth by giving money and general support to developing businesses without access to the stock market. Investors in initial public offerings (IPOs) essentially lend money to private businesses that are issuing shares to the public for the first time. The policy attribute relates not only to the particular policy environment but also to the success of government programmes and tax incentives. Regulators and governments are the typical stakeholders in this field. The technical firms, academic institutions, and

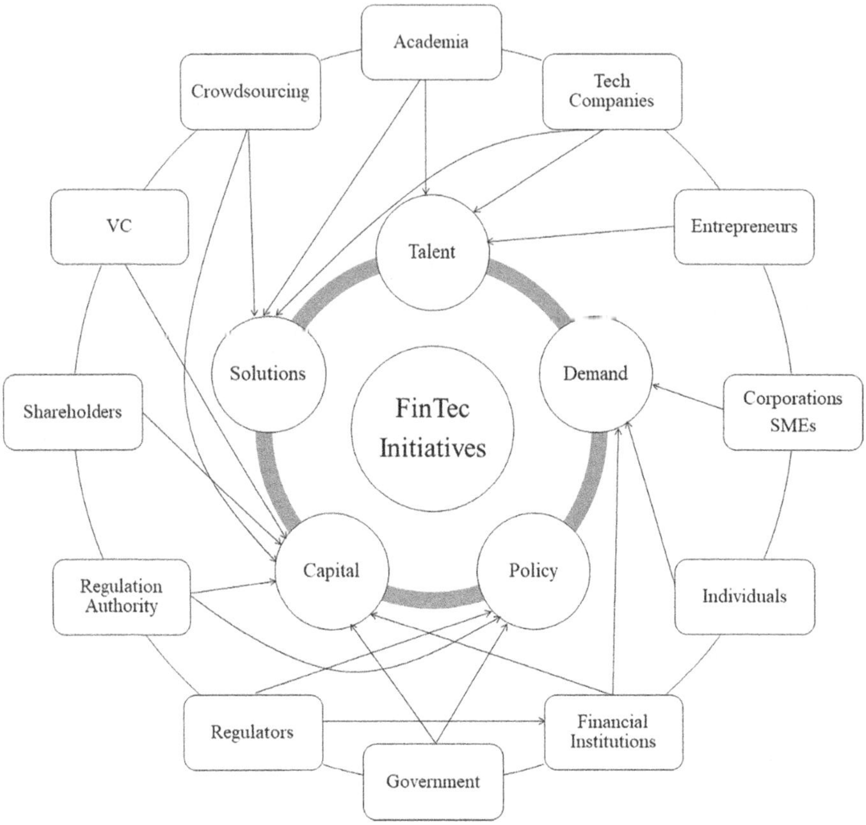

Fig. 1 The FinTech ecosystem (adapted from Nicoletti 2017 and EY 2016b)

perhaps crowdsourcing are all important factors in the solutions attribute. To influence the development of FinTech and move it in a useful direction, both entrepreneurs and regulators will need to make deliberate efforts. FinTech products, services, and methods can only expand and scale up through substantial customization of tools and processes that are built cumulatively on global FinTech intelligence (Mention 2019).

The FinTech companies are at the core of the ecosystem; whether they profit from it or not depends not only on the company's unique structure, talents, and ability to do so, but also on how well the channels connecting the various parts of the ecosystem function.

Focusing on FinTech as a concept is nearly impossible because it is evolving quickly, and definitions are becoming quickly out-of-date. It is always beneficial for traditional businesses to work with FinTech enterprises rather than competing with them. Due to continually shifting income streams and falling expenses, the true value of the majority of FinTech applications is still unknown (Langerveld 2017).

An analysis of the FinTech sector's topology was done by Arner et al. (2015). Five key sectors make up the FinTech sector today are finance and investment, operations and risk management, payments and infrastructure, data security and monetization, and client interface. The most investment-attractive services, according to an analysis of the value of investment in FinTech companies worldwide in terms of services, are finance and investment, payments and infrastructure, particularly peer-to-peer lending, online lending/scoring, online acquiring and mobile wallets, as well as personal financial management and planning.

According to the most recent EY FinTech Adoption Index (2019), money transfers (75% of active digitally active users have used services like peer-to-peer payments, non-bank money transfers, and in-store mobile payments at least once) and insurance (48% have used a premium comparison site, feeding information into an insurance-linked smart device, or buying products such as peer-to-peer insurance) were the most popular FinTech products in 2019. Savings and investment services, borrowing, and budgeting and financial planning all demonstrated significant growth potential.

There have been warnings about the effects of competition from information technology giants like Amazon, Apple, Facebook, and Google, even though it is widely acknowledged that financial technology firms have the potential to disrupt banking (McKinsey 2017; World Economic Forum 2017; Arnold 2018; KPMG 2021).

Banks still control the majority of the transaction payment business, together with Visa and MasterCard, although non-banks like PayPal, Apple, or Google tend to lead the way in terms of payment innovation (Vives 2017).

Until the 2016 filing season, when 14 banks, or 3% of all filers, done so, banks had not discussed the impact of FinTech on their operations. This number surged to 66 banks, or 14% of filers, in 2017 (Bunea et al. 2018). These filings show to be a valuable source of information on how banks view FinTech. Additionally, the information has the benefit of being management-certified and not anonymous when compared to survey data. Bunea et al. (2018) examined what banks have to say about FinTech in their yearly financial reports and discovered that they are mostly concerned about how FinTech will affect the lending, payments, and deposits industries as well as the planned bank charter for FinTech's. Cryptocurrencies, blockchain, and competition from Big Tech are far less of a concern for banks.

3 Disruptive Innovations

Since 1995, when it first appeared, the term disruptive innovation has become widely used to describe the way of operation and market conquest of many, primarily technological, start-up companies that have achieved global success. As stated by Baughman et al. (2015) disruptive innovation represents a catalyst for change that enables new technologies to be integrated into everyday life. Although the concept of disruptive innovation is widespread and often used, it should be emphasized that there is an obvious contrast between the widespread use of the concept in practice (including numerous discussions about it) and empirical academic research, which has not kept pace with the prevalence of this concept (Christensen et al. 2016). As Christensen (1997) states in his famous book *The Innovator's Dilemma*, disruptive technologies offer inferior products in mainstream markets. At the same time, they offer other features that few (and generally new) customers appreciate. The very idea of *disruption* means a process in which small companies with few resources can compete with large companies. Market leaders are usually focused on their most profitable market segments, while, on the other hand, they often ignore the needs of other customer segments. Disruptive companies are targeting neglected market segments. After positioning, disruptive companies begin to offer products with the performance required by major market segments while retaining all the advantages that led to their early success. When the main buyers start to accept the offers of new market entrants on a larger scale, then disruption occurs (Christensen et al. 2015). Disruptive technologies have two important characteristics. First, new technologies are often not even intended for mainstream customers, as they introduce products with attributes different from those historically valued by mainstream market segments. Second, the product attributes adopted by new customers improve at such a rapid rate that the new technology may later invade existing classic markets. However, when the main customers want new technology at that moment, then it is often too late for established companies. Pioneers of new technology already dominate the market (Bower and Christensen 1995). Disruption theory distinguishes disruptive innovations from sustaining innovations. So, the bottom line is that disruptive technologies are not aimed at improving existing products on the existing main market, as existing leading companies do through sustaining innovations, but they are actually aimed at neglected market segments or at the creation of completely new markets that eventually reach the main customers (Fig. 2). King and Baatartogtokh (2015) identified four key elements of the theory of disruptive innovation:

1. existing companies' base growth on sustaining innovation,
2. through the development of their products existing companies often overshoot customer needs,
3. existing companies have the ability to respond to the emergence of disruptive innovation but fail to exploit it., and
4. existing companies stumble due to disruptive innovations that have conquered the market.

In order to better understand the very concept of disruptive technologies, it is important to point out that disruptive technologies are not always the most advanced technologies. They are often based on existing technologies or business processes, offering new, alternative ways of their application.

Perhaps the most famous example of the disruptive impact of disruptive technologies relates to the Kodak. Kodak's business model was based on cross-subsidization. They sold the cameras at a lower price, thus creating a demand for films and chemicals. In this way, they ensured themselves continuous income

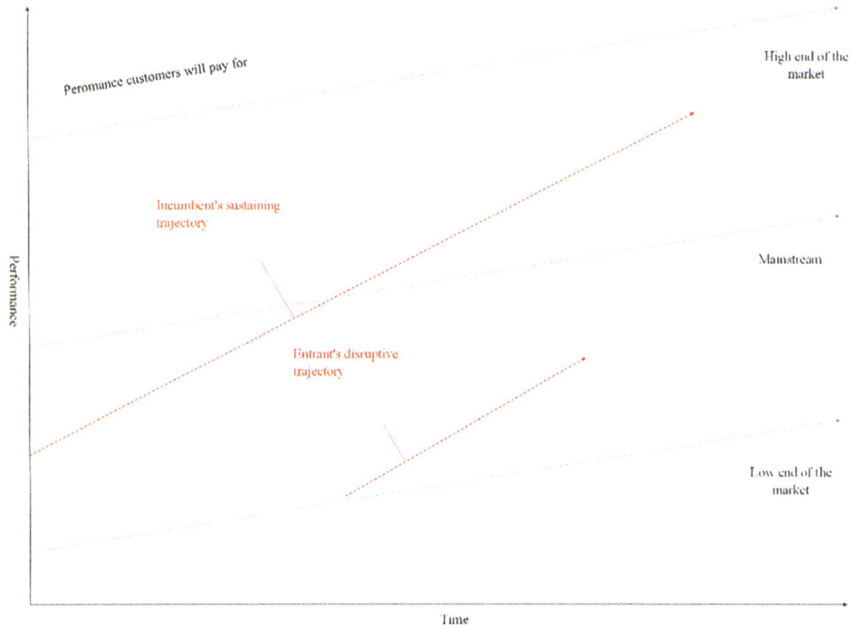

Fig. 2 The disruptive innovation model (adapted from Christensen et al. 2015)

throughout the entire period of using the photo camera. With the advent of digital cameras, Kodak experienced a drastic drop in film and chemical sales and filed for bankruptcy in 2012. What is most interesting in this story is that Kodak owns a significant number of patents related to digital cameras, but the company's management did not make a proper assessment of the new technology, which, like many other disruptive technologies, had a primitive form at the time. Christensen (1997) in *The Innovator's Dilemma* just asks this question: *Why great companies can fail?* He concludes that the reason is often that the management practices of leading people of established companies, which after all enabled them to become leaders in the industry, at the same time make it extremely difficult for the development of disruptive technologies, which ultimately steal their markets. Garud and Ahlstrom (1997) offered a slightly more subtle mechanism to explain how incumbent firms often overlook or underestimate the value of disruptive innovations. They state that the evaluation of new technology within a company is a social-cognitive process that is often not as objective as it is thought to be. The established criteria for evaluating technology eventually become the basis for constructing the reality of technology selection, and are often used without thinking, limiting what companies can see and blinding them to other possibilities. In this sense, the evaluation criteria that are taken for granted create what is called a technological black box. Also, domains and identities of organizational roles can jointly determine how quickly employees of existing companies react to disruption, whether they accept it and how innovative their responses are (Kammerlander et al. 2018).

The popularity of the term disruptive innovation has sometimes led to its misinterpretation and usage. Often, the typical incremental innovations associated with successful companies are viewed as disruptive. Christensen et al. (2015) cite the example of Uber, which is often mistakenly cited as an example of disruptive innovation. If we start from the fact that disruptive innovations are not initially aimed at the main customers until their quality reaches the standards of the main market segment, we can see that Uber has done exactly the opposite. He first built his position in the mainstream market and then turned to traditionally neglected clients. In addition, the service provided by Uber cannot be considered inferior to the existing service. On the contrary, it is more advanced in many segments. The fact that the company Uber really caused a disturbance in the market of taxi services probably leads to the description of its appearance on the market as a disruptive innovation. Therefore, Christensen et al. (2015) emphasize four points that are often overlooked when assessing whether an innovation is disruptive or not:

1. disruption is a process that cannot be viewed as a product at a fixed point in time,
2. disruptive companies often build business models that are very different from those of incumbents,
3. not every disruptive innovation leads to success, nor every company that disrupts the market was started by a disruptive innovation.
4. the phrase *disrupt or be disrupted* can sometimes mislead us

Such a strict selection in the assessment of innovations as disruptive or not, can harm the broad acceptability of the theory itself. After all, King and Baatartogtokh (2015) analysed 77 examples listed in Christensen's books *The Innovator's Dilemma* and *The Innovator's Solution*, wanting to determine how well these examples satisfy all four elements of the disruptive innovation theory. They showed that according to experts from the industry itself, only seven cases (9%) contain all four elements of the disruptive innovation theory mentioned earlier. In the era of digitization, innovations have a different path of acceptance and improvement compared to classical analogue innovations. The process of their introduction has been significantly accelerated, and products based on digital platforms have their own specific consumers, which can be called the community. Therefore, many innovations that may not meet all the traditional criteria for assessing whether they are truly disruptive innovations can still be considered disruptive in the way they affect the industry.

4 Disruptor of the Traditional Financial Industry

FinTech has gained attention in recent years, especially because of its potential to disrupt the landscapes of a number of financial institutions, intermediaries, technology companies, and businesses engaged in e-commerce in addition to banking (The

Economist 2015; Langley and Leyshon 2017; Hendrikse et al. 2018). Payments and cash transfers, crowdsourcing, and peer-to-peer lending are the industries that have experienced the most disruption, or at least those that are mentioned in the press the most. Global investment in FinTech businesses tripled from US$4.05 billion to US $12.21 billion between 2013 and 2014, outpacing the growth in venture capital investments as a whole (Accenture 2015). FinTech is being actively promoted in a number of international financial centres, such as New York, Luxembourg, Singapore, and Hong Kong, as offering opportunities for capturing new market share, and still there are ongoing discussions about whether the future of financial services would be marked by ruptures or redistribution (Lai 2020). A new era of convergence services is being ushered in by the quick growth of information and communications technology throughout the whole industry landscape. China is one of the developing nations in the financial industry and is going through an unparalleled level of financial and technological convergence (Shim and Shin 2016).

It is significant to point out that the majority of FinTech advancements have a global reach in order to assess the current situation of the market. The majority of items are created with a multi-country focus, which is the key reason for this. To reach a larger market, FinTech companies are publishing their products through digital channels. Due to the lack of a physical component in most FinTech products, the multi-country focus is possible (Brieske et al. 2015). Total investment capital per investment ratios reflects market confidence and expectations (ITA 2016; Koller et al. 2015). FinTech start-ups are receiving funding from more than just private investors. Some major banks are now doing so for strategic reasons (CB Insights 2017; EY 2016a; Skan et al. 2016). This suggests that major banks are becoming aware of the advantages and potential effects FinTech products may have on the established banking system.

By utilizing cutting-edge technologies, data science, and connectivity, FinTech companies have changed the way that money is traditionally transacted and have launched whole new financial products and services that are nearly universally available. Three billion people worldwide who have little or no access to financial instruments that could improve their lives can practically benefit from FinTech. Also, authorities might create sandboxes to encourage innovation and competition in the markets for financial services. In a nutshell, technological innovation contributes to cost savings, increased productivity, a larger clientele, better customer service, and risk management, and it is evident that artificial intelligence will be used in customer support in the future (Alam et al. 2019).

FinTech start-ups are a direct rival to established financial institutions. Since the emergence of payment FinTech companies around 2015, which provided superior value propositions like promotion, convenience, a wide selection of merchants, and many other areas where they started to have strong client acquisition levels, banks have already been disrupted (Siek and Sutanto 2019). Bunea et al. (2016) analysis of the first, limited group of institutions to openly acknowledge the threat presented by FinTech can only provide rudimentary insights into what makes these banks unique and what their future holds. The way many customers choose to do their banking has drastically changed thanks to the mobile phone. In reality, it has even made possible for certain people to have a bank account. Initiatives related to FinTech are quickly reaching new sectors and areas. A new form of currency called Bitcoin was introduced in 2009 by Satoshi Nakamoto (Skinner 2016). It is a type of digital currency that enables transactions to be carried out without the need of central banks or other middlemen. Digital currencies like Bitcoin have the potential to disrupt conventional payment methods as well. The creation of currency units in those digital currency systems, or cryptocurrencies, is controlled using encryption techniques and blockchain technology. This technology consists of a public digital database where transactions can be independently validated using a system of record blocks. With a large number of computers successively authenticating each transaction, it enables value to be transferred peer-to peer without the need for a middleman to confirm the transaction. Since it opens the door to numerous possible cost-saving solutions, blockchain technology has the potential to be disruptive. Additionally, it permits a currency that is not backed by the government or a reliable middleman, a role in which banks have developed expertise (Vives 2017). Among its many advantages, blockchain secures all transactions, whether they are between people or machines. Blockchain is still in its early stages and is changing its features in response to demand worldwide, and it needs an additional Internet component for data security in order to be reliable (Pompella and Matousek 2021).

The highly competitive financial services sector is problematic for both traditional banks and FinTech businesses (ACCA 2016; EY 2016a; McKinsey and Company 2016; PWC 2016; Skan et al. 2016). Both parties have the option of choosing to corporate or compete in order to do business sustainably. Skan et al. (2016) identified two categories of FinTech businesses. FinTech firms that are both competitive and cooperative, working to strengthen the positions of existing market players while aiming to replace banking products. The marketing approaches used by the two categories of FinTech companies vary. Competitive FinTech businesses concentrate mostly on market areas that have historically been less lucrative, come with large expenses, and are served primarily by traditional financial institutions. FinTech businesses compete by offering clients reduced costs while providing better experiences than their traditional counterparts (McKinsey and Company 2016; Skan et al. 2016). FinTech companies that work in collaboration with traditional financial institutions strive to assist them in modernizing their traditional banking business models to make them more financially viable. It is amazing that the majority of the contemporary collaborative FinTech companies initially had a competitive approach before switching to a collaborative one after failing to compete effectively (Skan et al. 2016). In 2014, the global split between competitive and cooperative FinTech investments was roughly one to three, but in 2015, it was practically already one to one. Between 2014 and 2015, the growth of aggressive FinTech investments was 23%, and the number of joint FinTech investments increased at a quicker rate, totalling 138% (CB Insights 2017).

Collaborative FinTech businesses require assistance from the traditional banking sector to develop. However, less than 10% of all deals included banks, according to CB Insights (2017). PWC (2016) mentioned the small amount of outside capital that banks have invested in cooperative FinTech firms. The low level of investments made by traditional banks is attributed to various operational factors. First, the majority of big banks have their own innovation divisions where they create fresh FinTech solutions, so there is no need to fund collaborative FinTech start-ups (Skan et al. 2016). Second, workers at conventional banks are resistant to change (EY 2016a). Third, banks now lack the necessary expertise to work with cutting-edge FinTech applications, and 20% of them believe they are only minimally skilled (Accenture 2015). Fourth, banks are having trouble altering their customary procurement, and 48% of banks believe they are not properly ready to incorporate FinTech applications. Fifth, traditional banks' technology infrastructure is comparatively out-of-date and unable to meet the demands of FinTech applications. Sixth, banks encounter financial difficulties that prevent them from making investments.

Targeting less lucrative niches by providing better experiences directly to customers, competitive FinTech start-ups have had some success. For instance, On Deck Capital offers quicker loans to SMEs, Square provides card services to microbusinesses, and eToro offers ordinary investors sophisticated trading tactics, frequently at a cost. Numerous financial services organizations are aware of how collaborative FinTech may support their own progress. FinTechs are increasingly eyeing incumbents as viable partners, from those who started out as collaborative players to those that did so after failing to effectively compete (Accenture 2016).

In reaction to new disruptive FinTech offers, industry incumbents like banks, insurance companies, or credit unions aim to use technology to change their traditional financial services. This is complicated, though, by the quick pace of technical development and long-standing organizational systems, creating significant research opportunities (Breidbach et al. 2019).

Insurance and asset management are also being pressured by FinTech developments. New calculative technologies are transforming customer behaviour, underwriting, and pricing of risks in the insurance industry, as well as developing new distribution and business models. By offering customized products and automated investing through robo-advisors, which are digital platforms that offer automated, algorithm-driven financial planning services with little to no human supervision, businesses may now target customers in new ways. As investors look for low-cost investment options, the flexibility to create a unique, diverse portfolio, and access to wealth management services formerly available only to the ultrawealthy, robo-advisors have grown in popularity (Lai 2020). Disruptive changes in the insurance sector are possible thanks to distributed ledger technologies which may help current insurers in their operations, but they may also give rise to peer-to-peer insurance networks that are more competitive (Lynn et al. 2019). When compared to side issues like whether Airbnb and Uber could be the forerunners of peer-to-peer forms of financial intermediation or if technology disruption in banking is a relevant concern, COVID-19 had a significant impact on reducing and focused attention on safety and health (Pompella and Costantino 2021).

Some have even predicted a radical upheaval of the banking and financial institutions, imitating the effects of Uber and Airbnb on established industries that were altered and disrupted. This line of reasoning gave rise to the phrase *Uberization of banks*, which refers to the expectation that traditional banking will undergo disruption in the same way that Uber did and is doing to the mobility sector (Pompella and Costantino 2021).

Palmié et al. (2020) study explains how the FinTech ecosystem has disrupted the financial services industry and describes what disruptive innovative ecosystems are in order to overcome this constraint. They explored the development of the FinTech ecosystem and presented a research agenda for the future on disruptive technologies and ecosystems. Overall, their research shows that innovative disruptive ecosystems not only need but also demand additional investigation.

Lai (2020) uses an actor-cantered approach to identify key actors in the developing FinTech ecosystem, which are divided into five main types, in order to look at how FinTech products and services are reshaping the intermediation function of banks and the ways in which banks have interacted with FinTech firms. Those types are (Lai 2020):

1. *Banks* that perform a variety of other financial service services in addition to offering loans and deposit facilities. These banks could be very sizable organizations with an international clientele, like HSBC, Citigroup, and Deutsche Bank, or they could be mid-sized regional or local institutions, like Santander, Macquarie, and DBS. These are frequently referred to as *incumbents* due to their established dominance over various banking and financial systems and sizable client base, although they are now up against growing competition from FinTech firms.
2. *Non-bank financial institutions* that provide financial services but do not hold a banking license, such as insurance businesses, venture capital firms, hedge funds, and asset managers. Even while several of their core services like robo-advising and peer-to-peer lending are also being impacted by FinTech applications, banks are typically perceived as being less *threatened* by FinTech firms than other financial institutions.
3. *Large technological firms* like Apple, Google, and Alibaba that are involved in the financial services industry but are not solely focused there. They are viewed as *disruptors* since they are non-financial companies providing financial services.
4. *Start-ups* are typically tiny businesses that are concentrated on a certain novel technology or procedure that has the potential to alter current financial relations or transactions. These are frequently quick-moving businesses that are new to the financial services industry and are frequently referred to as *disruptors*. Companies include Moven (retail banking), Prosper (peer-to-peer lending), Betterment (automated investment), Lemonade (insurance), and Stripe (mobile payments).
5. In order to make sure that *state entities* like regulators and government organizations' regulatory frameworks are current and effective, they collaborate with financial institutions and technology companies while amending or drafting them. In order to promote FinTech research and investment, several of them are also taking on promotional duties in terms of industry communication and outreach initiatives. Regulatory and promotional measures may change the level of competitiveness for incumbents and disruptors.

FinTech is obviously a *hot ticket* according to today's numbers and statistics. It demonstrates a significant increase in investments, income, and employment, and in 2016 it has already evolved from its disruptive beginnings into a distinct and unique industry (EY 2016b). FinTech projects are still in their early stages of development and vary to diverse degrees around the world according to the magnitude of investments and the sector's exceptional rate of growth.

Various geographic markets have different driving forces for FinTech innovations. FinTech benefits are based on increasing efficiency, lowering transaction costs, and creating value for both businesses and consumers in developed countries like the USA and Europe where banks have strong networks with corporate and retail customers. FinTech is typically driven by other pressing demands, such as financial inclusion and access to business working capital, in developing nations, where significant portions of the population are still unbanked, building on the legacy of microlending initiatives (Duncombe and Boateng 2009; Roy 2010). This implies that depending on who may have more clout or benefits, banks and technology companies will interact differently across different geographic markets.

Jiang et al. (2021) goal was to contribute knowledge to the continuing discussion about whether and how FinTech disrupts industries and/or creates chances for growth, particularly in relation to employment and labour demand. They found that jobs exposed to FinTech are also becoming more concentrated in different states and industries. However, to varying degrees, creative businesses and the finance sector are able to counteract the detrimental effects on the entire economy.

Market disruption is a possibility for tech businesses, but it does not always compromise regulation. According to Hodson (2021), FinTech banks in the UK and Germany disrupted retail banking without adopting the *ask forgiveness rather than permission* strategy preferred by digital start-ups like Uber. Before COVID-19, there was little regulatory disruption in the USA as the usage of video conferencing technology to deliver clinical health care was already rising (Andriola 2019). In the 2020, the Department of Justice in the UK opened a LawTech Sandbox, the programme that encourages cooperation between regulators and digital firms that are leading the use of artificial intelligence, machine learning, and other advancements in legal services. It is modelled after the FCA's regulatory sandbox (Tech Nation 2020).

FinTech efforts provide advantages, but there are also some possible drawbacks. Disruptive technologies frequently have drawbacks as a result of how they are used (Gilbert and Bower 2002). The environment in the case of FinTech projects increases the likelihood of negative outcomes. Deep dangers associated with laws exist for FinTech initiatives (Wehinger 2012). In general, technology makes it possible to cross traditional national boundaries. National borders are less important in the context of FinTech activities from a technological standpoint, but regulatory bodies on both sides are keeping a close eye. This is true in particular for issues related to taxation, customer data protection, and cross-national sovereignty. Although risk management-focused regulators are currently seen as a barrier to FinTech activities, there will likely be more collaboration between the financial services industry, FinTech firms, and regulatory officials in the future. Doing this is not simple. At this point in the development process, it might even be disastrous to block such a prospective industry transformation.

The cultural acceptance of technology by traditional banking institutions is a challenge (Nolan 2009). Without innovation in FinTech, there is a danger of technological complacency and ultimately technological decline in comparison to other nations. Financial institutions in some nations run the risk of losing competitive advantage by allowing their financial environments to become non-competitive in the international market if they don't take specific efforts to progress their financial technologies.

Banks face an additional challenge as a result of the development of FinTech, but this issue might also present an opportunity for banks to thrive in the future. Therefore, it is crucial for banks to start working with FinTech firms, especially in industries where FinTech firms offer services that are complementary to those of banks. Recent events have forced banks to raise their FinTech investments, revaluate their service distribution methods, further standardize their back-office operations, etc. Banks may be able to gain competitive advantages in the expanding market if FinTech is properly integrated into operations (Romānova and Kudinska 2016).

The investment community initially had doubts about the potential of FinTech's and the disruption trend they have sparked. Challenger banks and insurance aggregators' disruption has forced established companies to pay attention to the impact of FinTech and the threat it poses to their industry. Therefore, in order to expand their business and, in some circumstances, to outcompete the competition, financial institutions, major retailers, and telecom carriers are all trying to work together to buy these start-ups. Because they have the client base, technology, and functional know-how, as well as frequently a proprietary engine like a credit check engine, etc., successful start-ups have thus become an appealing acquisition target. Many of these organizations, both financial and non-financial, have begun to buy the most promising start-ups that fit their business model (Arjunwadkar 2018).

5 Conclusion

The financial services sector has undergone a significant transformation in recent years. It is becoming more challenging to close the technology gap between traditional enterprises and FinTech companies. Contextually, start-up businesses are seizing the spotlight by utilizing technology in order to get a competitive advantage. Any business engaged in the financial services sector that has adopted innovative business practices is included in the definition of FinTech, not only start-ups.

Both traditional organizations and FinTech enterprises may better comprehend the path of the sector overall by evaluating the key areas and ecosystems from a global perspective, adding to the evidence of the main economic trends that are now in play. FinTech efforts are a *hot spot* for investments and market size. The FinTech innovative mindset serves as a growth engine. The USA, integrating the ecosystems of Silicon Valley and New York while still functioning as separate hubs, and the

United Kingdom are currently in unchallenged leadership positions. China and Japan could have a very fascinating future. Sadly, continental Europe is still falling behind.

At a time when disruptive innovations are fundamentally upending many mature industries, well-known examples like Apple and Uber show that, at the moment, disruptive innovations frequently come from ecosystems or systems level rather than standalone enterprises. Unfortunately, the establishment and evolution of ecosystems in response to disruptive innovations has received less attention in the academic literature to date.

A global phenomenon, FinTech seek to innovate the financial services sector. FinTech make use of innovation with the goal of disrupting the market, particularly by eliminating established businesses like insurance firms and financial institutions through various business models. Pure and marginal innovations have been essential to the disintermediation process as a whole.

Due to their perception that FinTech companies are young and a minor threat, the banks, nevertheless, were anticipating it slowly or without much competition. The FinTech's digital approach, which adopted a client-centric mindset and developed a product that delivers its customers a high level of customer happiness, was not anticipated by the bank. Finally, despite the fact that the majority of their client segment is composed of bank customers, they still struggle with brand loyalty and brand awareness despite creating a digital payment wallet that is similar to the FinTech. As a result, FinTech is far ahead of banks, who are obliged to collaborate with FinTech firms in order to compete due to banks' subpar digital strategies.

The development of the blockchain architecture will handle the threats that were before inaccessible along with FinTech. Additional specialized work to create regulatory measures will aid in anticipating FinTech's reliance on blockchain technology. Businesses, FinTech entrepreneurs, and regulators should have a cogent and pragmatically grounded discussion about how FinTech trends are evolving, how FinTech offerings are changing supply and value chains, and how national regulatory frameworks are affecting cross-border investment and innovation performance across markets. Therefore, the disruptive innovations should be the focus of future research in order to determine their influence and significance, especially in financial systems.

In long term, the benefits of FinTech outweigh the risks by a wide margin. As their usage rises and more inclusive and open regulatory frameworks enable them to expand, FinTech technologies will only become more widespread in daily transactions. Now that incumbent financial institutions are forced to re-evaluate their market and strategic decisions, there are more opportunities for them to work strategically with FinTech start-ups. Last but not least, companies that create novel FinTech technologies see increases in operating efficiency and employment.

References

Abreu D, Brunnermeier MK (2003) Bubbles and crashes. Econometrica 53(9):1689–1699. https://doi.org/10.1111/1468-0262.00393

ACCA (2016) FinTech – transforming finance

Accenture (2015) The future of Fintech and banking. Accenture, 1–12

Accenture (2016) Fintech and the evolving landscape: landing points for the industry

Accenture (2020) Fintech fundraising grew strongly in most major markets in 2019. Accenture analysis finds Accenture Newsroom, 20 February

Alam N, Gupta L, Zameni AF (2019) Fintech an Islamic finance: digitalization, development and disruption. Palgrave Macmillan, Cham. https://doi.org/10.1007/978-3-030-24666-2

Andriola M (2019) Telemedicine and legal disruption. Health Law Policy Brief 13(2):1–29

Arjunwadkar PY (2018) FinTech: the technology driving disruption in the financial services industry, 1st edn. Auerbach Publications. https://doi.org/10.1201/9781351036504

Arner DW, Barberis JN, Buckley RP (2015) The evolution of Fintech: a new post-crisis paradigm? University of Hong Kong Faculty of Law Research Paper No. 2015/047, 1–44. https://doi.org/10.2139/ssrn.2676553

Arnold M (2018) Finance chiefs warn on big Tech's shift to banking: leading lenders fear internet giants will cherry-pick best parts of their business. The Financial Times

Barberis J (2014) The rise of FinTech: getting Hong Kong to lead the digital financial transition in APAC. Fintech Report. Fintech HK

Baughman AK, Gao J, Pan J-Y, Petrushin VA (2015) Multimedia data mining and analytics: disruptive innovation. Springer. https://doi.org/10.1007/978-3-319-14998-1

Bower JL, Christensen CM (1995) Disruptive technologies: catching the wave. Harv Bus Rev 73: 43–53

Breidbach CF, Keating BW, Lim C (2019) Fintech: research directions to explore the digital transformation of financial service systems. J Serv Theory Pract. https://doi.org/10.1108/JSTP-08-2018-0185

Brieske A, Dapp T-F, Garlan K, Sielecki M (2015) FinTech 2.0: creating new opportunities through strategic alliance. Deutsche Bank - Global Transaction Banking, 24

Brunnermeier MK (2009) Deciphering the liquidity and credit crunch 2007–2008. J Econ Perspect 23(1):77–100. https://doi.org/10.1257/jep.23.1.77

Bunea S, Kogan B, Stolin D (2016) Banks versus FinTech: at last, it's official. J Financ Transf 44: 122–131

Bunea S, Kogan B, Kund AG, Stolin D (2018) Fintech and the banking bandwagon. J Financ Transf 47:25–33

CB Insights (2017) The global FinTech report: 2016 in review

Christensen CM (1997) The innovator's dilemma: when new technologies cause great firms to fail. Harvard Business School Press, Boston

Christensen CM, Raynor ME, McDonald R (2015) What is disruptive Innovation? Harv Bus Rev 93(12):44–53

Christensen CM, McDonald R, Altman EJ, Palmer J (2016) Disruptive Innovation: intellectual history and future paths, working paper 17-057. Harvard Business School. https://doi.org/10.5465/AMBPP.2017.14218abstract

De Jonghe O (2010) Back to the basics in banking? A micro-analysis of banking system stability. J Financ Intermed 19(3):387–417. https://doi.org/10.1016/j.jfi.2009.04.001

Demirguc-Kunt A, Levine R (1999) Bank-based and market-based financial systems - cross-country comparisons. Policy research working paper series 2143, The World Bank. https://doi.org/10.1596/1813-9450-2143

Duncombe R, Boateng R (2009) Mobile phones and financial services in developing countries: a review of concepts, methods, issues, evidence and future re-search directions. Third World Q 30(7):1237–1258. https://doi.org/10.1080/01436590903134882

EY (2016a) Capital markets: innovation and the FinTech landscape. Ernst and Young Report

EY (2016b) UK Fintech: on the cutting edge. Ernst and Young Report
EY FinTech Adoption Index (2019) https://www.ey.com/en_gl/ey-global-fintech-adoption-index. Accessed 25 June 2022
Garud R, Ahlstrom D (1997) Technology assessment: a socio-cognitive perspective. J Eng Technol Manag 14(1):25–48. https://doi.org/10.1016/S0923-4748(97)00005-2
Gilbert C, Bower JL (2002) Disruptive change when trying harder is part of the problem. Harv Bus Rev 80(5):95
Hartmann P, Maddaloni A, Manganelli S (2003) The euro area financial system: structure, integration and policy initiatives. Oxf Rev Econ Policy 19:180–213. https://doi.org/10.1093/oxrep/19.1.180
Hendrikse R, Bassens D, Van Meeteren M (2018) The appleization of finance: charting incumbent finance's embrace of FinTech. Financ Soc 4(2):159–180. https://doi.org/10.2218/finsoc.v4i2.2870
Hochstein M (2015) FinTech (the word, that is) evolves. The American Banker. https://www.americanbanker.com/opinion/fintech-the-word-that-is-evolves. Accessed 23 June 2022
Hodson D (2021) The politics of FinTech: technology, regulation, and disruption in UK and German retail banking. Public Adm 99(4):859–872. https://doi.org/10.1111/padm.12731
Hwang SS (2014) What we need in the Fintech craze. LG CNS blog. http://www.lgcnsblog.com/technology/what-we-need-in-the-fintech-craze. Accessed 18 June 2022
ITA (2016) 2016 top markets report franchising overview and key findings, 1–7
Jiang W, Tang Y, Xiao RJ, Yao V (2021) Surviving the Fintech disruption (no. w28668). National Bureau of Economic Research
Kammerlander N, König A, Richards M (2018) Why do incumbents respond heterogeneously to disruptive innovations? Interplay Domain Identity Role Identity J Manage Stud 55(7):1122–1165. https://doi.org/10.1111/joms.12345
King AA, Baatartogtokh B (2015) How useful is the theory of disruptive innovation? MIT Sloan Manag Rev 57(1):77–90
Knewtson HS, Rosenbaum ZA (2020) Toward understanding FinTech and its industry. Manag Financ 46:1043. https://doi.org/10.1108/MF-01-2020-0024
Koller T, Goedhart M, Wessels D (2015) Valuation: measuring and managing the value of companies, 6th edn. Wiley
KPMG (2021) The pulse of Fintech H1 2021. https://home.kpmg/xx/en/home/insights/2020/02/pulse-of-fintech-archive.html. Accessed 30 June 2022
Lai KPY (2020) FinTech: the dis/re-intermediation of finance. Routledge Handb Financ Geogr:440–458
Langerveld D (2017) Fintech: current state and developments and potential in supply chain and logistics. Logistics and Fintech report
Langley P, Leyshon A (2017) Platform capitalism: the intermediation and capitali-zation of digital economic circulation. Financ Soc 3(1):11–31. https://doi.org/10.2218/finsoc.v3i1.1936
Levine R (2005) Finance and growth: theory, evidence and mechanisms. In: Aghion P, Durlauf S (eds) Handbook of economic growth, Part 1, vol 1. North Holland, Amsterdam, pp 865–934
Lynn T, Mooney JG, Rosati P, Cummins M (2019) Disrupting finance: FinTech and strategy in the 21st century, 1st edn. Springer International Publishing. https://doi.org/10.1007/978-3-030-02330-0
McKinsey (2017) The phoenix rises: remaking the bank for an ecosystem world. McKinsey Global Banking Annual Review 2017. McKinsey & Co
McKinsey & Company (2016) FinTechnicolor: the new picture in finance
Mention AL (2019) The future of fintech. Res Technol Manag 62(4):59–63. https://doi.org/10.1080/08956308.2019.1613123
Moore JF (1996) The death of competition: leadership and strategy in the age of business ecosystems. Harper Business, New York, NY
Nicoletti B (2017) The future of FinTech. Integrating finance and technology in financial services. Palgrave Macmillan, London. https://doi.org/10.1007/978-3-319-51415-4

Nolan S (2009) Kick-starting a customer-centric revolution. Manager: Br J Adm Manage 65:28–30
Palmié M, Wincent J, Parida V, Caglar U (2020) The evolution of the financial technology ecosystem: an introduction and agenda for future research on disruptive innovations in ecosystems. Technol Forecast Soc Chang 151:119779. https://doi.org/10.1016/j.techfore.2019.119779
Pompella M, Costantino L (2021) Financial innovation and technology after COVID-19: a few directions for policy makers and regulators in the view of old and new disruptors. Ekonomika 100(2):40–62. https://doi.org/10.15388/Ekon.2021.100.2.2
Pompella M, Matousek R (eds) (2021) The Palgrave handbook of FinTech and Blockchain. Palgrave Macmillan. https://doi.org/10.1007/978-3-030-66433-6
PWC (2016) Blurred lines: how FinTech is shaping Financial Services
Romānova I, Kudinska M (2016) Banking and fintech: a challenge or opportunity?. In: Contemporary issues in finance: current challenges from across Europe. Emerald Group Publishing Limited. https://doi.org/10.1108/S1569-375920160000098002
Roy A (2010) Poverty capital: microfinance and the making of development. Routledge, London
Schlechtendahl J, Keinert M, Kretschmer F, Lechler A, Verl A (2015) Making existing production systems Industry 4.0-ready. Prod Eng 9(1):143–148. https://doi.org/10.1007/s11740-014-0586-3
Schmidt RH, Tyrell M (2003) What constitutes a financial system in general and the German financial system in particular? Working paper series: Finance & Account-ing 111, Department of Finance. Goethe University Frankfurt am Main
Shim Y, Shin DH (2016) Analyzing China's fintech industry from the perspective of actor–network theory. Telecommun Policy 40(2–3):168–181. https://doi.org/10.1016/j.telpol.2015.11.005
Siek M, Sutanto A (2019) Impact analysis of Fintech on banking industry. In: 2019 international conference on information management and technology (ICIMTech). IEEE, vol 1, pp 356–361. https://doi.org/10.1109/ICIMTech.2019.8843778
Skan J, Dickerson J, Gagliardi L (2016) Fintech and the evolving landscape: landing points for the industry, 1–12
Skinner C (2016) How Fintech firms are using bitcoin blockchain and mobile technologies to create the internet of value. Marshall Cavendish International (Asia) Pte Ltd, Singapore
Tech Nation (2020) Meet the five UK lawtechs chosen to join first Lawtech Sandbox Pilot. Tech Nation, 8 December
The Economist (2015) The fintech revolution. The Economist. https://www.economist.com/leaders/2015/05/09/the-fintech-revolution. Accessed 18 June 2022
Van Horn JC (1978) Financial market rates and flows. Prentice-Hall, Englewood Cliffs
Venture Scanner (2021) Fintech 2021 summary. https://www.venturescanner.com/tag/fintech/. Accessed 27 July 2022
Vives X (2017) The impact of FinTech on banking. Eur Econ 2:97–105
Wehinger G (2012) The financial industry in the new regulatory landscape. OECD J: Financ Market Trends 2011(2):225–249. https://doi.org/10.1787/fmt-2011-5k9cswmzqp7d
World Economic Forum (2017) Beyond fintech: a pragmatic assessment of disruption in financial services. World Economic Forum Report

Cybercrime and Cyber Security in Fintech

Anastasija Despotović, Ana Parmaković, and Marija Miljković

Abstract This paper describes cybercrime in the field of financial technologies. There have been significant changes in payment systems caused by the development of Fintech and the increasing use of various digital and mobile technologies. Methods of protection against cybercrime are being developed in parallel with the development of new technologies, but cybercrime is also progressing at the same pace. The perpetrators are constantly finding new ways to abuse financial systems. Users of financial technologies must be aware of the potential risks of using financial technologies, only in that way will they be able to recognize and prevent potential threats. The increasing use of cryptocurrencies and the lack of legal regulations have led them to become a valuable target for criminals, and the number of crimes connected to cryptocurrencies is constantly growing. This paper aims to acquaint readers with the dangers of cybercrime and methods of protection against them. The first chapter of the paper is an introduction in which the concepts of cybercrime and cyber security are defined. The second chapter identifies and describes the threats and dangers of cybercrime in financial technologies. Chapter 2 deals with the analysis of current threats to financial systems as well as modern ways of protecting financial systems from cybercrime. How cyber-attacks manifest themselves and how attacks can be prevented are defined and explained. Different types of cyber-attacks are described in detail. The analysis led us to the conclusion that it is best to prevent cyber-attacks and that employee training is a very important factor in protecting the system so that they know how to prevent potential attacks and accidental security breaches. Chapter 3 analyzes the literature dealing with cybercrime and cybersecurity in the field of financial technologies. The literature states that banks were the first to introduce technological innovations into their operations, which led to the

A. Despotović · A. Parmaković (✉)
Faculty of Organizational Sciences, University of Belgrade, Belgrade, Serbia
e-mail: ana.parmakovic@stadaitsolutions.com

M. Miljković
Directorate for Telecommunications and Informatics J-6, Center for Command and Information Systems and Information Support, Belgrade, Serbia
e-mail: marija.miljkovic@vs.rs

S. Benković et al. (eds.), *Digital Transformation of the Financial Industry*,
Contributions to Finance and Accounting,
https://doi.org/10.1007/978-3-031-23269-5_15

revolution of technological progress in Fintech. Not only do banks participate in modern financial business, but a significant part of the business also consists of companies that specialize in the development and implementation of financial technologies. The fourth chapter deals with identified problems and potential solutions. Chapter 4 identifies problems and potential solutions in the field of financial technologies. The vulnerability of financial systems, how cyber-attacks take place, and their adaptation to modern business are analyzed. Based on the analysis, potential solutions to the identified problems are given and specific examples are given. The analysis led us to the conclusion that we must consider cyber risks in detail and give an adequate counter-response to each of their elements. The fifth chapter deals with cryptocurrencies. Blockchain technologies, their level of security, ways of endangering as well as their impact on financial operations are analyzed. The problem of lack of legal regulations in the field of cryptocurrencies is explained, as well as their impact on the growth of cybercrime in the field of financial technologies. The sixth chapter concludes the paper. The seventh chapter presents a list of references used in the paper. The main contribution of the paper is the systematic analysis of cyber threats and cybersecurity issues in the context of Fintech, resulting in a list of recommendations for various groups of stakeholders (banks, fintech companies, and end users).

Keywords Cybercrime · Cybersecurity · Financial technologies · Cryptocurrencies · Financial system

1 Introduction

Innovations in the field of technology always carry with them a certain type of risk, so it is necessary to foresee the risk factors before implementation and prevent them, prevent their manifestation in the process itself, and also prevent the appearance of new threats. The mentioned measures should be applied by every technologically developed company, especially companies that rely on the electronic business for a large part of their work. The aforementioned challenges are imposed by criminal entities in cyberspace who, we can safely say, adequately use the current technological development themselves. We see, therefore, that it is necessary to ensure the protection of vulnerable parts of the infrastructure and advanced defense of systems, servers, networks, computers, mobile devices, etc., which establishes a certain level of security in cyberspace. In which "cyberspace" represents the connection of computer networks, as it were, and the techniques of their protection "cyber security."

Cyber security (cyber security, cyber protection, digital security) is, in the simplest terms, the practical protection of devices, resources, and information (accounts, personal data, files, and of course money). To properly protect something, the most important thing is to ensure: confidentiality, that is, the independent possibility of controlling the authorization to access one's accounts, so that information does not leak; integrity of the data in our possession, i.e., knowledge that no one could change them without our permission; Access or the ability to access resources in our possession when we want it, that is, that access is not denied to us caused by cyber-attacks, such as DDoS or Ransomware. Opposing and avoiding malicious actions and their consequences requires analysis of the forms in which threats are manifested, and then synthesis of knowledge into responses to them. This is a particularly demanding job when we cannot determine the exact location of the malicious entities, and they are in most cases potentially close to us and possess the necessary means and information to carry out the attack. Employee education is crucial, to reduce the percentage of work errors, and also to train them for correct and ethical work.

There is no modus operandi, that is, a universal way of behavior of criminals in cyberspace, and thus not all directions of the spread of cybercrime can be described. However, as every criminal behavior needs to be defined by law, cybercrime (in legal regulations and high-tech crime) is most often described as any criminal offense in which the object, goal, or means of its execution is a computer, computer systems, networks, computer data, and/or their resources in material or electronic form. The convention on high-tech crime distinguishes four types of criminal acts, namely: acts against confidentiality, acts related to computers, acts related to the content, and acts related to copyright infringement.

As we emphasized at the beginning, technological development also influenced the more professional activities of criminals, and this trend did not bypass financial technologies either. Fintech as a new wave of financial business improvement provides numerous benefits, so user satisfaction is on the rise, but it also represents a very tempting area for criminal activities, primarily due to the constant flow of money, and material gain is one of the main motives for any criminal behavior. However, intangible consequences can also have a permanent impact on the business, in terms of loss of trustees, bad publicity, loss of protected information, etc. We realized that it is of great importance to protecting given values within financial institutions, and it is precisely this thought that guides us throughout our work.

2 Identification, Description of Threats and Dangers of Cybercrime in Fintech

The use value of money makes it one of the most tempting targets for cyber-attacks. Financial institutions that store a large amount of data about bank accounts and identities of users of financial services are frequent targets of attacks by cybercriminals.

The financial services sector increasingly relies on modern information and communication technologies to provide products and services to clients. The use of new technologies to a greater extent requires changes in procedures and regulations in the banking sector, including constantly changing rules on privacy and data protection, as well as cyber security requirements.

In a world of rapid technological changes, judicial authorities are introducing more rigorous data protection laws, individual responsibility is growing, and penalties for fraud are increasing. There are also many court cases related to intrusions into financial systems.

After detecting a large number of work interruptions in banks and companies, drafts are designed, and more adequate measures are taken to protect the system infrastructure and client privacy in the digital environment. There is an increased focus on business continuity, the resilience of the infrastructure is strengthened, and more modern methods of protection are applied.

Financial enterprises are evaluating the potential attack vectors they encounter daily. Special attention is also paid to the training of internal staff on the classic profiles of cybercriminals to gain a better insight into the threats they face knowingly or unknowingly.

Cyber-attacks in the financial sector are more destructive and pronounced compared to other sectors. Security threats can have a significant impact on the entire economy of a country or region. Money is generally the main motive for carrying out the attack. In addition, employees may be persuaded to provide vulnerable information to potential attackers in exchange for their gain.

2.1 The Most Significant Attacks in the Financial Sectors

Some of the most common cyber threats in the financial sector are Phishing, Ransomware, DDoS, Supply Chain, Bank Drops, and ATM Jackpotting.

2.1.1 Phishing

Phishing is a version of social engineering that misuses user data that including login credentials and credit card numbers. The attacker uses the spoofing technique to disguise himself as a trusted entity through a legitimate means of communication to deceive the victim. A potential victim receives a malicious email that may initiate the installation of malicious software on the targeted computer system or load a fraudulent web page that collects login credentials.

An attack can have devastating consequences, including unauthorized purchases and misuse of assets and identities. Installing malicious software on a large number of computers can initiate the creation of a foothold in corporate networks. In such a scenario, employees are compromised. They distribute malware within a closed environment and can be used as assets in large-scale attacks against appropriate targets. An organization exposed to such an attack suffers significant financial losses, reputation, and consumer trust.

Preventive computer protection against phishing attacks is the use of antivirus software. Automatic updating of the antivirus solution is essential, providing optimal protection and dealing with current security threats in real-time. Multi-factor authentication (MFA) is an important component of good identity and access management (IAM). MFA offers additional security by requiring additional verification factors in addition to the username and password requirements, thus allowing access to online resources and reducing the possibility of a successful cyber-attack. Note that having two different passwords is not considered two-factor authentication (Ramzan 2010).

Data backups at other locations prevent data loss in the event of an attack or equipment failure and are an important part of a successful disaster recovery plan.

2.1.2 Ransomware

Ransomware hacking groups often target financial industries for valuable customer information. The primary targets of the attacks were personal computers, but the attackers focused on corporations that store large amounts of confidential data about users, and often pay to unlock it.

The two most prevalent types of ransomwares are encryptors and screen lockers. Encryptors encrypt data on a system that is impossible to access without a decryption key. While the screen lock blocks access to the system noting that the entire system is encrypted.

Ransomware is a type of malware that encrypts data and blocks access to a computer system and data until the victim pays appropriate financial compensation. Infection usually starts with a malicious email. If a user opens an email or clicks on a malicious URL, the malicious software is installed and begins to encrypt essential files on the victim's computer. After the data encryption process, a notification is displayed on the compromised device. Encryption ransomware works by obfuscating the contents of user files using strong algorithms (Mohurle and Patil 2017). The notices contain a payment procedure to the attackers for the process of decrypting the compromised data. The request is time-limited and the appropriate financial compensation must be paid. To pay the ransom, the attackers use different methods of extortion to increase the pressure on the victims. The danger of leaking this data on the dark web can cause great damage to the reputation of companies that offer financial services and comply with ransom demands. After the payment has been made by the victim, the data is decrypted. There is a high probability that due to the paid fees, the victim will never receive the keys to decrypt the data. Experts think that no ransom should be paid, but many organizations have no choice. Payment is mostly made in cryptocurrencies.

Preventing ransomware attacks involves making backups and applying for adequate protection with security tools. Email protection tools are the basic line of defense, while endpoint data on workstations is a supplementary defense. Intrusion detection systems (IDS) are used to detect attacks. User training is important, but it is only one of several layers of "Defense in Depth" defenses.

2.1.3 DDoS Attacks

Despite the emergence of the cryptocurrency industry like Bitcoin and the constant growth trend of attacks on them, the financial field still suffers from a large number of Distributed Denial-of-Service (DDoS) attacks. The majority of DDoS attacks against targets in this sector hit the application and network layers of the TCP/IP reference model. DDoS attacks are a widespread potential threat to financial services because their attack domain is heterogeneous, including IT infrastructure, online trading platforms, user accounts, transaction websites, etc. This type of attack is implemented using so-called Bots and BotNets.

A botnet is a network of infected computers on the Internet that can be remotely controlled, used to send SPAM email, or organize DDoS attacks. A BotNet is also called a Zombie Network, where an individual computer is called a Bot or Zombie. A large number of computers around the world are believed to be part of one of the BotNet networks. These are mostly home PCs, without adequate Firewall and AntiVirus protection. They are also the starting point for launching DDoS attacks on financial companies.

Cybercriminals use various tactics to compromise and steal financial and private data. The Cybercrime as a Service (CCaaS) business model is used to implement DDoS attacks. It is designed so that an experienced cybercriminal builds advanced tools, software, and services to rent and sell to less experienced cybercriminals. As a result, attackers with limited expertise and a lower level of knowledge carry out attacks without much difficulty.

During the execution of the attack, the victim's server or network is flooded with fraudulent requests. Due to the high concentration of illegitimate requests from thousands of computers, attackers try to overload the computer network, servers, or some part of the IT infrastructure, thus preventing the normal functioning of systems and services. A successfully executed attack disables access to copper websites or Internet services. Customers become prevented from accessing and using their financial services and data. The consequences are loss of income, work of reputation, and violation of clients' trust in the functioning of the institution.

Large companies tend to protect themselves from security challenges, risks, and threats caused by the occurrence of DDoS attacks. Organizations implement effective security protections against DDoS attacks. The basic step in the protection process is to increase the bandwidth of the infrastructure. This method should be combined with other adequate means of protection. The use of hybrid cloud services increases security and provides optimal security due to the provision of unlimited bandwidth. It is crucial to create a DDoS Response Plan where every step is described in the event of an established attack, which provides additional security. The plan includes defined procedures, checklists in the system, and a qualified response team. A predefined plan provides a quick and efficient response. Time is a very critical factor in these cases. Every hour of downtime causes companies to lose serious amounts of money, so it is necessary to respond quickly to the incident.

2.1.4 Attacks on the Supply Chain

A supply chain attack is a type of cyber-attack that targets organizations that have potentially weak links in the supply chain. The supply chain primarily refers to the delivery of goods from the supplier through the manufacturer to the end user, networked individuals, organizations, technologies, services, resources, and activities that participate in the cycle from creation to sale of products. The weakest link and target of attack in this process are third-party suppliers, such as the financial or government sectors, that are closely related to the actual target.

An attack infiltrates a system to cause loss to the organization. Malicious programs are embedded in software or hardware that is trusted and already widely used, so the attacks themselves are very difficult to detect.

Proper third-party risk assessment is a priority and imperative to prevent supply chain attacks. By reducing the number of employees in the organization who are authorized to install software or introduce third-party hardware, the size of the attack can be reduced. Of particular importance is limiting access to confidential data and developing a stronger cyber security strategy.

2.1.5 Bank Drops

To hide the location and storage of stolen money, cybercriminals often store the stolen funds in fake bank accounts that they open with the stolen credentials of existing bank customers. The victim's complete user data is called "full" by cybercriminals. "Fullz" data can be purchased on the dark web and the price varies depending on the number of records. This data includes information about the potential victim, such as first name, last name, address, DOB (Date of birth), credit score, social security information, account numbers, driver's license number, etc. The patterns by which these attacks are carried out tend to shift to the digital wallet as more and more attackers choose cryptocurrencies that provide them with anonymity.

In response to this threat, financial institutions are required to perform special security checks on the credentials that have privileged users to open new accounts.

2.1.6 ATM "Jackpotting"

ATM Jackpotting is an attack on the physical and software vulnerabilities of Automated Teller Machines (ATMs) that ultimately have the ATMs disbursing cash. In this type of attack, cybercriminals suddenly get huge sums of money from ATMs (Kasanda and Phiri 2018). The money that the attacker steals is not tied to any bank account but is a cash payment of reserves from the ATM itself. The means used for this type of attack is a laptop or device that physically connects to the ATM and contains malicious software in the operating system that accesses and takes control of the ATM's main controls. The most common targets are stand-alone ATMs, which do not have strict supervision, adequate security, and updated software.

To prevent these increasingly sophisticated attacks, it is necessary to regularly update the software for better defense. Define a white list and lock the system to prevent the use of unauthorized programs and external media to prevent the entry of malicious software into the operating system of the ATM. Implement default passwords and update them. Then enable physical security and surveillance of ATMs to prevent unauthorized actions.

3 Literature Analysis

3.1 Fintech

There are many definitions of financial technologies, one of the most famous is: "Fintech is a new financial industry that applies various technologies to improve financial activities" (Schueffel 2016). The financial technology industry includes several innovative technologies based on powerful and complex analytical tools, advanced algorithms, software applications, big data as well as many other different functionalities (Spulbar et al. 2020). Fintech enables financial transactions to be carried out via digital devices such as mobile phones, tablets, computers. The application of financial technologies implies working on innovations and improving the quality of financial services by adapting technical solutions to different situations (Leong and Sung 2018). The goal of Fintech and the companies that deal with them is to help traditional companies implement modern technical solutions to improve their business. The use of different technologies and services is used to achieve the greatest possible efficiency so that clients are as satisfied as possible (Spulbar et al. 2020).

The connection between technology and the financial sector has a long history, from the introduction of the telegraph in the early 1800s to the first ATM installed by Barclays Bank in 1967, today we are in the Internet era, where technology is essential for both banks and customers (Arner et al. 2015). Banks are the most important part of the financial systems and they were the first to apply technological innovations to their financial systems. According to Nikkel, the idea of ATMs was a revolutionary idea at the time, as was the development of telephony systems on personal computers with modems to access banking applications. Since the expansion of the Internet in the 1990s, banks have developed online banking for consumers, while MasterCard has provided the latest technologies for online shopping (Nikkel 2020).

During the last decade, numerous companies dealing with financial technologies and cooperating with financial institutions have been formed. Fintech companies are taking advantage of financial technology to meet increasingly complex customer requirements, address compliance barriers, achieve high growth, and implement innovative business models (Pollari 2016). Financial technology advances facilitate financial inclusion, greater use of financial services enabling applications, reliability, and fairness of financial transactions, new market opportunities for smaller companies, and competitive advantage for entrepreneurial companies (Medeiros and Chau 2016). One of the main advantages of Fintech companies is that they reduce public distrust of the traditional financial industry because financial transactions are fast, secure, and transparent to the customer (Rooney et al. 2017). Banks cooperate with Fintech companies precisely for the above reasons. One of the problems that occur in the cooperation of banks with Fintech companies is the alignment of companies with the rigid structure of banks, as well as compliance with all procedures and regulations that banks must follow (Milne 2016). The biggest problem faced by banks that cooperate with Fintech companies is in the formation of common standards because they usually do business in different ways. Fintech innovations are characterized by many advantages, the most significant of which is the increase in customer satisfaction in the evolution of the global financial system. Significant changes in the financial sector have resulted in vulnerabilities that allow cyber-attacks, especially bank fraud. Potential risks related to the Fintech industry must be reduced by implementing the following activities: consumer and investor protection, clarity, and consistency of regulatory and legal frameworks (Spulbar et al. 2020).

3.2 Cybercrime

Cybercrime refers to any illegal activity that is carried out using a computer or the Internet (Avast 2022). Cybercrime is on the rise, and the emergence of new technologies such as AI, big data, and the cloud provides criminals with opportunities for new abuses of the system. Fintech start-ups, banks, and other financial institutions are at risk of various attacks, and the application of new technologies makes them targets for cybercriminals. Cybercrime includes certain categories, such as electronic fraud, cyber espionage, malware attacks, identity theft, cyberstalking, spam, copyright infringement, cyber terrorism, and computer viruses (Spulbar et al. 2020). Internet banking is a relatively new component of the banking system, very attractive, but also very vulnerable to cyber-attacks. Cybercrime activities are very difficult for law enforcement. Cybercrime brings great material damage, but non-material damage is also very significant (Antonescu and Birau 2014). Highlighting the non-financial consequences of cybercrime, such as the following: loss or violation of consumer trust, disparagement campaign based on negative publicity (bad image, public defamation, damage to reputation and prejudice), discontinuity and interruptions in business, reductions in productivity, compromising confidential customer data, unauthorized and prohibited access to various product innovations, misuse of intellectual property, as well as many other categories.

The main difference between Fintech start-ups and banks is that banks and other financial institutions invest large amounts of resources in the fight against cybercrime, data theft, and fraud defense and have established regulations to prevent cybercrime that poses a threat to the financial stability of the institution (Adeyoju

2019). Cybercrimes represent a financial loss for financial institutions and a reputational risk for them. Cyber breaches lead to loss of customers, reputation, revenue, brand, capital value, and higher operational costs for Fintech firms (Kopp et al. 2017).

Many tools that are legitimate help criminals in their abuses, such as cryptocurrencies and VPNs. VPN providers resist providing information to the police because they base their business on security and anonymity and refuse to admit that they are helping cybercriminals.

During the Covid-19 pandemic, users of financial services massively switched to conducting financial transactions via mobile devices, as a result of which there was an increase in the number of mobile banking trojans. A banking trojan/banking malware is a malicious computer program that attempts to gain access to confidential information stored or processed through online banking systems. A Trojan horse is any type of malicious program disguised as legitimate (Kopp et al. 2017). Malicious virtual applications represent one of the most prolific forms of cybercrime.

The shadow economy helps criminals achieve their abuses. The lack of regulation in many countries allows various services to conduct their business, such as cryptocurrencies and bulletproof hosters. The European Union has introduced the "5th Anti-Money Laundering directive" which regulates cryptocurrency transactions within the EU. There is no similar regulation at the global level (IOCTA 2021). Action to effectively fight cybercrime is based mainly on a clear and predictable legal framework. Enforcing rigorous cybersecurity standards is essential to reducing the effects of cybercrime (Spulbar et al. 2020).

3.3 Cyber Security

FinTech solutions rely heavily on technologies that are prone to hacking and data that is susceptible to abuse and manipulation, their combination can often lead to disastrous consequences (Adeyoju 2019). Cyber security can be defined as the security of information and the protection of electronic systems, networks, devices, programs, or data from theft or damage (Schatz et al. 2017). For the above reason, cyber security is one of the most important factors in financial technologies. As people and businesses around the world become increasingly dependent on modern technology, vulnerabilities to cyber-attacks such as corporate security breaches, phishing, blackmail, and social media scams are increasing. (Stevens 2018). Cyber security is the practice of defending computers, servers, mobile devices, electronic systems, networks, and data from malicious attacks, it includes the security of information technologies as well as the security of electronic information (Kaspersky 2022). Devices are increasingly connected and it poses an additional threat to cyber security and makes companies vulnerable to attacks. Companies that implement financial technologies are vulnerable to various attacks because they possess the confidential data of their customers. According to Najaf, the most common cyber security threats are Malware attacks, Data leakages, and Data integrity risks (Najaf et al. 2021).

The vulnerability of companies and the frequency of attacks have led to great efforts by experts and researchers to apply smart technologies such as artificial intelligence and other analysis tools to be able to counter cyber-attacks before they happen (Kang and Kang 2016). Smart programs and competent programmers are used to detect and classify malicious programs, stand up and address them, address their implications, and set protocols to prove the identity of users in the program (Al-Maksousy 2018). According to Davis, two types of risks are considered the strongest, the first are users of the system and others on the server side, where the data is stored (Davis 2017). Securing cyberspace is particularly difficult due to many factors: the ability of evil actors to operate from anywhere in the world, the existence of links between cyberspace and physical systems, and finally, the difficulty of reducing vulnerabilities and consequences in complex information networks (Al Duhaidahawi et al. 2020). Despite attempts to secure information infrastructure, employees in organizations still represent the biggest threat to cyber security, so it is necessary to focus on the behavior of employees in the organization. There is no one-size-fits-all solution to preventing cybercrime. Companies must regularly educate their employees about current threats so that there are no work errors that lead to phishing attacks or the installation of malware. A risk management plan is an important part of system protection. Threats must be assessed and an appropriate protection plan made.

To stay protected and safe from cyber-attacks, Fintech companies and banks must make continuous employee education a priority. They must train their staff and teams on data protection and disaster management, build and maintain a cyber security infrastructure designed to detect, withstand and repel cyber threats and report cyber-attacks promptly, as required by law (Adeyoju 2019).

3.4 Analysis of Research Results

There is no universal definition for Fintech, each author who deals with the mentioned field offers his own, which he believes should be generally accepted. The authors believe that the development of technology directly affects the financial systems and that they form a whole that cannot do without each other. Banks have always been the most important financial institutions and have always accepted the use of new technologies, in the past, it was ATMs, and in modern business, we can cite e-banking platforms as an example. Fintech enables greater involvement of the people, as it allows the people to do their financial affairs from home through various devices such as mobile phones, computers, or tablets. Fintech introduces significant changes in traditional business, resulting in new system vulnerabilities. Potential risks must be minimized. The authors agree that cybercrime is on the rise. New ways of conducting illegal activities and abusing fintech systems and technologies are constantly being found. The lack of legal regulations also affects the occurrence of cybercrime, because there are no legal regulations at the global level, in some countries e-business and fintech are just at their beginning, and therefore legal regulations. The consequences of cybercrime can be tangible and intangible. Companies that have suffered a security breach often suffer damage to their reputation, which is sometimes more difficult to recover than material damage.

The authors define cyber security as the protection of information and electronic systems from theft or damage. As fintech solutions rely heavily on technologies that are prone to hacking and various attacks, cyber security is one of its most important factors. Cyber security experts are putting a lot of effort into developing tools to prevent cyber-attacks and crime. Smart tools are used to detect and prevent unwanted system intrusions.

4 Identified Problems and Potential Solutions in Fintech

Before identifying the problem and stating possible solutions, it should be said that it is most profitable to assume and prevent any potential security threat, especially in the field of financial technologies. It is necessary to make an adequate assessment of potential risks and an empirical assessment of those risks that we may have exposed ourselves to in the past, without reacting correctly at that time. Thus, based on previous knowledge, we will be able to analyze their ways of acting and respond to them concretely.

In the past, financial fraud was based on transactions, from which entities defended themselves with regular and direct controls. Today, thanks to applications that exploit user data, identity-based fraud is more common. Also, their work is not monitored by appropriate supervisory bodies. With the development of financial technologies, the number of threatening entities also grows, because it is not entirely possible to provide the highest quality services in this area, without putting user security into question. Adding new user benefits and other functionalities makes it harder to protect trusted user data and increases system vulnerability. Now, more work must be done to prevent third-party intrusions, so that they do not provide themselves with access to protected data.

Confidentiality, integrity, availability, authentication, and non-repudiation are commonly cited as data protection objectives. Confidentiality presupposes the aforementioned prevention to prevent unauthorized data access, and it should ensure the privacy of the exchanged data. Integrity prevents unauthorized information from being changed so that the exchanged data reaches the final destination unchanged. Availability refers to the prevention of sabotage of access to information or resources of importance. Authentication prevents impersonation and non-repudiation is achieved precisely by preventing the masking of the entity from which the malicious activity originates; both objectives can be ensured by applying a digital signature.

Cyber-attacks in Fintech are a common occurrence. This is best seen through the establishment of cooperation between traditional financial companies (banks) and Fintech firms as modern financial providers, where the leakage or loss of data caused by cyber-attacks can have a fatal outcome. We are talking about user credentials and payment card data. In recent research, it is stated that this type of theft of data in the possession of banks is on the rise after the establishment of their cooperation with fintech companies because they are not able to adequately protect them (Ozili 2018).

Also, customized malicious attacks on SWIFT (Society for World Interbank Financial Telecommunication) are becoming more common. SWIFT is used for the international exchange of data between the banks of the world, through digitized communication. The system itself provides a degree of protection depending on the importance of the data exchanged, but recent research shows that even its systems are vulnerable to increasingly sophisticated attacks. The most exposed to them are banks that have established a regulator within Fintech, which allows its start-ups to conduct controlled experiments on their environment, thus creating an unstable environment suitable for hacker work.

These companies base their business on cloud computing, which does not have prescribed measures for saving data, which is why there is a potential loss of data. Cloud computing enables online payments, the use of digital wallets, and all in all, faster payment transactions. Protecting such business dynamics is a real challenge, requiring compliance with a whole range of security regulations and the use of adequate encryption techniques to protect sensitive information.

Concrete steps must be taken in the field of Fintech to improve the security situation and the protection of users. Potential solutions should integrate the importance of business priorities, but also their quality protection. In general, protection measures can be described as a continuous process that practically never ends and starts with prevention measures such as firewall, configuration, change of default credentials by the administrator, and the like. Then comes detection, i.e., detection of already damaged or attempted damage to the installed protection. Detection is achieved through continuous monitoring of the work of both external and internal factors. Also, for this purpose, intrusion detection systems are being developed, which, based on a memorized database, notice unusual activities and notify administrators about them. After which the reaction follows, i.e., taking steps to recover stolen data or restore the entire system if changes occurred during those detected unusual activities. It eliminates the consequences and it is desirable to return the system to its original, if not improved state.

The most commonly used answer to protect sensitive data is access control and for that purpose the use of the aforementioned cryptography, which enables communication even over an insecure communication channel by encrypting data so that an attacker cannot break the code. Risk reduction and prevention can also be established by physical methods, i.e., physical application of changes directly to the infrastructure, thus preventing further network damage. Then, by introducing access control lists that are used as a mechanism to protect the data warehouse and secure the cloud environment. They are applicable when exchanging different contents or when it is necessary to delete certain stored data. Based on all of the above, we can conclude that we must analyze cyber risks and provide an adequate counter-response to each of their elements.

4.1 Guidelines for Future Research in the Field of Financial Technologies

Fintech companies must coordinate their work with the banks and companies they cooperate with, to protect their business through joint efforts, especially from cyber-attacks. Also, compliance with legal frameworks and internal regulations is mandatory, especially the application of the Law on Consumer Protection and Electronic Commerce. It is also important to establish an economic balance between the promotion of innovations in financial technologies and the regulation of the traditional way of working in financial companies.

Future research related to financial operations and fintech should:

- Instruct fintech companies not to keep problems related to cyber security in business a secret, where they are difficult to access but to create an action plan with the help of the acquired knowledge in the event of a recurrence of cyber-attacks of the same or similar type.
- Study the impact of cyber security issues on fintech, as well as their impact on partnerships with banks. What are the assessments of traditional banks' trust in fintech, after taking measures to prevent cyber-attacks or after the consequences of a certain malicious action, if it happened.
- Expand the field of research using systematic econometric models, such as the ordinary least squares model or the probit model.

5 Cryptocurrencies

Blockchain is currently one of the most popular and significant technologies of today. Most people have heard of the term, but the concept behind it is still unknown and not clear enough. This technology is the basic model on which the operation of cryptocurrencies is based. Blockchain consists of a chain of records called blocks in which information is arranged in a certain order. Each block consists of a defined number of transactions, and each transaction is stored as the output of a hash function. A hash is an authentic address that is rewritten to each block in the process of its creation and any change in the block results in a change in its hash value.

Every work and decision is based on the agreement of all nodes of the network participating in the work of digital currencies. The processed data is encrypted with the help of cryptographic algorithms and functions to ensure user privacy and data integrity. Strong and complex encryption algorithms provide them with optimal protection.

The entire system of blocks and information is managed in a decentralized way, there is no central authority that performs the administration. In this way, there is no type of control by the government or any central entity, unlike other payment systems. As a result, we have that the third party, i.e., banks or government have no role in this concept (Hughes 2017).

Durability, robustness, reliability, and transparency are some of the characteristics of Blockchain. By design, Blockchain is designed to work as a medium of exchange online for purchasing goods and services and making payments.

One of the originally used cryptocurrencies in the world is the famous Bitcoin digital wallet founded in 2009. Bitcoin works on Blockchain technology and is used as a digital form of cash for payment. Its use is based on the trade of everyday things, there is also the possibility of larger purchases such as cars and real estate.

Physical money is transferred and exchanged in the real world, while cryptocurrency payments exist as digital entries in an online database that have a description and specific characteristics of the completed transaction. Crypto transactions are always successful, there are no delays and procedural costs.

Cryptocurrencies are forms of currency that exist in digital form and are stored in digital wallets. It is possible to buy them with the help of Digital wallets or trading platforms. They can be digitally transferred during trades in cyberspace, while blockchain technology stores and records the transaction and the new owner. The convenience of cryptocurrencies is that there is a record of all performed activities, i.e., the transfer of digital currency assets, and they are kept in a public ledger (digital ledger). After saving the data in the form of a digital ledger, the data is replicated on each node across the entire blockchain network, which makes it safer and impossible to change, hack, or defraud the system. The advanced coding method is used to store and transfer cryptocurrency data between wallets and public ledgers. Thanks to Blockchain technology, cryptocurrencies are immune to counterfeiting and reliable because every transaction is recorded. Verification is achieved by encryption by each node, i.e., member to complete the transaction. Cryptocurrencies got their name based on the application of cryptographic algorithms for the realization of transactions.

Digital transactions are encrypted, creating an undeniable, time-registered, and secure record of every payment, purposefully protecting against third parties with ulterior motives. Block sets record information about transactions, for example: who are the actors of the transaction, the direction of the transaction, and the amount of trade. This system is a peer-to-peer system that allows anyone regardless of location to send and receive payments (Hughes 2017).

Blockchain technology has the potential to transform the entire financial sector because it brings a significant number of benefits such as lower costs in the business, quick execution of transactions, the ability to review executed operations, and other advantages. Cryptocurrencies have revolutionized the world of finance and banking.

However, banks are afraid of the potential risks of this technology because there are almost no regulations regarding digital trade. One of the reasons for concern is the security and stability of cryptocurrency, which is why legislative entities are wary of any business in this area. The decentralized nature of the currency undermines the authority of central banks because there is a belief that they will be almost unnecessary in future operations.

There is also huge potential for economic growth, although there is a chance for criminal activity. Compliance guidelines should be defined to help banks bring innovation and efficiency to crypto-business.

Financial institutions should consider the crypto-competitor as a possible partner and become part of the crypto-industry. Banks could add the necessary security to this unregulated environment.

Banks must find a way to embrace this technology. By recognizing the potential benefits, they could improve financial services and alleviate current concerns.

Bitcoin has shown that the underlying security of its proof-of-work system is solid, however, there are limitations to this system. Limited scalability, high energy consumption, and unstable concentration of mining funds. There have been many scams from centralized brokers and promoters of cryptocurrency IPOs. Manipulation is very widespread in cryptocurrency exchanges. Money laundering and other criminal activities are serious problems in this area. Cryptocurrency is becoming the preferred payment method for all types of scams. The whole concept of digital currencies is widely accepted, but there is also an increasing rate of exploitation by hacker attacks and criminals who finance their illegal operations on the dark web.

6 Conclusion

Money in any form attracts unwanted attention from criminals. As a consequence of technological development, cash is in less and less use, thus the use of electronic money has grown. Countries like Sweden want to phase out physical money completely in the next 5 years and completely switch to the use of digital payments. The main advantage of digital payments and money transfers is that it is possible to easily follow the trail of money, which is not easy when using cash. Monitoring digital transactions significantly reduce the possibility of simple "money laundering," as well as the use of money in various illegal activities. As a result of these changes, criminals had to come up with alternative ways to continue their illegal activities.

Financial institutions, as well as financial technology companies, must prioritize the protection of their systems as they are prime targets due to the growth in the use of digital payments. Zero-day threats appear every day that cannot be prevented, therefore it is important to actively monitor all vulnerabilities in systems and remediate them in time. Unfortunately, no software can prevent all dangers and threats from unwanted intrusion into the system. The key to system protection is regular system maintenance and various employee training. Many organizations often neglect the training of employees, who can prevent a significant part of the attacks that we described in the second chapter. Companies must always stay abreast of the latest security technologies, as criminals are always finding new technologies and ways to carry out their crimes.

References

Adeyoju FIP (2019) Cybercrime and cybersecurity: FinTech's greatest challenges. Available at SSRN 3486277

Al Duhaidahawi HMK, Zhang J, Abdulreza MS, Sebai M, Harjan SA (2020) Analysing the effects of FinTech variables on cybersecurity: evidence form Iraqi Banks. Int J Res Bus Soc Sci 9(6): 123–133

Al-Maksousy HHL (2018) Applying machine learning to advance cyber security: network based intrusion detection systems

Antonescu M, Birau R (2014) Financial and non-financial implications of cyber-crimes in emerging countries. In: International conference emerging markets queries in finance and business EMQFB, 3rd edn, 29–31 October 2014, Bucharest, Romania, published in Procedia - Economics and Finance (Elsevier Journals), vol 32, pp 618–621. https://doi.org/10.1016/S2212-5671(15)01440-9. https://www.worldbank.org/en/. The World Bank official website. Accessed on 10.5.2022

Arner DW, Barberis J, Buckley RP (2015) The evolution of Fintech: a new post-crisis paradigm. Geo J Int L 47:1271

Davis JJ (2017) Machine learning and feature engineering for computer network security. Thesis. https://eprints.qut.edu.au/106914/1/Jonathan_Davis_Thesis.pdf. Accessed on 9.5.2022

https://www.avast.com/c-cybercrime. Accessed on 1.5.2022

https://www.europol.europa.eu/cms/sites/default/files/documents/internet_organised_crime_threat_assessment_iocta_2021.pdf. Accessed on 1.5.2022

https://www.kaspersky.com/resource-center/definitions/what-is-cyber-security. Accessed on 1.5.2022

Hughes SD (2017) Cryptocurrency regulations and enforcement in the US. W. St. UL Rev 45:1

Kang MJ, Kang JW (2016) Intrusion detection system using deep neural net-work for in-vehicle network security. PLoS One

Kasanda EN, Phiri J (2018) ATM Security: a case study of emerging threats. Int J Adv Stud Comput Sci Eng 7(10)

Kopp E, Kaffenberger L, Wilson C (2017) Cyber risk, market failures, and financial stability. International Monetary Fund

Leong K, Sung A (2018) FinTech (Financial Technology): what is it and how to use technologies to create business value in fintech way? Int J Innov Manage Technol 9(2):74–78

Medeiros M, Chau B (2016) Fintech-stake a patent claim? Intell Property J 28(3):303

Milne A (2016) Competition policy and the financial technology revolution in banking

Mohurle S, Patil M (2017) A brief study of wannacry threat: Ransomware attack 2017. Int J Adv Res Comput Sci 8(5):1938–1940

Najaf K, Mostafiz MI, Najaf R (2021) Fintech firms and banks sustainability: why does cybersecurity risk matter? Int J Financ Eng 8(02):2150019

Nikkel B (2020) Fintech forensics: criminal investigation and digital evidence in financial technologies. Forensic Sci Int: Dig Investig 33:200908

Ozili PK (2018) Impact of digital finance on financial inclusion and stability. Borsa Istanbul Rev 18(4):329–340

Pollari I (2016) The rise of Fintech opportunities and challenges. Jassa 3:15–21

Ramzan Z (2010) Phishing attacks and countermeasures. Handb Inf Commun Security:433–448

Rooney H, Aiken B, Rooney M (2017) Q. Is internal audit ready for blockchain? Technology Innovation. Manage Rev 7(10):41–44

Schatz D, Wall J, Schatz D, Wall J (2017) Security and law towards a more representative definition of cyber security towards a more representative definition of cyber security. J Dig Forensics
Schueffel P (2016) Taming the beast: a scientific definition of fintech. J Innov Manage 4(4):32–54
Spulbar C, Birau R, Calugaru T, Mehdiabadi A (2020) Considerations regarding FinTech and its multidimensional implications on financial systems. Revista de Sti-inte Politice 68:77–86
Stevens T (2018) Global cybersecurity: new directions in theory and methods. Politics and Governance. https://doi.org/10.17645/pag.v6i2.1569. Accessed on 9.5.2022.

Mobile Applications for Personal Finance Management: Technology Acceptance Perspective

Milos Mijić and Branko Ćebić

Abstract This paper deals with the perspectives of accepting mobile application technologies in the function of personal finance management. The paper uses the UTAUT2 model, a technology acceptance model that focuses on observing technology acceptance, focused on the user-consumer, and the acceptance of technical devices, applications, and services. For measuring user behavior UTAUT2 model includes the following elements (constructs): Performance Expectancy (PE); Effort Expectancy (EE); Social Influence (SI); Facilitating Conditions (FC); Hedonic Motivation (HM); Price Value (PV), and Habit (H). The paper will examine the following elements from the UTAUT2 model: Performance Expectancy (PE); Effort Expectancy (EE); Social Influence (SI); Facilitating Conditions (FC); Hedonic Motivation (HM); Price Value (PV); Habit (H). This paper aims to examine the readiness of an individual to accept and use new technologies of available mobile applications and their functionalities in personal finance management. The results should indicate the satisfaction of potential and existing users of mobile applications for personal financial management and the acceptability of the mentioned applications from the UTAUT2 model, by users. The contribution of this paper is reflected in the fact that research on this topic is being conducted for the first time in Serbia.

Keywords Technology acceptance perspective · Personal financial management · Financial literacy · UTAUT2 model

1 Introduction

Today, every individual wants to live without debt so that he does not work until old age and in order to survive and educate his children. Every living being should therefore be aware of the importance of their financial planning and management

M. Mijić (✉) · B. Ćebić
Academy of Applied Studies Šabac, Šabac, Serbia
e-mail: branko.cebic@vipos.edu.rs

S. Benković et al. (eds.), *Digital Transformation of the Financial Industry*, Contributions to Finance and Accounting,
https://doi.org/10.1007/978-3-031-23269-5_16

(Munohsamy 2015). The best way to start growing your money is to manage it wisely (Bitethegram 2020). Financial management helps us improve our standard of living which leads to good health and a significant reduction in financial stress. In addition, it enables an individual to make better financial decisions, which reduces poverty and debt and increases savings (Bhatt 2011a, b). It is essential for every individual to know the importance and benefits of personal financial management leading to a stress-free life. Many of us have not been taught the importance of money management throughout our lives. We have not learned to save and invest. Just knowing the importance of managing personal finances is not enough, but we need to take steps to plan, organize, and manage our personal finances. Many of us are in debt, have no idea how we got into it, and don't know how to begin solving our financial problems (Scott 2009). Today, we can break the vicious cycle by teaching young people to better manage their finances. The goal of any personal finance management is that our income is greater than our expenses so that we can then use the excess money to achieve some of our desires and goals. Personal finances greatly affect all areas of our lives. That's why personal finance management (McDowell, CB, SlidePlayer, n.d.) today appears as a need of every individual who generates income. For the successful management of personal finances, it is important to recognize the extent to which money management and budgeting are important for personal and professional success. It is important for every individual to manage his money properly so that he can avoid unnecessary waste of money and secure a certain financial future for himself through the achievement of his life goals. Successful money management requires the development of a personal financial plan so that we can track our money, protect ourselves from debt or keep debt under control, protect ourselves from misuse in order to avoid additional stress that can endanger our health and ensure a certain financial future.

2 Review of Literature

2.1 Personal Finance

Finance and personal finance management in the broadest sense refers to money management, how we earn or spend, how we save and invest our money, but also refers to the handling of financial products such as loans, insurance, private pension, investments, and others (Herbut 2021). Personal financial management is dealing with our financial situation in a responsible way in order to achieve financial independence (UMBC Money Matters Seminar, n.d.; Bhatt 2011a, b). At a basic level, personal financial management means gaining an understanding of your personal financial situation in order to make the most of your personal assets, both in your daily life and in planning for your future. Of course, you should keep in mind that property depends to some extent on where you live and what your cost of living is. Cost of living is essentially the amount of money we need to cover basic living expenses such as food, housing, commuting, and even healthcare (Skills YouNeed

2022). Personal finance is a term that refers to money management, saving, and investing. The term often refers to an entire industry that provides financial services to individuals and households and advises them on financial and investment opportunities. They relate to meeting personal financial goals (Kenton 2022). Personal finance refers to financial planning and control of personal financial flows—inflows and outflows of cash with the aim of maximizing individual well-being (King and Carey 2017). Money management is done in all areas of life. Financial management also includes personal financial management that helps us manage our family's finances, which is budgeting, saving, investing, debt management, and other aspects related to personal money where an individual can achieve personal goals (Bhatt 2011a, b). Personal finance management is the process of controlling income and planning expenses through a detailed financial plan, where the money that comes in is monitored and its rational use is controlled. In a world where funds and investments move quickly and we connect our bank accounts to numerous services and make purchases at the touch of a button, financial management is a more complex concept than ever before. In order to maximize the use of the money available to us, we must think strategically (Skills YouNeed 2022). Managing our own budget allows us to see the real state of our finances, and to allocate the money we have in accordance with needs and priorities. By analyzing our income and cash flow, we can see how much money has to be invested in basic expenses, taxes, etc. The basic assumption of quality management of personal finances is that the individual (or his agent) is sufficiently financially literate, that they have the knowledge to control financial flows and to regularly review their financial status and success, and that they implement adequate actions for previously defined personal financial plans (King and Carey 2017). Financial experts agree that, even if people today have much more money than a few generations ago, the amount of knowledge about managing that money is no greater today than it used to be (Fogarty 2012). For the successful management of personal finances, Munohsamy (2015) highlights the importance of financial management and suggests a way in which each individual can take steps to properly manage their finances. It talks about the level of awareness of financial management in Brunei with the aim of creating awareness among people about the importance of planning and managing personal finances, but also to educate readers on how to plan and manage their finances. According to Munohsamy (2015), such activities would indirectly affect the development of the nation. Personal Financial Management (PFM) is a term used to describe the software that powers many different personal finance and mobile banking tools. Since it first started operating in 1983, the software has evolved and expanded beyond its original purpose to reduce and simplify bill payment. As customer behavior and needs evolve, so will the PFM software and the applications it powers (Tymkiw 2022).

In addition to the usual mobile applications for mbanking, which users receive from parent banks, today there are also a large number of independent mobile applications for managing personal finances. Mobile PFM apps for the individual can be a tool for effective budgeting and controlling impulsive spending. These applications are characterized by easy handling, high level of functionality, and data visualization. Some of the most important functionalities of PFM applications are:

recording of income, recording of expenses, creation and monitoring of the planned budget (difference between planned and realized), preparation of financial reports, bill payment reminder (notification), data backup. There are also applications on the market that offer the user the connection of his bank accounts, and even services for payment and monitoring of transactions, such as Mint (mint intuit, n.d.), which implies that PFM mobile apps cover all aspects of personal finance. Ease of use is one of the advantages of PFM applications, and is a key factor for simultaneously and easily performing multiple financial tasks. Data visualization is very important and is present in most PFM mobile applications, because this is what makes them simple and attractive for users. Overview dashboards and statistical data displayed in diagrams make information understandable and easy for further analysis.

According to Servon and Kaestner (2008), organizing financial literacy training, using PFM applications, can help low- and middle-income individuals to be more effective financial actors. These apps help track the user's spending and can provide personalized advice to deal with unplanned financial expenses. Marketing company "Fact.MR Market Research Company's" (2021) report on the Personal Finance Mobile App Market, among other things, states that personal finance mobile apps reached 1.3 billion downloads in the second quarter of 2020, and registered exponential increase in the frequency of application usage. The increasing share of smartphones in developing countries gives a satisfactory picture of the growth in the adoption rate of mobile applications for PFM. Also in the report of the company Fact.MR Market Research Company (2021) it is stated that at the global level more than 75% of the surveyed smartphone users used at least one application to manage their finances. During this extensive user research, it was found that users are more inclined to use mobile apps than websites. Mobile applications for personal finance make it easier to use by offering all the necessary financial services and services in one place and at the user's fingertips. According to the results, 6 out of 10 users preferred personal finance apps, while 4 users prefer websites for managing personal finances. It is concluded that mobile applications for PFM represent a significant benefit for the user because they raise the level of financial literacy.

To make the most of your income and savings, it is important to become financially literate so that you can distinguish between good and bad advice and make smart decisions (Kenton 2022).

2.2 *Financial Literacy*

During the last decades, there have been significant changes and transformation of the market of goods and services. Such a situation was greatly contributed by the great progress in the development of communication and IT technologies. Their development and progress has led to a change in the entire system and direction of the financial services industry, including banks, insurance companies, stock exchanges, and other service providers. Despite the fact that information is readily available, numerous studies show that users of financial services still struggle with the basics of financial literacy. Many citizens are not prepared for the current financial crisis because they face a lack of understanding of the basic principles of good financial decision-making and the responsibility that each decision entails (Đikanović 2013). Certain financial literacy helps us successfully overcome various challenges in the field of personal finance management. We can transfer our acquired knowledge to our family members and our friends and acquaintances. The term financial literacy refers to a number of important financial skills and business concepts (Fernando 2021). It can help protect individuals so that they do not become victims of financial fraud or various types of criminal acts that are increasingly common (Mastercard NuData Security 2021). Financially literate people are generally less susceptible to financial fraud because the acquired knowledge provides them with adequate help in achieving various life goals, such as saving for education and retirement or other responsible use of credit or running their own business. Financial literacy is the ability to understand and effectively use various financial skills (Fernando 2021) and knowledge that help a person to achieve progress. The essence of financial literacy is a good understanding of the issues related to it: how money is earned and spent; which are active and passive income or expenses; what is a loan and how to use it; how money loses value (inflation) and increases (investment); how to plan a budget and prioritize expenses; how to set financial goals and save money for the future. It includes personal financial management, budgeting and investing. Financial literacy is at the core of our relationship with money and requires lifelong learning. Financial literacy is also defined as knowledge and understanding of financial concepts and risks, as well as the skills, motivation and confidence to apply that knowledge and understanding in order to make effective decisions to improve individual and societal financial well-being (OECD 2016). This definition reflects the need both to understand financial reasoning and behavior and to measure the knowledge and concepts acquired in relation to personal finance (OECD 2019). Research has identified financial literacy as a factor contributing to individual well-being (AFG 2019). An unsustainable debt burden may be more likely to accumulate, either due to poor spending decisions or a lack of long-term preparation. This situation can lead to bad credit, bankruptcy, foreclosure, and other negative consequences (Fernando 2021). Today, there are more opportunities than ever for those who want to educate themselves about the world of finance. One example is the US government-sponsored Commission on Financial Literacy and Education, which offers a wide range of free educational resources (US Department of the Treasury 2021). Developing one's financial literacy to improve personal finances involves learning and practicing various skills related to budgeting, debt management and payment, as well as understanding debt, credit and investments (Kumar and Shaun O'Brien 2019). Considering the importance of finance in modern society, a lack of financial literacy can have major negative consequences for an individual's long-term financial success. Unfortunately, research shows that financial illiteracy is very common. According to the Financial Industry Regulatory Authority (FINRA), 66% of Americans are financially illiterate in America (Financial Industry Regulatory Authority 2021). Research has shown that the French have heterogeneous financial knowledge. The majority of respondents, 78% of them, believe that financial education should be taught at school. If in the future financial and budgetary education were really taught in school, 65% of the French believe that the acquired knowledge in that subject would enable the reduction of over-indebtedness and the situation of financial stability (IFOP 2016). Allianz (2017) conducted a comprehensive survey in November 2016, in 10 European countries: Austria, Belgium, France, Germany, Italy, the Netherlands, Portugal, Spain, Switzerland, and the United Kingdom. The analysis carried out on 1000 respondents showed that France, Portugal, and Italy showed a low level of financial literacy. Further research has shown that more efforts should be made to improve the overall financial literacy of societies. At the same time, the focus should be on women and younger people who have shown a low level of financial literacy (hellofuture 2022). In 2017, in the Russian Federation, an agreement was concluded on the introduction of the principles of financial literacy into educational standards. With this agreement, Russia is committed to increasing the financial literacy of the population in cooperation with the Central Bank, the Ministry of Finance, and the Ministry of Education of the Russian Federation (Advisor, 2020). As part of the joint project of the Ministry of Finance of the Russian Federation and the World Bank, the course "Financial Literacy" was prepared. The goals of the course are to increase financial literacy and use the acquired knowledge and skills in everyday life (MUEGN, n.d.). According to Đikanović (2013), the focus of educational activities should primarily be young people, pupils, and students. The financial preparedness of young people is essential to their well-being and is essential to their economic future. Young people should be financially educated in order to acquire the necessary financial knowledge that will enable them to be in a better position in making timely and adequate investment decisions in their lives. Many receive their financial education more at home than at school. Parents and family have a much greater influence on the financial education of young people. Numerous researches have shown that almost half of students who studied personal finance for an entire semester did not take seriously the importance of this type of education. Such results were probably influenced by the fact that most of them were minors or were freshmen. They most likely have not been exposed to many financial decisions. For these reasons, their motivation to become financially literate must be encouraged (Đikanović 2013). This motivation can be influenced by PFM applications and currently there are many applications on the market that aim to educate young people (children and teenagers) how to manage their personal finances. Examples of such applications are: Greenlight (Debit Card for Kids and Teens, n.d.), Plan'it Prom (Google Play, n.d.), BusiKid, (BusyKid, n.d.).

2.3 Technology Acceptance Model

The evolution of theories and models of technology acceptance, which began at the beginning of the twentieth century, is still ongoing. It took place in different theoretical perspectives, such as cognitive, affective, motivational and behavioral intentions and reactions of individuals (Hernandez 2017; Weeger and Gewald 2013).

Recently, the unified theory of technology acceptance and use has been used as one of the most developed and intensive models for testing technology adoption and acceptance. This model is accepted as robust and reliable for application on different technologies. It is viable even after any modification on it. It has a minimal amount of complexity consistent with its limited number of constructs and moderating variables that make it applicable and understandable for studying acceptance behavior for any new technology (Momani 2020). In the field of software engineering, the adoption, acceptance, and behavior of information systems is part of software quality activities, and since the 1970s has attracted attention as an initial step for the use and realization of technologies. Currently, understanding the causes of user acceptance/ rejection of any new technology has become an integral task in the life cycle of any information system (Silva and Dias 2007; Sivathanu and Pillai 2019). Theories and models of technology acceptance are constructed as a framework for studying methods of understanding and acceptance of new technologies by users (Fishbein and Ajzen 1975). The actual use of any information system implicitly refers to the existence of the intention to use it. The continued use of the information system depends on the belief that the information system must be accepted by the user and that the continued use of the information system that comes after its acceptance depends on the user's satisfaction with the system. This means that in the organizational environment, there must be greater investment in information technology (Hong et al. 2006). With the ever-increasing development of technology and its integration into the private and professional life of users, the decision to accept or reject it still remains the subject of numerous investigations. All research dealing with the technology acceptance model (TAM) indicates the popularity of the model in the field of technology acceptance (Marangunić and Granić 2015). The technology acceptance model emerged from behavioral psychology. He is one of the first models of accepting the use of technology, which included psychological factors (Alharbi and Drew 2014). The special feature of the TAM model compared to other models is precisely the inclusion of psychological factors that can predict and explain user behavior during the process of accepting the use of technology (Teo and Zhou 2014). The TAM model has undergone numerous changes to become a key model in understanding predictors today. Despite the evident continuous progress in discovering new factors that could significantly influence key TAM variables, there are still many unexplored areas of potential application of the model that could provide insight into the near and long-term future, allowing users to see possible trends and upcoming behavior based on already existing data (Marangunić and Granić 2015). TAM was developed out of concern that workers were not using the information technology (IT) available to them (Davis 1989; Davis et al. 1989). Its creators concluded that the key to increasing usage was to first increase IT acceptance. The assessment was determined by asking individuals about their future intentions to use IT. Knowing the factors that shaped one's intentions would allow organizations to manipulate those factors to promote acceptance and thereby increase IT usage (Holden and Karsha 2010). Davis' 1986 Technology Acceptance Model (TAM) (Davis 1986) is quite simple and is still one of the leading theoretical models applied in the field of information systems and computer technology. This model assumes a mediating role of perceived ease of use and perceived usefulness variables in the complex relationship between system characteristics (external variables) and probability of system use (system success indicators). Based on the theory of deliberate action, Davis et al. (1989) developed a technology acceptance model, TAM (The Technology Acceptance Model) to determine which factors encourage people to accept or not accept information technology. According to the definition of the TAM model (Davis 1989), the two most important expectations of an individual about the use of information technology are perceived usefulness of the system (Perceived Usefulness) and perceived ease of use (Perceived Ease of Use). Perceived usefulness of a system is defined as the degree to which the user believes that the use of a particular system would increase his performance at work. This definition is based on the expectation-value model, which is defined in the basis of the theory of deliberate action. By definition, perceived ease of use is defined as the degree to which a person believes that using a particular system would be effortless or not. External variables or external impulses (External Variables) represent different technical characteristics of the system. They directly condition perceived usefulness and ease of use (Davis 1989). Based on the perceived ease of use and usefulness of the system, users develop an attitude (Attitude Towards Use) and an intention (Intention to Use) that influence the actual use of the system (Actual Usage). Perceived usefulness of a system is the strongest predictor of an individual's intention to use information technology (Davis 1989). The existence of these basic factors of the TAM has proven over time to be insufficient to fully explain the technology acceptance process. A critical review of TAM highlighted the need to include, in addition to the basic constructs of the model, other external factors in order to provide a better insight into the model and a clearer understanding of the technology acceptance process (Legris et al. 2003). The existence of only the basic constructs of the TAM model gives partial information about the opinion of individuals about a technology.

2.4 UTAUT Model (Unified Theory of Acceptance and Use of Technology)

More recently, numerous research efforts have been made to consolidate theoretical data on IT acceptance. Several research works have been done that could provide answers to the most important and effective limitations of theories and models of technology acceptance depending on the review and comprehensive analysis of previous research (Lee et al. 2003; Moghavvemi et al. 2013; Williams et al. 2015). Previous theories and models have discussed the behavior of individuals and their ability to accept and adopt new technologies according to some constructs and variables. These theories are focused on the psychological and behavioral points of view of technology users. Out of a total of 32 constructs listed in existing theories, studies have shown that a maximum of 7 of them can determine the intention of

Table 1 Definitions of constructs of the UTAUT model (Momani 2020)

Constructs	Definition
Performance expectancy	The capability of the technology to providing benefits and enhancing the performance to the user according to his/her expectations (Venkatesh et al. 2003, p. 447)
Effort expectancy	User expectations about the ease of use of technology (Venkatesh et al. 2003, p. 450)
Social influence	The expected influence of others on the user to start and continue using the technology (Venkatesh et al. 2003, p. 451)
Facilitating conditions	The expected level of organizational and technical infrastructure that can support the use of technology (Venkatesh et al. 2003, p. 453)
Behavioral intention	The expectation of the user's intention to perform plans and decisions regarding the use of technology (Venkatesh et al. 2003)

behavior or use (Momani 2020). It was hypothesized that 4 of them have a direct impact on the adoption intention and on the acceptance of the technology by users. Those constructs are: expected performance, expected effort, social influence, facilitating conditions. It was found that the other 3 constructs do not have a direct influence on the intention to use or the use of technology (Fuksa 2013). Based on the most significant constructs from the previous eight theories and models, Venkatesh et al. (2003) set up a new model called the Unified Theory of Acceptance and Use of Technology (UTAUT) (Table 1).

UTAUT is a new but promising theory. The first tests of UTAUT explained an impressive 70% of the variance in the intention to use the technology and about 50% in its actual use (Holden and Karsha 2010).

2.5 UTAUT2

During the last ten years, researchers have shifted the focus of research on technology acceptance to the user-consumer and to the acceptance of technical devices, applications, and services. Consumers themselves are responsible for the costs that can be crucial to the acceptance of the technology. They have previously learned behaviors, habits. Very often they expect the use of technology to give them enjoyment and satisfaction (Venkatesh et al. 2012). They therefore extend the theory on the UTAUT model by positing the Extended Unified Theory of Technology Acceptance and Use, UTAUT2 (Fig. 1). Venkatesh et al. 2012 hereby advance their initial theory of the UTAUT-model from 2003 and extend it with three more constructs that directly influence intention to use and use of technology. Those constructs are: *Hedonic motivation*; *Price Value,* and *Habit.* Hedonic motivation as a factor implies fun or pleasure that occurs during the use of a certain technology. It has a significant impact on the acceptance and use of technology. The authors of UTAUT2 believe that the cost value of the technology used is significant when looking at the intent and use of the technology. They argue that users perceive the

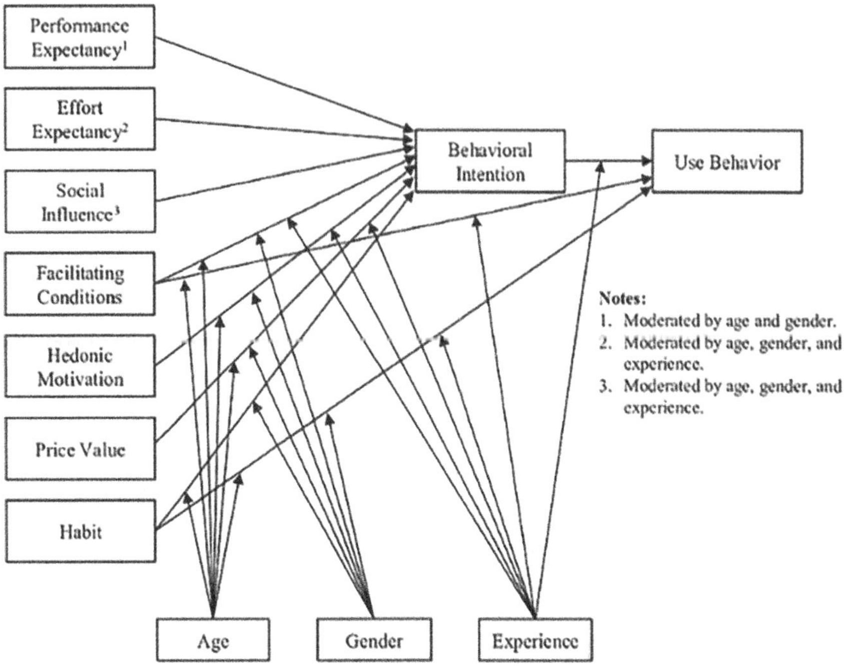

Fig. 1 Model of general theory of acceptance and use of technology 2 (UTAUT2) (Venkatesh et al. 2012)

quality of technology according to the price range and therefore consider that price value is a significant predictor of intention to use and technology use. The last added factor is the habit formed through experience in using the technology. It refers to users' perceptions of the use of the technology they use (Venkatesh et al. (2012). For the purpose of measuring the behavior of technology users, the taken constructs (elements) and the connections between them as determined by Venkatesh in the UTAUT2-model are (Venkatesh et al. 2012):

- *Performance Expectancy (PE)* determines the user's belief that the use of the solution will be more effective and productive. The construct is moderated by gender and age.
- *Effort Expectancy (EE)* indicates the user's assessment of the effort to achieve proficiency in using the selected solution. The effect of this variable will be moderated by gender, age, and experience.
- *Social influence (SI)* shows the individual's belief that his environment will support the use of the solution. This construct is influenced by all three indirect moderators—gender, age, and experience.
- *Facilitating conditions (FC)* are defined as "the degree to which an individual believes that there is an organizational and technical infrastructure that supports

the use of the system" (Venkatesh et al. 2003) and the construct is moderated by experience and age.
- *Hedonic motivation (HM)* determines an individual's expectation or experience that using a solution seems pleasant or fun and is moderated by age, gender, and experience.
- *Value for money (VM)* represents the individual's assessment that the use of the solution will be profitable in relation to monetary compensation (e.g., good value for money invested). It is moderated by age and gender.
- *Habit (H)* determines the user's assessment of how much, taking into account previous experience, the use of the solution will become a daily routine for him, and it is moderated by age, gender, and experience.

The UTAUT2 model is the latest model that has been gradually adopted to explore various issues such as self-service technology, smart mobile device adoption, learning management software acceptance, and the healthcare industry.

3 Research Methodology

The research model is set according to the UTAUT-2 model and includes all seven elements (performance expectancy, effort expectancy, social influence, facilitating conditions, hedonic motivation, price value, habit). The conducted research was done on the primary data that was collected by survey, online interview technique. The questionnaire consisted of three groups of questions. The first group (four) of questions related to the socio-demographic characteristics of the respondents, i.e., gender, age, work status, and education of the respondents. The next group of questions related to the level of monthly income, personal finance management, as well as whether the respondents are familiar with and whether they use mobile applications for personal finance. The third part of the questionnaire consisted of 25 statements. The statements in the survey questionnaire were taken from the relevant literature and adapted for the needs of this research. They are grouped into seven variables according to the UTAUT2 model (Venkatesh et al. 2012). Additionally, the variable BI, (Behavior Intention), was inserted as the eighth variable, the dependent variable. Respondents expressed their degree of agreement on a five-point Likert scale (1—completely disagree, 5—completely agree). The online survey was conducted in the period from May 25 to June 20, 2022 (119 respondents in the Republic of Serbia were surveyed). The analysis of the collected primary data was performed in the statistical data processing program *SPSS v. 20* (*The Statistical Package for the Social Science*). From the statistical analyses, descriptive statistical analysis (for the sample structure), reliability analysis, and correlation and regression analysis were carried out. The sample is segmented according to gender, age, education, work status, and amount of monthly income. Table 2 shows the structure of the sample and the socio-demographic characteristics of the respondents.

Table 2 Display of demographic data

Description	Category	Percentage	Number
Gender	Female	70.6	84
	Male	29.4	35
Age	18–25	43.7	52
	26–35	16.8	20
	36–45	16	19
	46–55	9.2	11
	56 and more	14.3	17
Level of education	Secondary education	35.3	42
	Higher vocational education	64.7	77
Working status	Student	42.9	51
	Manager, entrepreneur	6.7	8
	Professor, doctor, engineer	23.5	28
	Worker	25.2	30
	Pensioner	1.7	2
Income in a month	Less than 50.000 din.	23.5	28
	From 50.000 to 70.000 din.	20.2	24
	From 70.000 to 100.000 din.	16.8	20
	More than 100.000 din.	18.5	22
	I don't want to make a statement	21	25

In the research, seven hypotheses adopted according to the UTAUT2 model were set. Through the element of performance expectancy, existing and potential users of mobile personal finance applications express their expectations, and this element suggests that individuals will use application services if they believe they will have positive outcomes (Venkatesh et al. 2003). Performance expectancy actually measures the degree to which the user believes that accepting and using mobile application services will help him plan and manage his daily and monthly budget. In the field of mobile applications, more research has been done so far on the acceptance of mobile application technology for banking (m-banking) according to the UTAUT2 model. Users of m-banking believe that the element of performance expectancy is one of the most important indicators (indicators) of behavioral intention (Baptista and Oliveira 2015; Basri 2018). Based on the above, it was assumed that the expected performance affects the intention of users to use the services of mobile applications for managing personal finances, and the following hypothesis was put forward:

H1: Performance Expectancy (EP) has a positive effect on the intention to use mobile applications for personal finance management by end users.

According to the theory of the UTAUT2 model, the effort expectancy required to use mobile applications smoothly affects the user's intention to use those applications. In relation to the effort expectancy, users who find mobile applications easier to use become more ready for all m-banking services (banking transactions) (Lin

2011). The relation that the effort expectancy affects the intention to use the personal finance management application was assumed and the following hypothesis was defined:

H2: Effort Expectancy (EE) has a statistically significant influence (positive influence) on the intention to use mobile applications for managing personal finances by end users.

Environmental influence reflects the notion that user behavior is influenced by how peers, friends, or family members value the use of mobile apps for managing personal finances. The influence of the environment is especially important in the early stages of acceptance and application of new technology when most users have no experience or information about the technology, and therefore rely on public opinion (Marinkovic and Kalinic 2017). In fact, it is about the influence of people from the individual's immediate environment on his behavior, related to a certain activity. Similar research has confirmed that social influence (environmental influence) is directly related to an individual's intention to use mobile banking services (Bhatiasevi 2016; Tan and Leby 2016). The mentioned element was singled out as the most significant when it comes to the intention to use mobile banking services (Venkatesh and Zhang 2010; Yu 2012). Since the element of environmental influence is a significant indicator of the user's intention to use, the following hypothesis was put forward:

H3: Social Influence (SI) has a statistically significant influence (positive influence) on the intention to use mobile applications for managing personal finances by end users.

The fourth examined element from the UTAUT2 model is facilitating conditions. Under facilitating conditions, the subjective assessment (potential and existing, I don't know whether to state this everywhere or just use the user) of mobile application users on the existence (possession) of necessary resources, user competencies, instructions for using mobile applications for financial management is observed. Facilitating conditions are defined as the degree to which an individual believes that the organizational and technical infrastructure can support the use of the system (Venkatesh et al. 2003). The use of mobile application technology requires the availability of appropriate resources, knowledge, and technological infrastructure, i.e., it is logical to assume that an individual's intention to use mobile applications for managing personal finances largely depends on these conditions. Also, in terms of facilitating conditions, benefits can be represented by online tutorials or demo (trial) versions of mobile applications, and contribute to a greater likelihood of accepting mobile applications for managing personal finances. Therefore, the following hypothesis was assumed:

H4: Facilitating conditions (FC) have a statistically significant effect (positive effect) on the intention to use mobile applications for managing personal finances by end users.

Hedonic motivation is the first element added to the UTAUT2 method and is defined as fun or pleasure derived from the use of technology (Venkatesh et al. 2012). This element determines the individual's expectation or experience, and refers to the enjoyment or happiness that results from using the technology. Hedonic motivation has a significant influence on the intention to use and acceptance of a certain technology. Based on the above, the following hypothesis is put forward:

H5: Hedonic motivation (HM) has a statistically significant influence (positive influence) on the intention to use mobile applications for managing personal finances by end users.

The authors of the UTAUT2 model believe that the price value of the technology used is significant when considering the intention to use, acceptance and use of the technology. They claim that users perceive the quality of technology according to the price range, and therefore consider that price value is an important and significant predictor of intention to use (Venkatesh et al. 2012). The element of price value is positive if the benefits of using mobile applications for managing personal finances are greater than the associated costs. From the above, the following hypothesis is put forward:

H6: Price value (PV) has a statistically significant influence (positive influence) on the intention to use mobile applications for managing personal finances by end users.

The last added factor is the habit that arises through experience in using technology and refers to users' perceptions of the use of the technology they use (Venkatesh et al. 2012). It is viewed as previous behavior, and is measured as the degree to which the user believes that the behavior is automatic. Habit reflects the multiple results of previous experiences and the frequency of behavior in the past is considered one of the main determinants of current behavior (Ajzen 2002). Therefore, the following hypothesis is put forward:

H7: Habit (H) has a statistically significant influence (positive influence) on the intention to use mobile applications for managing personal finances by end users.

Some of the mentioned assumptions (hypothesis) were empirically proven by Zhou et al. (2010), Witeepanich et al. (2013), as well as Afshan and Sharif (2016). Baptista and Oliveira hypothesized the relationship between the elements of the UTAUT-2 model and the intention to use mobile banking and the acceptance of mobile banking technology. They found that expected performance, hedonic motivation, price value, and habit directly and significantly influence intention to use. Given the recent paper on UTAUT-2 model, Hew et al. 2015 found that PE, EE, FC, HB, and HM had significant effect on BI to use mobile applications. Gao, Li, and Luo made an empirical study on wearable technology acceptance and they showed that PE, HM, EE, and SI were positively associated with individual's intention to adopt healthcare wearable devices. The reliability of the questionnaire was tested using the Internal Consistency Method. The method refers to the range in which the variables measure the same thing and the internal consistency of the measurements is checked. In this paper, the Krombach coefficient α was applied. In order to design a reliable measuring instrument, the aim is for the results on similar items to be connected, that is, to be internally consistent, but also for each of them to fully contribute unique information. No questionnaire is absolutely valid or absolutely reliable, but we always try to make the Cronbach coefficient α as high as possible.

Correlation analysis was used to measure the degree of linear relationship between two variables. The closer the correlation coefficient is to unity in absolute value, the stronger the correlation between phenomena. Given that the paper observed one feature of the element of the observed set and only analyzed the structure and properties of the set according to that feature, a regression analysis was performed because in practice there is often a need to monitor two or more features at the same time and to examine whether there is mutual influence between them.

4 Results and Analysis

On the basis of the research carried out on primary data collected through a survey, online interview technique, certain information was obtained based on which it can be seen that the majority of respondents are female, 84 of them (70.6%), and 35 are male (29.4%). In the sample, the majority of respondents are between 18 and 25 years old, 43.7% of them, 16.8% of respondents are between 26 and 35 years old, and 16% are between 36 and 45 years old. The fewest respondents are in the group from 46 to 55 (9.2%), while 14.3% of respondents are aged 56 and over. When it comes to the educational structure, most respondents, 64.7%, have higher education, 35.3% of respondents have secondary education. The questionnaire was mostly filled out by students (42.9%), while employees of various occupations made up 55.4% of the sample, and 1.7% were pensioners. According to the amount of monthly income, almost each of the four mentioned groups is equally represented (Table 2), and 21% of respondents did not want to declare their income. In the part related to personal finances, the majority of respondents, 62.2%, answered that they did not need any help in terms of efficient cost planning, daily budget management, and saving money. The remaining respondents need help the most in order to save money. Also, more than half of the respondents, 57.1%, answered that there are no problems of a financial nature. When asked if they are familiar with mobile applications for managing personal finances, the majority of respondents, 39.5% of them, answered that they are familiar with them, but do not use them. Unfortunately, only 10% of respondents answered that they use applications or plan to use them in the near future. A third of those surveyed, 33.6% stated that they were not familiar with mobile applications for managing personal finances (PFM), but they would like to find out and learn more about them. Almost a fifth, 16.8% answered that they are not familiar with and are not interested in using PFM mobile applications. What is positive is that almost half of the respondents, 45.4%, use the services of mobile banking applications. Analysis of the reliability of the survey on a group of

Table 3 Reliability of the scale

Variable	Cronbach's Alpha
Performance expectancy (PE)	0.922
Effort expectancy (EE)	0.932
Social influence (SI)	0.844
Facilitating conditions (FC)	0.920
Hedonic motivation (HM)	0.942
Price value (PV)	0.902
Habit (HB)	0.951
Behavior intention (BI)	0.818

Source: Author's calculation based on SPSS

Table 4 Correlation analysis

	BI	PE	EE	SI	FC	HM	PV	HB
BI	1	0.768**	0.462**	0.606**	0.472**	0.746**	0.675**	0.852**
PE	0.768**	1	0.542**	0.641**	0.562**	0.790**	0.567**	0.681**
EE	0.462**	0.542**	1	0.556**	0.794**	0.626**	0.580**	0.474**
SI	0.606**	0.641**	0.556**	1	0.527**	0.685**	0.496**	0.455**
FC	0.472**	0.562**	0.794**	0.527**	1	0.603**	0.527**	0.463**
HM	0.746**	0.790**	0.626**	0.685**	0.603**	1	0.586**	0.731**
PV	0.675**	0.567**	0.580**	0.496**	0.527**	0.586**	1	0.612**
HB	0.852**	0.681**	0.474**	0.455**	0.463**	0.731**	0.612**	1

Source: Author's calculation based on SPSS
**It means that correlation is significant at the 0.01 level

characteristics involves the calculation of Cronbach's alpha coefficient. The obtained values of this coefficient range are from 0 to 1. When the value is greater than 0.7, it is considered that the reliability and consistency of the claims is adequate (Hair et al. 2014). The test reliability results are given in Table 3. The Cronbach's Alpha values obtained are greater than 0.8 (ranging from 0.818 to 0.951) and indicate that all 8 variables observed in this research have very good internal consistency.

In order to determine the strength of the relationship (degree of linear dependence) between the variables, a correlation analysis was performed, the results of which are shown in Table 4. Based on the obtained values of the Pearson correlation coefficient, it can be concluded that there is a statistically significant positive relationship at the 0.01 level (probability 99%) between all variables. The obtained correlation coefficients have a positive sign (+), which indicates that with an increase in the value of one variable, the value of another variable also increases, i.e., that as the value of one variable decreases, the value of the other variable also decreases. Correlation analysis indicates that the variable Behavior Intention has a strong correlation with most of the variables, while there are moderate correlations with two variables, Facilitating Conditions and Effort Expectancy.

In order to test the research hypotheses related to the influence of the independent variable (variables of the UTAUT2 model) on the dependent variable (Behavior

Table 5 Simple regression analysis—(Dependent variable—Behavior Intention)

Independent variable	R^2	β	*t*
Performance expectancy	0.590	0.778**	12,965
Effort expectancy	0.214	0.480**	5642
Social influence	0.367	0.722**	8235
Facilitating conditions	0.223	0.438**	5795
Hedonic motivation	0.556	0.743**	12,115
Price value	0.455	0.748**	9885
Habit	0.727	0.791**	17,634

Source: Author's calculation based on SPSS
**It means that correlation is significant at the 0.01 level

Intention), a simple regression analysis was performed, and the results are shown in Table 5.

The results of the regression analysis show that all independent variables of the UTAUT2 model have a statistically significant positive influence on users' intention to use the services of mobile applications for managing personal finances, with the strongest influence of the variables Habit ($b = 0.791$) and Performance Expectancy ($b = 0.778$). The variables Price Value ($b = 0.748$), Hedonic Motivation ($b = 0.743$), and Social Influence ($b = 0.722$) have approximately the same high (strong) influence, while the variables Facilitating Conditions ($b = 0.438$) and Effort Expectancy ($b = 0.480$) have the weakest (smallest) influence on users' intention to use mobile applications for managing personal finances. To determine whether two variables are functionally related, the coefficient of determination, R^2, is determined. It is interpreted as a descriptive measure of the strength of the regression relationship, which measures how well the regression line fits the data. The determined value of the coefficient of determination (Rsquare) indicates that 72.7% of the variability of the dependent variable Behavior Intention is explained by changes in the Habit variable. The coefficient of determination R^2 is statistically significant. The next independent variable with a statistically significant impact is Performance Expectancy, and 59% of the variability of the dependent variable is explained by changes in this variable. The coefficient of determination R^2 is statistically significant. Another independent variable with a statistically significant impact is Hedonic Motivation, and 55.6% of the variability of the dependent variable was explained by changes in this variable. The coefficient of determination R^2 is statistically significant. For the independent variables Price Value (45.5%), Social Influence (36.7%), Facilitating Conditions (22.3%), and Effort Expectancy (21.4%), which have a smaller statistically significant influence on the dependent variables Behavior Intention, it can be said that the variability cannot be explained by the regression line and that they are under the influence of unidentified factors. The values of the coefficient of determination, percentages of variability of the dependent variable in relation to other independent variables, are given in Table 4 (R^2). *Hypothesis test for correlation coefficient.* The result of hypothesis testing (result of simple regression analysis) indicates that all the hypotheses cannot be rejected, i.e., that they can be accepted. The status of the set hypotheses is shown in Table 6.

Table 6 Results of hypotheses testing

Hypothesis	Status
H1: ***Performance expectancy*** *has a statistically significant effect on the intention to use mobile applications for managing personal finances by end users*	Hypothesis accepted
H2: ***Effort expectancy*** *has a statistically significant influence on the intention to use mobile applications for managing personal finances by end users*	Hypothesis accepted
H3: ***Social influence*** *has a statistically significant effect on end users' intention to use personal finance management mobile applications*	Hypothesis accepted
H4: ***Facilitating conditions*** *have a statistically significant influence on the intention to use mobile applications for managing personal finances by end users*	Hypothesis accepted
H5: ***Hedonic motivation*** *has a statistically significant effect on the intention to use mobile applications for managing personal finances by end users*	Hypothesis accepted
H6: ***Price value*** *has a statistically significant effect on the intention to use mobile applications for managing personal finances by end users*	Hypothesis accepted
H7: ***Habit*** *statistically significant impact on the intention to use mobile applications for managing personal finances by end users.*	Hypothesis accepted

5 Conclusion

The paper describes the theoretical foundations of: models of technology acceptance, financial literacy, functionality of mobile applications for managing personal finances, with the aim of checking the willingness of individuals to accept and use the technology of mobile applications for managing personal finances in the surveyed population. The research is based on the theory of acceptance and use of technology. Nowadays, among the models and theories in the literature related to the acceptance and use of technological innovations, the UTAUT2 model is often used. The goal of the work was to, using all the elements from the UTAUT2 model, identify the key influences among the respondents that will indicate the intention of the respondents to accept and use the services of mobile applications for managing personal finances. The results of this research indicate that 5 out of 7 elements (Habit, Performance Expectancy, Price Value, Hedonic Motivation, Social Influence) of the UTAUT2 model have a key role in the individual's intention to use technologies. Statistical analysis shows that the elements Habit and Expected benefit are the most important determinants of the acceptance of mobile application technology for personal finance, while the elements Expected effort and Facilitating conditions have the weakest influence on the intention to use. Considering the current social circumstances in which the individual is mostly guided by the expected benefit when accepting new technology, where the realized benefit implies the creation of a habit of use, and bearing in mind the already existing habit of daily use of the mobile phone for other activities and applications, such results could be expected. The impact of expected effort is difficult to examine in a sample where most respondents did not use the services of the mentioned applications. Most of the most popular personal finance mobile apps have functionalities that are fully user-friendly, easy to use and have high utility. The research results agree with previous research in the field of mobile technologies. This study is important because it continues to examine the influence of elements according to the UTAUT2 model on the acceptance of mobile application technology. In contrast to previous studies, which mainly refer to the acceptance of mobile application technology for banking (mbanking)—or the acceptance of mobile banking technology—this study deals with the perspective of accepting PFM applications, as a future trend and way of managing personal finances. It also confirms the influence of the elements of the UTAUT2 model on the acceptance of mobile application technology. In the literature, the Habit element usually has a significant and positive effect on the adoption of mobile or online innovations (Gao et al. 2015; Wong et al. 2014; Escobar-Rodriguez and Carvajal-Trujillo 2014). For the element expected performance it was pointed out that it has the strongest influence on intention to use (Baptista and Oliveira 2015; Basri 2018), while the weakest element is expected effort. So, this study also confirmed the positive relationship between all elements of the UTAUT2 model that influence the acceptance of a certain technology, in this case mobile applications for managing personal finances. The obtained results show that the perspective of technology acceptance is positive. The positive implications also refer to the intention of most respondents to educate themselves in order to gain more knowledge about managing personal finances, where only the use of mobile applications for PFM can help to overcome personal finance problems more easily. In the domestic literature, there are few studies of an empirical nature that deal with the topic of personal finance, that is, the use of smartphones as personal finance assistants. Although the majority of the surveyed population consisted of people with a university degree, the vast majority of respondents were not aware of the existence of mobile applications for personal finance, and those who were aware mostly did not use them. From the above, as well as based on the positive impact of all seven elements on the intention to use, a proposal for future research could refer to the testing and use of a specific mobile application for PFM, in a certain period of time, with a group of users. The analysis of the obtained results would also be done according to the elements of the UTAUT2 model. For future research, demographic characteristics such as gender and age should also be included in order to examine their moderating effect. Like many studies, this research has limitations. The most significant limitation concerns the sample size. Future research should be conducted on a larger sample, and this created measuring instrument could be used for future research in this area. In the future, the financial literacy of each individual should develop and follow the trends in the development of technology. Residents should be trained in the direction of successful management of personal finances and promote the role, possibilities, and advantages of mobile applications for managing them.

References

AFG (2019) U: Livret Blanc. Education financière, des épargnants éclairés; acteurs de l'économie de demain. https://hellofuture.orange.com/en/financial-competence-a-model-for-measuring-financial-literacy-around-the-world/. Accessed 10 May 2022
Afshan S, Sharif A (2016) Acceptance of mobile banking framework in Pakistan. Telematics Inform 33(2):370–387. https://doi.org/10.1016/j.tele.2015.09.005
Ajzen I (2002) Residual effects of past on later behavior: habituation and reasoned action perspectives. Personal Soc Psychol Rev 6(2):107–122
Alharbi S, Drew S (2014) Using the technology acceptance model in understanding academics' behavioural intention to use learning management systems. Int J Adv Comput Sci Appl 5(1): 143–155
Allianz (2017) U: are you financially literate?. https://www.allianz.com/en/press/news/studies/170127-are-you-financially-literate.html. Accessed 10 Jun 2022
Baptista G, Oliveira T (2015) Understanding mobile banking: the unified theory of acceptance and use of technology combined with cultural moderators. Comput Hum Behav 50:418–430. https://doi.org/10.1016/j.chb.2015.04.024
Basri S (2018) Determinants of adoption of mobile banking: evidence from rural Karnataka in India. Int J Trade Glob Markets 11(1/2):77–86. https://doi.org/10.1504/ijtgm.2018.09249
Bhatiasevi V (2016) An extended UTAUT model to explain the adoption of mobile banking. Inf Dev 32(4):799–814. https://doi.org/10.1177/0266666915570764
Bhatt B (2011a) U: Financial Management Importance. (From) http://www.blognbuzz.com/financial-management-importance.html. Accessed 12 Apr 2022
Bhatt B (2011b) Financial management importance. (From). http://www.blognbuzz.com/financial-management-importance.html. Accessed 12 Apr 2022
Bitethegram (2020) U: 5 tips on personal financial management. https://bitethegram.com/5-tips-on-personal-financial-management/. Accessed 10 Apr 2022
BusyKid (n.d.) U: the app for learning, the card for fun! https://busykid.com/. Accessed 10 Jun 2022
Davis FD (1986) A technology acceptance model for empirically testing new end-user information systems: theory and results. Doctoral dissertation. MIT Sloan School of Management, Cambridge, MA
Davis FD (1989) Perceived usefulness, perceived ease of use, and user acceptance of information technology. MIS Q 13(3):319–340
Davis FD, Bagozzi RP, Warshaw PR (1989) User acceptance of computer technology: a comparison of two theoretical models. Manag Sci 35(8):982–1003
Debit Card for Kids and Teens | Greenlight (n.d.) U: Learn to earn, save and invest together. https://greenlight.com/. Accessed 10 Jun 2022
Đikanović Z (2013) U: Finansijska pismenost, Conference: OBRAZOVANJE I RAZVOJ. https://www.idn.org.rs/biblioteka/Obrazovanje_i_razvoj.pdf. Accessed 2 May 2022
Escobar-Rodriguez T, Carvajal-Trujillo E (2014) Online purchasing tickets for low cost carriers: an application of the unified theory of acceptance and use of technology (UTAUT) model. Tour Manag 43:70–88
Fact.MR Market Research Company (2021) U: Personal Finance Mobile App Market. https://www.factmr.com/report/personal-finance-mobile-app-market. Accessed 5 Jun 2022
Fernando J (2021) U: financial literacy. https://www.investopedia.com/terms/f/financial-literacy.asp. Accessed 2 May 2022
Financial Industry Regulatory Authority (2021) U.S. survey data at a glance: financial knowledge and decision-making. https://www.usfinancialcapability.org/results.php?region=US. Accessed 10 Jun 2022
Fishbein M, Ajzen I (1975) Belief, attitude, intention, and behavior: an introduction to theory and research. Addison-Wesley
Fogarty M (2012) U: save, invest, grow. Readers Digest. March 2012

Fuksa M (2013) Mobile technologies and services development impact on mobile internet usage in Latvia. Proc Comput Sci 26:41–50. https://doi.org/10.1016/j.procs.2013.12.006
Gao Y, Li H, Luo Y (2015) An empirical study of wearable technology acceptance in healthcare. Ind Manag Data Syst 115(9):1704–1723
Google Play (n.d.) U: plan'it prom. https://play.google.com/store/apps/details?id=com.sevendesigns.planitprom&hl=en&gl=US. Accessed 10 Jun 2022
Hair FJ, Black CW, Babin JB, Anderson ER (2014) Multivariate data analysis. Pearson Education Limited, Harlow
hellofuture (2022) U: Financial competence, a model for measuring financial literacy around the world. A review of models for measuring financial literacy, ad-dressing their strengths and limitations from an educational perspective. https://hellofuture.orange.com/en/financial-competence-a-model-for-measuring-financial-literacy-around-the-world/. Accessed 5 Jun 2022
Herbut K (2021) Vodič upravljanje ličnim finansijama, Beogradski fond za političku izuzetnost, 2021. Beograd
Hernandez AA (2017) Green IT adoption practices in education sector: a developing country perspective. Int J Sociotechnol Knowl Dev 9(3):1–16. https://doi.org/10.4018/IJSKD.2017070101
Hew JJ, Lee VH, Ooi KB, Wei J (2015) What catalyses mobile apps usage intention: an empirical analysis. Ind Manag Data Syst 115(7):1269–1291
Holden RJ, Karsha B-T (2010) U: the technology acceptance model: its past and its future in health care. J Biomed Inform 43(1):159–172
Hong S, Thong JYL, Tam KY (2006) Understanding continued information technology usage behavior: a comparison of three models in the context of mobile internet. Decis Support Syst 42(3):1819–1834. https://doi.org/10.1016/j.dss.2006.03.009
IFOP (2016) Education financière: Connaissances et pratiques des Fran-çais. Rapport. https://www.ifop.com/publication/education-financiere-connaissances-et-pratiques-des-francais/. Accessed 10 May 2022
Kenton W (2022) U: personal finance. https://www.investopedia.com/terms/p/personalfinance.asp. Accessed 2 May 2022
King J, Carey M (2017) Personal finance. Oxford University Press. https://oxforduniversitypress.app.box.com/v/he-9780198748779
Kumar R, Shaun O'Brien S (2019) Federal Reserve Bank of San Francisco. U: "2019 findings from the diary of consumer payment choice". Accessed 10 Jun 2022
Lee Y, Kozar KA, Larsen KRT (2003) The technology acceptance model: past, present, and future. Commun Assoc Inf Syst 12:50. https://doi.org/10.17705/1CAIS.0125
Legris P, Ingham J, Collerette P (2003) Why do people use information technology? A critical review of the technology acceptance model. Inf Manag 40(3):191–204
Lin HF (2011) An empirical investigation of mobile banking adoption: the effect of innovation attributes and knowledge-based trust. Int J Inf Manag 31(3):252–260. https://doi.org/10.1016/j.ijinfomgt.2010.07.006
Marangunić N, Granić A (2015) Technology acceptance model: a literature review from 1986 to 2013. Univ Access Inf Soc 14:81–95. https://doi.org/10.1007/s10209-014-0348-1
Marinkovic V, Kalinic Z (2017) Antecedents of customer satisfaction in mobile commerce: exploring the moderating effect of customization. Online Inf Rev 41(2):138–154. https://doi.org/10.1108/oir-11-2015-0364
Mastercard NuData Security (2021) 2020 fraud risk at a glance. Accessed 10 Jun 2022
McDowell CB SlidePlayer (n.d.) U: personal financial management. https://slideplayer.com/slide/12074634/. Accessed 10 Apr 2022
mint intuit (n.d.) U: managing money, made simples. https://mintintuitcom/. Accessed 4 Jun 2022
Moghavvemi S, Salleh N, Abessi M (2013) Determinants of IT-related innovation acceptance and use behavior: theoretical integration of unified theory of acceptance and use of technology and entrepreneurial potential model. Soc Technol 4(2):243–260. https://doi.org/10.13165/ST-13-3-2-01

Momani A (2020) U: the unified theory of acceptance and use of technology: a new approach in technology acceptance, July 2020. Int J Sociotechnol Knowl Dev 12(3):79–98. https://doi.org/10.4018/IJSKD.2020070105

MUEGN (n.d.) U: Školski program finansijske pismenosti. Program finansijske pismenosti. Akademska postignuća, srednja diploma. https://muegn.ru/bs/literatura/programma-po-finansovoi-gramotnosti-v-shkole-programma-povysheniya-finansovoi.html. Accessed 10 Jun 2022

Munohsamy T (2015) U: personal financial management Institut Teknologi Brune. https://wwwresearchgatenet/publication/279198054_Personal_Financial_Management. Accessed 2 May 2022

OECD (2016) U: Cadre d'évaluation de la culture financière de l'enquête. PISA 2015. https://hellofuture.orange.com/en/financial-competence-a-model-for-measuring-financial-literacy-around-the-world/. Accessed 2 May 2022

OECD (2019) U: PISA 2018 financial literacy framework. https://hellofuture.orange.com/en/financial-competence-a-model-for-measuring-financial-literacy-around-the-world/. Accessed 2 May 2022

Scott J (2009) The importance of personal money management (from). http://www.moolanomy.com/2066/the-importance-of-personal-money-management/. Accessed 10 Apr 2012

Servon, J. L., Kaestner, R. Consumer financial literacy and the impact of online banking on the financial behavior of lower-income bank customers, J Consum Aff, Vol. 42, No. 2, 2008, pg. 271–305

Silva PM, Dias GA (2007) Theories about technology acceptance: why the users accept or reject the information technology? Braz J Inf Sci 1(2):69–86. https://doi.org/10.36311/1981-1640.2007.v1n2.05.p69

Sivathanu B, Pillai R (2019) Leveraging technology for talent management: foresight for organizational performance. Int J Sociotechnol Knowl Dev 11(2):16–30. https://doi.org/10.4018/IJSKD.2019040102

Skills YouNeed (2022) U: Personal Financial Management. https://www.skillsyouneed.com/rhubarb/personal-financial-management.html#google_vignette. Accessed 5 Jun 2022

Tan E, Leby LJ (2016) Behavioural intention to adopt mobile banking among the millennial generation. Young Consum 17(1):18–31. https://doi.org/10.1108/yc-07-2015-00537

Teo T, Zhou M (2014) Explaining the intention to use technology among university students: a structural equation modeling approach. J Comput High Educ 26(2):124–142

Tymkiw C (2022) U: Personal Financial Management (PFM). https://www.investopedia.com/personal-financial-management-pfm-5181311. Accessed 2 May 2022

U.S. Department of the Treasury (2021) Financial Literacy and Education Commission. https://home.treasury.gov/policy-issues/consumer-policy/financial-literacy-and-education-commission. Accessed 10 May 2022

Venkatesh V, Zhang X (2010) Unified theory of acceptance and use of technology: U.S. Vs China. J Glob Inf Technol Manage 13(1):5–27. https://doi.org/10.1080/1097198x.2010.10856507

Venkatesh V, Morris MG, Davis GB, Davis FD (2003) U: user acceptance of information technology: toward a unified view. MIS Q 27:425–478

Venkatesh V, Thong JYL, Xu X (2012) Consumer acceptance and use of information technology: extending the unified theory of acceptance and use of technology. MIS Q 36(1):157–178

Weeger, A., & Gewald, H. (2013): Examining social and cognitive aspects Determining Physician's adoption of electronic medical records. In: Proceedings of the 21st European conference on information systems. Academic, pp 1–14

Williams MD, Rana NP, Dwivedi YK (2015) The unified theory of acceptance and use of technology (UTAUT): a literature review. J Enterp Inf Manag 28(3):443–448. https://doi.org/10.1108/JEIM-09-2014-0088

Witeepanich C, Emklang N, Matsmak J, Kanokviriyasanti P, Chanvarasuth P (2013) Understanding the adoption of Mobile banking services: an empirical study. In: Proceedings of the 4th international conference on engineering, project, and production management. Bangkok, Thailand: the Sukosol. 2013, pp 282–291. October; 23–25

Wong CH, Wei-Han Tan G, Loke SP, Ooi KB (2014) Mobile TV: a new form of entertainment? Ind Manag Data Syst 114(7):1050–1067

Yu C (2012) Factors affecting individuals to adopt mobile banking: empirical evidence from the UTAUT model. J Electron Commer Res 13(2):104–121

Zhou T, Lu Y, Wang B (2010) Integrating TTF and UTAUT to explain mobile banking user adoption. Comput Hum Behav 26(4):760–767. https://doi.org/10.1016/j.chb.2010.01.013

Digital Payment Systems for Small to Middle-Sized Enterprises in Serbia

Miodrag Šljukić

Abstract The last twenty years have been characterized by the development of digital payment systems driven by innovations, deregulation, and the increased importance of technology users. This led to the appearance of many new products and actors in this field. This article reviews the current digital payment systems and their implication for SMEs (small to middle-sized enterprises) and entrepreneurs. The main objective is to identify and classify current payment technologies, and their trends, and explore their application in SMEs and entrepreneurs in Serbia. The following research questions are formulated: (1) what is the level of application of current payment methods in SMEs and entrepreneurs in Serbia, and (2) what prevents the spread of digital payment methods in these organizations? Research has been done on a sample of 108 SMEs and entrepreneurs from all regions of Serbia. The results show that digital payment methods' usage depends on the transaction's role. The biggest obstacle to the spread of digital payment technologies is the cost of implementation and use. The most significant benefits are improved administration, transaction speedup, and a reduced rate of errors. The research contributes by identifying the most frequently used digital payment systems and practical problems and suggesting possible solutions.

Keywords Payment ecosystem · Digital payment technology · Mobile payments · Internet banking

1 Introduction

The payment system is every system used for clearing financial transactions by transferring monetary value. It includes instruments, institutions, people, rules, procedures, standards, and technologies that enable such exchange (Bossone and

---

M. Šljukić (✉)
Faculty of Organizational Sciences, Belgrade, Serbia

S. Benković et al. (eds.), *Digital Transformation of the Financial Industry*, Contributions to Finance and Accounting,
https://doi.org/10.1007/978-3-031-23269-5_17

Cirasino 2001). The need for a digital payment system appears when the money in the form of credit, i.e., payment promise, is used.

Digital payment systems are the evolution of traditional payment systems and rely on them a lot. Paper payment instruments have their digital twins, while digital payment systems based on payment cards use the infrastructure developed within traditional systems. These payment systems use electronic payment instruments, and the whole transaction is often done in a virtual space. Digital payment systems are an integral part of electronic commerce and one of the main drivers of their development. And vice versa: developing digital payment systems influences the volume and characteristics of e-commerce business models. The main feature of digital payment systems is innovation. Deregulation of payment services has led to the appearance of new actors in this market: fintech companies, payment specialists, and large technology companies. The main trends include the rise of mobile payments and new payment methods. Some key improvements are increased speed of transactions, merging of different applications and services into one digital super-wallet, the development of P2P payments, usage of new technologies like blockchain, open banking, social network payment, etc. (Mondres 2018).

Numerous legislative acts regulate payment systems in Serbia. The basis for developing the digital payment systems is Law on Electronic Signature and Law on Electronic Document because they level the legal status of electronic and paper documents, which is the basis for digital payments. Other laws make conditions for faster and broader inclusion of Serbia in international commerce and financial flows easing the transfer of money abroad and reducing administrative work. This is particularly significant for SMEs lacking finances and technical expertise in this area.

The subject of this research is the payment systems in SMEs and entrepreneurs in Serbia. The goal of the study is to identify and classify contemporary payment methods in the world and Serbia, point out the trends in this area, and identify the benefits and problems that Serbian SMEs and entrepreneurs have in their practical implementation. The research was conducted on a sample of 108 SMEs and entrepreneurs from all regions of Serbia. Based on the subject and goal of the study, the following research questions are defined:

Q1: What is the level of employment of digital payment systems in SMEs and entrepreneurs in Serbia?

Q2: What are the obstacles to the spread of digital payment systems in SMEs and entrepreneurs in Serbia?

The remaining of this article consists of five chapters. The first chapter, the Literature review, describes the payment ecosystem and shows the leading contemporary technologies in the field. Also, the current situation in the area of payment services in Serbia is introduced in this chapter. Chapter Methodology describes the procedure and instruments which are used in the research. Chapter Results presents the research findings, while Discussion provides a critical view. Chapter Conclusion once more emphasizes the main results of the study and its contribution and gives the answers to the research questions. Also, limitations and possible future research are presented in this chapter.

2 Literature Review

According to the standard definition from biology, an "ecosystem is a complex community of the living beings, their physical environment and all of their interrelations within defined space" (Encyclopedia Britannica n.d.). This analogy is used in other areas, so we talk about the payment ecosystem. It emerges whenever somebody wants to buy something from another person. The shape of the ecosystem depends on where buyer and seller meet, the type of goods exchanged, the kind of delivery of goods, time, place, and payment instrument.

Bank for International Settlements (BIS) defines a payment instrument as "any instrument which provides its owner transfer of funds" (Phillphass 2003). According to FCA, payment instruments are any personalized devices or a set of instructions agreed upon provider and user of the financial service that the user uses for the payment initiation. European central bank defines a payment instrument as a "tool or a set of procedures which enable the transfer of funds from payer to payee. Payer and payee can be the same person" (European Central Bank n.d.).

The money transfer from the buyer to the seller is made through the funds transfer system. BIS defines funds transfer systems as "instruments, organizations, operational procedures and information-communication systems used for initialization and transfer of payment information from payer to payee and transaction settlement" (BIS 2001). According to the European Central Bank, the funds transfer system is a "formal agreement based on private agreement or the legislature which has multiple users, common rules and standardized agreements for transfer and netting or settlement of monetary liabilities which arise among its members" (European Central Bank n.d.). Similar definition comes from Law on Payment Services of the Republic of Serbia in article 2 which defines payment system as "system for transfer of monetary assets between participants of the system with written and standardized procedures and rules for processing and netting and settling payment orders in the payment system which apply to all participants in the system" (Law on Payment Services 2018).

A digital payment system is a form of financial exchange between buyer and seller, made using electronic communications. It is an integral part of e-commerce that enable simple and easy money transfers from buyer to seller, including information about executed transactions. Digital payments are made using the internet or mobile channels. According to Ahmed et al. (2019), a digital payment system must provide atomic transactions, privacy, and security. It must be safe from fraud, available at any moment, cost-efficient, and capable of integration with similar systems. Abrazhevich (2001) states that the digital payment system is expected to be accepted by its users, easy to use, secure, reliable, scalable, and efficient. Users must be assured that the money and information are safe from theft or misuse, and their anonymity must be guaranteed. The system should have an option to convert funds to another system. Money flow and fund sources should be traceable, and the system should be able to conduct specific operations, even if not online.

A key driver of the evolution of payment is technological development. General technology development in the last 50 years had a trend of minimization, capacity increase, networking, mobility, and omnipresence. Compared to mainframe computers, PC became prevalent in the 1980s and 1990s thanks to the development of hardware with larger capacity and performances. Today the central role belongs to smart mobile devices: phones, tablets, laptops, IoT, etc. The transition from simple accounting applications to AI systems capable of complex operations illustrates the dynamics of software development in the same period. The number and the influence of technology users (buyers and sellers) in that period constantly grew relative to the number of service providers (banks and technology companies). Such a trend was enabled by but also conditioned digitalization of payment instruments, including money itself, speeding up money circulation with massive usage of digital payment methods. During that period, payment cards were the dominant payment instrument, but recently, payment methods that use alternative identification methods arose, and real-time payment became standard (Deloitte 2018). Significant drivers of this trend are the customer's expectations and legislative changes oriented toward open banking and fintech companies (Shah et al. 2016). This has led to the inclusion of large technology companies working for the financial sector and payment services specialists in the payment systems. Thanks to this, a lot of services that were exclusive to large corporations became available to SMEs. Traditionally payment systems were rigid and oriented to the product. In contrast, modern payment systems are oriented toward the customer and integrated into other banking services through online banking applications (Deloitte 2018).

There are numerous ways to classify digital payment methods. According to Ahmed et al. (2019), depending on the instrument used, digital payment systems can be classified as e-cash systems, e-cheque systems, and systems based on e-cards. Metha (2015) classifies digital payment systems as e-cash systems, e-cheque systems, net banking, e-wallet, smart cards, online systems based on credit cards, and payment gateway systems. Cash-based systems are transferable and independent of their network or device. E-cheque systems use e-cheques as payment instruments. It is a digital form of the paper cheque, protected with a PIN and digitally signed, usually used for micro-payments. A payment gateway is an e-commerce service that allows sellers to accept payments that buyers make over the internet safely. Bons and Alt (2015) use the type of currency, process, and types of participants in the transaction as a criterion for classification. E-payments can be classified as payments in real currency, payments in virtual currency, and other services of digital payments. Most digital transactions are made in real currency. They include money transactions, credit transactions using e-banking or m-banking, direct debit, card transactions, and e-money. EU defines e-money as the value represented by the claim from the issuer, which is kept in the electronic form issued on the acceptance of funds in an amount not smaller than the issued money value and accepted as a means of payment from the other participants (European Commission 2009). Virtual currency is all payment means not regulated by government agencies. Payment methods based on virtual currencies can be closed or open. Closed virtual schemes have limited interaction with the real economy and are mostly irrelevant to real-world sellers. Opened transactions can appear as a one-way schema that enables buyers to earn virtual currency but cannot convert it to real money, like pre-paid credit for a mobile phone. Two-way opened virtual-currency-based schema, like bitcoin, allows conversion to real money.

Based on earlier classifications, Sahut (2008) identified two main categories of digital payments: payments based on accounts and payments based on e-money. Account-based payments can be further divided into payments by card, e-cheque, e-mail, mobile payments, and other micropayment methods. Virtual money-based payments include payments made by e-wallet, virtual wallet, and virtual currency. A payment card is an instrument of cashless payment in the form of plastic in standard dimensions, usually linked to the owner's account (Muthurasu and Suganthi 2019). There are three types of cards: prepaid, debit, and credit cards. Payment by card is the most often payment method on the internet. Systems based on e-mail are designed for SMEs and P2P transactions. They are used in micro and international payments. Mobile payments are all the payments conducted by mobile devices, including online buying, money transfers, or buying in a store. It includes mobile applications, mobile wallets, NFC (near field communication), soundwaves, MST (Magnetic Secure Transmission), QR (quick response), SMS (Short Message Service), payment using a mobile network provider, and mobile banking. A mobile wallet is software for keeping information about payments and codes for different payment methods and websites. There is a trend to use mobile wallets for other mobile payment services because users prefer integrated services. NFC payments are contactless payments that use NFC technology for data exchange between two devices near each other (Brophy 2021). QR payments are made by scanning codes that can be printed on paper or displayed on a screen. QR codes can keep large amounts of information encrypted and read even if damaged, which makes them suitable for scanning with a mobile device. MST generates a magnetic signal and sends it to a card reader. Payments using mobile network providers are prevalent in countries where the level of inclusion of the population in the banking system is low. In such a situation, mobile phones replace cards, and telecommunication company becomes payment institution. Services of m-banking can be accessed by using specialized bank applications. To use an e-wallet and virtual wallet, a user must first deposit the money into the bank account. Then the money is converted to digital money and transferred to the wallet on the device. A virtual wallet is a piece of software, while an electronic wallet is a hardware.

SMEs can achieve significant improvement in their business by choosing the right payment system in a way that ensures benefit, raises the company's asset, improves efficiency, and optimizes processes. Cash flow management and transaction recording are the core of every business. That is why optimizing the payment process is the focus of the company's effort to improve efficiency and profitability. Digital payment systems go beyond simple funds transfers. When choosing a digital payment system, SMEs should consider all the benefits, like integrating bills and payments between two sides and avoiding settling open items, accounting and reporting tools based on automatically generated data, etc.

B2B payments are the connection point of SMEs with their business partners. In each of these points, it is possible to use tools to create additional value. SMEs often have problems digitizing their business to incorporate digital payments. The most often barriers in this process are ignorance and lack of trust in innovations. Other barriers include the lack of knowledge about benefits provided by digital payments and the lack of capabilities to finance the transformation of payment methods or employee training. On the other hand, SMEs that have already accepted digital payment methods must be aware that not all types of digital payments are equal and hence must choose the one that best suits their business model (Deloitte 2018).

A survey from Australia and New Zealand (Deloitte 2018) showed that 85% of survey respondents had benefited from paying and accepting digital payment methods. The most beneficial was an improvement in cost control and administration, the reduced time needed to process and execute transactions, and reduced transaction costs compared to traditional payment methods. Almost half of the respondents stated that the total cost of doing business was reduced to half after employing digital payment. The study concludes that the digital payment system, no matter which side SME takes in the transaction, leads to improvements thanks to business process automatization, reduced time the workforce is engaged, a drop in the number of errors, and better control of the payment process.

Digital payment systems in Serbia are regulated by the Law on Payment Services which has been valid since 2018. This law defines basic terms and determines conditions and means of payment services, e-money, and payment systems. According to it, e-money is "electronically stored money value which makes money claim to the issuer of that money, issued after the receipt of money funds for execution of payment transactions and acceptable by individuals or enterprises which are not issuers of that money." E-money institution is "enterprise located in the Republic of Serbia with the license issued by National Bank of Serbia for issuing e-money." The same act defines a payment system as a "system for transfer of money funds between participants of this system with written and standardized procedures and rules for processing and netting and clearing payment orders in the payment system which applies to all participants in that system." Payment services providers can be a bank, e-money institutions, payment institutions, NBS (National Bank of Serbia), Treasury, and public postal operators. Banks, e-money institutions, public postal operators, NBS, and Treasury, can issue e-money. The Law on Digital Assets has been in use since June 2021. It defines a digital or virtual asset as a "digital record of value which can be digitally purchased, sold, exchanged or transferred and which can be used as a means of exchange or for investment, not including digital records of the currencies which are legal payment means." Virtual currency is "the kind of digital asset which was not issued and for whose value does not guarantee central bank" and which is "not necessarily linked to the legal mean of payment and has no legal status of money or currency, while accepted as a mean of exchange by individuals or enterprises (Law on Digital Assets 2020)."

According to the data published by NBS, by the end of the first quarter of 2021 in Serbia, more than 9.1 million payment accounts existed, almost 1.8 million other types of payment accounts, and nearly 46,000 e-money accounts. In the same period, more than 9.6 million cards were used, including more than 80 thousand cards with e-money. During the first quarter of 2021, more than 300 thousand phone payments were made, almost 3.2 million payments over the internet, and nearly 2.3 million mobile payments. Also, more than 101 million payment transactions were made, of which almost half (more than 49 million) were initiated digitally, mainly using internet banking (36 million) and mobile banking (12 million). Over 7.3 million transactions totaling 20 billion dinars were instituted in the first quarter of 2021 to buy goods and services. 98% of these transactions were made using cards, while 2% were made using e-money. About 73% of this number of transactions was denominated in Serbian dinar, while euro and dollar transactions made around 13% each. When expressed in value, 62% of transactions were made using Serbian dinar, 23% in euros, and 12% in US dollars. In the same period, 21 million transactions were made using cash tellers totaling 270 billion dinars, 250 billion of which were cash withdrawals. During the same period, 80 million transactions were made on POS devices totaling 180 billion dinars (NBS 2021).

The Statistical Office of the Republic of Serbia (Kovačević et al. 2020) conducted a survey in 2020 on a sample of 2800 households. Almost five million, 94.1% of the population of Serbia, use a mobile phone, and 74.3% use a computer. Eighty one percent of households have an internet connection, an increase of over 8% compared to 2018. Most internet users are in Belgrade, followed by Vojvodina. More than 72% of respondents used a computer in 2020, while 3.2 million use a computer every day. More than 78% of the population of Serbia uses the internet, which is a 2% increase compared to 2019. 3.75 million people use the internet every day. Of all active internet users, 71.2% have an account on a social network. Forty three percent of respondents never bought goods or services online. Of those buying online, 55.6% did not spend more than 50 euros, mostly in transactions with domestic sellers. The same research included 1270 enterprises from the Republic of Serbia, of which 1007 (79%) were SMEs. Only 19.3% of them employ ICT experts. Mobile internet connection is used by 77% of SMEs and 91.1% of large enterprises. Websites have 84.4% of SMEs and 95% of large enterprises.

3 Methodology

Considering the goal of the research and the type of data used, this research can be classified as quantitative and descriptive. It was conducted from March 16th to April 10th, 2022. Data was gathered using the questionnaire, which was available to respondents in electronic format on Google Forms. Each respondent was sent an e-mail requesting to participate in the research and a brief explanation of the research goal, context, and guidelines.

Research units are SMEs and entrepreneurs who are registered on the territory of the Republic of Serbia. Respondents were chosen randomly from the list of SMEs and entrepreneurs acquired from the Serbian Business Registers Agency. An instrument for data gathering is comprised of demographic data, questions related to the use of digital payment systems when collecting claims, and questions that relate to the use of digital payment systems that organization uses when paying. All questions, except the last, are closed type. Questions 1–5, 8, 10, 12, and 13 are answered by choosing one answer, while questions 6, 7, 11, and 14 were multichoice. Questions 9, 15, and 16 are five-level scales going from Not at all to Very much. The last question is open and gives respondents a choice to state their suggestions for digital payment improvements. This question was not processed statistically but is part of the discussion.

Data is processed using the statistical package R 4.0.5. Statistical methods are descriptive and inferential statistics. Results are presented graphically and in tables of frequencies and proportions.

4 Results

The sample consists of 108 SMEs and entrepreneurs from 20 counties of Serbia which are grouped into four economic regions defined by the Regional Development Act. Sample structure by regions is shown in Fig. 1 left, while sample structure by the organizational form is shown on the right part of Fig. 1.

Figure 1 shows that the number of respondents from Belgrade and Vojvodina is approximately the same as well as that from the other two regions. Most of them, 33 (31%), come from the region Vojvodina where Novi Sad is leading, with 13 respondents. In contrast, the least number of respondents come from South and Eastern Serbia—19, with Nis leading the region with 5 respondents. There are 69 (64%) entrepreneurs and 39 (36%) SMEs in the sample.

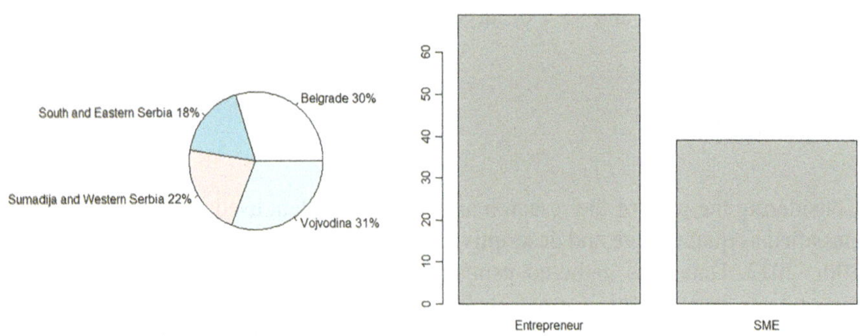

Fig. 1 Left: sample structure by the location of respondents, right: sample structure by the organizational form

Table 1 Cross-overview of the number of ICT experts by the size of the organization

ICT/Size	0	1–5	5+	Total
1–9	66 (85.7%)	22 (84.7%)	1 (20.0%)	89 (82.3%)
10–49	9 (11.7%)	2 (7.7%)	3 (60.0%)	14 (13.0%)
50–99	1 (1.3%)	1 (3.8%)	1 (20.0%)	3 (2.8%)
100–149	1 (1.3%)	1 (3.8%)	0	2 (1.9%)
Total	77	26	5	108

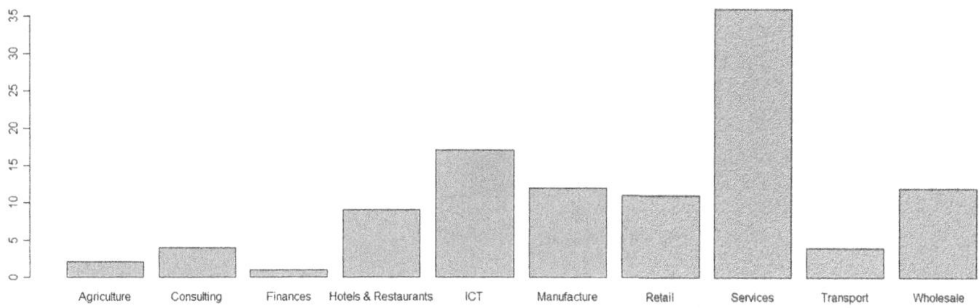

Fig. 2 Sample structure by industry

Table 1 gives a cross overview of the number of ICT expert employees and the organization's size. In the columns is the number of ICT experts employed, while in the rows is the organization's size.

Most SMEs and entrepreneurs, 77 (71%), do not employ ICT experts. Of those 31 (29%) who use ICT experts, the most organizations, 22 (71%) employ between 1 and 5 ICT experts. These organizations employ between 1 and 9 workers, most of whom are in the ICT business—14 (64%). Figure 2 shows the sample structure by industry.

Most SMEs and entrepreneurs in the sample are in the services, 36 (33%) and 17 (16%) are in the ICT sector. These two groups make up almost half of the sample. Figure 3 shows the internet and mobile banking usage level in the sample.

Internet banking is more often used than mobile banking. Questioning account balance and turnover, receiving statements, and paying using internet banking are used evenly. Receiving reports about account balance and notifications about transactions are the most often used mobile banking services. Figure 4 shows the kind of internet presence of organizations in the sample.

SMEs and entrepreneurs mostly use website and social networks to publish information about their goods and services. Twenty three (21%) respondents have e-shop on the web, and 11 (10%) use e-shop on social networks for selling their products and services. Thirty (28%) organizations do not have an internet presence. Of them, 27 (90%) are entrepreneurs. Only 7 out of 23 (30%) SMEs and entrepreneurs in retail or wholesale have a web store, while 3 (13%) have stores on social networks.

Fifty (46%) SMEs and entrepreneurs state that internet presence is of little importance to them, in contrast with 15 (14%) who think the internet significantly

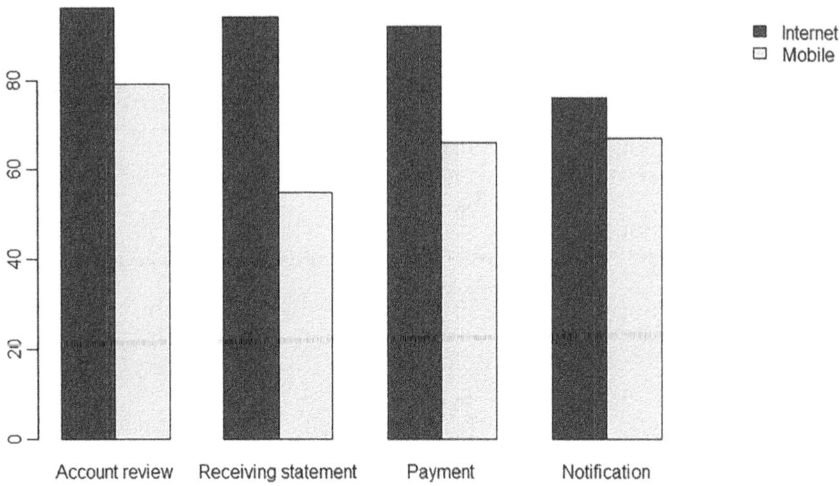

Fig. 3 Internet and mobile banking usage in SMEs and entrepreneurs

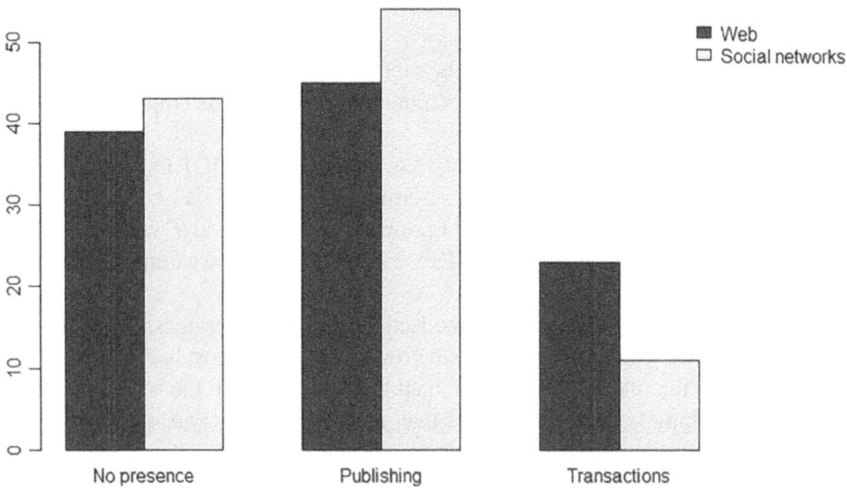

Fig. 4 Kind of internet presence of SMEs and entrepreneurs

influences their business. The median significance of internet presence is the same for entrepreneurs (Md = 2, $n = 39$) and SMEs (Md = 2, $n = 69$). Considering the organization's size, those with 10–49 employees consider the internet presence more significant (Md = 3, $n = 20$) than other groups, while internet presence is the least important for the minor organizations with 1–9 employees (Md = 2, $n = 88$). The results of the Mann–Whitney U test showed that this difference is statistically significant, $U = 620.00$, $z = -2.19$, $p = 0.03$, $r = 0.21$. The importance of internet

Table 2 The significance of internet presence regarding the location of the selling market

Significance	Sells abroad	Does not sell abroad	Total
Not at all	3 (5.4%)	14 (26.9%)	17 (15.7%)
Small	31 (55.3%)	19 (36.6%)	50 (46.3%)
Average	13 (23.2%)	13 (25.0%)	26 (24.1%)
Large	9 (16.1%)	6 (11.5%)	15 (13.9%)
Very large	0 (0.0%)	0 (0.0%)	0 (0.0%)
Total	56	52	108

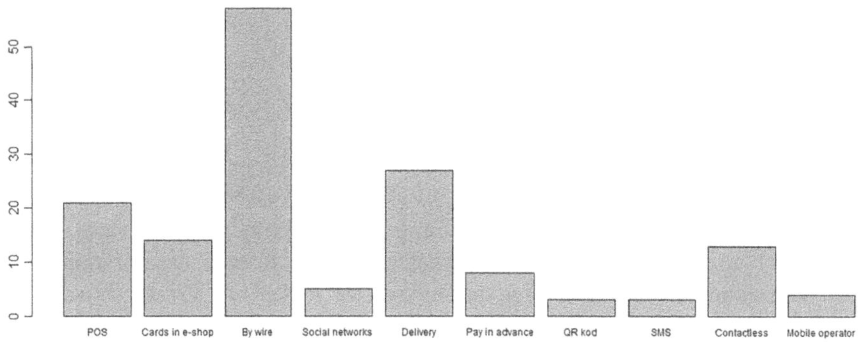

Fig. 5 Use of digital services for collecting claims from the sale

presence regarding the location of the sales market (domestic or abroad) is shown in Table 2.

Fifty-six (52%) organizations have buyers abroad, while 52 (48%) do not sell abroad. Of those who sell abroad, 31 (55%) consider internet presence unimportant. Respondents who do not sell abroad predominantly think that internet presence is of average or below-average significance to them, 46 (88%). The result of Mann–Whitney test shows no significant difference between two groups (Md = 1, $n = 56$ and Md = 2, $n = 52$) $U = 1208.00$, $z = -1.63$, $p = 0.10$, $r = 0.16$. The level of usage of digital services when collecting claims from the sale is shown in Fig. 5.

When the claim collection is done digitally, SMEs and entrepreneurs most often use P2P and wire services (E-banking, PayPal, Skrill, etc.) 57 (53%) and on delivery 27 (25%). Only 3 (3%) respondents use QR codes or SMS for collection. Most respondents, 61 (56%), use only one digital service when collecting claims from the sale, while 18 (17%) do not use digital payment methods. Of 23 retail and wholesale organizations, 14 (61%) accept credit cards. Wire transfer uses 37 (66%) of 56 respondents who have buyers abroad.

Approximately an equal number of organizations buy, 55 (51%), and do not buy 53 (49%) the goods and services over the internet. More organizations do not import goods and services, 61 (56%), than those who buy from abroad, 47 (44%). Figure 6 shows the most used digital payment methods SMEs use when paying for goods.

The most often used method for paying for goods and services is by wire and P2P payments 54 (50%), followed by payment by card in e-shops 39 (36%) and POS

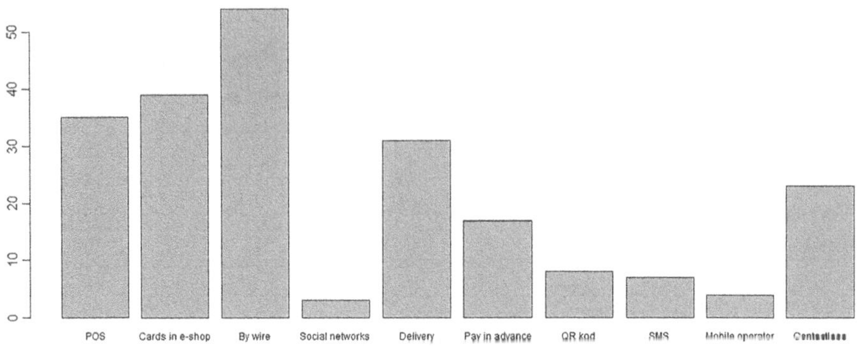

Fig. 6 The most often used digital payment services for buying

devices 35 (32%). Payment on social networks is the rarest payment method used in the sample, with only 3 (3%) organizations using it. Most SMEs and entrepreneurs, 47 (44%), use one payment method for paying for goods and services, while 14 (13%) respondents do not use digital payments. If only organizations that purchase goods and services over the internet are looked at (56), the most often used payment method is wire transfer and P2P payments (34, 61%), card in the e-shop (33, 59%), card on POS devices, (25, 47%), and payment on delivery, (24, 43%). Organizations that buy goods and services from abroad (56) most often for payment use wire transfer and P2P payments (29, 52%), cards in e-shops (28, 50%), and cards on POS devices (20, 36%).

When estimating benefits from digital payment methods, the highest median score and consistency (Md = 4, IQR(3–5)) were given to better administration, the speed of transaction, and error rate reduction. The result of the Friedman test shows that the difference in perceived benefits is statistically significant, $\chi 2$ (8, 108) = 114,07, $p = 0{,}00$. The intensity of the problem respondents face when using digital payment methods was also estimated on the five-level scale. The biggest problems with digital payment methods (Md = 5, IQR(4–5)) are higher costs and significant resistance to the change of old payment methods. Fear of fraud (Md = 5, IQR(3–5)) is also significantly high. The result of the Friedman test shows that the difference in perceived problems is statistically significant, $\chi 2$ (4, 108) = 18,65, $p = 0.00$.

5 Discussion

The number of ICT experts in SMEs and entrepreneurs is relatively small. When organizations from the ICT industry are excluded, 85% of the sample do not employ ICT specialists. This may be due to the lack of ICT experts in the labor market, the high costs their employment implies, or the outsourcing of these activities.

Internet banking is dominant compared to mobile banking in listing transactions, receipt of reports, and payments, while mobile banking is mainly used for receiving notifications about transactions. This result is expected since financial listings and payment orders require devices with larger screens, which can explain the affinity for using desktop computers for these activities. On the other hand, most people have mobile phones or other mobile devices suitable for receiving text or e-mail messages.

Survey results show that the dominant type of internet presence is information publishing on website or social networks without a direct sale. This indicates a relatively low perception of the significance of direct electronic sales. Almost 10% of respondents use only social networks, which can be explained by the technical simplicity of use and higher price of website development compared to the usage of social networks. Organizations have a dominantly average and below-average perception of internet presence significance, no matter if they have buyers abroad or not. This is somewhat unexpected since it should be easier for those who export to communicate using the internet. A possible explanation lies in the general climate toward e-business which is only at the beginning in Serbia. About a quarter of respondents have direct sales over the internet as e-shops. Almost a third (30%) of organizations from retail and wholesale sell goods and services using e-shops. These data indicate that the understanding of e-commerce in SMEs and entrepreneurs, even those whose primary business is commerce, is still developing. That has implications for the level of development of digital payments in these organizations. Possible causes for such a state are the lack of ICT experts in organizations and the lack of knowledge on management in SMEs about the advantages of e-commerce and digital payment systems.

Seventeen percent of organizations do not provide digital payment methods to their buyers, while most organizations offer only one way. The most often used method is wire transfer and P2P services. Using newer technologies like QR codes, mobile network providers, text messages, and contactless payments is very rare. An unexpectedly small share of organizations from retail and services (61%) offer payment by card on POS devices. The most often cited reasons are the lack of need since the buyers do not use cards for payment and the high fees banks charge for this kind of payment. Almost all organizations that sell abroad provide payment using P2P transfer.

On the other hand, organizations use numerous digital payment methods when paying for goods and services. Most often, organizations use one payment method, while 13% of organizations do not use digital payment methods. Paying by wire and P2P payment services are the most often used, followed by cards in e-shops and POS devices. The number of services used for paying is larger than the number used for collecting claims. This suggests that e-commerce and digital payments are more used for purchasing than for selling, i.e., that e-commerce is more developed in large companies that are suppliers to SMEs and entrepreneurs.

The most significant benefit of digitalization is improved administration, transaction speed, and error rate reduction. This may suggest that due to insufficient integration of payment systems with in-house systems, other benefits are not visible enough or do not exist at all. On the other hand, high costs, fear of fraud, and resistance to change are perceived as the biggest obstacles to switching to digital payment systems.

The last question gave the respondents a choice to give their opinion on digital payments in their business. Most problems are regarded as high fees charged by banks for using digital payment systems, above all for using POS devices and processing transactions in the e-shop. Also, a lack of motivation for use and education on digital payment technologies on the buyers' side was emphasized. The design of software solutions should be better, especially regarding the speed and easiness of digital transactions. There is also a fear of fraud. The advantage of digital payments is the option to make transactions from the office. This can also be seen in the widespread usage of internet banking. Micro and macro environments of SMEs and entrepreneurs also contain obstacles to spreading digital payment systems. Some of them are:

- since banks charge fixed fees on POS device usage, many small shops and restaurants perceive it as a significant risk.
- redesign of the country's payment system has been done very recently, and a lot of it is still not alive in practice.
- lack of ICT experts and the consequent high price of their engagement in organizations. In this context, the organization's size is essential because SMEs and entrepreneurs have significant problems attracting additional human resources. The lack of expertise in ICT reduces the opportunities for spotting and utilizing the benefits of digital payments. That is why many SMEs do not see the reason for digitizing payments. Also, problems with integrating digital payments with legacy information systems dissimulate their implementation.
- people are generally ignorant of the options provided by digital payment methods, leading to a small number of participants in transactions.

Overcoming these problems is a long-term process. The financial market's development with its payment services segment enabled by changed regulations will inevitably lead to adopting of new payment technologies. The solution to these problems requires more ICT in the curriculum. That will reduce the gap between ICT knowledge demand and ICT experts' supply. Developing the domestic ICT industry and software solutions can reduce costs and increase technology usage in domestic organizations. In the short term, the government and organizations should increase marketing efforts. Also, reducing bank fees would lead to more use of digital payment methods.

6 Conclusion

This research revealed digital payment systems SMEs and entrepreneurs in Serbia use in their business, their perception of the benefits digital business provides, and obstacles that prevent wider usage of these systems. The types of digital payment systems used by SMEs and entrepreneurs depend on their role in transactions. The biggest perceived obstacle to using digital technology is the increase in costs. At the same time, benefits are better administration, an increase in the speed of transactions, and a reduction in error rate.

Q1: What is the level of usage of digital payment systems in SMEs and entrepreneurs?

Almost all SMEs and entrepreneurs surveyed use internet banking to receive reports, insight into balance and turnover on the accounts, and send payment orders to a bank. Mobile banking is used less often, primarily for receiving notifications about transactions. Most organizations use only one payment method when charging for goods and services, and the most often used method is wire transfer and P2P services. Newer technologies, including QR codes, mobile network operators, text messages, and contactless payments, are rarely used in this role. When paying, organizations use more digital payment methods. The most often used are wire transfer and P2P services, payment by card in the e-shop, and on POS devices.

Q2: What are the obstacles to the broader use of digital payment systems?

The biggest obstacle stated by the respondents is high bank fees and the weak motivation of buyers to use digital payments. An insufficient number of ICT experts makes the digital transformation of payment systems harder, which is evident with SMEs and entrepreneurs who do not have the financial and organizational resources to employ them. Research showed that there is resistance to changing old ways of payment, fear of fraud paying over the internet, and a lack of knowledge about procedures and legislature in payment services related to digital payment.

This research contributes by providing management insight into the status of digital payment systems in Serbia. Results indicate less often used services, which can point out market possibilities for SMEs and entrepreneurs from the ICT area who develop services for e-commerce and digital payments. The research emphasized the need for education about the benefits of digital payment systems, revealed the problems related to the digitalization of the payment system, and suggested possible overcome.

Further research in this direction should include banks, payment providers, and software companies. That would give a better image of the environment in which SMEs and entrepreneurs do their business and provide a better explanation of their problems which reduce the level of use of digital payment systems.

References

Abrazhevich D (2001) Classification and characteristics of electronic payment systems classifications of payment mechanisms: state of the art. LNCS 2115:81–90

Ahmed A, Aziz A, Muneeb M (2019) Electronic payment system: a complete guide. J Multidiscipl Sci 1(2):1–17. https://doi.org/10.33888/jms.2019.121

BIS (2001) Core principles for systemically important payment systems (Issue January). Bank for International Settlements
Bons RWH, Alt R (2015) E-commerce online payments. Int Encyclopedia Dig Commun Soc 1–16. https://doi.org/10.1002/9781118767771.wbiedcs062
Bossone B, Cirasino M (2001) The oversight of the payments systems: a framework for the development and governance of payment systems in emerging economies. The World Bank
Britannica, T. Editors of Encyclopedia (2022) ecosystem. Encyclopedia Britannica. Retrieved from https://www.britannica.com/science/ecosystem
Brophy M (2021) NFC payments: everything you need to know about contactless payments. Fit Small Business. Retrieved from https://fitsmallbusiness.com/nfc-payments/
Deloitte (2018) SME digital payments new opportunities to optimize. The Paytech Revolution Series 1–32
European Central Bank Glossary. https://www.ecb.europa.eu/services/glossary/html/glossp.en.html
European Commission (2009) Directive 2009/110/EC (E-Money Directive). Official Journal of the European Union, 7–17
Kovačević M, Šutić V, Rajčević U, Milaković A (2020) ICT usage in the republic of Serbia. Statistical Office of the Republic of Serbia Belgrade 2020
Law on Digital Assets (2020) RS Official Gazette 153/2020
Law on Payment Services (2018) RS Official Gazette. 44/2018
Metha K (2015) Social media marketing in India. Int J Res Anal Rev 2(3):33–44
Mondres T (2018) The present and future payments ecosystem. ABA Bank J 110(2):38
Muthurasu DC, Suganthi DM (2019) An overview of digital library. Glob J Res Anal:1–2. https://doi.org/10.36106/gjra/8906567
NBS | Statistics (2021) NBS. https://nbs.rs/sr/ciljevi-i-funkcije/platni-sistem/statistika/
Phillphass (2003) Bank for International Settlements – Committee on Payment and Settlement Systems, A glossary of terms used in payments and settlement systems (2003), p 38 1 (Issue March)
Sahut JM (2008) Internet payment and banks. Int J Bus 13(4):361
Shah A, Roongta P, Jain C, Kaushik V, Awadhiya A (2016) Digital payments 2020: the making of $500 billion ecosystem in India, pp 1–52

Digital Payment Systems on High-Speed Railway Belgrade–Novi Sad with a Comparative Analysis

Danijela Stojanović and Nenad Stanisavljević

Abstract The subject of this research is the implementation of new digital payment systems and digital services on the newly built first high-speed railway in Serbia with a speed of 200 km/h between Belgrade and Novi Sad, which opened for traffic in March 2022, as well as on other Serbian railroads in passenger railway traffic today. The authors analyze the results achieved by selling train tickets via digital payment systems on the high-speed railway Belgrade–Novi Sad, nominally and by income, as well as passenger remarks on the functionality of this way of doing business. The paper quantitatively and qualitatively compares digital payment systems of passenger railway traffic on Serbian railroads today with the beginning of their implementation fifteen years ago, as well as the experiences of international railway administrations and organizations. The research aims to analyze the forms and means of applying digital payment systems on Serbian railways in the previous decade and define the level reached in the railway sector today. Based on all these analyses, the research describes and proposes the directions for further development of digital payment systems in the railway sector in Serbia.

Keywords Digital payment systems · Railway sector · High-speed railway · Passenger railway traffic · E-card · Mobile terminal

D. Stojanović (✉)
Institute of Economic Sciences, Belgrade, Serbia
e-mail: danijela.stojanovic@ien.bg.ac.rs

N. Stanisavljević
Infrastructure of Serbian Railways, Belgrade, Serbia
e-mail: nenad.stanisavljevic@srbrail.rs

S. Benković et al. (eds.), *Digital Transformation of the Financial Industry*, Contributions to Finance and Accounting,
https://doi.org/10.1007/978-3-031-23269-5_18

1 Introduction

Contemporary information technology, the development of the Internet and mobile technologies has contributed to the transformation of many branches of industry (Tomić and Stojanović 2018; Stokić et al. 2019; Stojanović and Domazet 2020; Stanisavljević et al. 2022). Thanks to the development of IoT and mobile technologies, a wider community has acquired the possibility to define problems and offer solutions in many areas of social activity (Bogdanović et al. 2021; Stojanović et al. 2020; Petrović et al. 2017, 2022) including railway traffic (Zhong et al. 2021).

With the development of information technology, the financial sector has been transformed and new financial services have been established throughout society (Turban et al. 2015; Hannoon et al. 2021). Electronic payment began back in the 1970s, and during the 1990s, electronic trade has appeared, which means performing various types of business transactions electronically. The mass purchase and sale of products and services via the Internet began in the twenty-first century (Turban et al. 2009; Abrazhevich 2001).

By applying modern information and mobile technologies, conditions for improving the level and quality of services in passenger railway traffic have been created (Chen et al. 2018; Rodríguez et al. 2021). The development of electronic business in passenger railway traffic based on intelligent internet devices should raise the quality, efficiency, and rationality of railway services to a significantly higher level, and provide more passenger satisfaction and a better journey on trains (Kalathas and Papoutsidakis 2021; Gangwar et al. 2017). Improving business processes in railway traffic affects economic and social development (Van de Voorde and Meersman 2017; Jabłoński and Jabłoński 2020).

Unlike the traditional purchase of railway train tickets at ticket counters in booths at railway stations, the IoT-based electronic business model facilitates the purchase of train tickets online, directly on the carrier's website or using a special application. The purchase of train tickets online is possible using mobile phones or computers, with a digital record of the railway ticket that can be read on a validator (Alam et al. 2021; Sheeja et al. 2022).

Railways in Europe and the world, whether they are modern railway administrations or in developing countries, have been paying more attention to the improvement of electronic train ticket payment systems in the past twenty years. In recent years the priority of international railway organizations has been represented by the global and multi-transport implementation of electronic train ticket issuing systems (Winarko and Giri 2022; Erdei 2021).

Railway traffic in Serbia has been in very poor condition in recent decades, especially regarding passenger transport. The average speed of trains on Serbian railways was about 40 km/h and due to poor infrastructure on sections of a few hundred kilometers, slow speeds of 10–20 km/h were introduced. Passenger wagons and locomotives were outdated and often broke down in need of repair, so train departures were canceled. Because of this, passengers lost their trust in trains and turned to other means of transport, so the transport of passengers by rail was increasingly reduced.

Thanks to the comprehensive process of modernization of Serbian railways worth about five billion euros, which the government of Serbia began about ten years ago, about 900 km of railway tracks were reconstructed, 51 new electric motor and diesel motor trains, the first high-speed railway track in Serbia between Belgrade and Novi Sad was built, and work continued towards Subotica and the state border with Hungary. By reconstructing the railway tracks, procuring new rolling stock and the construction of the first high-speed railway in Serbia, traffic and technical-technological conditions were created for the intensive development of forms and methods of implementation of digital payment systems and digital services on the newly built first high-speed railway, as well as on other Serbian railroads (Stojanović et al. 2022).

2 Background

Thanks to the development of the Internet and mobile technologies, many industrial and economic branches were transformed, which is recognizable in banking, for example. Internet and mobile banking have completely changed the banking business, providing new channels of distribution and accessibility of banking services, reduced costs, and the cooperation between mobile operators and banks has intensified (Tomić and Stojanović 2018). The development of modern information technologies and the transformation of banking services has changed the way many industrial branches and services work, including public transport.

Ten years ago, when the development of the railway digital train ticket sales system was only beginning, the authors analyzed the evaluation of the operating system for the sale of train tickets and the functioning of the railway train ticket system (Fan et al. 2012). High-speed railways are a branch of transport which has been rapidly developing in Europe in the last decades. The integration of national systems in a strong trans-European network of railway systems has become the transport priority of the European Union, including the technical harmonization and integration of services, which includes seating reservation systems, ticket sales and information (Kos and Urbanek 2014).

Although e-ticketing is predominant in the air transport industry, the German Railway ("Deutsch Bahn Mobiliti"), as one of the largest transport networks, has successfully implemented an electronic ticket strategy in an open access system (Ng-Kruelle et al. 2006). Today, the German Railway ("Deutsch Bahn") in its offer of services regarding passenger traffic has an online digital railway ticket for transportation, and almost all of their services can be purchased online. The railway ticket purchased online can be saved on a mobile phone in PDF format, loaded onto the application via the DB Navigator or printed, and can be booked immediately before travel. The DB Navigator application provides the passenger with all travel information in real time, including information on which part of the platform the train will stop. Railway ticket verification is performed by scanning the QR code (www.bahn.de, 2019).

Via online German Railway platforms and the DB Navigator application, it is possible to buy train tickets today for trains on French railways and in cross-border traffic between these two countries. Via online and mobile sales channels of German Railways services of Italian and Austrian Railways can be purchased, including Austrian night trains starting their journey or ending their route in Germany. Thanks to this, train travel in Europe is much easier, more comfortable, more attractive and more accessible.

French railways have a digital train ticket with a bar code, which is obtained when booking and paying for services. Passengers can be registered on the French Railway website and download an application for purchasing e-tickets, which facilitates easy booking, storage or replacement of a train ticket and is shown in digital form via mobile phone on the train before traveling (www.sncf.com, 2019).

One way to improve public transportation is implementing and integrating electronic tickets, which allows you to combine different types of transport using one ticket. This makes public transport easier to use and more attractive for users (Kos-Łabędowicz 2014). However, although the integrated ticket payment system is one of the goals of EU transport policy, so far only a few European countries have developed such integrated systems. On the level of the European Union, a unique system for online reservation was not created, but even so, e-ticketing will be an important path for selling tickets in traffic in the forthcoming period (Scărişoreanu 2020).

3 FSM: Full-Service Model

Today, most railway companies and distributers of railway services have ownership of the IT distribution systems they use. At the same time, their passengers have a growing need for flawless solutions to purchase train tickets and travel. Therefore, the railway companies must cooperate and offer comprehensive solutions for train tickets, with the aim of creating an accessible and efficient distribution system for railway train tickets.

A number of European railways and organizations developed a joint "Full-Service Model" (FSM), as a unique IT frame of support for the distribution of railway passenger products and improving customer access to European railway tickets.[1] It is a private industry initiative, which aims to facilitate online distribution services in favor of passengers and offer traveling solutions from door to door.

The "Full-Service Model" includes railway companies in passenger transport and train ticket sellers. They have developed an Open-IT framework, which can be

[1] https://tsga.eu/fsm

integrated into already existing distribution systems, and is open for all companies that offer travel services or travel distribution.

This initiative was launched in 2013 by executive directors of passenger railway companies who are members of the Community of European Railways, together with the European Technology and Travel Services Association, the European Association of Travel Agents and Tour Operators, and the International Rail Transport Committee.

The aim is to simplify the railway ticket reservation/booking process for passengers, to simplify and reduce distribution costs for railway companies and distributors, and therefore increase the competitiveness of the railway as an ecological and convenient transportation system. Using coordinated specifications, railway companies that want their products distributed by other railway operators or train ticket sellers, will no longer have to develop bilateral customized IT interfaces with them. Thanks to the "Full-Service Model," there will be savings in expenses and a new step will be made towards further improving direct train ticket sales.

4 The Roadmap for Selling Railway Tickets

The Community of European Railway and Infrastructure Companies (CER) published a Road map for the sale of railway tickets in October 2021. It deals with the further improvement of passenger services during planning, reservations/booking and international travel by rail. Even though there are many online platforms today where passengers can purchase train tickets for international railway traffic, passenger expectations are increasing. This obliges railway companies to constantly improve the international issuing of railway train tickets.[2]

International railway administrations assembled in the Community of European Railway and infrastructure companies (CER) plan to fully digitalize train tickets by 2025. The long-term vision of this international railway organization is to provide travelers with a flawless user experience by 2030 when seeking, choosing and purchasing railway transport and services. Passengers will have access to comprehensive, reliable and simple online information regarding train schedules, prices and the purchase of train tickets for intercity and international railway traffic. They will be easily accepted throughout Europe.

[2] www.cer.be

4.1 An Electronic Database for Train Ticket Control

The International Union of Railways (UIC) has developed an electronic database for ticket control (ETCD), which will enable the issuing and control of passenger train tickets in a series of countries.

The International Union of Railways offered a centralized system of control of passenger train tickets in real time, which can be used by railway companies around the world. The goal is to achieve an online exchange of ticket control information between railway carriers and railway ticket issuers.[3]

4.2 Asian Railways

On Indian railways, the e-ticket is a large part of all train tickets reserved online throughout this country, and this service is widely accepted among students of the main Indian technical colleges (Swamy 2012).

The authors also dealt with passenger perceptions in their research regarding the quality of electronic services on the Taiwanese high-speed railway website (Cheng 2011).

On the high-speed railway Shanghai–Nanjing the convenience of purchasing train tickets is one of the most significant correlates of passenger satisfaction with railway services (Zhen et al. 2018).

4.3 Railways in the Region

When it comes to railways in the region, HŽ (Croatian Railway) passenger transportation[4] introduced at the end of 2016 their offer of selling train tickets online, as part of an integrated system of sales and train ticket reservations instead of manual ticket printing in the train by conductors who received mobile terminals, and ticket machines were placed at railway stations.

Slovenian Railways[5] have introduced an online issuing system for train tickets at the end of 2018 and 4000 train tickets were issued in the first 4 months.

---

[3]https://uic.org

[4]www.hzpp.hr

[5]www.sz.si

4.4 Railways in Developing Countries

As for the growth of developing countries, the railway traffic system plays a key role, which is why there is a need to optimize the processes in railway transport, especially when it comes to the purchase of train tickets.

Therefore, in Nigeria, the online system was effective in air transport, so an electronic system for issuing train tickets has been implemented using HTML, PHP, CSS, JQuery, Java script, and Bootstrap codes for a quick response to the train ticket verification process (Sani et al. 2019).

The Bangladesh Railway has introduced an electronic service for issuing train tickets in 2009, so that a quarter of train tickets in this country is sold electronically, online or by SMS, as many as 98% of users today are very satisfied, satisfied, or moderately satisfied with electronic ticket payment (Rahman et al. 2018), and an analysis on how to increase women's satisfaction with e-ticket services of Bangladesh Railways was performed (Ferdous et al. 2022).

4.5 E-Ticketing in Railway Freight Transport

Although online ticket payments are dominant in passenger transport, with the development of this traffic system e-ticketing has been increasingly applied in freight transport, such as using and implementing e-ticketing technology for the electronic monitoring of construction material delivery (Nipa et al. 2019).

5 The Beginning and Development of e-Ticketing in Serbian Railways

The development of electronic trade and e-ticketing on "Serbian Railways" in passenger railway traffic began in 2004. In that year, on September 12th, marking the occasion of 120 years of Serbian railways joining the European Reservation System (EPA) they began operating at Belgrade Station.

5.1 The European Reservation System (EPA)

"Serbian Railways" were the first in Southeastern Europe to join the EPA system. Thanks to this electronic system, passengers could buy tickets and reservations in Belgrade, sold by international railway administrations, for any international railway destination. International railway administrations were included in a unique

European reservation system, and the passenger paid for train documents in the place where he bought them.

A year later, the unique railway company in Serbia "Serbian Railways," on the 15th of September, on the day of the railway workers, put into operation the application "Electronic Issuing of International Train Tickets." Thanks to this new application, the first train ticket that was sold at the time in international passenger traffic was Niš–Munich. "Serbian Railways" was the first to take advantage of this application in Southeast Europe, thanks to which the experts of Serbian railways received the greatest domestic award in the field of IT "Discobolos."

5.2 *Electronic Issuing of International Train Tickets*

For the first time, on the 9th of December 2007 when the new Train Schedule arrived, it became possible for passengers in Serbia to book places on intercity and international trains on the internet, at the official institutional "Serbian Railways" website.[6] Until then, it was only possible to book seats on passenger trains on intercity and international railway traffic via the call center or electronic mail.

"Serbian Railways" on May 9, 2008 began the e-ticketing operation for the very first time, a new system for cashless train ticket purchases on the Internet. This new offer for Serbian railway passengers was made available on the company website www.zeleznicesrbije.com. In this way, Serbian railways updated their services in passenger transport in order to keep up with travel conditions on the European railway system (Stojanović and Stanisavljević 2010). The train tickets could be purchased via e-ticketing for trains on route between Serbia and Montenegro. The e-ticketing offer of Serbian railways then included the possibility of booking and buying reservations for seating and beds on trains that traveled from Belgrade, Niš, Novi Sad, and Subotica to destinations in Montenegro, as well as the purchase of train tickets from all "Serbian Railway" stations which were on the route of these trains.

One of the first electronic train tickets of Serbian railways was purchased by credit card in Hongkong, for a ticket and bed on the route Podgorica–Belgrade. The problems that occurred at the beginning of the implementation of e-ticketing on Serbian Railways were: difficulty in using the application because of a large number of simultaneous accesses to the system, as well as the realization of financial transactions, because many international banks did not have the dinar (RSD) as a currency.

And while on Serbian railroads, e-ticketing users from abroad almost exclusively purchased and paid for train tickets on the internet, passengers from Serbia mainly went for the standard procedure of pre-booking train tickets, which did not include the purchase and payment of train tickets by credit card. The real technological and

[6] www.zeleznicesrbije.com

material capabilities of "Serbian Railways" were a limiting factor for the further development of purchasing electronic train tickets. Therefore, the number of train tickets sold via the Internet was extremely small, almost insignificant. Therefore, since May 2008 until the end of 2009, only 264 train tickets were sold on the Internet. This means that only every 9591th visitor of the "Serbian Railways" website bought a train ticket over the Internet.

By comparison, Slovak Railways sold as many as 53,652 tickets online in 2009, which is 0.81% of the total number of train tickets sold in this country. Slovak Railways earned 572,820 euros from the sale of train tickets over the Internet, and as much as 86% of visitors of their company website[7] bought a ticket electronically. "Serbian Railways" took a new step forward in the field of e-commerce and e-ticketing in April 2009, winning a software solution for access to the EPA system. The experts of Serbian Railways did so in cooperation with German Railways, which also verified this system.

"Serbian Railways," which was a unique railway company until then, was restructured in 2015, which also had an impact on the development of digital train ticket payment systems in passenger transport. From "Serbian Railways," the following were separated and established as special companies "Infrastructure of Serbian Railways" (for maintaining public railway infrastructure), "Serbia Train" (for passenger transport), and "Serbia Cargo" (for railway freight transport). Restructuring the railway sector in Serbia and the establishment of a joint-stock company for railway transport of passengers "Serbia Train" also influenced the functioning and development of digital systems for purchasing train tickets. "Serbia Train" continued the business activities in passenger transport of the former "Serbian Railways," but the restructuring of the railway sector required formal, organizational and technological changes, as well as a certain period of time, for the further improvement and development of e-ticketing on Serbian railways.

5.3 E-Ticket (Ekarta): Online Ticket Sales in Intercity Traffic

Thus, in 2018, "Serbia Train" offered customers a service which enabled them to buy a train ticket in intercity passenger traffic online. The application for online train ticket sales was located on the website of the carrier www.srbvoz.rs. The sale of train tickets via digital payment systems in the first phase was only possible on the route Belgrade Center–Vršac–Belgrade Center. The Belgrade Center–Vršac route was selected because of the quality of the transport service, which included new diesel motor trains, introduced into traffic at that section, travel time, the number of departures on a daily basis, respect for the train schedule, and a competitive price of the transport service.

[7] www.slovakrail.sk

The railway transport organization "Serbia Train" has enabled service users to buy train tickets for intercity passenger traffic via the Internet. The application was on the carrier's website. The users decided on a route, return tickets, as well as the category of wagons they are traveling in (first or second class) using the application (Pavlović et al. 2020). The personal data were then entered, as well as any identification cards which enabled the passenger to receive a train ticked at a discount price, and an email address and a password for the purchased train tickets. After that, the whole process of payment and purchase of train tickets ended on the website of a commercial bank. After confirming the transaction, the passenger receives confirmation of the successful purchase of the train ticket and a ticket in PDF format on their email address, which must be printed during the trip.

At the end of 2018, the application for purchasing train tickets via mobile devices "*Ekarta*" could be downloaded for free from the Play Store, as well as from the *AppStore*, for the *IOS* version. Tickets purchased on these applications did not have to be printed, they were already saved in the profile of the user on the application itself. The passenger showed the train ticket on the screen of his mobile device, and the conductor read it on their mobile terminal.

6 Construction of the First Serbian High-Speed Railway Belgrade–Novi Sad, with a Speed of 200 km/h

The first high-speed railway in Serbia, for trains running at a speed of 200 km/h, was built on the Belgrade–Novi Sad section and was opened for traffic on March 19, 2022. It is the first phase of construction of the international railway project for high-speed railways of 200 km/h Belgrade–Budapest, as a large and significant investment and infrastructure project in this part of Europe. It is the first cross-border project marking the cooperation between China and Central and Eastern European countries, which is jointly implemented by Serbia, Hungary, and China. On the high-speed railway between Belgrade–Budapest, as planned, travel between these two capital cities will last less than 3 h.

Construction of a high-speed railway from Belgrade–Budapest is the first cross-border project marking the cooperation between China and Central and Eastern European countries, which is jointly implemented by Serbia, Hungary, and China. When the high-speed railway from Belgrade to Budapest is completed, train travel on this international route will last less than three hours. The high-speed railway Belgrade–Budapest is part of the global project "One Belt–One Road" representing the infrastructure connection of Europe and Asia, which was initiated by China (Stojanović et al. 2022).

Reconstruction, modernization, and the construction of a high-speed railway Belgrade–Novi Sad–Subotica–State border with Hungary (Kelebija)–Budapest, include the reconstruction of an existing one-track railway and the construction of another track, in order to form a modern two-track high-performance railway for mixed (passenger and freight) traffic with speed of up to 200 km/h. The high-speed railway through Serbia from Belgrade to Subotica and the state border with Hungary is 183 km long. The high-speed railway from Belgrade to Novi Sad was completed, 75 km long. The construction of a high-speed railway between Novi Sad and Subotica is 108 km long, which should be completed according to plan by the end of 2024.

The construction of a high-speed railway Belgrade–Novi Sad costs nearly 1 billion dollars, it is funded by the loan facilities and budget of the Republic of Serbia, and the project investor is the joint-stock railway infrastructure management company "Infrastructure of Serbian Railway." The high-speed railway Belgrade–Novi Sad is electrified, equipped with modern safety signals and telecommunication devices, as well as a European Traffic Control System ETCS-level 2, which is the highest level of regulation for high-speed trains. All railway junctions and tracks on high-speed railways are leveled, and a physical and noise barrier has been set up along the length of the high-speed railroad. All train stations between Belgrade and Novi Sad have been reconstructed or new ones have been built, furnished, with new and extended platforms, underpasses, canopies and other station objects, equipped with modern equipment.

At the Belgrade Center railway station, a new Dispatch Center was built for electronic monitoring of train traffic on the high-speed railway. In addition to the newly built high-speed railway between Belgrade and Novi Sad, "Serbia Train" has procured three new trains running at a speed of 200 km/h from the Swiss company "Stadler." These are modern, two-storey, electric motor sets with a total of 316 seats, trains of exceptional comfort and modern design, at a higher technological and security level. The new trains received the promotional name "Soko" *(falcon).*

The entire high-speed railway system between Belgrade and Novi Sad has provided fast and efficient travel between these two cities for passengers, comfort and quality of travel, the highest level of service in passenger railway transport and traffic safety. The first train that ran between Belgrade and Novi Sad, traveled 33 min between these two cities, 3 min faster than it was scheduled.

From the establishment of regular high-speed railway traffic between Belgrade and Novi Sad, every day there was a total of 36, then 40, and from May 1, 2022, 64 departures of passenger trains of three different categories *(Inter City, Regio Express and the Regio)*, depending on the number of stations where "Soko" stops. With an aim to reinstate passenger confidence in the railway and to affirm the first Serbian high-speed railway and train "Soko" at a speed of 200 km/h between Belgrade and Novi Sad, passengers can, until the end of May 2022 obtain promotional train tickets in one direction at a price of 300 dinars (about 2.5 euros).

For just a little less than 5 months, a total of almost a million passengers have traveled on the high-speed railway between Belgrade and Novi Sad.

Fig. 1 Application for online ticket sales (Source: www.srbvoz.rs)

7 Digital Payment Systems on the High-Speed Railway Belgrade–Novi Sad

Improving the speed and efficiency of travel, the quality of transport service and comfort, and raising traffic safety to the highest level on the high-speed railway Belgrade–Novi Sad was accompanied by the modernization of the system for selling train tickets to passengers. In addition to the classic systems of selling train tickets at railway ticket offices or through mobile terminals used by conductors, "Serbia Train" has developed and improved digital channels for the sale of train tickets, through which train tickets can be purchased in internal passenger rail traffic, with the construction of the high-speed railway (Fig. 1).

Digital ticket sales channels include an application for online ticket sales, ticket sales via mobile phones, and ticket machines.

7.1 Online Sale of Train Tickets

There are two ways to sell train tickets online:

(a) through the "Serbia Train" website (www.srbvoz.rs),
(b) via mobile phones, via the "Serbia Train" application.

The application for the online sale of train tickets enables the purchase of train tickets in internal passenger rail traffic. The "Serbia Train" application is available for Android and iOS platforms via mobile phones. It is available for free through the *App Store* and *Google Play*. Online purchase of train tickets through the application is realized quickly and easily through five steps that need to be done.

The first step involves the selection of a train. It includes the answer to the questions whether it is a round trip or a one-way trip, which route you are traveling on, date and time of travel, class, and number of passengers, the basis of which the train ticket price is calculated (Fig. 2).

The second step includes information about the passenger: name, surname, and date of birth. Train tickets purchased online are non-transferable, and ticket control is performed based on a personal document. Then there is the login to the online shopping system, along with the previously registered email and password. If the customer does not have an open account for buying a train ticket online, it is necessary to register first.

The fourth step involves agreeing to the terms and conditions of purchase. And at the end, a new website is opened through which the customer is forwarded to Bank Intesa, where the payment process is carried out, and the purchase is completed.

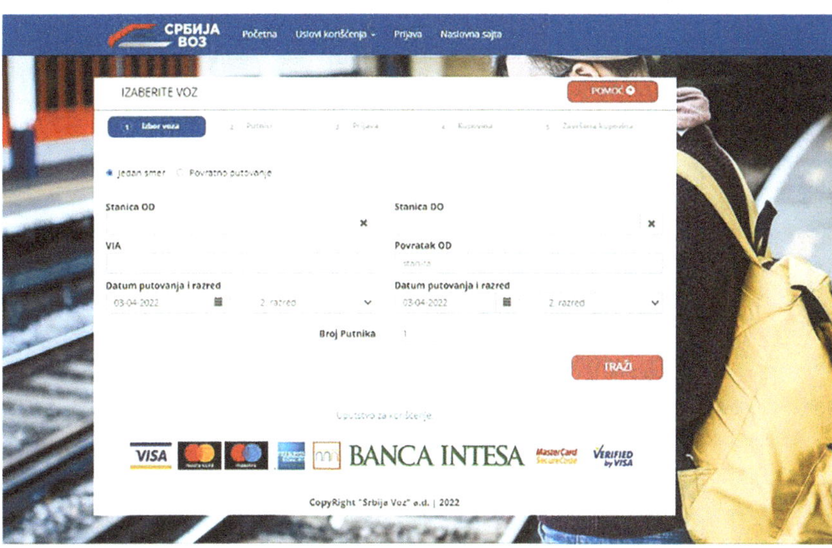

Fig. 2 The payment process on website. Source: www.srbvoz.rs

Train tickets purchased through the "Serbia Train" website in PDF format are delivered by email to the email address specified during registration. That message confirms the successful purchase of a train ticket for the route, the selected travel date, the number of passengers, and the train class. The train ticket in PDF format is attached to the email, which must be printed and taken with you on the train.

Tickets purchased with mobile phones through the "Serbia Train" application do not need to be printed. When checking train tickets, the passenger shows the train ticket to the conductor on the screen of his mobile device, and the conductor reads it through mobile terminals.

For the first time, the railway company for passenger transport, "Serbia Train," acquired ticket machines for selling train tickets.

Six ticket machines were installed on the route of the high-speed train Belgrade–Novi Sad, two each in the railway stations Belgrade Centar, Novi Beograd, and Novi Sad.

7.2 *Sale of Train Tickets Through Digital Sales Channels*

The authors of this paper analyzed the sale of train tickets on the high-speed railway Belgrade–Novi Sad from April 18 to July 27, 2022. In the period mentioned, 521,930 train tickets were sold for high-speed trains (Fig. 3).

A total of 216,251 train tickets were sold at the railway ticket offices, i.e., 41% of the total number of train tickets sold. Through the mobile terminals used by train conductors, another 51,707 train tickets were sold, i.e., 10% of the total number of train tickets sold. This means that a total of 267,958 train tickets, or 51% of the train

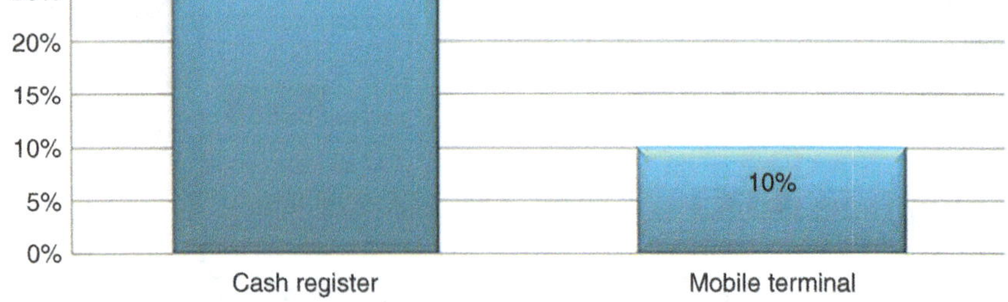

Fig. 3 Traditional payment channels for train tickets. Source: authors' compilation

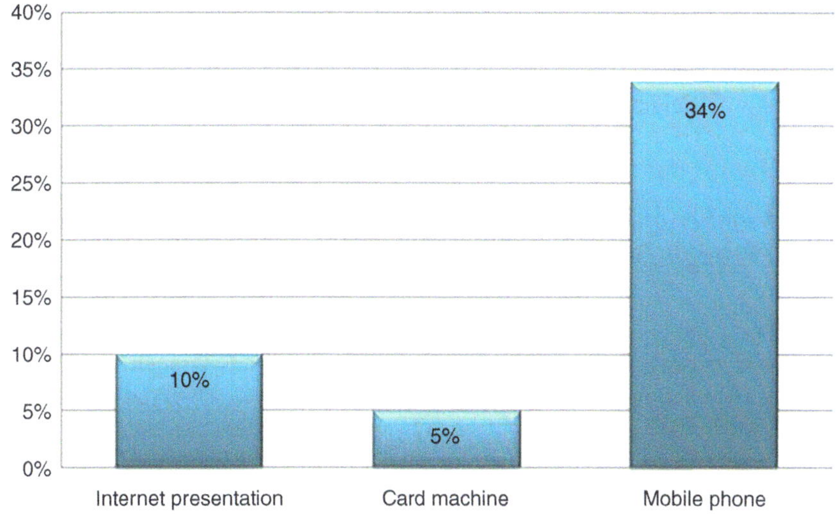

Fig. 4 Digital channels for paying train tickets. Source: authors' compilation

tickets sold on the high-speed railway, were sold through classic train ticket sales systems in the specified period.

Digital channels for the sale of train tickets include sales through the Internet, mobile phones, and ticket machines. Regarding digital media for the sale of train tickets on the high-speed railway, 175,820 train tickets were sold via mobile phones, or 35% of the total number of 50,805 train tickets, or 10% of the full tickets sold, were sold through the online ticket sales application on the "Serbia Train" website. And finally, 27,347 train tickets were sold at six ticket machines in the mentioned period or 5% of the total number of train tickets sold. In the mentioned period, a total of 253,972 train tickets were sold through digital channels for the sale of train tickets on the high-speed railway, i.e., 49% of the total number of train tickets sold.

Such a high percentage of train ticket sales through digital media can be the result, on the one hand, of the construction of a high-speed railway between Belgrade and Novi Sad and the improvement of the quality of transport services on this route, but on the other hand, the improvement and development of digital ticket sales systems. Such a high percentage of the sale of train tickets through digital media can also indicate the increase in the number of younger passengers between Belgrade and Novi Sad. They use their mobile phones more for applications and online shopping. Such a high percentage of the use of digital media for the sale of train tickets may also indicate a change in the structure of passengers using the high-speed railway (Fig. 4).

In any case, this ratio of ticket sales by traditional (51%) and digital (49%) systems on the high-speed railway Belgrade–Novi Sad is completely different from what was expected. It changes the public's usual opinion about users of passenger rail transport services. It can be assumed that thanks to the modern, fast, comfortable, and high-quality transport on the high-speed railway Belgrade–Novi Sad, the structure of passengers has changed. Based on this information, the authors of the paper in the coming period will analyze the passenger structure on the high-speed railway Belgrade–Novi Sad according to a number of different parameters.

7.3 Number of Passengers per Station with Tickets Purchased Through Digital Sales Channels

The paper's authors analyzed the number of passengers at railway stations on the high-speed railway Belgrade–Novi Sad who bought tickets through digital sales channels (internet, mobile phone, ticket machine). Data were observed from March 25 to July 27, 2022. There are thirteen railway stations where passenger trains stop on the route of the high-speed line: Beograd Centar, Novi Beograd, Tošin Bunar, Zemun, Zemunsko Polje, Batajnica, Stara Pazova, Nova Pazova, Inđija, Beška, Sremski Karlovci, Petrovaradin, and Novi Sad.

The most significant number of passengers who bought tickets through digital sales channels in the specified period was at the Novi Sad railway station—131,687 passengers, 41.8% of the total number of passengers on this route in the specified period. Then follow the railway stations Belgrade Center—109,532 passengers, which is 35%, and New Belgrade—46,837 passengers, which is 14.9% of the total number of passengers who bought tickets through digital sales channels (Fig. 5).

These are the three largest railway stations on the Belgrade–Novi Sad high-speed railway. Passengers at these three stations who bought train tickets through digital sales channels make up 91.7% of the total number of passengers who bought train tickets through digital sales channels. Then follows the Indjija station with 6957 passengers who bought train tickets online, which is 2.2% of the total. At the same time, at Stara Pazova station, there were 3879 passengers who bought train tickets online, and in Tošina bunar, 3270 passengers. With online purchased train tickets, which is about 1% of the total.

Batajnica, Beška, Nova Pazova, Petrovaradin, Sremski Karlovci, and Zemun's railway stations were between 0.5 and 0.7% of passengers with train tickets purchased through digital sales channels. The fewest passengers with train tickets purchased through digital sales channels were at the Zemunsko Polje station—445 of them in total.

7.4 Passengers About Digital Channels of Train Ticket Sales

Immediately after the completion of the construction of the high-speed railway and the establishment of regular railway traffic at a speed of 200 km/h, the "Infrastructure of Serbian Railway" opened a new service for citizens to complain and report

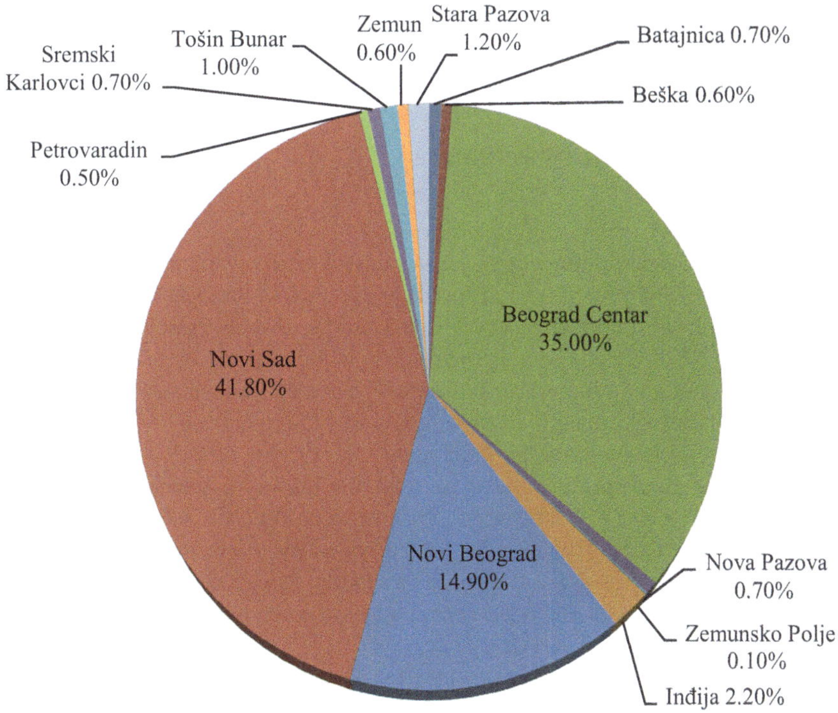

Fig. 5 Number of passengers per station with tickets purchased through digital sales channels. Source: authors' compilation

problems on the Belgrade-Novi Sad high-speed railway. A separate email address has been opened: brzepruga.primedbe@srbrail.rs. Through this email, citizens could report all the problems they encountered on the high-speed railway, from the state of the railway infrastructure to the behavior of the railway staff.

The goal of opening this email was to enable direct and fast communication with users of the high-speed railway so that the railways could react quickly and eliminate objections based on the collected information. In this way, the highest quality of services, the layout and appearance of railway facilities, the state of the railway infrastructure, and the comfort and convenience of traveling by trains at a speed of 200 km/h should be maintained and preserved. In the first month since the opening of the newly built high-speed railway Belgrade–Novi Sad, passengers, and service users submitted a total of 64 comments and objections.

Out of that number, only four objections related to the application for the online sale of train tickets, which is only 6.25% of the total number of emails received. Of those four remarks, two were related to the fact that the application did not provide the possibility that the departure and return are not on the same day. One was that there is no information about the remaining number of accessible seats on the train and that there is no schematic display in the application seats, so passengers can choose which seat they want. In a short period, service users could have information about the number of accessible seats on the train on the high-speed railway.

8 Future Research Directions

In the next five to six years, "Infrastructure of Serbian Railways" will modernize and build another thousand kilometers of new railroad tracks. Within this framework, a railway will be built for 200 km/h speeds between Novi Sad and Subotica, then a high-speed railway from Belgrade to Niš and further towards Preševo, as well as a railroad from Niš to Dimitrovgrad. The reconstruction of a section of the Belgrade–Bar railroad through Serbia was also planned—between Valjevo and Vrbnica.

Also, the railway company for passenger traffic "Serbia Train" will continue to modernize its fleet, therefore the procurement of 18 new electric motor trains is currently being implemented. Based on this, this railway company plans further dynamic development of its transport services, in accordance with the needs and interests of passengers. This includes the improvement of electronic business and digital payment systems in passenger railway traffic, in accordance with the development of information technologies and an increase in the interest of passengers for this form of transportation services.

The authors of this paper will continue to monitor and investigate the development of digital payment systems for train tickets and the entire electronic business of passenger railway transport in the following period. This implies that the authors will quantitatively and qualitatively analyze future indicators of digital train ticket sales on the high-speed railway between Belgrade–Novi Sad, both in relation to the total number of passengers transported in this section and in relation to the previous use of this passenger service. The authors will also address passenger experiences regarding the use of digital payment systems on the high-speed railway of Belgrade–Novi Sad in future research and analyze which passenger categories use digital train ticket payment systems more often.

Also, the authors will analyze the development of a digital system of train ticket payments on trains and railroads in Serbia, a comparative analysis in relation to the indicators and level of e-ticketing on modern European railways and railways in the region. And finally, in all their future research in this area, the authors will define weak and critical points of the digital train ticket payment system based on analysis, and indicate the ways of solving and overcoming them.

All research and analysis that the authors will implement in the coming period, will aim to improve and develop electronic trade, digital train ticket payment systems, and e-ticketing. In this way, the authors will contribute to the overall progress of railway passenger transport, including increasing the quality of services, number of passengers and revenues, and therefore the entirety of railway traffic in Serbia.

9 Conclusion

The development of modern information technologies has encouraged the establishment of new financial services throughout society. Thanks to this, conditions for improving the level and quality of services in passenger railway traffic, which are based on the implementation of modern information and mobile technologies and intelligent internet devices were created. In the 1970s, electronic payment begins, and in the 1990s electronic trade, so that mass purchase and sales of products and services began in the twenty-first century. Unlike the traditional purchase of railway train tickets at ticket counters, the IoT-based model has enabled online train ticket purchases, using mobile phones or computers.

Railways in Europe and the world, whether they are the most modern railway administrations or in developing countries, have been paying more and more attention to improving electronic train ticket payment systems in the previous twenty years. In recent years, the priority of international railway organizations is represented by a global and multi-transport implementation of electronic train ticket issuing systems.

The development of e-ticketing in Serbian Railways begins in 2004, by joining the European reservation system, and then continues to develop with the system of electronic issuing of international train tickets, e-ticketing for cashless train ticket payments over the Internet and *Ekarta*—online train ticket sales in intercity traffic.

However, the development of electronic sales of train tickets in Serbia was largely prevented by the extremely poor condition in which the railway system in our country found itself. In March 2022, a newly built high-speed railway was opened for traffic at 200 km/h between Belgrade and Novi Sad, and three modern and comfortable new high-speed trains were procured, which crossed this distance in only 33 min. In this way, the quality of transport services on this section of the Belgrade international highway Belgrade–Budapest was raised to a higher level.

On the high-speed railway connecting Belgrade–Novi Sad an electronic train ticket payment system was developed via application, and for the first time on the network of Serbian railroads in stations along this section, machines are placed for selling train tickets. The results of online train ticket sales show that passengers in large numbers have opted for this type of purchase. This has certainly been influenced by the traditional advantages of purchasing train tickets online, such as saving time and money, or the simplicity and comfort of electronic business. However, the development of e-ticketing on Serbian railways in the previous almost two decades has shown that electronic payment systems cannot be successfully developed without quality transportation services. Therefore, the quality of transport services on the high-speed railway Belgrade–Novi Sad, new infrastructure for speeds of 200 km/h, modern and comfortable trains, the speed and comfort of travel between these two cities is the best guarantee of development and the increasing implementation of electronic train ticket payments via the application.

The authors of the work indicate that the electronic train ticket payment system in Serbia needs to fit into the plans and directions of development of the international railway system. They confirmed by their research that the construction of a high-speed railway, and significantly increasing the quality of transportation services, has contributed to the development of digital train ticket payment systems on Serbian railroads and defined that e-ticketing improvement is an important segment of the overall progress of railway passenger transportation and railway traffic in Serbia as a whole.

Acknowledgements This work was supported by the Ministry of Education, Science and Technological Development of the Republic of Serbia (institutional funding of the Institute of Economic Sciences).

The authors of the paper thank the joint-stock company for railway passenger transport, "Serbia Train" for the quantitative and qualitative data on passenger transport on the Belgrade–Novi Sad high-speed railway.

References

Abrazhevich D (2001) Classification and characteristics of electronic payment systems. In: International conference on electronic commerce and web technologies, pp 81–90

Alam S, Chowdhury M, Siddique AB (2021) A user-friendly android application featuring smart ticketing system and destination announcement for metro rail based rapid transport system in Bangladesh. In: 3rd international conference on electrical and electronic engineering, ICEEE 2021, pp 29–32

Bogdanović Z, Labus A, Barać D, Naumović T, Radenković B (2021) Challenging E-learning in higher education via Instagram. In: Rocha Á, Reis JL, Peter MK, Cayolla R, Loureiro S, Bogdanović Z (eds) Marketing and smart technologies. Smart innovation, systems and technologies, vol 205, pp 479–491

Chen R, Long W-X, Fellow M, Li C, Member S (2018) Development trends of mobile communication systems for railways. IEEE Commun Surv Tutor 20(4):3131–3141

Cheng YH (2011) Evaluating web site service quality in public transport: evidence from Taiwan high speed rail. Transp Res Part C: Emerg Technol 19(6):957–974

Erdei A (2021) Application of electronic ticketing at the Hungarian railway. J Tour Res 27:58–69

Fan L, Liu X, Wang J (2012) An evaluation of the operation of the railway E-ticketing system. iBusiness 2012(02):164–167. https://doi.org/10.4236/IB.2012.42019

Ferdous Z, Islam FF, Rahman FN, Rumi MH (2022) Customer satisfaction of Bangladesh railway E-ticketing system. Bangladesh J Pub Adm 30(1):2664–4622

Gangwar N, Semwal T, Nair SB (2017) CARE: an IoT based system for passenger service and comfort in railways. 2017 9th international conference on communication systems and networks (COMSNETS), pp 55–62

Hannoon A, Al-Sartawi AMAM, Khalid AA (2021) Relationship between financial technology and financial performance. In: The big data-driven digital economy: artificial and computational intelligence, vol 974, pp 337–344

Jabłoński A, Jabłoński M (2020) Social perspectives in digital business models of railway enterprises. Energies 13(23):1–20

Kalathas I, Papoutsidakis M (2021) Predictive maintenance using machine learning and data mining: a pioneer method implemented to Greek railways. Designs 5(1):1–18

Kos B, Urbanek A (2014) Areas of using telematic tools in the high speed rail integration process in Europe. Commun Comput Inf Sci 471:341–349

Kos-Łabędowicz J (2014) Integrated e-ticketing system – possibilities of introduction in EU. Commun Comput Inf Sci 471:376–385

Ng-Kruelle G, Swatman PA, Kruelle O (2006) E-ticketing strategy and implementation in an open access system: the case of deutsche bahn. Inf Technol Tour 2

Nipa TJ, Rouhanizadeh B, Kermanshachi S (2019) Utilization and implementation of the E-ticketing technology to electronically track the delivery of construction materials. CSCE Annual Conference

Pavlović Z, Banjanin M, Vukmirović J, Vukmirović D (2020) Contactless ICT transaction model of the urban transport service. Transport 35(5):500–510

Petrović L, Stojanović D, Labus A, Bogdanović Z, Despotović-Zrakić M (2017) Harnessing edutainment in higher education: an example of an IoT based game. In: The 12th international conference on virtual learning, Sibiu, Romania-Europe, pp 318–324

Petrović L, Stojanović D, Mitrović S, Barać D, Bogdanović Z (2022) Designing an extended smart classroom: an approach to game-based learning for IoT. Comput Appl Eng Educ 30(1):117–132

Rahman Z, Mahmad MM, Hasan P, Shampa S (2018) Impact of public service innovation on public satisfaction: a study on railway e-ticketing

Rodríguez A, Sañudo R, Miranda M, Gómez A, Benavente J (2021) Smartphones and tablets applications in railways, ride comfort and track quality. Trans Zones Anal Measure 182:109644

Sani Y, Mariann T, Mamman A (2019) Web-based E-ticketing system for booking and reservation for railway transportation using quick response codes. I-Manager's J Inf Technol 8(4):8–17

Scărişoreanu DI (2020) Integrated e-ticketing: solution to make public transport more attractive than personal cars transport 3 unified modeling language. Int J Transp Syst 5:25–30

Sheeja R, Umaeswari P, Bibin C, Nishanth R, Chandana SH (2022) Local train ticketing system using web services AIP Conference Proceedings, 020022

Stanisavljević N, Stojanović D, Petrović L (2022) Open innovation and crowdsourcing: challenges and opportunities for Serbian railways. E-Bus Technol Conf Proc 2(1):36–41

Stojanović D, Domazet I (2020) Use of information technologies in educational purposes-case from Serbia. Econ Anal 53(2):68–78

Stojanović D, Stanisavljević N (2010) Elektronska trgovina u "Železnicama Srbije." In: X Međunarodna Konferencija E-Trgovina 2010, pp 167–172

Stojanović D, Bogdanović Z, Petrović L, Mitrović S, Labus A (2020) Empowering learning process in secondary education using pervasive technologies. Interact Learn Environ:1–14

Stojanović D, Jovičić E, Stanisavljević N (2022) The role and significance of Chinese investments in the modernization of railway infrastructure in Serbia. In: Bhuiyan M, Beraha I (eds) Opportunities and challenges for multinational enterprises and foreign direct investment in the Belt and Road Initiative, pp 194–216

Stokić A, Stojanović D, Bogdanović Z, Despotović-Zrakić M, Radenković B (2019) Enhancing the customer relationship management in public libraries: findings from three developing countries. Library Hi Tech 37(2):251–272

Swamy RN (2012) Popularity of E-ticketing system of Indian railways: a survey based approach. Indian J Pub Adm 58(1):69–81

Tomić V, Stojanović D (2018) Trends and innovations in mobile banking. In: Digital transformation, pp 290–310

Turban E, King DR, Lang J, Lai L (2009) Introduction to electronic commerce

Turban E, King D, Lee JK, Liang T-P, Turban DC (2015) Electronic Commerce. https://doi.org/10.1007/978-3-319-10091-3

Van de Voorde E, Meersman H (2017) Transport research for a changing and sustainable future. Int J Transp Econ:11–23

Winarko HB, Giri IPS (2022) The digital payment service automation attributes model: empirical evidence of railway public transport. In: Handbook of research on big data, green growth, and technology disruption in Asian companies and societies, pp 138–152

Zhen F, Cao J, Tang J (2018) Exploring correlates of passenger satisfaction and service improvement priorities of the Shanghai-Nanjing high speed rail. J Transp Land Use 11(1):559–573

Zhong G, Xiong K, Zhong Z, Ai B (2021) Internet of things for high-speed railways. Intell Converged Netw 2(2):115–132